BEREAVEMENT

Studies of grief in adult life

Fourth edition

Colin Murray Parkes and Holly G. Prigerson

PENGUIN BOOKS

PENGUIN BOOKS

Published by the Penguin Group
Penguin Books Ltd, 80 Strand, London WC2R ORL, England
Penguin Group (USA) Inc., 375 Hudson Street, New York, New York 10014, USA
Penguin Group (Canada), 90 Eglinton Avenue East, Suite 700, Toronto, Ontario, Canada M4P 2Y3
(a division of Pearson Penguin Canada Inc.)
Penguin Ireland, 25 St Stephen's Green, Dublin 2, Ireland (a division of Penguin Books Ltd)
Penguin Group (Australia), 250 Camberwell Road, Camberwell, Victoria 3124, Australia
(a division of Pearson Australia Group Pty Ltd)
Penguin Books India Pvt Ltd, 11 Community Centre, Panchsheel Park, New Delhi – 110 017, India
Penguin Group (NZ), 67 Apollo Drive, Rosedale, North Shore 0632, New Zealand
(a division of Pearson New Zealand Ltd)
Penguin Books (South Africa) (Pty) Ltd, 24 Sturdee Avenue, Rosebank, Johannesburg 2196, South Africa

Penguin Books Ltd, Registered Offices: 80 Strand, London WC2R ORL, England

www.penguin.com

First published by Routledge 2010
Published in Penguin Books 2010
1

www.greenpenguin.co.uk

Penguin Books is committed to a sustainable future
for our business, our readers and our planet.
The book in your hands is made from paper
certified by the Forest Stewardship Council.

CONTENTS

List of Figures   vii
List of Tables   viii
Foreword to the First Edition by John Bowlby   ix
Foreword to the Fourth Edition by Robert Jay Lifton   xi
Acknowledgements   xiii
Introduction   xiv

1 The cost of commitment   1

2 The broken heart   15

3 Trauma   33

4 Attachment and loss   48

5 Continuing bonds   68

6 Anger and guilt   90

7 Changing the assumptive world   100

8 Complications of grief   122

9 Determinants of grief I: Kinship,
   gender and age   137

10 Determinants of grief II: Mode of death   152

11 Determinants of grief III: Personal
   vulnerability   164

12 Determinants of grief IV: Social and
   cultural influences   181

13 Helping the bereaved I: Bereavement
   support: History and evaluation   193

14 Helping the bereaved II: Types of help
   for types of problem   220

15 Helping the bereaved III: Sources of help   238

16 Reactions to other types of loss   252

17 Disasters   267

   Appendices   279
   Organizations Offering Help to the Bereaved   305
   Recommended Further Reading   307
   References   309
   Index   337

FIGURES

1 Changes in indicators of grief over two years
post-bereavement   280

2 Mortality rate of widowers after bereavement
as a percentage of rate for married men over ten years
post-bereavement   281

3 Sedative consumption, before and after bereavement,
in forty-four widows in two age groups   291

4 Scores of insecure attachment × overall distress
in 181 persons referred for psychiatric help after
bereavement   293

5 Anxious/ambivalent attachment scores correlated
with other variables   294

6 Score of separations from parents during childhood
correlated with other variables   295

7 Avoidant attachment scores correlated with
other variables   296

8 Disorganized attachment scores correlated with
other variables   297

9 Mean grief/loneliness scores × age group × living
alone or with others   298

10 Severity of emotional disturbance in twenty-five
widows during the first three months of bereavement   298

11 Mean General Health Questionnaire scores before
and after intervention in bereaved persons in two
therapy groups and a control group   300

12 Mean outcome scores in three groups of
hospice bereaved   304

TABLES

1   Psychiatrist's predictions of cervical cancer and biopsy
    diagnosis in fifty-one women admitted for investigation
    of suspicious smear test   281
2   London Study: Intercorrelation of health indices
    and anger in twenty-two widows   282
3   The Yale Bereavement Study: Prolonged grief disorder
    (PGD) at six months predicts impairment at
    thirteen months   285
4   London Study: Correlation (r) between
    mean year scores on psychological measures among
    twenty-two London widows   287
5   Tests of moderation for targeted population   299

FOREWORD TO THE
FIRST EDITION

Some ten years ago a young psychiatrist wrote from the Maudsley Hospital calling my attention to Darwin's work on grief. This proved of great value to me. Soon we had met and discovered that our thoughts were running along similar lines. When opportunity offered, therefore, we joined forces and a happy, mutually productive partnership has followed. During these years, despite uncertain financial support, Colin Murray Parkes has devoted himself without reserve to unravelling the problems of grief and mourning. In this admirable book we have the fruits of his labours.

Considering the attention given to the subject by Freud half a century ago and the classical work of Lindemann in the early 1940s, it is remarkable that psychiatrists have been so long in recognizing bereavement as a major hazard to mental health. Not until this past decade has any sustained research been mounted, and hitherto few books on grief have been published by psychiatrists.

In the understanding of an illness a turning-point comes when the pathological processes of the illness can be seen as intensifications, deviations, of prolongations of processes that occur in health. In keeping with this rule, the increased understanding of grieving and its pathological variants available today is a direct result of our greatly increased knowledge of the processes of grieving that occur in ordinary people. To this advancing knowledge Dr Parkes has made major contributions. As this book goes to press the detailed findings of studies he has conducted in the United Kingdom from the Tavistock Institute of Human Relations and in the United States from Harvard Medical School are being published in the scientific journals.

Not only has Dr Parkes furthered our scientific understanding of grieving, but he has played an active part in trying to develop means whereby bereaved people can be helped. Through his clinical work with bereaved patients and his studies of widows, and in work for St Christopher's Hospice, Sydenham, and for Cruse, the national organization for widows and their children, he has had extensive experience of the problems of which he writes and, in addition, close working relations with members of the helping professions concerned with them. Thus, in a way the Tavistock especially values, he has given attention equally to the promotion of scientific understanding and to the development of professional skills based upon it.

This book, then, provides at once an authoritative description of what today we believe we know about grieving, in both its healthy and its less-healthy forms, and a guide to all those whose everyday living and professional work bring them into contact with bereaved people. It is certainly the first book of its kind, and for many years to come is likely also to remain the best.

John Bowlby
1972

FOREWORD TO THE FOURTH EDITION

I have been reading and learning from Colin Parkes' work on death, grief, and loss for more than a half century. During that time Parkes has emerged as the predominant world authority on the nature and consequences of bereavement. What few of us at first realized, but Parkes understood from the beginning, is that the experience of grief and loss has relevance for every conceivable level of psychological function.

Bereavement provides a middle ground between ordinary experience and potential psychological impairment. It is in itself by no means pathological, as its manifestations are to be expected with every significant loss. But it is also a key to understanding the large phenomenon of depression, which is so central to what we call psychopathology and to psychological experience in general. In demonstrating so sensitively what happens to people in bereavement, Parkes illuminates much about the human condition.

Parkes' insights, now in association with his co-author Holly Prigerson, have been drawn mostly from individual-psychological behavior. But they readily extend to collective experience as well. During the mid and late 1960s, when I was writing up my study of atomic bomb survivors in Hiroshima, I found wisdom in Parkes' 1955 paper published in the *British Medical Journal*, 'Effects of bereavement on physical and mental health – A study of the medical records of widows'. From reading that and his subsequent publications, and from talking with Parkes himself, I gained better understanding of how Hiroshima, during the years after the bomb, became a city of collective mourning.

In 1967 I had the privilege of joining with Parkes in the now legendary seminar conducted by John Bowlby at the Tavistock Clinic. It was clear to me that, while Bowlby was the senior figure and director of the seminar, he had enormous respect for Parkes' findings, and that those findings had great importance for the developing principles surrounding attachment and loss that came to have so much influence in psychiatry and psychoanalysis, in Great Britain and throughout the world. And in my own work, when I sought to conceptualize basic psychiatric emotions in relation to a focus on death and the continuity of life, I turned to the original 1972 edition of *Bereavement* for clinical, theoretical, and evolutionary understanding.

Parkes' studies of bereavement have had considerable influence on work with war veterans, especially concerning Americans who fought in Vietnam. The latter were survivors who, like the widows and widowers in Parkes' studies, struggled with the meaning of their death encounter. Parkes' work even helped illuminate behavior during combat, when angry grief could combine with misguided military policies to produce the atrocities so emblematic of that war. And when a committee of American psychiatrists sat down to formulate the nature of post-traumatic stress disorder, we were greatly influenced by Parkes' detailed observations on the varied manifestations of grief and loss.

Beyond the clinical and scientific knowledge contained in this volume is what could be called profound psychological generosity. Throughout his career, Parkes has been willing to bring not only empathy, but what could be called sympathetic affinity, to those experiencing the most painful forms of loss. I was moved but not entirely surprised to learn of Parkes' recent involvement in studying and making known to the world some of the terrible psychological details of the genocide in Rwanda. That work in turn led him to participate in systematic explorations aimed at preventing mass killing and genocide. Such larger concerns come naturally to a man who has long insisted upon taking in so much of human suffering in the service of alleviating it. The new edition of this volume includes old and new insights about bereavement, and about the humane frontiers of clinical and psychological work.

Robert Jay Lifton
2009

ACKNOWLEDGEMENTS

The studies that form the basis of this book were carried out with the support of the Mental Health Research Fund (now the Mental Health Trust), the Department of Health and Social Security, the Tavistock Institute of Human Relations, the London Hospital Medical College and the US National Institute of Mental Health Grants 1RO1MH-12042; MH56529 (HGP) and MH63892 (HGP) and from the National Cancer Institute CA106370 (HGP).

Thanks are due to the staff of the Bethlem Royal and Maudsley Hospitals, the Tavistock Institute and Clinic, the Laboratory of Community Psychiatry of Harvard Medical School, and St Christopher's Hospice, Sydenham, and especially to the late John Bowlby, without whose support, guidance, and constructive criticism the work would never have been possible.

Others who have made a special contribution include Richard Brown, Gerald Caplan, Marlene Hindley, Margaret Napier, and Robert Weiss. The late Olive Ainsworth criticized the drafts, Janice Uphill typed my illegible manuscripts and Rosamund Robson gave editorial assistance.

Thanks are also due to Professor John Romano for permission to include the case study on page 54 and to Henk Schut for permission to use his data for Figure 11.

But most of all, thanks are due to the numerous bereaved people who agreed, at a time of great distress, to talk to a stranger in the hope that their experience could be of value to others.

We gratefully acknowledge permission to quote from the following publications: Joan Didion's '*The Year of Magical Thinking*' (Random House), Susan Hill's '*The Springtime of the Year*' (Sheill Land Associates), C.S. Lewis' '*A Grief Observed*' (CS Lewis Co. and Faber & Faber), Marjorie Pizer's poem '*Lament for Glen*' (Pinchgut Press), and David Sutton's poem '*Not to be Born*' (peterloo Poets).

INTRODUCTION

When a love tie is severed, a reaction, emotional and behavioural, is set in train, which we call grief. This book is about grief; more particularly, it is about what happens to the survivors when a person dies.

The loss of a husband or wife is one of the most severe forms of psychological stress, yet it is one that many of us can expect to undergo at some time in our lives. At other times we may be expected to give comfort and support to relatives or friends who are themselves bereaved. This unpleasant thought may well prompt us to shrug off the whole nasty subject and look for lighter reading – for what can one say? And yet grief, like any other aspect of human behaviour, is capable of description and study, and when studied it turns out to be as fascinating as any other psychological phenomenon.

Books about the psychology of sex are seldom pornographic and, for similar reasons, a book about grief need not be doleful. The very act of thinking objectively about distress places us at one remove from the distress. This applies as well to the sufferer as to the helper, and Eastern mysticism is much concerned with the development of means of dissociating oneself from one's own suffering.

It would seem to follow that a book that helps people to think about grief may make both the experience and the witnessing of grief less unpleasant.

But if dissociation is a necessary part of clear thinking it may also be a defence against thinking. The focusing of attention on one aspect of a situation automatically excludes from attention other aspects. Even 'clinical detachment' can be used as a defence. It is a recurrent problem for those in the 'helping professions' that in order to function effectively, to 'enjoy' being a good doctor, nurse, clergyman, lawyer, or whatever, they must allow themselves to approach and, to a degree, share the distress of those they are attempting to help.

People vary widely in the extent to which they can do this. Some, who have, perhaps, more 'basic trust' in life, can tolerate a high level of involvement; others will avoid, in every possible way, any potential source of anxiety. But for most of us, whose tolerance lies somewhere between these extremes, two things are crucial: the magnitude of the distress and our own confidence in our ability to cope with it. As long as we feel that our participation is worthwhile we shall find ourselves able to tolerate high levels of disturbance in others without disengaging.

Confidence in our ability to cope with the distress of others can be, and normally is, obtained by a process of attunement. By repeated exposure we gradually discover what we can do to alleviate distress and how much of it is inevitable and insurmountable.

The study of psychology cannot replace such experience but it should facilitate and deepen our understanding of it and enable us, through understanding, to deal more effectively with the problems posed by suffering.

When grief is looked upon as a valid and, in its own right, interesting topic of study, it becomes possible to treat it in a way that neither trivializes it nor puffs it up; to treat it, in effect, as another part of the life-space, which must be examined, understood, and assimilated.

This book describes, in succession, the nature of the principal components of the reaction to bereavement, the effects of bereavement upon physical and mental health, the reaction to stress in general, the highly specific 'search' component that characterizes grieving and shows it to be an inevitable part of love, the ways in which we gradually make real the fact and implications of loss, the part played by feelings of anger and self-reproach, and the gradual discovery of new meaning and identity. It then discusses the morbid or atypical forms that grief may take, and considers the several factors that affect the course of grief and the means by which this course can be modified. In the penultimate chapter, bereavement is looked at as one among many major transitions, each of which constitutes a period of challenge and readjustment, and in the final chapter we examine how this combined knowledge can be utilized in responding to the awesome challenges for caregivers faced with natural and man-made disasters.

Psychosocial transitions are the times when we reassess our picture of the world and our means of being a part of it. They are experienced as impinging upon us but their effects include major changes in the heartland of the self. At such times we are uniquely open both to help and to harm. We need protection, reassurance, time to recoup, and help in developing blueprints for the future. Those who are in a position to meet these needs must expect to find the recipient of their help defensive, sensitive, vulnerable, and unreasonable. Even so, a little help given at a time of transition will often be more effective than help given at other times and, in the long run, it will be appreciated more.

Successive editions of this book have been necessary every ten years or so because of the growth of knowledge that has taken place. The advent of computerized databases brought with it rapid access to thousands of papers on bereavement and some of them have helped us to a greater understanding and changed our ways of helping the bereaved.

As a result it has been necessary to change our minds about a few things, and to extend our thinking about others. One problem is the increasing sophistication of the research methods and statistical analyses that are now employed. It was this, together with considerable respect for her work, which prompted Parkes to invite Prigerson to join him as co-author of this volume. Prigerson has played a major part in The Yale Bereavement Study that has provided a firm scientific basis for diagnosing the most frequent and distressing complications of bereavement.

Several theoretical models have received attention in recent years and, while we question claims that they constitute a new paradigm for understanding bereavement, they deserve attention. These include a greater understanding of the ways in which people can discover new meaning in their lives after a major loss, a greater recognition of the extent to which attachment to loved people continues after their death ('continuing bonds'), and a growing interest in the positive assumptions and attitudes that make for resilience.

Perhaps the most remarkable technical advance in the decade has resulted from the discovery of ways of studying the moment-to-moment changes in the human brain in action. Up to now, much of the human brain has remained *terra incognita*. One can only compare these recent discoveries to those of the early explorations of the earth and heavens.

Thanks to the wonder of fMRI scanning it is now possible to anatomize a pang of grief. We shall see how this work confirms the theory that grief involves parts of the brain that we share with other species. Although this work is in its infancy we have no doubt that, in the years to come, scientists will map out the neuroanatomical basis of grief and its consequences for mental functioning. It is, to coin a phrase, time for us to get our heads round our brains.

Another area that has developed in recent years has been cellular chemistry and physiology. It is now possible to remove living cells from the human body and to demonstrate that those arising from bereaved people are functioning less efficiently than those from non-bereaved. Are they grieving?

It is also possible to identify the chemical messengers that trigger or inhibit the nervous pathways that have been discovered by fMRI scanning. This opens the door to possible future use of medications to correct malfunction in these pathways.

All this is difficult stuff, but we have done our best to make it comprehensible for the reader and, as in previous editions, have continued to place the technical aspects of the research in the appendices.

Of more immediate importance for the practice of bereavement care has been the publication of a large number of well-conducted evaluations of bereavement services. The results have disappointed any expectation that we might have had that most bereaved people will obtain lasting benefit to their physical and mental health from the kind of bereavement counselling that is now widely available. The good news is that most people come through bereavement well, without the need for substantial help from outside their network of family and friends; for the minority who do not, effective interventions are now possible. This book will attempt to make use of the best available evidence to enable the reader to identify those who need help, to provide that help where possible, and to steer others towards special sources of help for special problems.

Colin Murray Parkes
Holly G. Prigerson

1

THE COST OF COMMITMENT

> The mourner is in fact ill, but because this state of mind is
> common and seems so natural to us, we do not call mourn-
> ing an illness.
>
> Melanie Klein, 1940

Although Sigmund Freud contributed little to our understanding
of bereavement it is interesting to find that his discovery of psycho-
analysis, and the subsequent development of psychotherapy, origin-
ated from the study of a bereaved young lady. Anna O. was an
intelligent, imaginative girl of twenty-one, who sought help from
Freud's friend and colleague Dr Josef Breuer. A puritan in a purit-
anical family, Anna led a monotonous existence enlivened by the rich
fantasy world she created for herself. Although she is described as
moody and obstinate, she was a sympathetic person, fond of helping
the sick and passionately devoted to her father.

Her mental illness took the form of a succession of psychosomatic
and dissociative symptoms including headaches, 'absences', para-
lyses and anaesthesia in her limbs. These came on during her father's
terminal illness and got worse after his death. Breuer came to see her
each day and treated her by encouraging her to talk about her fantasies. These were always sad and usually involved a girl sitting
beside a sick-bed. After the father's death the symptoms got worse
and the stories became more tragic. Breuer discovered that each
symptom was related to a particular disturbing event, and tended to
improve when Anna had succeeded in discussing the event that was
associated with it.

When the anniversary of her father's illness arrived, Anna O. began
to relive, during her 'absences', the traumatic events of the preceding
year. These episodes were precipitated by any reminder of that year

and their accuracy was authenticated by reference to her mother's diary. It was at this time that a number of severe and obstinate symptoms disappeared dramatically after she had described the events that, Breuer concluded, had given rise to them. Breuer reinforced these recollections by causing her to relive experiences by means of hypnosis. Thus, the crucial observation of a link between a traumatic loss and the symptoms which followed, gave rise to what Breuer called the 'talking cure'.

Sigmund Freud, who knew Breuer well, was greatly interested in this case and made use of the 'talking cure' himself. Breuer, on the other hand, did not pursue his discovery. He had devoted so much time and interest to this one attractive girl that his own marriage was affected. According to Ernest Jones (1953, 1955), Breuer, when he realized the extent of his involvement with this patient, abruptly brought the treatment to an end. Anna, who was by now strongly attached to Breuer, responded to this latest loss by becoming distressed and developing a fresh crop of dramatic symptoms, among them a hysterical childbirth or 'pseudocyesis'. The subsequent course of her illness was not as uneventful as Breuer's account leads one to suppose. She appears to have continued to have 'absences' for some years and to have been admitted to a mental institution on at least one occasion – here she is said to have 'inflamed the heart of the psychiatrist in charge'. She never married, remained deeply religious, became the first social worker in Germany, founded a periodical, and started several institutes (Zangwill, 1987).

A description of the case of Anna O. was published jointly by Breuer and Freud in 1893, in a paper entitled 'On the Psychical Mechanisms of Hysterical Phenomena', along with a series of cases treated by similar means. Although Breuer lost interest in the 'talking cure', Freud took it up with enthusiasm. He made a virtue of the personal relationship between patient and physician and believed that improvement often depended upon this. Hypnosis he eventually abandoned because it interfered with this relationship and because he found the method of 'free association' equally effective in the recovery of memories of traumatic events.

With hindsight it seems likely that, by encouraging and rewarding Anna's fantasies, Freud and Breuer may have perpetuated her problems. Indeed, Freud soon found that the recovery of recent memories, in this and other cases did not necessarily relieve symptoms. He therefore encouraged his patients to recall earlier periods of their lives, and he claimed that he discovered the memories of primal events in their childhoods, which he believed to have been the critical determinants of mental illness. Already by 1898, five years after the publication of the paper mentioned above, Freud had become convinced of the importance of sexual experiences in childhood and thenceforth he took less interest in the recent experiences of his patients. Nevertheless, he never gave up the view that major psychic traumata, occurring in childhood or in adult life, can be responsible for neurotic illness. He gave evidence to this effect before a commission set up by the Austrian military authorities after the First World War to investigate the harsh treatment of war neuroses by their own doctors.

We have dwelt on Freud's contribution because of its great influence and also because we believe that it is more than a coincidence that the breakthrough to which Breuer's talking cure gave rise resulted from the investigation of a case of mental illness arising at the time of the loss of a father. There is no doubt that the symptoms that Anna O. developed resulted from a combination of causes, some relating to her father's threatened or actual death, others to her own personality and early life experiences. Her father's illness and death can be regarded as the precipitating circumstances without which the illness would probably not have arisen – at least not in the form it actually took. Thus, by examining the relationship between a recent precipitating event and the particular symptoms that followed it, Breuer and Freud made a contribution to our understanding of psychopathology.

Few other attempts have been made to do just this, perhaps because the connection between a particular event and a particular symptom is often difficult to trace. Nevertheless, we believe that where major stresses are concerned (and loss of a close relative is normally a major stressor) this approach fully justifies its results.

A bereavement by death is an important and obvious happening which is unlikely to be overlooked. Less obvious forms of loss, and losses that take place some time before the onset of an illness, may be overlooked. Even if they are not, it is less easy to demonstrate that there is a causal connection between them and the illness. And even if a causal connection can be assumed, the precise nature of this connection needs to be understood.

If, by studying the clear-cut case where causation is undoubted, we can learn more about the chain of causation and its precise consequences it may eventually be possible to understand other types of case by starting from the consequences and working backwards towards the causes.

TRAUMATIC STRESS

The field of post-traumatic stress has come to prominence in recent years thanks to the recognition of a complex of symptoms, which are likely to arise when people experience severe threats to their lives or witness peculiarly horrifying scenes. It has been termed Post-Traumatic Stress Disorder (PTSD). PTSD accounted for much of the mental illness found among veterans of the war in Vietnam and, although it had been described after many other situations in the past, it was that event, more than any other, which forced psychiatrists to acknowledge the existence of PTSD as a diagnosis. The distinctive features of PTSD are haunting memories of the traumatic event that are so vivid that the sufferer feels as if they are experiencing the trauma again and again. These occur during the day or at night in the form of recurrent nightmares. They are so painful that people will go to great lengths to avoid any reminder that will trigger them off. They feel as if they are waiting for the next disaster and are constantly jumpy and on the alert.

Clearly PTSD differs from the other psychological reaction to major traumatic events, grief. Despite Freud's insistence on the importance of mourning (1917), the reaction to bereavement had been little studied by psychiatrists until recent years. Grief, after all, is a normal response to a stress that, while rare in the life of each of us, will be experienced by most sooner or later; and it is not commonly thought of as a mental illness. But what is a mental illness?

GRIEF AND MENTAL DISORDER

Bereaved people often fear that they are going mad and organizations for the bereaved take pains to reassure them that grief is not a mental disorder but a 'normal' response to bereavement. While this is an understandable and well-meant response it perpetuates two fallacies, that mental disorders are forms of insanity and that they are abnormal. In fact, only a very small proportion of people diagnosed with mental disorders are insane, mad or psychotic and most mental disorders are normal ways of reacting to life circumstances and situations that are themselves abnormal.

Nor is it true that mental disorders are incurable or that only psychiatrists are qualified to treat such conditions. Most psychiatric conditions improve over time even without treatment and those treatments that are necessary can usually be given by psychologists, counsellors, or members of primary health care teams.

The assertion that because grief will be experienced by most of us sooner or later it cannot be said to be an illness is not valid. There are many illnesses that most of us experience: chicken pox, measles, even the common cold. If a bruise or a broken arm, the consequence of physical injury, is within the realm of pathology, why not grief, the consequence of a psychological trauma?

But doctors don't treat grief, you may say. In fact they do. There are indications that many people go to their doctor for help after a bereavement, and a large proportion of their complaints, as we shall show, are expressions of grief. Even those who do not seek help are not necessarily 'well'; people suffer various physical complaints without requesting help, and there are numerous minor ailments such as warts, bruises, or burns for which professional care is unnecessary.

Illnesses are characterized by the discomfort and the disturbance of function that they produce. Grief may not produce physical pain, but it is very unpleasant and it usually disturbs function. Thus newly bereaved people are often treated by society in much the same way as a sick person. Employers expect them to miss work, they stay at home, and relatives visit and talk in hushed tones. For a time, others take over responsibility for making decisions and acting on their behalf. When grief is severe, bereaved people may be disabled for weeks, and relatives worry about them; later they may say, 'I don't know how I lived through it'.

On the whole, grief resembles a physical injury more closely than any other type of illness. The loss may be spoken of as a 'blow'. As in the case of a physical injury, the 'wound' gradually heals; at least, it usually does. But occasionally complications set in, healing is delayed, or a further injury reopens a healing wound. In such cases abnormal forms arise, which may even be complicated by the onset of other types of illness. Sometimes it seems that the outcome may be fatal.

This said, in view of current prejudice, it would do more harm than good to label those who suffer a major loss as mentally ill. That term would only be justified if the symptoms were so lasting, severe, and disabling that it was to the patient's advantage to provide them with the treatments and privileges that accompany illness. We shall see, in the course of this book, that there are indeed a minority of bereaved people who meet these criteria. But even they can be reassured that their psychiatric disorder is not madness or incurable, it is a psychological condition that can be diagnosed and treated.

Since the first edition of this book was published the influential *Diagnostic and Statistical Manual* of the American Psychiatric Association (1987, 1994) has included 'Bereavement' among a group of 'Other Conditions that may be the focus of clinical attention'. In this way they allow it to be taken into consideration without committing themselves to a diagnosis.

In many respects, then, grief can be regarded as an illness. But it can also bring strength. Just as broken bones may end up stronger than unbroken ones, so the experience of grieving can strengthen and bring maturity to those who have previously been protected from misfortune. The pain of grief is just as much a part of life as the joy of love; it is, perhaps, the price we pay for love, the cost of commitment. To ignore this fact, or to pretend that it is not so, is to put on emotional blinkers, which leave us unprepared for the losses that will inevitably occur in our lives and unprepared to help others to cope with the losses in theirs.

We know of only two functional psychiatric conditions whose cause is known, whose features are distinctive, and whose course is usually predictable, and those are PTSD and grief. Yet PTSD is a relatively new discovery and grief has been so neglected by psychiatrists that, until recently, it was not even mentioned in the indexes of most of the best-known general textbooks of psychiatry. The diagnostic systems that are in use in psychiatry grew up without reference to these conditions.

When knowledge is lacking regarding the aetiology and pathology of a disease, it is standard medical practice to classify it by its symptoms. This is what has happened in psychiatry. It is the principal presenting symptom that usually determines the diagnosis, and because psychiatric patients usually complain of emotional disturbance, the diagnostic labels contain the names of the emotions involved. Thus we have anxiety states, phobias, depressive reactions, depressive psychoses, and so on. The system would work better if there were not so many patients who exhibit one feature at one time and a different one at another. This leads to strange combination terms such as phobic anxiety, anxiety-depression, schizo-affective disorder, or, as a last resort, to pan-neurosis or personality disorder. When asked how to classify psychiatric problems that follow bereavement, most psychiatrists say 'depression', and certainly depression is a common feature. Yet more prominent is a special kind of anxiety, separation anxiety, which is discussed at length in Chapter 4. In fact, it is fair to say that the pining or yearning that constitutes separation anxiety is the characteristic feature of the pang of grief. If grief is to be forced into the Procrustean bed of traditional psychiatric diagnosis, therefore, it should probably become a subgroup of the anxiety states. This said, separation anxiety should not be confused with general anxiety, and prolonged grief disorders have quite different patterns of symptoms from Generalized Anxiety Disorders (GAD; Prigerson *et al.*, 1996). Furthermore, separation anxiety is not always the symptom that causes a bereaved person to seek help and it may be that PTSD and grief will open the door to a new classificatory system. We shall return to these issues in Chapter 8.

THE PROCESS OF GRIEVING

Although there is a tendency for the features of grief to diminish over time, the symptoms of grief do not all appear from day one and then fade away, there is a pattern to the process of grieving. It involves a succession of clinical pictures, which blend into and replace one another, and which vary greatly from one person to another, one family to another and even one culture to another. In this book we shall see how numbness, commonly the first state, gives place to pining, and pining is often followed by a period of disorganization and despair until, in the long run, this too declines as acceptance grows. Many people use the term 'recovery' to describe this time although we are all, to some extent, permanently changed by the losses in our lives; a widow does not go back to being the same married person that she was, even if she remarries (Bowlby and Parkes, 1970; Maciejewski *et al.*, 2007; Prigerson and Maciejewski, 2008; and Appendix 1).

Each of these states of grief, has its own characteristics and there are considerable differences from one person to another as regards both the duration and the form of each state. Furthermore people can move back and forth through the states so that, years after a bereavement, the discovery of a photograph in a drawer or a visit from an old friend can evoke another episode of pining. In the light of this variation we no longer use the term 'phases of grief' as this gives too rigid a framework and it is not surprising that some have questioned the existence of the phases of grief (Wortman and Silver, 1989). Nevertheless, more recent quantitative research (see Appendix 1) has confirmed that there is a tendency for the symptoms that distinguish these phases to peak in the order given above (Maciejewski *et al.*, 2007), however, one phase does not have to end before the next can begin and there is considerable overlap between them. In the American study, which included a wider age range than the younger widowed sample from London, many bereaved people were able to accept the reality of bereavement from the start and yearning was the most prominent negative feature throughout the first two years of bereavement. For these reasons we no longer consider the 'phases of grief' to be a very useful concept. Perhaps its greatest value has been to draw attention to the fact that grief is a process through which people pass and that, in doing so, most tend to move from a state of relative disorientation and distress to one of growing understanding and acceptance of the loss (Prigerson and Maciejewski, 2008).

We said earlier that grief is not a common stress in the lives of most of us. In saying this we should, perhaps, have written grief with a capital G. Losses are, of course, common in all our lives. And in so far as grief is the reaction to loss, grief must be common too. But the term grief is not normally used for the reaction to the loss of an old umbrella. It is more usually reserved for the loss of a person, and a loved person at that. It is this type of grief that is the subject of this book, and this type of loss is not a common event in the lives of most of us.

Even bereavement by death is not as simple a stress as it might, at first sight, appear to be. In any bereavement it is seldom clear exactly what is lost. The loss of a husband, for instance, may or may not mean the loss of a sexual partner, companion, accountant, gardener, baby-minder, audience, bed-warmer, and so on, depending upon the particular roles normally performed by this husband. Moreover, one loss often brings other secondary losses in its train. The loss of a spouse is often accompanied by a considerable drop in income, and this may mean that the widow or widower must sell his or her house, change his or her job (if s/he has one), and move to a strange environment. The need to learn new roles without the support of the person upon whom one has come to rely, at a time when others in the family, especially children, are themselves bereaved and needing support, can place a major burden on a person over and above the fact of the bereavement itself.

Of course, not all of the changes that follow bereavement are losses. In the ongoing flux of life human beings undergo many changes. Arriving, departing, growing, declining, achieving, failing – every change involves a loss and a gain. The old environment must be given up, the new accepted. People come and go; one job is lost, another begun; territory and possessions are acquired or sold; new skills are learnt, old abandoned; expectations are fulfilled or hopes dashed – in all these situations individuals are faced with the need to give up one mode of life and accept another. If they identify the change as a gain, acceptance may not be hard, but when it is a loss or a 'mixed blessing' they will do their best to resist the change. Resistance to change, the reluctance to give up possessions, people, status, expectations – this, we believe, is a major component of grief.

An important contribution to our understanding of grief has been made, in recent years, by Stroebe and Schut (1999) who see grief as involving two orientations, a loss orientation and a restoration (or change) orientation. When oriented towards loss we look back, when oriented towards restoration we look forward. Since it is not possible to look back and forward at the same time, bereaved people must oscillate between these two orientations. We shall see how these two orientations reflect two quite different, but overlapping, psychological processes, one reflecting the continuing attachment to the lost person, the other the need to change a whole set of assumptions and habits of thought as we move forward in life.

A death occurs at a particular time and place. Of course it may have been anticipated. An illness can drag on over a great length of time and sometimes people have been functionally dead for months before their physical death. Nevertheless, it is, in our experience, rare for there to be no reaction to the death itself. Even when patients have been unconscious for weeks and the doctors, in their alienation, have come to regard them as 'vegetables', relatives continue to visit and hope. Even when the relatives say that they know there is no hope, they betray the expectation that something can be regained or retained of the old relationship. That they may continue to do this after the death is a fact that is not generally recognized. But there are good grounds for regarding the death itself as the crucial event after which grief can normally be expected to occur. And for all that has just been said, bereaved people do have enough in common to make it worth while to look at bereavement as a whole and to map out the course of events that tend to follow it.

Apart from grief, two other factors that often play a part in determining the overall reaction to a bereavement are stigma and deprivation.

STIGMA

By stigma we mean the change in attitude that takes place in society when a person dies. Every widow discovers that people who were previously friendly and approachable become embarrassed and strained in her presence. Expressions of sympathy often have a hollow ring and offers of help are not followed up. It often happens that only those who share the grief or have themselves suffered a major loss remain at hand. It is as if the widow has become tainted with death in much the same way as the funeral director.

In some societies the taboo on bereaved people can be more explicit. In a paper entitled 'A Little Widow is a Dangerous Thing', Cochrane (1936) wrote:

> Among the Shuswap of British Columbia widows and widowers in mourning are secluded and forbidden to touch their own bodies; the cups and cooking vessels which they use may be used by no one else. They build a sweat house by a creek, sweat there all night and bathe regularly, after which they must rub their bodies with branches of spruce. No hunter comes near such mourners, for their presence is unlucky . . . Thorn bushes are used for bed and pillow, and thorn bushes are also laid around their beds.

The Agutainos of Polawan also find the widow a dangerous thing:

> She may only go out at an hour when she is unlikely to meet anyone, for whoever sees her is thought to die a sudden death. To prevent this she knocks with a wooden peg on the trees as she goes along, warning people of her presence. It is believed that the very trees on which she knocks will soon die (ibid.).

In the circumstances it is not surprising that many societies have found it most convenient to send the widow into the next world along with her husband. Ritual suicide has been widespread, appearing in Asia, Africa, America, and Australia. Cochrane cites traces of it in Europe also.

In our society we have less fear of the newly bereaved, but we still find it difficult to accept their need to mourn, and when forced to meet them we find ourselves at a loss. Geoffrey Gorer (1965), in his study of grief and mourning in Britain, said, 'Mourning is treated as if it were a weakness, a self-indulgence, a reprehensible bad habit instead of a psychological necessity'. We do not burn our widows, we pity and avoid them. In similar vein Illich (1977) has described bereavement as a form of 'Consumer Resistance'.

DEPRIVATION

Deprivation implies the absence of a necessary person or thing as opposed to the loss of that person or thing. A bereaved person reacts to both loss and deprivation. Grief is the reaction to loss, loneliness the reaction to deprivation. Deprivation means the absence of those essential 'supplies' that were previously provided by the lost person. Our understanding of the supplies provided by love relationships is still scanty. In a sense they are the psychological equivalents of food and drink. People are necessary to people, and the loss of a loved husband, wife, or child leaves behind a gap. Our needs for interaction with a loved person are presumably rooted in instinctual needs for pair bonding and brood rearing. They include much more than sexual intercourse and the suckling of the young. John Bowlby (1969) discussed at length the evolution of attachment behaviour. He suggested that at the time of its evolution 'protection from predators' was one of the most important functions of attachments between human beings. Although there is no longer any good reason for a widow to fear attack by hyenas, it is no surprise to find that the lack of a close attachment to another person is often associated with a subjective feeling of insecurity and danger. We shall see, in later chapters, that fears of separation, and the insecurity that results, sometimes persist into adult life and increase vulnerability to bereavement.

When we add to these instinctual supplies the supplies of information, comfort, money, sex, and other things that may derive from love objects in our complex society, it is clear that bereavement is likely to be followed by deprivation.

The cultural evolution that has made marriage and similar partnerships integral parts of our social organization has done little to ensure that the functions that they perform will be adequately carried out after their dissolution. Increasing disregard of formal mourning has meant that bereaved individuals get little support from society at large and from their own families in particular. Automatic remarriage to the husband's eldest brother (levirate marriage), once the custom among Jews, may not have solved the problem of mourning, but it must have ensured that many of the essential needs of the widow were met. Loneliness, poverty, rolelessness, sexual frustration, and absence of the security that comes from sharing responsibilities are a few of the ongoing feelings that stem from deprivation. They can be expected to continue as long as the deprivation continues and to end when alternative sources of supply are found. Widows who no

longer have small children must learn to live alone and it is no surprise to find that, in Lopata's (1979) study of widows in Chicago
who had been bereaved for an average of eleven years, half said that
'loneliness' was their greatest problem.

THE ROOTS OF GRIEF

Loss, change and deprivation are so inseparably bound together that
it is not possible to study one without the others. One can postulate
that the pangs of grief, will be greatest shortly after the loss, and will
then decline, leaving behind the reaction to deprivation, but people
even get used to being deprived.

There is one thing, however, that justifies us in treating bereavement as a unitary stress and paying less attention to secondary losses,
deprivation, role change, and stigma, that is the observation that
grief is so powerful a reaction that, for a time, it overshadows
all other sources of difficulty. '. . . for my particular grief', says
Brabantio, 'Is of so floodgate and o'erbearing nature, That it engluts
and swallows other sorrows, And it is still itself' (*Othello*, I.iii).

Attachment and personality

How someone copes with the challenge of change in their life will
determine not only their view of the world but their view of themselves. It is no exaggeration to assert that personality is both a result-
ant and a determinant of change. From the moment of their birth
children relate to the world around them. We are born with an innate
bias to develop behaviour patterns that, if all goes well, interlock
with the behaviour patterns of our mother and produce the first
attachment. We usually learn that our cry can be expected to fulfil its
biological function of attracting our mother. Before long we have
learned to charm by smiling and to maintain attachment by clinging.
As our size and strength increase and we begin to crawl or toddle,
our propensity to follow mother becomes apparent. From now on
we can maintain a safe proximity to her at will, but we can also
wander away. If we become aware that we have lost mother we will
cry and search restlessly and she will respond to our cry and come in
search of us.

In most human communities it is the mother to whom this first
attachment takes place and most of the research, which was initiated
by Bowlby's important work, 'Child Care and the Growth of Love'

(1953), has focused on her as the indispensable parent. More recently it has been shown that fathers and others can be satisfactory substitutes for the natural mother provided that they provide consistent care. Hence the term 'mother' throughout this book should be taken to refer to the person who is the primary carer.

So far there is nothing peculiarly human about the infant's behaviour. Other animals have the same or similar ties to their mothers. But already differences will be emerging and there is reason to believe that the manner in which the mother responds to the baby's attachment behaviour can determine how the baby henceforth behaves. The innate behaviour patterns that emerge in early childhood are soon modified, refined, or extinguished by experience. For instance, it has been shown experimentally that a baby's propensity to smile at a human face will gradually disappear if the human face consistently fails to smile back. Similarly, the 'bathroom treatment' for crying babies works on the assumption that, if you ignore a baby's cry for long enough it will stop crying. There are numerous studies of the effect of separating child from mother and these all point to the conclusion that such separations are potentially harmful to the developing child. Pathological effects seem most likely to occur if (a) the separation is prolonged, (b) no mother-substitute is available, (c) the child is in pain or its movement is restricted, (d) it is in an unfamiliar environment, and (e) it is between six months and three years of age at the time of the separation. The recognition of the importance of this combination of circumstances has given rise to major reforms in the care of young children in hospital, which include, in many hospitals, the admission of the mother along with the young child. (Details of the various studies that support these findings, and those that follow, are given in Bowlby's influential trilogy 'Attachment and Loss', published in 1969, 1973, and 1980).

The mother of a two-year-old child is a mobile base from which forays can be made into a semi-familiar world. The child is both attracted and repelled by the unfamiliar component in this world, but it is the proximity of mother that will determine whether a new object or person is approached or avoided. Periods of clinging tend to alternate with periods of exploration at a safe distance from mother, but if a stranger should appear or the child should suddenly realize that it has gone beyond the safe distance it soon 'returns to base'.

To young toddlers, therefore, mother is a haven of safety. The behaviour that attaches them to her ensures their protection and has evolved for that reason in human beings just as it has in a wide range of other species.

It is from this personal bond between mother and child that all subsequent relationships develop, and it is probably no exaggeration to say that what the toddler learns about mother governs its expectations of future relationships. Erikson (1950) has spoken of the 'basic trust' that may or may not arise in the mind of young children, and how this will influence their future attitudes not only to people but to the world in general and to changes occurring within it. By basic trust Erikson meant the development in the child of a confident expectation that when mother leaves she will return, that when she is needed she will be there, that if it cries out or searches for her she will be found.

Trust in others and trust in the world can be cemented or shattered by experiences at any stage in life, and literature abounds with tales of people who have been embittered by fate. Usually the happy ending comes when faith is restored by the love of another. But there are those who seem doomed to disappointment, and too often one finds that these people lack that basic trust which should arise in early childhood: intolerant of separation or change, they cling too hard to what they have, or, losing it, avoid all human involvement for fear of further disappointment.

The import of these remarks will become clear when we come to consider the consequences in later life of severing those personal bonds that succeed, and to some degree resemble, the primal tie to the mother. We shall not be surprised to find elements of the same behaviour patterns that were found in childhood and are found, to some extent, among a wide range of beasts, birds, and teleost fishes.

2

THE BROKEN HEART

> He only without framing word, or closing his eyes, but earnestly viewing the dead body of his son, stood still upright, till the vehemence of his sad sorrow, having suppressed and choaked his vitall spirits, fell'd him starke dead to the ground.
>
> Montaigne's description of the death of John,
> King of Hungaria

Is grief a cause of death? You will not find grief on a death certificate, not today. But the notion that one may die of grief is a popular theme among novelists, and it is not long ago that it was a recognized cause of death. Thus, in Dr Heberden's Bill classifying the causes of death in London during the year 1657 we find:

Flox and Small Pox	835
Found dead in the streets, etc.	9
French Pox	25
Gout	8
Griefe	**10**
Griping and Plague in the Guts	446
Hang'd and made away 'emselves	24

Such figures would today be dismissed as examples of medical mythology, but is there in fact any evidence that grief is sometimes a cause of death?

GRIEF AND BEREAVEMENT MORTALITY

There is, of course, no doubt that psychological factors play a part in many illnesses, but it is only in rare cases of 'vagal inhibition' and in so-called voodoo deaths that they appear to be the sole cause of death. Vagal inhibition is a pseudoscientific term sometimes used by doctors for the cause of death following a sudden emotional shock. A classic example is provided in the story of some students who held a mock trial and sentenced a man to death. He was led to the place of execution, blindfolded, and hit on the back of the neck with a towel – whereupon he died. Not dissimilar are the numerous well-authenticated cases of death from witchcraft. Although the witchcraft can take many different forms, such deaths seem to follow a general pattern. The 'victim' is told that the appropriate ritual curse has been carried out; if he has faith he at once becomes deeply depressed, stops eating, and within a few days is dead. In neither the vagal inhibition type of death nor death from witchcraft is there any post-mortem finding that explains the phenomenon.

Such occurrences are fortunately very rare, but there is other evidence of the effect of psychological factors on mortality among the unhealthy and ageing. Aldrich and Mendkoff, for instance, discovered a major increase in mortality among chronically sick patients when a Chicago Home for Incurables was closed for administrative reasons. Of 182 patients who were relocated in other homes, thirty were dead within three months – a mortality rate five times greater than expectation. Mortality was highest among those patients whose grasp on reality was most tenuous, particularly among the thirty-eight whom Aldrich rated as 'psychotic' before relocation, of whom twenty-four died within a year (Aldrich and Mendkoff, 1963).

Apart from a few isolated cases of doubtful authenticity, we have come across no evidence that phenomena such as these are responsible for death following bereavement. The examples have been quoted simply to remind the reader that psychological factors can have profound effects even on healthy people.

For many years it has been known that widows and widowers have a higher mortality rate than married men and women of the same age. But then so have bachelors and spinsters, and it is not unreasonable to suspect that some of the fitter widows and widowers remarry, thereby ensuring that those who remain will have a relatively high mortality rate (Johnson *et al.*, 2000).

This explanation might certainly account for an increased mortality rate among the widowed population as a whole, but it would not explain the peak of mortality in widowers during the first year of bereavement as discovered by Michael Young and his colleagues (Young, Benjamin, and Wallis, 1963). They found an increase in the death rate among 4486 widowers over the age of fifty-four of almost 40 per cent during the first six months of bereavement. This dropped off rapidly thereafter to around the mortality rate for married men of the same age. (Further details are given in Appendix 2.)

Since this study was published, a number of other studies of the mortality of bereavement have confirmed these findings. Reviewing fifteen longitudinal studies Stroebe and Stroebe (1993) concluded, 'The bereaved are indeed at higher risk of dying than are non-bereaved persons. This seems to apply not only to the widowed but also to other bereaved relatives. Highest risk occurs in the weeks and months closest to loss'.

Several studies (reviewed by Stroebe and Stroebe, 1993), have confirmed that widowers are more vulnerable to death following bereavement than widows. This said, widows may also be at risk, as confirmed by a major study by Mellstrom *et al.* (1982) who found a highly significant increase in the death rate among widows during the first three months of bereavement and among widowers during the whole of the first year. The life expectancy of widowers was reduced by one and a half years and that of widows by six months. Among parents losing a child it is the mothers who have been found to be at greater risk than fathers (Li, Mortensen, and Olsen, 2003). Possible explanations for these gender differences will be considered on page 147.

Of other types of bereavement Rees and Lutkins (1967) and Li *et al.* (2003) have found an increased mortality among parents who have lost a child, Roskin (1984) among grandparents who have lost a grandchild and Tomassini *et al.* (1998) among twins whose twin has died, with the highest rates in identical, monozygotic, twins.

Causes of death after bereavement

Several diseases contribute to the higher mortality in the bereaved, but the most frequent cause of death is heart disease. The research by Young *et al.* (1963) on the death rate among widowers was used as the basis of a further study (carried out by Parkes, Benjamin, and Fitzgerald, 1969) of the causes of death among these same widowers as revealed on their death certificates. It was soon apparent that three-quarters of the increased death rate during the first six months of bereavement was attributable to heart disease, in particular to coronary infarction and arteriosclerotic heart disease (see Appendix 2). This is confirmed in Mellstrom's study and further confirmation comes from a study of sudden cardiac deaths in women aged between twenty-five and sixty-four (Cottington *et al.*, 1980). They were six times more likely to have suffered the death of a significant other person than were women in a healthy control group.

The origin of the term 'broken heart' goes back to biblical times. 'Bind up the broken hearted', says Isaiah, and the idea seems to have persisted ever since that severe grief can somehow damage the heart. Benjamin Rush, the American physician and signatory of the Declaration of Independence, wrote in his *Medical Inquiries and Observations upon the Diseases of the Mind* (1835): 'Dissection of persons who have died of grief, show congestion in, and inflammation of the heart, with rupture of its auricles and ventricles'. Rupture of the heart is, of course, a rare condition, but when it does occur it is usually caused by a coronary infarction. All of which leads us to suspect that the old physicians may not have been as foolish as we suppose. (In case any bereaved reader is now clutching his chest and preparing to call an ambulance, may we hasten to point out that palpitations and a feeling of fullness in the chest are normal concomitants of anxiety and that bereaved people often experience them without developing heart disease.)

The fact that bereavement may be followed by death from heart disease does not prove that grief is itself a cause of death. We do not even know whether bereavement causes the illness or simply aggravates a condition that would have occurred anyway. Perhaps widowers tend to smoke more or to alter their diet in a way that increases their liability to coronary infarction. Even if emotional factors are directly implicated we still have to explain how they affect the heart. Stress is known to produce changes in the blood pressure and heart rate, in the flow of blood through the coronary arteries, and in the chemical constituents of the blood. Any of these changes could play a part in precipitating clotting within a diseased coronary artery and thereby produce a coronary infarction, but without further research we can only speculate.

One other interesting finding can be seen in the graph (Figure 2) shown in Appendix 2. If the widowers in our study survived for four years after their spouse's death their mortality rate dropped to below that of married persons of the same age. A similar finding has been reported by Lichtenstein, Gatz, and Berg (1998) in a well-conducted study in which twins who had lost a spouse were compared to their married twin. As in our study, death of the spouse was followed by a sharp rise in mortality in the first year of bereavement but a mark-edly decreased rate (compared with the married twin) in those who survived for more than 4 years. Two explanations are possible, either the bereaved people became more physically resilient than married people over the years, or those who died were already sick and/or at risk prior to their bereavement, which had the effect of bringing forward a death that would eventually have occurred in any case.

Most studies have not shown an increase in deaths from cancers following bereavement, but cancers can take a long time to kill and there are few long-term follow-ups of bereaved populations. An exception is Levav's 20-year follow-up of 6284 Israeli parents who lost an adult son in an accident or at war. They found a significant increase in deaths from cancers of the lung, blood and skin. They were also able to show that parents who already had cancers at the time of their bereavement were more likely to die from the cancer and died sooner than those whose cancer developed after their bereavement (Levav *et al.*, 1988). Thus bereavement may reduce resistance to cancer.

Other causes of the increased mortality after bereavement are sui-cide, cirrhosis of the liver, infectious diseases, and accidents.

Psychological factors influencing the increased mortality after bereavement

Four longitudinal studies have shown an increased risk of suicide among bereaved people (Bojanovsky, 1980; Bunch, 1972; Kaprio, Koshkenvuo, and Rita, 1987; McMahon and Pugh, 1965). This is greatest during the first week of bereavement when Kaprio *et al.* showed a ten-fold increase in suicidal deaths among women and a sixty-six-fold increase in men. Parents and sons are at risk as well as spouses (Bunch, 1972).

Increased mortality from accidental and other violent deaths was reported by Jones and Goldblatt (1987) and by Mellstrom *et al.* (1982). This finding may be explained both by lack of self-care, newly bereaved people often have difficulty concentrating on driving and some take deliberate risks, and by excessive consumption of alcohol, which is a contributing factor to many violent deaths.

Four large-scale studies have shown that it is the most stressful bereavements that carry the greatest risk of mortality. In one, deaths caused by illnesses associated with 'risk-taking' (e.g. alcoholism, tobacco and accidents) predicted an increased mortality in the bereaved spouses (Martikainen and Valkonen, 1996), in a study of parents who had lost a child the greatest increase in mortality was found among mothers whose child had died unexpectedly and from unnatural causes (Li *et al.*, 2003). Among people whose spouse had died at home, those with the highest 'caregiver burden' also had the highest rates of mortality (Christakis and Allison, 2006) and a very similar study of elderly bereaved people showed that, even controlling for the health of the bereaved person before bereavement, those with high levels of caregiver strain had a mortality rate over the first four years of bereavement that was 63% higher than that of those who were not responsible for care or did not find it a strain (Schulz *et al.*, 2001).

Could bereavement mortality be reduced?

In an important review of evidence, Osterweis, Solomon, and Green (1984) pointed out that, of the three principle causes of bereavement-related death (suicide, cirrhosis of the liver, and cardiac events), 'All three conditions often have clinical antecedents (depression, alcoholism, and cardiovascular disease) that could be detected before or very shortly after bereavement, thus identifying three high-risk groups for whom early intervention might be useful'.

In all known societies it is friends and families who provide most of us with psychological support after bereavement and it is fascinating to learn that, in a sample of 503 elderly British widows and widowers who were followed up for six years after bereavement, factors associated with high death rates were: (1) having nobody to telephone; (2) not having seen all of one's grandchildren during the first six months of bereavement; and (3) having no live brothers or sisters (Bowling, 1988). This is but one among many papers showing the benefits of social support on health after bereavement (see Chapter 12 and Parkes, 2006, for further details). Clearly we need to cherish the old folks if we want them to live long and contented lives.

Another type of intervention that may reduce mortality is remarriage. Thus Helsing, Comstock, and Szklo (1982) found that widowers who remarried had a mortality rate substantially lower than widowers who did not remarry and lower even than the rates among married men in the control group! However, it may well be that this reflects the effects of good health on eligibility rather than the effects of remarriage on health.

It seems likely that measures aimed at reducing the stress of bereavement will also help to reduce mortality. Hospices are well known for their support to patients and their families and Christakis and Iwashyna (2003) found a significantly lower mortality among widows whose husband died in a hospice by comparison with deaths in other settings. They do not report the cause of death in these cases and they may well result from the influence of lower levels of stress on the heart, but there is also some evidence that the number of suicides among the relatives of patients dying at St Christopher's Hospice, Sydenham, UK, has diminished since the introduction of a bereavement service (this is described in more detail on page 242).

OTHER EFFECTS OF BEREAVEMENT ON HEALTH

Many studies have shown that bereavement is associated with an increased risk to both physical and mental health. In Britain, under the National Health Service (NHS) each member of the British population is registered with a general practitioner (GP) who keeps a standard medical record. Most wives are registered with the same GP as their husband. This makes NHS records a valid source of information about the health of widows and widowers who experience increased rates of consultation with GPs during the first year of bereavement (Charlton *et al.*, 2001; Parkes 1964). Other studies have shown similar increases in hospital admissions (Laditka and Laditka, 2003) and overall health costs (Prigerson, Maciejewski, and Rosenheck, 2000).

Physical health

Lindemann's interest in bereavement as a topic worthy of study was triggered by his observation of an association between losses and the onset of ulcerative colitis (1945). What other effects does bereavement have upon health? Many physical and mental illnesses have been attributed to loss. Usually the attribution is based on the observation that the illness in question came on shortly after a loss. But since losses of one sort or another occur in the lives of all of us, a chance association between illness and loss is always possible. Furthermore, the distinction between physical and psychological symptoms soon breaks down. In the rest of this chapter we discuss, first, the types of condition that are commonly brought to the attention of a physician or GP, and we then go on to look at the symptoms reported by bereaved psychiatric patients. It will soon be obvious that there is a considerable overlap.

As we have seen above, heart conditions explain much of the increased mortality and several studies have shown an increased incidence, after bereavement, of congestive heart failure (Chambers and Reiser, 1953), hypertension (Santic *et al.*, 2006; Wiener *et al.*, 1975), and sudden cardiac arrests (Engel, 1971).

Some of the better studies of the psychosomatic effects of loss have come from the Strong Memorial Hospital in Rochester, USA, where a group of psychiatrists developed the theory that it is the feelings of helplessness and hopelessness that may accompany loss that are responsible for physical illness. In one remarkable study, women suspected of having cancer of the womb were 'diagnosed' by a psychiatrist with striking accuracy (see Appendix 3). These women had been admitted for investigation after a routine vaginal smear had revealed the presence of ugly-looking cells that might or might not indicate cancer. At this stage nobody knew whether a cancer was present or not, and a biopsy was necessary to prove or disprove such a diagnosis. The psychiatrist, who was as ignorant as anyone of the true situation, interviewed each woman and asked her about her feelings about any recent losses in her life. When he found evidence of both loss and feelings of helplessness or hopelessness he predicted that this woman would, in fact, be found to have cancer. In 71 per cent of cases his diagnosis proved to be correct.

The sceptic will point out that perhaps, unbeknown to the doctor, these women did have an inkling of their true diagnosis and it was this knowledge that influenced their feelings or their tendency to recall recent losses in their lives. Similar bias could conceivably explain the high rate of losses reported to Cooper and Farragher (1993) by women with breast cancers. Even so, the evidence from the studies of cancer deaths cannot be explained away and, as we shall see, more recent studies of the underlying causes of cancer provide an explanation for these findings.

High rates of loss have also been reported in a number of other conditions. Thus Klerman and Izen (1977), reviewing an extensive literature, in addition to cardiovascular diseases, list acute closed-angle glaucoma, cancer, Cushing's disease, disseminated lupus ery-thematosus, idiopathic glossodynia, pernicious anaemia, pneumonia, rheumatoid arthritis, thyrotoxicosis, tuberculosis, and ulcerative col-itis. More recently non-epileptic seizures (Reuber *et al.*, 2007), and a rare condition that causes painful bruising, autoerythrocyte sensitiza-tion syndrome (Gundogar *et al.*, 2006), have been added to the list.

In retrospective studies of this type the investigator starts with a person who is sick, or suspected of being sick, and attempts to find out the number and severity of any losses suffered prior to the onset of illness. They can then be compared with the number and severity of losses suffered by a control group of healthy people. Such studies always carry a risk of retrospective bias, depressed or grieving people may recall losses more readily than healthy persons because they take a more pessimistic view of the world and interpret life events as losses rather than minor blips or challenges. Another way of proceeding is to start with people who are known to have suffered a particular loss and to follow them up in order to find out what illnesses are contracted thereafter. This approach has been adopted in several studies of bereaved people. For example, seventy-two East London widows were interviewed by Peter Marris on average two years after they had been bereaved; thirty-one (43 per cent) thought that their general health was now worse than it had been before bereavement (Marris, 1958). In another study by Hobson (1964), a similar proportion of widows (seventeen out of forty) from an English market town made the same assertion. According to both these studies the number of complaints attributed to bereavement was very large. Headaches, digestive upsets, rheumatism, and asthma were particularly frequent.

In one study of the case records of eight London GPs, Parkes was able to identify forty-four widows who had been registered with their GP for two years before and one and a half years after bereavement (Parkes, 1964). Three-quarters of these widows consulted their GPs within six months of bereavement and this was a 63 per cent increase over the number who had consulted them in a similar period prior to bereavement. The largest increase was in consultations for anxiety, depression, insomnia, and other psychological symptoms, which were clearly attributable to grief. But it was surprising to find that the rise in consultations for such symptoms was confined to widows under sixty-five years of age. Older people did not, apparently, consult their doctor about these matters. Consultations for physical symptoms, however, had increased in all age-groups, most notably for arthritis and rheumatic conditions. Psychological factors are known to play a part in rheumatism, but many of these widows had osteoarthritis, a condition that takes years to develop. It seems therefore that, as with coronary infarction, the bereavement probably did not originate the condition but aggravated one that was already present. It is possible, too, that the widows were using their arthritis as an excuse to visit their doctor and that the higher consultation rate reflected a need for help which had little to do with their physical state (these findings are discussed in more detail in Appendix 4).

A useful series of studies which does not rely on the widow consulting her doctor was carried out by Maddison and his colleagues from the University of Sydney, Australia (Maddison, 1968; Maddison and Viola, 1968; Maddison, Viola, and Walker, 1969). They devised a postal questionnaire containing fifty-seven questions about symptoms and health care over the preceding year. This was completed by 132 American and 221 Australian widows thirteen months after bereavement, and by control groups of married women. All were under the age of sixty. Of the total sample of widows, 28 per cent obtained scores indicating 'marked' deterioration in health, compared with only 4.5 per cent of the married women.

Symptoms that were commoner in the bereaved than in the married groups included nervousness, depression, fears of nervous breakdown, feelings of panic, persistent fears, 'peculiar thoughts', nightmares, insomnia, trembling, loss of appetite (or, in a few, excessive appetite), loss of weight, reduced working capacity, and fatigue. All these symptoms are common features of grief and it is not surprising to find them complained of by a group of newly bereaved widows. But Maddison *et al.* found also, in the widows, excessive incidence of symptoms that were less obviously features of grieving. These included headache, dizziness, fainting spells, blurred vision, skin rashes, excessive sweating, indigestion, difficulty in swallowing, vomiting, heavy menstrual periods, palpitations, chest pains, shortness of breath, frequent infections, and general aching.

Many of Maddison's findings have subsequently been confirmed in a study of sixty-eight young Boston widows and widowers under the age of forty-five, which Parkes carried out with Ira Glick, Robert Weiss, Gerald Caplan, and others at Harvard Medical School. (This study is henceforth referred to as the Harvard Study. The findings are reported in more detail in Glick, Parkes, and Weiss, 1974, and Parkes and Weiss, 1983.) These unselected widows and widowers were interviewed fourteen months after bereavement and compared with a control group of sixty-eight married men and women of the same age, sex, occupational class, and family size. The bereaved group showed evidence of depression and of general emotional disturbance as reflected in restlessness and insomnia, and in having difficulty in making decisions and remembering things. They also consumed more tranquillizers, alcohol, and tobacco than they had done prior to bereavement. They were distinguished from the non-bereaved group by the frequency of their complaints of physical symptoms indicative of anxiety and tension; however, they did not show, as older bereaved subjects have shown in other studies, a large increase in physical ailments.

Four times as many bereaved as non-bereaved had spent part of the preceding year in hospital, and the bereaved group sought advice for emotional problems from ministers, psychiatrists, and (occasionally) social workers more often than did the non-bereaved. Over the years mutual-help groups and organizations making use of bereavement volunteers have sprung up in many countries and have become the primary source of support to bereaved people. In a study of 161 family caregivers of patients who died under the care of American palliative home care services (termed 'hospice' in the USA) 30 per cent made use of a bereavement service during the first six months of bereavement (Cherlin *et al.*, 2007). Yet more recently numerous sources of help have become available on the Internet and are likely to become the first place from which bereaved people will seek for information and support. (Further details are given in Appendix 19, and in Chapter 9.)

In conclusion, we think we can justly claim that many widows and widowers seek help during the months that follow the death of their spouse, at the time when this study was carried out and, probably still today, the professional persons to whom they most often go are medical practitioners. We accept the evidence that bereavement can affect physical health, and we shall consider how this can be explained later, but most of the complaints which take people to their doctors are reflections of anxiety and tension rather than of organic disease. In such cases the most important role for the doctor may be to reassure people that they are not sick rather than to label them as sick. Other sources of help will also need to be considered and may themselves reduce the effects of bereavement on the survivor's health.

Recent research into the endocrine and autonomic nervous system, together with neuro-physiological studies of brain function, are beginning to shed light on the underlying links between body and mind that explain both transient and lasting problems following bereavement. Before considering these let us look at some of the psychological problems.

Bereavement and mental health

Is there also evidence that bereavement can lead to frank mental illness? The results of Parkes' first studies, which were carried out in the early 1950s, have been amply confirmed by later studies and it is the latter that we shall summarize here.

A recent review of eleven studies involving 3481 widowed individuals and 4685 non-widowed controls during the first year of bereavement, showed that almost 22 per cent of the widowed were diagnosed as suffering Major Depressive Disorder and there were also increased risks of Panic Disorder and Generalized Anxiety Disorder (Onrust and Cuijpers, 2006). Vulnerability to depression may not be confined to human beings, and Goodall (1971) has described very similar reactions, which sometimes ended fatally, among bereaved chimpanzees!

Post-Traumatic Stress Disorder (PTSD), which was described above, is, as we might expect, most common following unexpected and horrific types of bereavement. Schut, de Keijser, and van den Bout (1991) followed up 281 people under the age of 66 who had lost a partner. He assessed them at intervals across the first 25 months of bereavement using a questionnaire to measure the presence of the classical symptoms of PTSD (as described in the American Psychiatric Association's *Diagnostic and Statistical Manual*, 1987). Although only 9 per cent met these criteria throughout the period of follow-up nearly a half met them at some time during the two years. PTSD was also diagnosed at four months after bereavement, in 5.7 per cent of parents who lost a child (Barry, Kasl, and Prigerson, 2002) and during the first year after bereavement, in 12 per cent of the widows reviewed by Onrust and Cuijpers (2006).

Problems in grieving. From the case records of the bereaved psychiatric patients in Parkes' study in 1964, it became apparent that, at the time of their admission to hospital, which usually took place about a year after bereavement, many of them were still grieving. What is more, their grief had often taken an unusual form, either being more severe and prolonged that usual, or being delayed and/or complicated in ways which will be described. In these patients grief was an integral part of the illness that had brought them into psychiatric care.

In other cases, however, the mental illness did not seem to involve grieving. For instance, several patients who had always been heavy drinkers had developed alcoholic psychoses after the death of a close family member. Here the symptoms were the symptoms of alcoholism, and if there was any persisting tendency to grieve this was not an obvious part of the clinical picture. Bereavement, in these cases, had been the 'last straw', resulting in the breakdown of individuals whose previous adjustment had been precarious.

This study (henceforth referred to as the Case-note Study) revealed quite clearly the important part that bereavement can play in producing mental illness. It also indicated that the mental illnesses that follow bereavement often seem to comprise pathological forms of grieving, which are specific to bereavement. In other cases, however, they comprise non-specific reactions, which might have been triggered by a variety of life events. The study of bereavement has led, not only to a better understanding of pathological grief but also to a greater understanding of these other events and their consequences. Bereavement is, after all, the most severe life event that most of us can expect to experience.

The most frequent form of pathological grief is **Prolonged Grief Disorder**. This has been found in 11.3 per cent of American widows by six months after bereavement, following deaths from natural causes, and confirmed in a similar study of the widows of men dying from cancer (Latham and Prigerson, 2004). It will be described, along with other psychiatric disorders in Chapter 8.

Despite these problems it is important to recognize that the majority of bereaved people are resilient and come through the process of grieving without lasting damage to their physical or mental health. Indeed they may grow in maturity and emotional stature. This is particularly the case among older bereaved people for whom most bereavements are relatively timely.

Bonanno *et al.* (2002) in a study of 205 widows and widowers over the age of 65, used a measure of 'depression' as an indicator of distress. They found that over a half reported little depression during the 18 months after the death, 11 per cent reported a high level of depression at 6 months after bereavement but this had improved by 18 months and only a quarter reported high levels at both 6 and 18 months after bereavement. It would be wrong to attribute all of the depression to the bereavement and many of these people had been depressed before the death, sometimes because of the burden of caring for a sick person and often in anticipation of the coming loss.

Most of the studies described above have concerned themselves with the first few years of bereavement but what of the long term? Data on this is hard to come by, not only because it takes a long time to carry out long-term studies and few investigators have the stamina and resources to carry them out, but also because, as time goes by, other life events tend to occur in the lives of all of us and it becomes increasingly difficult to know for sure what contribution each one of them has made to our current problems. A follow-up study of the bereaved parents of children who had died from cancer showed that, 4–9 years later, 25 per cent thought that their grief was still 'unresolved' and this group reported significantly worse physical and mental health than those whose grief was 'resolved' (Lannen *et al.*, 2008). Loss of a spouse or partner, however, seems less crippling. In a large-scale study of 14,000 American men and women who were followed over a twelve-year period those who became widowed during the first two years of the study were compared with the rest and the investigators concluded, 'It may be comforting to know that human beings are highly adaptable creatures, and that, in the long run, the majority of us will be able to cope even with the most distressing and disruptive events' (McCrae and Costa, 1993).

RESEARCH INTO BEREAVEMENT

In order to understand better the ways in which bereavements can lead to psychiatric disorders and to initiate programmes of prevention or treatment we must look more closely at the ways people react to bereavement, the circumstances in which problems can arise and the actions that can be taken to influence the situation, to reduce pathology and encourage psychological growth.

Since this has been the main thrust of our research over the years we shall first describe four of the major studies to which reference will be made throughout this volume. We refer to them as Parkes' 'London Study', 'Bethlem Study', 'Harvard Study' and 'Love and Loss Study'. We then outline a fifth major programme of study carried out by Prigerson and her colleagues at Yale University, which will be referred to as 'The Yale Bereavement Study'.

Case notes are not the most reliable source of research data, and while many of the case histories which Parkes studied contained a full and convincing account of the patient's reaction to bereavement there were others in which the reaction was not described in any detail. Obviously, a more systematic investigation of bereaved psychiatric patients was required. Research was needed, too, to determine what is a 'normal' or 'typical' reaction to bereavement.

Two studies were undertaken with these aims in view, the Bethlem Study and the London Study, and they form the principal sources of information for Chapters 3–8 of this book. **The London Study** (Parkes, 1970), to which reference has been made above (page 23), was carried out after the Bethlem Study, but it will simplify matters if it is discussed first.

It is sometimes said that psychiatrists get a distorted view of life because they see only people who have failed to master the stresses they encounter. The London Study was an attempt to find out how an unselected group of twenty-two London widows under the age of sixty-five would cope with the stress of bereavement. It was undertaken with the intention of establishing a picture of 'typical grief' among young and middle-aged widows. Older widows were excluded because, as we explain in Chapter 9, there is reason to regard grief in old age as rather different from the grief of young people. Whatever the cause of this, it would have confused the overall picture too much to include older people in this survey.

Widows who agreed to help were brought to Parkes' attention by their GPs. These GPs had been asked to refer every woman in their practice who lost her husband and not to pick out those with special psychological difficulties. However, there were some widows who were not referred, either because they refused to take part or because the GP did not want to upset them. On subsequent inquiry, GPs did not think that these widows differed to any marked extent from those who were referred, and it appears that those who were interviewed were a fairly representative sample of London widows.

They were seen by Parkes at the end of the first month of bereavement, and again at the third, sixth, ninth, and thirteenth months, a minimum of five interviews in all. Essentially Parkes was studying the first year of bereavement. However, in order to include but not be over influenced by the anniversary reaction, he carried out the 'end-of-year' interview one month late. This enabled him to obtain an account of the anniversary reaction and also to get an idea of how the widow was adjusting now that this crisis was past. Parkes writes:

> At the outset I had some misgivings about the entire project. It was not my wish to intrude upon private grief and I was quite prepared to abandon the study if it seemed that my questions were going to cause unnecessary pain. In fact, discussion of the events leading up to the husband's death and of the widow's reaction to them did cause pain, and it was quite usual for widows to break down and cry at some time during our first interview; but with only one exception they did not regard this as a harmful experience. On the contrary, the majority seemed grateful for the opportunity to talk freely about the disturbing problems and feelings that preoccupied them. The first interview usually lasted from two to three hours, not because I had planned it that way but because the widow needed that amount of time if she was to 'talk through' the highly charged experiences that were on her mind. Once she found that I was not going to be

embarrassed or upset by her grief she seemed to find the interview therapeutic and, although I took pains to explain that this was a research project, I had no sense of intrusion after the first few minutes of the initial contact.

(For a more detailed consideration of the ethical aspects of research in bereavement, and some guidelines for readers who may wish to carry out their own research, see Parkes, 1995b.)

The aim of the **Bethlem Study** (Parkes, 1965a, 1965b) was to investigate reactions among people seeking psychiatric help after bereavement most of which were found to be atypical. Interviews were obtained between 1958 and 1960 with twenty-one bereaved patients at the Bethlem Royal and Maudsley Hospitals. Of the twenty-one patients, four were male and seventeen female. Most of them were seen soon after entering psychiatric treatment, at which time they had been bereaved for an average of seventy-two weeks (the range was from 4 to 367 weeks).

In both the London Study and the Bethlem Study bereaved people were asked to tell the interviewer, in their own words, about their bereavement and how they reacted to it. Questions were kept to a minimum and simply ensured that comparable information about critical events was obtained in each case. Some notes, particularly records of significant verbatim statements, were taken at the time and some assessments were made immediately after the interview. These were recorded on a survey form, which was also used as an *aide-mémoire* during the interview.

Following these two studies, which revealed, respectively, typical and atypical forms that the reaction to bereavement can take, the **Harvard Study** was carried out. This investigation (referred to above, pages 24–25, and described in full in Glick *et al.*, 1974, and Parkes and Weiss, 1983) had a rather different object in view. It had been established that grief normally follows a certain pattern but that pathological variants sometimes occur, and the team now wanted to discover why most people come through the stress of bereavement unscathed whereas others suffer lasting distress and physical or mental illness. They also wanted to see if it was possible to identify, at the time of bereavement, those who would be likely to get into difficulties later. Since previous research (reviewed in Chapter 9) had shown that the health risk was greatest in young widows, they focused attention on people under the age of forty-five who had lost a spouse. And because widowers had rarely featured in earlier investigations they included a group of them in this one. Forty-one widows and nineteen widowers were contacted by letter and telephone, and visited, in their homes, three to six weeks after bereavement, and again fourteen months after they had been bereaved, at which time an assessment was made of their health. The results of this predictive study are discussed in Chapter 9. Subsequent work on both sides of the Atlantic has now confirmed many of the findings.

The Harvard Study confirmed Parkes' expectation that American widows would be found to react to bereavement in a similar manner to the British widows who had been the subjects of his earlier studies. These studies were not carried out to prove or disprove any particular theory, but inevitably Parkes felt constrained to group certain features together and to attempt an explanation of the process of grieving which would make sense of the data.

The reader will have noted that the choice of widows and widowers under the age of 65 in the London Study, and under 45 in the Harvard Study, plus the fact that both studies were carried out over forty years ago, in relatively wealthy parts of the West, introduces several biases that make it unwise to regard their reactions to bereavement as typical of all bereaved people. For reasons that will become apparent, these people suffered unusually severe losses, indeed they were selected for study because younger bereaved people were expected to be at risk.

While carrying out these studies Parkes continued to see bereaved people in his role as a clinical psychiatrist and was able to develop a questionnaire with the aim of discovering what distinguished those people who seek psychiatric help after bereavement from bereaved people who do not. The results of that study have been published in 'Love and Loss: The roots of grief and its complications' (Parkes, 2006); they have confirmed many of the results of the earlier studies and revealed love and grief as two sides of the same coin. We refer to this as the '**Love and Loss Study**'. Problems in loving commonly give rise to problems in grieving. Just how they do this will become apparent in the course of this book.

Meanwhile, in **The Yale Bereavement Study**, Prigerson and her colleagues studied the psychiatric complications of bereavement. In order to place these on a systematic footing they developed a questionnaire, the Index of Complicated Grief (ICG; Prigerson *et al.*, 1995b), that has been subjected to rigorous tests of its validity and reliability, further details of which are given in Chapter 8 and Appendices 1 and 5. The ICG has now been used in many parts of the world and in a variety of circumstances. It has now been superseded by a simpler but equally valid 13-item Prolonged Grief index

(PG-13). Prigerson and her colleagues have also undertaken clinical studies that have enabled them to develop a set of criteria for diagnosing the most frequent form of complicated grief, Prolonged Grief Disorder. There is growing support for her hope that this will become accepted as the standard for diagnosis and included in the two major diagnostic manuals, the American Psychiatric Association's *Diagnostic and Statistical Manual* (DSM) and the World Health Organization's *International Classification of Diseases* (ICD). These criteria will be considered in Chapter 8.

JOHN BOWLBY AS APPRECIATED BY COLIN PARKES

When, in 1959, I first reviewed the scientific literature on loss and grief I was struck by the absence of any reference in it to the common observation that non-human animals, in their reaction to loss, show many of the features that are evident in human beings. One of the few people who have made this point is Charles Darwin, who, in *The Expression of the Emotions in Man and Animals* (1872), described the way in which sorrow is expressed by animals, young children, and adult human beings. His work caused me to formulate a 'biological theory of grief', which has not required major modification.

My preliminary formulation, which formed part of a dissertation for the Diploma in Psychological Medicine, had no sooner been submitted to the examiners than I was lent a duplicated copy of a paper which showed that many of the conclusions I had reached had been reached quite independently by the late John Bowlby. Bowlby's review of the effects of maternal deprivation in childhood had appeared as a World Health Organization monograph in 1951 and had been followed by a series of papers aimed at clarifying the theoretical questions to which it gave rise. By 1959 Bowlby was well set in working out a comprehensive theory, the first part of which was already in print. I sent him a copy of my own dissertation at that time and subsequently (in 1962) joined his research staff at the Tavistock Institute of Human Relations. From that time until Bowlby's death in 1992 our collaboration was close and I made use of many of his ideas. These biographical details are mentioned because I am no longer sure which of us deserves the credit (or blame) for originating many of the ideas that make up the overall theory on these pages. All that I can say, with confidence, is that my debt to John Bowlby is great.

3

TRAUMA

No one ever told me that grief felt so like fear. I am not afraid,
but the sensation is like being afraid. The same fluttering
in the stomach, the same restlessness, the yawning. I keep
on swallowing.

C. S. Lewis, *A Grief Observed* copyright © C.S. Lewis Pte.
Ltd. 1961. Published by Faber & Faber Ltd.

Lady Percy to her Lord:

Tell me, sweet lord, what is't that takes from thee
Thy stomach, pleasure, and thy golden sleep?
Why dost thou bend thine eyes upon the earth,
And start so often when thou sit'st alone?
Why hast thou lost the fresh blood in thy cheeks
And given my treasures and my rights of thee
To thick-eyed musing and cursed melancholy?
In thy faint slumbers I by thee have watch'd,
And heard thee murmur tales of iron wars;
. . .
Thy spirit within thee hath been so at war,
And thus hath so bestirr'd thee in thy sleep,
That beads of sweat have stood upon thy brow,
Like bubbles in a late disturbed stream;
And in thy face strange notions have appear'd,
Such as we see when men restrain their breath
Henry IV, Part One, Act II, Sc. 3

In this chapter we begin to piece together the evidence that explains
the complex reactions of human beings to the loss of a loved person.
To do that we need to examine the roots, in human anatomy and
physiology, of our emotions and behaviour, and its origins in the
non-human animals from which we have evolved.

Every thought and feeling that we experience arises out of chemical and electrical changes in the brain and a great deal has been learned about these in recent years. Indeed it would take us beyond the scope of this book to attempt to put together all of the fascinating findings of research in this rapidly developing field. Rather we have selected some key studies of special relevance to our understanding of bereavement.

STRESS

For many years research workers have studied and written about stress. The term has been used to characterize the effect of virtually any novel or unpleasant experience. Human beings and animals of all shapes and sizes have been tricked, confined, terrified, mutilated, shocked, puzzled, embarrassed, challenged, stumped, overwhelmed, confused, or poisoned in a wide variety of experimental conditions in attempts to track down the consequences of this ubiquitous phenomenon. Numerous books and articles describe the results of these experiments.

The outcome of this work has turned out to be more complex than it first appeared. One reason for this complexity is the body's ability to correct its own imbalances. A sharp change in one substance in the blood stream will trigger off a feed-back loop that counteracts its effects thereby maintaining homeostasis and preventing escalation. Likewise, messages from our sense organs are constantly streaming into the brain, where they set off other feed-back loops to limit, or turn them off, and prevent the brain from being overwhelmed.

One finding, however, has stood the test of time, in 1929 Cannon published a book, *Bodily Changes in Pain, Hunger, Fear and Rage*, which demonstrated that, whether an animal is preparing to fight or flee, it will show a single overall physiological response. This response includes changes in body functions under the control of the sympathetic part of the autonomic nervous system and the endocrine glands (which secrete chemical messengers that trigger a variety of responses). The outcome is to improve muscular perform-ance (increase heart and respiratory rate, transfer blood to the muscles from other organs, increase muscular tension), improve vision (by dilation of the pupil and retraction of the eyelids), assist heat loss (increase sweating), cause the bristling of hair characteristic of 'threatening' (by contraction of erector pili muscles), and mobil-ize reserves of energy (convert glycogen in the liver to glucose).

Stress also results in inhibition of activities of the parasympathetic system, which controls digestion and other non-priority functions (by stopping the flow of saliva, relaxing the bowel and bladder, reducing the flow of secretion in the bowel, and increasing the tone of the sphincter muscles). This body of knowledge is now taught as a part of elementary physiology. Clearly, sympathetic stimulation and parasympathetic inhibition have the useful function of putting the animal into a state of readiness for instant action. Unfortunately for human beings in the world today, these bodily reactions are seldom useful, indeed they make it difficult for us to remain calm and hide our feelings and they are often misinterpreted as symptoms of malfunction.

These physical effects arise at times of stress but they often persist after the alarm is past because of the chemical substances, such as adrenaline (epinephrine), that continue to circulate in the blood for varying lengths of time. Foremost among these is cortisol, another chemical messenger; when released from the adrenal gland (under the influence of corticotrophin from the pituitary), this mobilizes stores of fuel, adjusts the immune response system and has other subtle effects on the operation of the brain.

While most people are familiar with the fight/flight response, less has been written about a third alternative, inhibition of movement or 'freezing'; yet this too may improve an animal's chances of surviving if other alternatives are thought to be unlikely to succeed. Tourists visiting game reserves on foot are regularly warned that, if a lion or rhinoceros approaches, they should not, on any account, run away as this will trigger immediate pursuit. Recent research has demonstrated the existence of two similar but distinct chemical messengers (corticotrophin-releasing factors; CRF 1 & 2) that, when released in the hypothalamus, induce the pituitary gland to trigger either flight or freezing. In human beings the latter passive response to stress is now thought to be associated with feelings of helplessness and depression (Hammack et al., 2003).

Arousal

Much has been learnt of the mechanisms in the brain that govern arousal and attention. Partly this is a question of the amount of brain that is active at a given moment. During sleep, for instance, most of the central nervous system is at rest, as is evidenced by the regular synchronous electrical discharges that can be recorded from the majority of its parts. As the level of consciousness increases and the animal wakes up, a characteristic pattern of desynchronization occurs in larger and larger areas until in periods of intense activity nearly every part of the brain seems to be involved in the general process of perceiving, thinking, and directing actions.

The parts of the brain that seem to be most closely associated with the control and direction of 'arousal', as this whole process has been termed, are the reticular formation and the limbic system. They control not only the level of arousal but the particular areas of the brain that are aroused. Stimulation of the reticular formation, for instance, has been shown to produce, first, curiosity, then successively, as the intensity of stimulation increases, attention, fear, and panic.

A tacit assumption is often made that measures of heart rate, galvanic skin response, and sweating, which were once thought to indicate alarm, are in fact measures of arousal. Although the fit between these measures of sympathetic activity and the electro-encephalographic measures is not perfect, it is rare to have a highly aroused brain without the signs that sympathetic stimulation is present.

This is hardly surprising when one considers that in order to become fit for instant action an animal must be fully aroused. Does it follow, then, that any animal that is fully aroused is in a state of fear or rage? Common experience suggests that it does not, and reports of individuals who have been in extreme situations, even in situations that would be expected to evoke great fear, commonly indicate that it is only after the crisis is past its peak that the participant becomes aware of any 'feelings' at all. During the period of intense activity they are so preoccupied with the task in hand that emotion is redundant (at least, that is how it seems in retrospect). Parkes writes, 'Having once been threatened by a man with a loaded revolver I can bear witness to this fact. I was able in that situation to note the signs in myself of autonomic disturbance – rapid beating of the heart, dryness of the mouth, and a general increase in tension – at the same time, however, I was not consciously afraid'.

It should be clear, from what has been said, that there are three distinct components in the overall response to extreme situations: level of arousal, autonomic disturbance, and emotional reaction. While there is a tendency for the three to go together, the correspondence between them is not perfect and measurement of one cannot be taken as a precise index of the other two.

Emotions

Emotions are commonly assumed to cause behaviour but, as we have seen, they often follow it. In alarming situations powerful emotions are soon likely to arise but the character of the emotion will be determined by our appraisal of the situation rather than preceding that appraisal. If we appraise the situation as one in which we may well be hurt or defeated then fear is likely to predominate, if we anticipate that a fight is necessary, and that we have a reasonable chance of winning, anger is the more likely emotion. If we are confident of our ability to master the situation, the predominant emotion is likely to be one of triumph or elated excitement. If the situation is seen as our own fault, or likely to lead to humiliation, then a reaction of shame is to be expected. In many situations the outcome is uncertain and we may experience mixed or rapidly changing emotions.

Although it is not possible for non-human animals to tell us what they are feeling, and psychologists have rightly been reluctant to attribute human emotions to non-human animals, that does not mean that we can assume that non-humans do not have feelings and emotions. Evidence from neuroanatomical studies show that parts of the brain that evolved very early in evolution play a significant part in generating emotions in all species.

In 1937, the neuroanatomist James Papez demonstrated that emotion is not a function of any specific brain centre but of a circuit that involves four basic structures, interconnected through several nervous bundles: the hypothalamus, the anterior thalamic nucleus, the cingulate gyrus and the hippocampus. This circuit, acting in a harmonious fashion, is responsible for the central functions of emotion (affect), as well as for its peripheral expressions (symptoms).

In recent years much has been learned about the changes in the brain that are associated with emotional expression. The techniques of computed tomography (CT), positive-emission tomography (PET) and magnetic-resonance imaging (MRI) scanning have improved our knowledge of the anatomy of the brain, but it is functional MRI (fMRI) scans that allow us, for the first time, to study the brain in action. Through this technique moment-to-moment changes in blood flow, indicating cerebral activity in each part of the brain, can be measured and linked to emotional and other reported experience.

Interrelationships

To sum up the principal components on the inactive/active dimension we can set out three levels of arousal alongside their psycho-physiological and behavioural outcomes, thus:

Central nervous system	Synchronous electrical activity of most parts of CNS	Partial desynchronization	Desynchronous electrical activity of most parts of CNS
Autonomic nervous system	Sympathetic inhibition; parasympathetic activity	Mixed picture	Sympathetic activity; parasympathetic inhibition
Subjective emotion	None	Interest; apprehension	Anger, shame, fear, depression or excitement
Behaviour	Asleep; unresponsive	Moderate activity; alert	Hyperactivity, hyper-sensitivity or withdrawal

This simplistic picture can be said to apply to all human beings at all times. But most of us spend most of our life in the middle and on the left-hand (inactive) side of the picture and can tolerate only brief periods on the right-hand side. Situations that tend to produce alarm are regarded as stressful, and if they continue for more than a short period of time we experience a sense of strain. (In physics a stressor exerts stress on an object in which it produces strain. The same terminology would seem applicable to psychology and physiology.)

Recent research into opioid peptide systems in the brain, which are known to be affected by stress, opens a new area for future studies since these are very likely to be affected by bereavement (Hamner, 1994).

THREAT AND LOSS

What are the characteristics of the situations that produce alarm in animals and human beings? While any unfamiliar or unpredictable situation is potentially alarming, there are certain types of situation that are especially so. These include situations involving the absence of an escape route or 'safe' place, or the presence of particular danger signals which the individual is 'set' to recognize at any time (cries, sudden movements or sounds, etc.). Absence of a safe escape route, lack of a haven or home in which the individual can feel secure, or, in social animals, absence of fellow members of the species who normally provide or share defence (e.g. parents or mate) can increase the likelihood that a particular situation will be objectively dangerous and will give rise to a state of alarm with all the signs described above.

Patients faced with life-threatening illnesses and members of their families are likely to experience high levels of anxiety, which may even meet criteria for psychiatric illness (Bambauer *et al.*, 2006). To this must be added one other category of situation capable of producing a high state of alarm, that is threat to or separation from a child or other dependent person to whom we are attached.

All these situations threaten the security of the individual and they include situations of loss. A woman who loses her husband has good cause for alarm. Not only has she lost a source of protection but she is likely to be exposed to novel situations and problems in her new role as widow for which she may be quite unprepared. She no longer has a confidant with whom she can discuss matters, yet she will probably have to take over many additional responsibilities and roles that were formerly her husband's. It will hardly surprise us to find her showing signs of alarm.

In fact this has been found to be the case. In the London Study it was clear that, for most of the widows, the world had become a threatening and potentially dangerous place. During the first month of bereavement nearly all (eighteen out of twenty-two) said that they felt restless, and the degree of restlessness fell off only gradually during the year. Restlessness and increased muscle tension went together, and assessments of restlessness and tension made at the time of our interviews were highly intercorrelated (see Appendix 6; Table 4).

There are indications from many sources that the grieving person is in a state of high arousal during much of the time and that this occasionally approaches panic. Fourteen of the twenty-two London widows described episodes of feeling panicky. One widow, for instance, found her 'nerves on edge' and trembled a great deal; she stayed with her sister throughout the first month of her bereavement, but whenever she returned home or even when left alone she felt scared and panicky. Although brief episodes of alarm occur in all our lives from time to time and do not cause more than transient distress, the persistence of lasting full arousal can have a variety of consequences that are detrimental to health.

Loss of appetite and weight, difficulty in sleeping at night, digestive disturbances, palpitations, headaches, and muscular aches and pains all seemed to reflect a general disturbance in the nervous control of bodily processes in the direction of stimulation of sympathetic activity and inhibition of parasympathetic or vegetative activities. Thus nineteen of the twenty-two London widows lost their appetite during the first month of bereavement and in fifteen this brought about recognizable loss of weight. Insomnia was mentioned by seventeen widows and was severe in thirteen; difficulty in getting to sleep at night and a tendency to wake early or during the night were also reported. Twelve widows took sedatives during the first month of bereavement and five were still taking them a year later.

The loss of interest in food and dryness of the mouth that were typical during the early weeks of bereavement were usually associated with a sense of fullness or a lump in the 'pit of the stomach' (epigastrium), often with belching and heartburn. As one widow put it, 'The whole thing has hit my stomach'. Headaches, which were mentioned by over half the widows during the first month of bereavement, were usually described as a sense of 'tension' or 'pressure' in the head. Similar symptoms of autonomic disturbance have been found by other researchers, notably by Maddison (see Chapter 2, page 24).

Around two-thirds of the London widows had a sense of time passing very quickly. They seemed to be 'on edge' and described themselves as 'jumpy' and 'irritable'. 'I get all tuned up'; 'I'm always on the go'; 'I'm at the end of my tether, I can't cope but I know I must'; 'I feel all in a turmoil inside'; 'My nerves are on edge'; 'I can't pin myself down to anything'; 'Stupid little things upset me' – these comments give a good picture of the overall restless anxiety that was found.

Anger and irritability are discussed more fully in Chapter 6, but it is worth noting at this point that assessments of these features made at the time of the interviews correlated closely with assessments of restlessness and tension (Appendix 6; Table 4) and with the widow's own assessment of her state of health as bad (Appendix 4).

The evidence suggests, then, that bereavement is a stressful situation and that the generalizations that stem from earlier research into stress are likely to hold good in the case of bereavement. The symptoms described above are symptoms of strain. They occur in many different types of stress situation and there is nothing about them that is specific to bereavement. They are the reason given by many widows for consulting their doctor after bereavement, and they are all symptoms with which doctors are very familiar.

Further research has confirmed many of the findings outlined above. The secretion of adrenaline (epinephrine) and noradrenaline (norepinephrine) from the inner part of the adrenal gland (the medulla) is associated with compensatory changes in the secretion of other (corticoid) hormones from its surface (cortex). In a recent summary Hall and Irwin (2001) conclude: 'Changes indicative of acute heightened arousal (e.g. cortisol & catecholamine, altered immunocompetence & sleep disturbance) are commonly seen in anticipatory bereavement and during the first few months after a loss. More enduring alterations . . . have also been observed'.

Similar changes in corticoid hormones have been found in free-ranging female baboons following the death of close female relatives (Engh *et al.*, 2006). In baboon societies individuals spend much time in mutual grooming. This provides comfort and cements social relationships as well as reducing infestation with parasites. Engh *et al.* discovered a sharp rise in mutual grooming in bereaved baboons, they conclude:

> Even in the presence of familiar troop-mates and other relatives, females experienced a stress response when they lost specific companions, and they apparently sought to alleviate it by broadening and strengthening their social relationships.

All of the physiological changes resemble those that occur in severe anxiety and depression. They are influenced by many factors in addition to bereavement and cannot be used as reliable measures of grief.

THE IMMUNE RESPONSE SYSTEM

What of the more serious disorders, the infections and cancers to which some bereaved people seem to be susceptible? Can we deduce a possible physiological explanation for these? Some of the most important research to have been conducted in recent years concerns the body's 'immune response system'. This is a complex system of physical and chemical functions, which influences our natural resistance to infections, to damaged cells and to cancer cells arising within us.

It operates in part through two types of lymphocyte in the blood, T-cells and B-cells. We can now remove blood from a bereaved person and observe that these living cells behave more sluggishly when their host is bereaved. Schleifer and his colleagues (1983) found that the function of both types of cell was markedly suppressed in fifteen widowers during the first two months after the death of their wives. Similar findings have been obtained by Bartrop *et al.* (1977), although the changes that they studied were confined to the T-cells. Bereavement can also impair the action of the 'natural killer cells', which, as the name implies, play a part in destroying alien cells (Irwin and Weiner, 1987; Pettingale, Hussein, and Tee, 1994). Although these changes usually disappear after a few months they sometimes continue for as long as six months in those with lasting depression (Gerra *et al.*, 2003).

These studies at last provide us with the beginnings of an explanation for some of the effects of bereavement on health, but they do need to be interpreted with caution. Certainly we should not assume that the changes in the immune system that have been found after bereavement are peculiar to that situation, similar changes can occur following other types of stress and the severity of the response is more closely related to the intensity of depression than it is to the intensity of grief *per se* (Calabrese, Kling, and Gold, 1987; Schleifer *et al.*, 1984). Other factors associated with the immune response are disturbed sleep and PTSD (Ironson *et al.*, 1997). Whatever the cause of these findings it is reassuring to learn that the natural killer cells of people who receive social support were less affected by the bereavement than were those of people without social support (Esterling, Kiecolt-Glaser, and Glaser, 1996).

Since AIDS is a disease of the immune response system it is no surprise to find that HIV-positive people are vulnerable to the effects of bereavement on the immune response system (Kemmeny and Dean, 1995; Kemmeny *et al.*, 1995). Interestingly, in HIV-positive bereaved people, the immune impairment is less marked if they have an 'active' as opposed to a 'passive' coping style (Goodkin *et al.*, 1996). We return to consider the implications of this on page 286.

The fact that physiological reactions and psychosomatic symptoms are not stressor specific does not justify us in ignoring the special nature of the stress situations that produced them or the highly specific psychological symptoms that accompany them. Physiology may not enable us to distinguish between 'fight' and 'flight', but it is clearly of great importance to the individual to choose correctly between these alternative actions. It is behaviour, rather than physiology, that determines the outcome of a stress situation.

CRISIS

The study of stress situations has been advanced by the development of 'crisis theory', a body of theory that has important implications in the fields of preventive psychiatry and community mental health. It derives largely from the work of Gerald Caplan and his colleagues at the Laboratory of Community Psychiatry, Harvard Medical School (see Caplan, 1961, 1964). Caplan used the term 'crisis' to cover major life stresses, of limited duration, which endanger mental health. Such crises disrupt the customary modes of behaviour of the people concerned, alter both their circumstances and their plans, and impose a need for psychological work, which takes time and effort. They present the individual with the opportunity and obligation to abandon old assumptions about the world and to discover new ones, and they thereby constitute a challenge.

Empirical observations reveal that under mild to moderate stress most people learn rapidly and are likely to accept the need to change more readily than at other times in their life. They also tend to seek help more willingly than at other times, and other people are more prepared to offer it. The support that society offers its suffering members during periods of crisis is often considerable though it may be relatively short term.

When the strain exceeds a certain threshold of severity (which varies from one individual to another), our efficiency and learning capacity falls off rapidly and individuals find themselves unable to cope with the situation and overwhelmed by it. They may persevere in useless activities which are inappropriate to the present situation, but may have been successful in the past, or they may panic and behave in a thoroughly disorganized and fragmented manner. In such circumstances old ideas and assumptions may be adhered to rigidly, and offers of help, which would involve an acceptance of the need to change, are repudiated. 'I'll never believe he's dead and you can't make me', said one widow.

These two types of response, which have been observed in many different studies, are analogous to Cannon's 'fight/flight' response in so far as 'fight' involves an approach to the problems and difficulties whereas 'flight' involves withdrawal and the avoidance of problem solving.

It seems that most animals have an inborn propensity to pay attention to unfamiliar or alarming stimuli. Subsequently, the decision to approach or to withdraw is made, depending upon the characteristics of the stimulus, the individual, and the environment. This is the first and most important decision that an animal must make in the situation, and survival may well depend on it. It is, moreover, a situation in which instinctive mechanisms are of limited value. A monkey may be born with a fear of 'snake-shaped' objects, but its decision to approach or avoid such an object will soon be determined by experience. In fact it may be that learning is never more rapid than in situations in which the decision to approach or withdraw must be made. Approach is likely if the unfamiliar or alarming stimulus is not too alarming and if it occurs in a situation in which the animal feels 'safe'. Intruders upon one's territory are more likely to be approached, and perhaps threatened, than are the same individuals when met on their own territory. Because our survival depends upon our ability to learn about danger it should not surprise us if memories of life-threatening or other terrifying situations tend to persist even when the danger is past.

Human beings bring to this age-old situation, not a terrifying and dangerous set of teeth and claws, but a highly efficient memory and decision-making mechanism capable of guiding their approach to any problematic situation. It is this success in 'attacking' problems in advance that has given us a distinct advantage over other species. It also leaves us with the need to anticipate events that may never happen and to prepare ourselves in retrospect for disasters that are already past. In other words we are the only animal who worries and agonizes.

MEMORY AND POST-TRAUMATIC STRESS

Recent research (Brewin, 2001) has shown that there are two types of memories, both of which are involved in situations of danger. 'Situationally Activated Memories' (SAM), as the name implies, are triggered by the constellations of smells, feelings, images, sounds and tastes that are associated with a dangerous or traumatic situation. They arise through the functioning of a small, almond-shaped nucleus in the midbrain, the amygdala, and are stored in the non-dominant hemisphere of the brain. 'Verbally Activated Memories' (VAM) are a much more sophisticated type of memory, facilitating reasoning and verbal communication. They arise more slowly through the functioning of the hypothalamus and the dominant hemisphere of the brain. It is during our sleeping hours that SAM is normally transformed into VAM and stored in the dominant hemisphere, where it is accessible to introspection and linked with other memories (Hull, 2002).

Between them the two memory systems enable a rapid response to emergencies and a more considered response to more persistent dangers. However, they do not always work smoothly together. Within the hypothalamus there is an area termed the dentate nucleus that is extremely sensitive to cortisol. Some individuals respond to traumatic situations by a surge of cortisol that has the effect of 'blowing a fuse' in the dentate nucleus (Jacobs, Van Praag, and Gage, 2000; Manji, Drevets, and Charney, 2001). This causes the hypothalamus to malfunction, SAM is not transformed into VAM and this gives rise to 'flashbacks' in which the traumatized person repeatedly experiences horrific images and feels as if they are reliving the experience all over again. While these images are usually memories of the event they can also arise from a vivid imagination of what happened, even if the event was not witnessed. These experiences are so painful that the sufferer will go to great lengths to avoid any reminders that will trigger them. This is believed to be responsible for the phenomenon of PTSD.

The techniques that human beings adopt to cope with emergent situations may involve approach or withdrawal, or elements of both. The theory of psychic defence rests on the assumption that there is a limit to the amount of anxiety an individual can tolerate and that when this limit is reached individuals will defend themselves by withdrawing, psychologically, from the situation that evokes the anxiety. Is it too large a jump for us to see in this behaviour an echo of the physical withdrawal of an animal in a situation of danger? In neither case does withdrawal necessarily imply failure or defeat, although it may do so. In both cases withdrawal is assumed to reduce the danger of being overwhelmed, and anxiety is the subjective accompaniment of real or imagined danger.

We may control anxiety by shutting ourselves up in a safe place (usually our home), avoiding people and situations that will remind us of the trauma, and deliberately filling our minds with thoughts and activities that will distract us from the horror. But it is a paradox that, *in order to avoid thinking about something, we have to think about it*. That is to say, at some level, we remain aware of the danger that we are trying to avoid. Hence it should not surprise us if attempts at avoidance commonly fail. In sleep and at times of relaxed attention painful memories tend to float back into our mind and sufferers from PTSD find themselves reliving the trauma yet again.

Henry consulted Parkes two months after several members of his family had been killed in the ferry boat *Herald of Free Enterprise*. He recalled how he had left his family below and was smoking a cigarette on the top deck when the boat suddenly heeled over and then capsized outside Zeebrugge harbour. His immediate reaction was to save his own life. He managed to smash a window and escaped onto the outside of the boat that was now lying on its side and half submerged. Only now did he realize that his family were still below. In his alarm he tried to climb back into the ship but was deterred by a fellow survivor who warned him, 'You'd never get out of there alive'.

Henry remained on board for five hours, helping with the rescue operation and watching anxiously as each new survivor emerged from the ship. But none of his own family came out alive and, in the course of the next two weeks he was to identify the bodies of four of them as, one by one, they were recovered from the wreck.

Throughout this period he exerted a rigid control and he was still not crying two months later when he was persuaded to seek psychiatric help. At this time he was tense and tremulous, chain-smoking to control his nerves and feeling numb and depressed. He was easily upset by loud noises and was particularly sensitive to the sound of rushing water. He had shut himself up at home and seldom went out. His surviving daughters feared that he might kill himself.

Three months after the disaster a heavy thunderstorm took place and, when Parkes saw him the following day, Henry appeared haggard and exhausted. 'It was the thunder', he said, 'It was the same noise that the boat made as it turned over. I heard the children screaming'. He then related, in great detail and with the tears pouring down his cheeks, his memories of the disaster. Parkes reports, 'The experience was so vivid that I too felt caught up in the situation. After a while I said, "You're still waiting for them to come out aren't you?" '

This case illustrates well the features of PTSD. As long as Henry succeeded in avoiding the thoughts of what had happened he could not escape from the memories that were constantly threatening to emerge. In this case the thunderstorm acted as a trigger to his Situationally Activated Memories and allowed him to begin the process of converting them to Verbally Activated Memories by verbalizing them. In other cases more systematic approaches are needed to overcome persistent PTSD. These will be discussed on pages 222–3.

PTSD, as we have seen, gives rise to intrusive memories and avoidance. Hall *et al.* (1998) have shown that high scores of these symptoms, in bereaved people, are associated with poor sleep during the early, non-dreaming period of the night, and this, in turn, is associated with small numbers of natural killer cells. Just how this fascinating link between mind and body can be explained remains to be discovered.

CONCLUSIONS

Just how a human being reacts to a particular stressor depends on many things: on the person's inherited sensitivity to stress; on the characteristics of the stressor; on the individual's repertoire of coping techniques; on how the situation is perceived in the light of previous experience; on the capacity to tolerate powerful emotions; and on the need to maintain self-esteem.

In these circumstances it is hardly surprising that behavioural responses to stress vary widely. The number of interacting factors that determine behaviour and the difficulty in accurately assessing each of them have long been major bars to progress in understanding human behaviour. In studying bereavement we have the opportunity to hold constant one of these factors, the life event, and this makes it easier to unravel the interaction between the others.

The reaction to bereavement, as we have seen, includes components that we can term non-specific, they can be caused by factors other than bereavement. Hence bereavement evokes arousal and the responses that characterize the alarm reaction; it may also evoke intrusive memories or fantasies and it may cause approach or avoidance behaviour. The form these responses take will be partly stressor specific (i.e. they will derive from the nature of the situation) and partly subject specific (i.e. they will derive from the personal predispositions of the subject).

In the next five chapters of this book we attempt to describe and explain the stressor-specific components in the reaction to bereavement. In later chapters studies of the subject-specific factors will be considered.

4

ATTACHMENT AND LOSS

Over a number of years K. Kollwitz worked on a monument for her younger son who was killed in October 1914. His death became for her a sort of personal obligation. Two years later she noted in her diary: 'There's a drawing made, a mother letting her dead son slide into her arms. I could do a hundred similar drawings but still can't seem to come any closer to him. I'm still searching for him as if it were in the very work itself that I had to find him'.

Catalogue to an exhibition of the works of K. Kollwitz,
London 1967

THE NATURE OF ATTACHMENTS

John Bowlby, who is generally regarded as the father of attachment theory, described the elements of behaviour that characterize attachments between infants and their mothers. He divided them into those behaviours that maintain attachment (smiling, babbling, clinging and following) and those that bring about reunion when separated (crying and searching).

Bowlby went on to show how each element developed in the course of the first year of life (Bowlby, 1969). It is easy to see how these behaviours increase the child's chances of survival in a dangerous world and it is no coincidence that similar patterns of attachment evolved in all social animals. Babies do not need to be taught to cry, but, like all instinctual behaviour patterns, crying can be modified by learning from the moment of its first inception.

Since the impulse to cry and to search, is necessary to survival, we should not be surprised to find that these impulses, and the emotion of separation anxiety, which goes with them, remain an element of

the reaction to losses later in life, even when our reason tells us that
the person lost cannot be regained.

THE PANGS OF GRIEF

The most characteristic feature of grief is not prolonged depression
but acute and episodic 'pangs'. A pang of grief is an episode of
severe anxiety and psychological pain. At such times lost people are
strongly missed and the survivors sob or cry aloud for them.

Pangs of grief begin within a few hours or days of bereavement
and reach a peak at about four months (Maciejewski *et al.*, 2007).
In Joan Didion's case they started seven or eight hours after her
husband's sudden death. 'Grief is different. Grief has no distance.
Grief comes in waves, paroxysms, sudden apprehensions that weaken
the knees and blind the eyes and obliterate the dailiness of life'
(Didion, 2005, p. 27). At first they are very frequent and seem to
occur spontaneously, but as time passes they become less frequent
and take place only when something occurs that brings the loss to
mind. Finding a photograph in a drawer, meeting a mutual friend of
the lost person, waking up alone in a double bed – happenings such
as these precipitate attacks of anxious pining.

From their studies of infants separated from their mothers,
Robertson and Bowlby (1952) called this the phase of yearning and
protest. Subsequently Bowlby and Parkes (1970) described a phase
of 'yearning and searching for the lost figure' in the grief of adults.
Protest is discussed in Chapter 6, but it should be noted in passing
that the anger that this word implies peaks a little later, at about five
months post-bereavement (Maciejewski *et al.*, 2007). We found that
feelings of panic, a dry mouth, and other indications of autonomic
activity are particularly pronounced during these pangs of grief. Add
to these features deep sighing respiration, restless but aimless hyperactivity, difficulty in concentrating on anything but thoughts of loss,
ruminations around the events leading up to the loss as well as loss
of interest in any of the people or things that normally give pleasure
or claim attention, and one begins to get a picture of this distressing
and distressed state.

Pining or yearning – a persistent and obtrusive wish for the person who is gone, a preoccupation with thoughts that can only give
pain – why should one experience such a useless and unpleasant
emotion? The answer to this question gives the key to this whole
phase of grief and to much that follows it. Pining is the subjective

and emotional component of the urge to search for a lost object. We maintain that an adult human being has the same impulse to search that is shown by many species of social animal.

THE URGE TO CRY AND TO SEARCH

Lorenz (1963) has described the effects of separating a greylag goose from its mate:

> The first response to the disappearance of the partner consists in the anxious attempt to find him again. The goose moves about restlessly by day and night, flying great distances and visiting places where the partner might be found, uttering all the time the penetrating trisyllabic long-distance call . . . The searching expeditions are extended farther and farther and quite often the searcher itself gets lost, or succumbs to an accident . . . All the objective observable characteristics of the goose's behaviour on losing its mate are roughly identical with human grief. . . .

Bowlby (1961; our italics) has reviewed the literature covering the reaction to bereavement in jackdaw, goose, domestic dog, orang-utan, and chimpanzee. He summarizes his conclusions as follows:

> Members of lower species protest at the loss of a loved object *and do all in their power to seek and recover it*; hostility, externally directed, is frequent; withdrawal, rejection of a potential new object, apathy and restlessness are the rule.

The value of such behaviour for the survival of both individual and species is obvious, crying and searching both making it more likely that the lost one will be recovered. In the meantime the separated individual is in a state of danger and must be prepared to fight or to flee should the need arise; hence the importance of an alarm reaction at this time.

In his study of the vocalization of the young vervet monkey, Struhsaker (1967) described no less than five varieties of 'lost call'. Spectrographic analysis reveals that the characteristics of these calls make them both penetrating and capable of accurate directional location over long distances. Similar studies have not, as far as we know, been carried out with the human infant, but most mothers are well able to distinguish the characteristics of the various cries of their babies. Darwin (1872) paid careful attention to the ways in which human beings and animals give visible expression to their emotions. Weeping was for him 'the primary and natural expression, as we see in children, of suffering of any kind'. Sobbing, he believed to be the partial expression of weeping – the cry is muted but the spasmodic inspiratory movement remains, as is clearly seen in the young child shortly before or after weeping. Darwin suggested that the contortion of the muscles about the eyes is necessary to protect the eyes from the rise in venous pressure that accompanies any forced expiration (it can also be discovered in laughing, shouting, etc.).

In the adult human being the facial expression of grief is seen as a compromise between the urge to cry aloud and the urge to suppress such inappropriate and ineffective behaviour. Thus the raising of the inner aspect of the eyebrows, wrinkling the forehead and the base of the nose, produces an expression similar to that of a person looking upwards towards a bright light – someone attempting to shield their eyes from the light by lowering the eyelashes but, at the same time, to look at the light by raising the brows. The resulting contraction of antagonistic muscles produces a characteristic expression that is also seen when the sorrowing person suppresses the impulse to cry aloud.

Similarly, the depression of the angles of the mouth is alleged to be necessary in crying in order to enable the maximum amount of sound to be emitted. In the sorrowing adult the mouth is not widely opened but the angles of the mouth are drawn down. Irregular sighs are thought to represent the inspiratory spasms of crying or sobbing, and the term 'choked with grief' reflects this.

Speculative though details of Darwin's theorizing may be, his general hypothesis that the expression of grief in the human adult contains elements of behaviour patterns which are more fully expressed in young children and social animals is illuminating. Just which components derive from which behaviour patterns is likely to remain a matter for conjecture but there can be little doubt that a large part of the expression of grief is derived from the urge to cry.

To say that what we see on the face of a bereaved person is no more than a suppressed cry, however, is an oversimplification. Maturing human beings learn to do more than hide their feelings. They learn to express them in ways that convey to their fellows shades and textures of meaning, which may be very much more subtle than those conveyed by the crying child. In most circumstances in which one human being has become separated from another it is neither necessary nor appropriate for both to cry aloud. The facial expression that Darwin describes, coupled with restless searching and verbal requests for help, is sufficient to excite the serious concern and cooperation of others. The suppressed cry has thus become part of a ritualized social signal system, which is still only partially under the control of the will but which enables the separated individual to evoke and direct the help of others in an orderly and constructive manner. Only when searching is useless and reunion impossible, as in the statistically infrequent event of loss by death, does the involuntary expression of grief lose its utility. In such circumstances bereaved people may attempt to 'hide their feelings' with varying degrees of success. The extent and consequences of their success are discussed in Chapter 5; the extent of their failure is the subject of this chapter.

THE GRIEVING CHILD

Before we return to the pining adult let us take one more look at the child during the same phase of grief. We quote from an article by James Robertson (1953) in which he described the behaviour of healthy children aged between fifteen and thirty months on admission to hospital or to some residential institution.

> In this initial phase, which may last from a few hours to seven or eight days, the young child has a strong conscious need for his mother and the expectation, based on previous experience, that she will respond to his cries. He is acutely anxious that he has lost her, is confused and frightened by unfamiliar surroundings, and seeks to recapture her by the full exercise of his limited resources. He has no comprehension of his situation and is distraught with fright and urgent desire for satisfactions only his mother can give. He will often cry loudly, shake his cot, throw himself about, and look eagerly towards any sight or sound which might prove to be his missing mother.

Each of the components described in the preceding pages is here; alarm, protest, crying, and searching. But note that what Robertson is describing is not just the effects of losing mother; it includes the effects of being lost oneself. This child is in a strange environment; its need for its mother is therefore greater than would be likely if it had been at home.

Familiar territory, mother, and other attachment figures, all share 'home valency' (Meyer-Holzapfel, 1940), and in the absence of one the tendency to cling to the others is stronger than usual. The young child who has achieved mobility moves within an orbit the centre of which is mother. In unfamiliar surroundings the orbit is small and the child will tend to cling to the mother. In familiar surroundings the child moves within a wider orbit and can tolerate intermittent separations when mother disappears altogether, provided that she is not gone for too long and that no change in the situation stimulates a demand for her return. As the child grows older and more and more of the world becomes familiar, it normally learns to tolerate greater degrees of separation and at the same time develops attachments to a number of other individuals who have now taken on some of the home valency. Nevertheless, it seems that the desire for attachment figures persists as does the desire for a safe and familiar environment. Separation from either or both of these gives rise to behaviour which, in the normal course of events, ensures their return or the return of the individual to them. It is this behaviour that tends to take place during the yearning phase of grief.

THE GRIEVING ADULT

Bereaved adults are well aware that there is no point in searching for a dead person, but we maintain that this does not prevent them from experiencing a strong impulse to search. Because they recognize that searching is irrational, they tend to resist the suggestion that this is what they want to do. Some bereaved adults, however, have ready insight into the irrational components of their own behaviour.

> 'I can't help looking for him everywhere . . . I walk around searching for him . . . I felt that if I could have come somewhere I could have found him', said one London widow, a week after the death of her husband. She had thought of going to spiritualist meetings in the hope of getting in touch with her dead husband, but decided against it. Another of the London widows said, 'I'm just searching for nothing'; and another, 'I go to the grave . . . but he's not there. It's as if I was drawn towards him'.

Several bereaved psychiatric patients in the Bethlem Study were aware of the urge to search. Most of them were mothers who had lost children. An Australian woman had lost her adoptive son and her true son in the war. Their deaths were announced within a few weeks of each other. When told of her son's death, she refused to believe it and eventually persuaded her husband to bring her to England in search of the boy. On arrival she thought she saw him coming towards her on the stairs. She became very depressed and cried for the first time since her bereavement.

Another mother received a message that her son had been killed in action in Belgium. She reacted severely and four years later, when the war was over, persuaded her husband to take her to visit her son's grave in order to make sure that he was dead. Returning home she said, 'I knew I was leaving him behind for ever'.

Two other women interviewed in the Bethlem Study reported conscious searching for a dead person. One, a mother, described how she repeatedly went into the bedroom in search of her dead baby. The other, a widow, had repeatedly gone to the kitchen door to look for her husband. She found this behaviour so painful that she resisted it: 'I think, there's no good going into the kitchen, he'll never come back'.

Children who have persisted in a search for lost parents extending into adult life have been described by Stengel (1939, 1943), who believed that some wandering fugues are the result. Adoptive children often 'keep alive' the hope of finding their true parents. One in the United States had spent large sums of money in hiring private investigators to locate his mother. A striking change occurred when he succeeded in finding her. She crossed the American continent to stay with him and, although she did not live up to his idealized expectations, their relationship did become quite good. Moreover, his restless anxiety which had been present for many years diminished considerably.

In the examples quoted above, searching was quite manifest, but the majority of the bereaved people studied by Parkes were not consciously aware of the need to search. In order to show how their behaviour nevertheless revealed the urge to search, it is necessary to look more closely at what searching entails.

SEARCHING AND PERCEPTION

Searching is a restless activity in which one moves towards possible locations of a lost object. The person who is searching has to select places in which to look, move towards them, and scan them; what is to be seen must also be selected.

'Selecting what to see' is an important part of perception. At every moment of every day sense organs in all parts of a person's body are sending back 'messages' to the central nervous system. These messages arise from within and without the body itself. In states of low arousal (e.g. during sleep) only a very small proportion of them reaches consciousness; in states of high arousal a larger porportion does so. But even when a a person is alarmed, only a small number of the total pool of sensations attain conscious levels of attention.

Those messages that do reach consciousness are the residue of a barrage. One can picture them as having to pass a series of filters which cut off those that are irrelevent or capable of being acted upon at an unconscious level. By the time a message reaches conciousness it has not only passed a series of filters but undergone a process of organization which links it with memories of similar previous experiences; it has already undergone a preliminary process of recognition. A word on a page is not perceived as a succession of of black and white shapes which must be interpreted before they can be understood; it is already a concept by the time it attains consciousness. This preconscious recognition accounts for the difficulty we have in spotting misprints in a manuscript – our brain has already been 'set' to anticipate and to perceive the correct spelling; the misprints have been filtered out before reaching consciousness. (There are five deliberate misprints in the last two paragraphs.)

The development of a perceptual set to see one thing and ignore another is necessary to any behaviour. It is essential in searching if the lost object is to be 'seen' and recognized. Searchers carry in their mind a picture of the lost object. As each possible location is approached, sensations derived from that location are matched with the picture. When a fit, however approximate, is made, the object seen is 'recognized', attention is focused upon it, and further evidence is sought to confirm the initial impression.

COMPONENTS OF SEARCHING

A woman is searching anxiously for her son; she moves restlessly about the house looking in places in which she thinks he might be found. She appears distraught and is unaware that her hair is dishevelled. She is thinking constantly of the boy and, when she hears a creak on the stair, immediately associates it with him. 'John, is that you?' she calls. The components of this behaviour are:

1   Alarm, tension, and a state of arousal.
2   Restless movement.
3   Preoccupation with thoughts of the lost person.
4   Development of a perceptual set for that person.
5   Loss of interest in personal appearance and other matters that normally occupy attention.
6   Direction of attention towards those parts of the environment in which the lost person is likely to be.
7   Calling for the lost person.

Each of these components is to be found in the behaviour of bereaved people. The first two items, which are not peculiar to searching behaviour, have already been discussed. The special quality of pining or separation anxiety, which is the subjective accompaniment of the alarm reaction, is reflected in the special quality of the restless hyperactivity. This has been well described by Lindemann (1944; our italics):

> The activity throughout the day of the severely bereaved person shows remarkable changes. There is no retardation of action and speech; quite to the contrary, there is a rush of speech, especially when talking about the deceased. There is restlessness, inability to sit still, moving about in an aimless fashion, *continually searching for something to do.* There is, however, at the same time, a painful lack of capacity to initiate and maintain normal patterns of activity.

We contend that the searching behaviour of the bereaved person is not 'aimless' at all. It has the specific aim of finding the one who is gone. But bereaved people seldom admit to having so irrational an aim and their behaviour is therefore regarded by others, and usually by themselves, as 'aimless'. Their search for 'something to do' is bound to fail because the things they can do are not, in fact, what they want to do at all. What they want is to find the lost person.

There are several reasons for the restlessness. As we have pointed out, restlessness is a part of the alarm reaction. It is also associated with anger and will need to be reconsidered in that context. One young woman who was interviewed by Parkes after the death of her de facto husband was repeatedly glancing over her right shoulder. She did this, she said, 'because he was always on my right'. In her case the repetition of this activity seemed to represent an abortive search. A widow who wrote for advice to Cruse Bereavement Care, the British organization, described how she not only felt but acted upon a restless need to search: 'Everywhere I go I am searching for him. In crowds, in church, in the supermarket. I keep on scanning the faces. People must think I'm odd'.

Preoccupation with thoughts of the lost person and with the events leading up to the loss is a common feature in bereaved people. 'I never stop missing him', said one widow, and the tendency to return again and again to thoughts of the lost person was still present in most of the London widows a year after bereavement.

IMAGES OF THE DEAD

These memories were remarkable for their clarity. The dead person would be pictured exactly as he was when alive. Usually he would be 'seen', for instance, in his accustomed chair, and the memory would be so intense as almost to amount to a perception: 'I keep seeing his very fair hair and the colour of his eyes'; 'I still see him, quite vividly, coming in the door'; 'I can always see him'. A similar clarity was often present in memories of the husband's voice or touch: 'I can almost feel his skin or touch his hands', said one widow.

At other times, particularly at night or when attention was relaxed, the bereaved woman would go over in her mind the events of the past in which the lost person took part. During the early months of bereavement, and again as the anniversary of the death approached, memories of the last few weeks of the patient's life were common: 'I go through that last week again and again'; 'I find myself going through it'. The experience was sometimes so clear that it was almost as if the bereaved person was reliving the events of a year ago. 'A year ago today', said a widow of sixty, 'was Princess Alexandra's wedding day. I said to him, "Don't forget the wedding." When I got in I said, "Did you watch the wedding?" He said, "No, I forgot." We watched it together in the evening except he had his eyes shut. He wrote a card to his sister and I can see him so vividly. I could tell you every mortal thing that was done on all those days. I said, "You haven't watched anything." He said, "No, I haven't." '

When these memories are of unhappy or horrific events, that the person would prefer to forget, they have consequences that are very different from those that result from happy memories. In fact, as we saw in Chapter 2, the bereaved may complain that the memories of traumatic events interfere with their ability to think about and to grieve for the person who has died. It seems that we must make a distinction between grief and traumatic stress reactions and that the thing that distinguishes the two is the character of the images that come to occupy the attention of the bereaved. A mother, who had woken to find her baby dead beside her, sat in the cemetery for hours recalling her dead baby with his glazed eyes and dry mouth. Painful illnesses or accidental deaths that cause mutilation of the dead person, leave behind correspondingly painful memories. On the other hand, a peaceful death and a post-mortem appearance of repose or contentment is remembered with gratitude and is unlikely to spoil the other memories of the person who has died. An exception to this general rule was found in one woman whose husband had been married twice: she had always been jealous of his first wife and after her husband's death she remarked bitterly, 'He looked so happy in death it made me think he was with her'.

If recollections in the early stage of bereavement gave pain, happier memories often came to replace them. One widow, who was initially haunted by a vivid recollection of her husband's face after death, described how, as time passed, this memory faded and was replaced by a picture of him 'when he was normal'.

MISPERCEPTIONS

It is postulated that maintaining a clear visual memory of lost people facilitates the search by making it more likely that they will be located if, in fact, they are to be found somewhere within the field of search. It constitutes a part of the perceptual set for the lost person, by which incoming information from the sense organs is scanned for evidence of the lost object.

If a woman is set to perceive certain classes of object then it is likely that she will also misperceive those objects more often than usual. Ambiguous impressions will be interpreted to fit the looked for object and attention will be focused upon them until the mistake has been corrected.

Such occurrences are common after bereavement, as studies by Rees (1971) and Kalish and Reynolds (1973) have shown. Widows in the London Study often described illusions of having seen or heard their dead husband. These illusions usually involved the misinterpretation of some existing sight or sound. 'I think I catch sight of him in his van, but it's the van from down the road', said one. Other widows reported identifying a man in the street – as he came closer they would realize their mistake. A creak at night was interpreted as the husband moving about the house and a sound at the door as the husband coming home. Widows who had been accustomed to listen out for their husband during his last illness would hear him cough or call out. Such illusions, though disturbing at the time, were not more frequent among psychiatrically disturbed subjects and cannot be regarded as anything but a part of the normal reaction to bereavement. Nevertheless, they are sometimes of such vividness that people need to be reassured that they are not an unusual feature.

Although the pangs of grief and the urge to search are very powerful they are not present all of the time. The pang passes, the need to cry aloud diminishes and, for a while, the bereaved can turn their thoughts to other things. Bereaved people oscillate back and forth between grieving and the other demands of life, eating, sleeping, caring for surviving children, etc. This oscillation has received much attention from psychologists and has been termed the 'Dual Process of Grieving' (Stroebe, Schut, and van den Bout, 1994). It needs to be understood if we are to make sense of the problems that arise when it goes wrong.

Between the pangs of grief life may appear to go on as usual but, in fact, that is not the way it feels. The appetites and enthusiasms that normally involve us are severely depleted and much of our behaviour seems governed by habit rather than desire. Newly bereaved people often show little concern for food, sleep, personal appearance, work, or family. Although no systematic information was sought regarding sexual feelings, it was Parkes' impression that sexual appetite, too, is diminished during the early stages of bereavement. This, however, is not always the case, and an increased need for someone to cling to can sometimes lead to increased sexuality (Swigar, Bowers, and Fleck, 1976).

LOCATING THE DEAD

Being alert, restless, preoccupied, and set to find the lost person, the griever directs attention to those parts of the environment that are most closely associated with that person. At least half of the London widows admitted that they felt drawn towards places associated with their husband and most reluctant to leave the home where he had lived; they treasured possessions and parts of the house that were especially 'his', and tended to return repeatedly to them. One widow said, 'I walk around all where we used to go', and two others expressed the feeling that they must hurry home whenever they went out, because their husband would be waiting. One of these terminated a visit to her sister prematurely because she felt that she had left her husband too long.

Another kept going through her husband's clothes, feeling in the pockets and gazing at them. She remarked that it was here that the smell of her husband lingered most strongly and she found this very evocative of his presence. A London widow regularly wore her husband's dressing-gown. This, so she said, seemed to bring him closer. A thirteen-year-old girl who had lost her father angered and disgusted her mother by taking his pyjama jacket to bed with her at night. Photographs, pipes, wallets, and other 'close' personal possessions were often prominently displayed in places where the bereaved person preferred to be. Favourite pieces of furniture, 'his chair' for instance, were objects of special reverence. One widow had found that she could not get away from the notion that her husband was still sitting in his chair. She would sit in her own chair and find herself frequently gazing at his. This was so much of an interference with her other activities that she felt she had to do something to prevent it. The solution she finally adopted was satisfying and extremely simple: she sat in his chair herself.

When someone is lost the most natural place to look for them is the place where they were last seen. Following a loss by death this is the place where they died. Many bereaved people are aware of mixed feelings; on the one hand, they feel drawn towards the hospital or other place of death, on the other hand, their memories of the painful events that took place, along with recognition that the patient's bed will now be empty, or occupied by someone else, may make it hard to return. In the end a visit to the ward where the person died, may be seen as a step forward if it leads to a greater acceptance of the death. Likewise, following a road traffic accident some will avoid the place where it took place while others feel drawn to it and may even construct roadside memorials. Clark and Franzmann (2006) suggested that roadside memorials also enable bereaved people to achieve a sense of empowerment and control by challenging the authority of church and government.

Most widows liked to visit their husband's grave and several spoke of the almost uncanny attraction that drew them to the cemetery. They would think of him as being located in or around the grave and feel concern for his comfort if the weather was inclement. 'It's terrible if it's raining. It's as if I want to pick him up and bring him home.' One widow who had had her husband cremated explained this on the grounds that the local cemetery was occasionally flooded during wet weather and her husband had always been 'frightened of water'. She had a fantasy of all the corpses 'floating around in their coffins' and wouldn't have liked this for her husband.

On the whole, the sense of the dead person being located in his place of burial was less strong when he had been cremated. One widow whose husband had been a municipal gardener arranged for his ashes to be scattered in the public park where he had worked. Subsequently she visited the place frequently. Even the container in which the ashes had been placed had become numinous; it was placed on a table in the widow's sitting-room, an object of fascination and awe.

At Aberfan, in Wales, where 116 children died when a water-laden coal tip inundated a school in 1966, visiting the burial place of the children became an important part of the life of bereaved mothers, and the wish to stay close to the dead children was the reason given by many parents for not moving out of the village. This was despite the fact that the disaster fund made a grant to each bereaved family to enable those who wished to do so to buy a house elsewhere.

People who attempt to avoid painful reminders of the dead person by moving away often come back, and the bereaved person who avoids reminders is aware of a sense of being pulled in two directions. One widow, for instance, moved into the back bedroom of her house to get away from her memories, but found that she missed her husband so much that she moved back into the front bedroom 'to be near him'. Two widows felt drawn towards the hospital where their husbands had passed their final illnesses, and one found herself walking into the hospital ward before she realized that he was not there. Another thought of her husband as being upstairs in the bed in which he had remained for many months before his death. She found herself listening out for him and sometimes thought she heard him calling for her.

Spiritualism claims to help bereaved persons in their search for the dead, and seven of the bereaved people who were included in Parkes' various studies described visits to séances or spiritualist churches. Their reactions were mixed: some felt that they had obtained some sort of contact with the dead and a few had been frightened by this. On the whole they did not feel satisfied by the experience and none had become a regular attendee at spiritualist meetings.

REUNION

A more drastic solution to the problem of grief is suicide. This is sometimes considered as a way of achieving reunion with the dead; it may also be seen as an end to present alienation and misery. As we saw in the last chapter, several investigators have found an association between suicide and bereavement. In Parkes' studies, ideas of suicide were often expressed. Many of the London widows went through a period during which they felt they 'might as well be dead'. Typically they would say, 'If it wasn't for the children I might consider it' – but in fact only one had made any sort of suicidal attempt and that was very half-hearted.

Among the bereaved psychiatric patients there was one, a girl of twelve, who had been admitted to hospital because of serious weight loss after the death of her mother. She had refused to eat and her father had said, 'You'll become like Mummy', whereupon she replied, 'That's just what I want to do. I want to die and be with Mummy'. Death was seen as a possible means of succeeding in her search for her mother.

CALLING

There remains one other accompaniment of searching which must be considered here. Calling for the lost person, while not strictly an essential part of searching, is often associated with it.

'Dwight, where are you? I need you so much', wrote Frances Beck (1966) in her *Diary of a Widow*. Crying is, of course, a frequent feature of grief and sixteen of the twenty-two London widows cried when discussing their bereavement with Parkes a month after the death of their husband. The fact that they cried does not, of course, mean that they were necessarily crying for their husbands. Crying is an expression of helplessness, which can arouse sympathy and offers of help in many situations. On occasion, however, the object to which the cries of these widows were directed was quite clearly the husband. Faced with the fact that she would never have her husband back again, one widow shouted out, 'Oh Fred, I do need you', and then burst into tears. A bereaved mother cried out for her dead baby during the night, and a nurse called to her dead sister at night and dreamt repeatedly that she was searching for her sister but could not find her.

In the London Study tearfulness was closely associated with

preoccupation with thoughts of the lost husband (see Appendix 6; Table 4), and this finding seems to suggest that, whatever other factors contributed to cause these widows to cry, an important one was these memories.

GOAL-DIRECTED BEHAVIOUR

In order to get the search for a lost person into perspective we have to bear in mind that a great deal of human and animal behaviour contains elements of searching. Searching fills the gap between aims and object. Traditional psychology has paid little attention to this category of behaviour and it is only with the advent of ethology (the study of animal behaviour) that the significance of searching has been recognized.

In analysing goal-directed behaviour ethologists have found it useful to divide it into the successive acts that make it up. A particular set of circumstances gives rise to behaviour A; this behaviour alters the situation and calls forth a fresh behaviour pattern, B; this further alters the situation until, if all goes well, the goal is achieved and the behaviour sequence is terminated. It obviously helps if the animal knows what its 'goal' is, but that is not necessarily the case. The robin who feels impelled to collect pieces of dead grass, fly with them to a tree and weave them together, may have no idea why it is building a nest.

Stimuli that guide behaviour towards a set goal are termed 'orienting stimuli' and stimuli that bring the sequence to an end 'terminating' or 'consummatory stimuli'. Similarly, behaviour that leads towards a set goal is termed 'appetitive behaviour', and the final, more or less stereotyped, activity with which a behaviour sequence terminates has been called 'consummatory behaviour'.

This classification works well enough for behaviour such as coitus, and eating and drinking, which have as their goal a specific change in the organism. There are, however, some types of goal situation that are continuous over time, e.g. occupation of territory, incubation of eggs, or maintenance of proximity to mother. In such cases there is no consummatory behaviour and achievement of the goal situation initiates a different type of ongoing activity, the effect of which is to ensure that the goal situation will be continued.

Either type of behaviour sequence can fail to reach its goal. This may occur because the goal cannot be reached by the means employed or because more pressing stimuli distract attention and initiate a different behaviour sequence having higher priority in the hierarchy of goals. In the former case the behaviour is said to be frustrated. C. S. Lewis (1961) has described the frustration of the mourner:

> I think I am beginning to understand why grief feels like suspense. It comes from the frustration of so many impulses that had become habitual. Thought after thought, feeling after feeling, action after action, had H [his wife] for their object. Now their target is gone. I keep on, through habit, fitting an arrow to the string; then I remember and I have to lay the bow down. So many roads lead through to H. I set out on one of them. But now there's an impassable frontier-post across it. So many roads once; now so many culs-de-sac.

In every appetite there is an element of searching for the right fit between perception and action; and in the appetitive behaviour that mediates attachment to a human being the search element is more explicit. We speak of love as a 'bond' or 'tie'. The strength of a tie is its resistance to severance. The behaviour patterns mediating attachment ('attachment behaviour') are patterns of interaction: clinging, smiling, following, searching, calling, and so on. They have been described at length by Bowlby (1969). Some of these patterns, such as smiling and clinging, are best regarded as 'maintenance behaviour' and require the presence of the object for their evocation. Others, such as calling and searching, are appetitive activities and occur only in the absence of the object.

The goal situation to which these behaviour patterns normally give rise is the optimum proximity of the loved person. When this is achieved the appetitive behaviour ceases. But if the loved person is permanently lost, appetitive behaviour will tend to persist and with it the subjective discomfort that accompanies unterminated striving. This is what is experienced as frustration. (The term 'frustration' is used to indicate both the situation of a person or animal whose appetitive behaviour is balked and the subjective discomfort which results.)

HABITS

It is not only behaviour patterns mediating attachment that are evoked following bereavement. Many other behaviour patterns require the presence of the lost person for their termination although they are not themselves examples of attachment behaviour. Some of these are habits or activities established over the years, in which both parties shared or which depended for their relevance on both parties being alive: laying the table for two, washing up together, or making decisions about expenditure, leisure activities, etc. When these patterns are initiated after the death of one party, a sense of frustration quickly follows. But alternative means of coping are usually available and the bereaved person soon learns to wash up alone and plan his or her own activities. When, however, attachment behaviour is evoked (as when a woman misses her husband in bed or finds herself waiting for him to come back from work), no substitute is acceptable. It is this that accounts for the persistence of the impulse to search long after habits such as laying the table for two have been unlearnt. C. S. Lewis is right in regarding the persistence of habit as a cause of frustration, but it is not the only cause. The suspense he describes would seem to indicate the expectation that something is about to happen. To the griever the only happening that seems important is the return of the one who is lost. And in social animals, from their earliest years, the principal behaviour pattern evoked by loss is searching.

THE NEUROPHYSIOLOGY OF GRIEF

Recent technology now makes it possible to study what happens in the brain during a pang of grief and these findings are in keeping with our theory that the pang of grief is the emotional accompaniment of searching for a lost person.

Since all thought uses chemical energy, and this energy is obtained from oxygen in the blood, mental activity evokes a demand for blood; this leads, within 1–5 seconds, to an increase in blood flow in the parts of the brain that are active. Functional magnetic resonance imaging (fMRI) is a way of visualizing, on a computer screen, the magnetic changes in the brain that accompany these changes in blood flow. The imaging is so precise that we can now identify activity within areas of 2–4 cubic millimetres. This has enabled researchers to evoke pangs of grief by exposing bereaved persons to pictures of the lost person and words that bring home the pain of separation while studying what goes on in their brains. These studies show that several parts of the brain, which have been shown to be responsible for processing of familiar faces, visual imaging, memory retrieval, the processing of emotion, and regulation of the autonomic nervous system, play a part in the pang of grief.

When bereaved people with Prolonged Grief Disorder (PGD) were compared with others without the disorder, although both showed activity in the same pathways as described above, only the PGD group showed a pattern of brain activity in an area concerned with intense seeking for a reward. This same area is implicated in drug addiction in which similar cravings are experienced. Seeing the image of the dead person may, for a moment, raise the hope of reunion. But this hope is normally rapidly dashed by the realization (via the higher pathways) that reunion is impossible. Maybe PGD sufferers have more difficulty than others in giving up hope. For references to the research and more details of these important studies see Appendix 7.

IS GRIEF INEVITABLE FOLLOWING LOSS?

Wortman and Silver (1989) have suggested that distress, and by implication grief itself, is not inevitable following a loss but it is clear from their paper that they are confusing 'distress' with depression, which is certainly *not* inevitable. Anthropological studies have failed to reveal any society in which people do not show some sign of grieving although there is great variation in the ways in which this is expressed (Rosenblatt, Walsh, and Jackson, 1976). The only apparent exceptions to the rule seem to be people with little or no attachment to the person who has died, and they cannot be said to have suffered a loss at all. Of course people can avoid, deny and repress their feelings and some of the ways in which they do this will be considered in the next chapter. In a recent study Bonanno *et al.* (2002) have challenged the assumption that grief is a necessary response to bereavement and that, sooner or later, 'grief will out'. They support this claim from a sample of widows over the age of 65, 46 per cent of whom had low scores of depression at both six and eighteen months after bereavement. While there is no reason to doubt their claim that these people were 'resilient', the absence of information about the intensity of grief during the first few weeks of bereavement invalidates any claim that they did not grieve. Furthermore there were 5 per cent who had low scores of depression at six months but higher scores a year later.

Bonanno *et al.*'s work is important for the light that it throws on the roots of resilience. Their study also confirms the common observation that, in elderly people, particularly among those whose partner suffered a long illness, high levels of depression often precede bereavement, which, in some cases, may even come as a relief. We shall return to further consideration of these issues in later chapters.

5

CONTINUING BONDS

... They think they see their dead friends continually in
their eyes, observantes imagines ... 'all the year long' as
Pliny complains to Romanus, 'methinks I see Virginius, I
hear Virginius, I talk with Virginius, etc.'
Robert Burton, *The Anatomy of Melancholy* (1621)

Despite the words of the marriage ceremony, which promise attachment 'until death us do part', it is clear, from our own and other studies, that attachment does not cease when a loved person dies. This observation has been referred to as the 'continuing bond' with the deceased and has received much attention since Klass, Silverman, and Nickman edited their book on this subject in 1996. Although this phenomenon was described clearly in the first, and all subsequent editions of *Bereavement: Studies of grief in adult life*, it is only now receiving the attention that it deserves. We shall see how the continuing attachment to the dead person takes several forms, some of which facilitate adjustment and others that delay or complicate it.

FINDING

When appetitive behaviour is frustrated, as we have seen, there results an increase in the intensity and persistence of that behaviour. But even when pining is most intense something may happen to mitigate the pain of grief. Some sight or sound will be misperceived and, for a moment, it seems as if the search is at an end. Or the bereaved person may feel that the lost one is near at hand without actually perceiving them. Sometimes this mitigation occurs spontaneously, at others it is the bereaved themselves who find ways to reduce the pain of grief and of traumatic memories.

Widows interviewed by Parkes have spoken of the comfort they derive from putting a bolster beside them in the bed at night or from pretending to themselves that their husband can hear their prayers. 'I talk to him and quite expect him to answer me', said one widow. A certain 'willing suspension of disbelief' is necessary to allow such pretences to succeed and there is always the danger that one may 'wake up' to the emptiness of it all. But it seems that many bereaved people get comfort from such behaviour.

The commonest means of mitigating the pain of grieving comprises the maintenance of a feeling or impression that the bereaved person is nearby although they may not be seen or heard. A comforting sense of the persisting presence of the lost husband was reported by fifteen of the twenty-two London widows. To some extent this seemed to allay restlessness and pining. Thus one widow said, 'I still have the feeling he's near and there's something I ought to be doing for him or telling him'. Often the dead person was not in any particular place: 'He's not anywhere in particular, just around the place; it's a good feeling'; 'Spiritually he's near'; 'I still feel that he's around'.

Just as the child feels braver when mother is nearby, so the widow tends to feel more secure when the sense of her husband's presence is strong: 'When I'm washing my hair, it's the feeling he's there to protect me in case someone comes in through the door'.

One is reminded of comparable behaviour in animals whose circumstances allow the initiation but not the termination of appetitive behaviour – sooner or later, in partial or complete form, the missing behaviour sequence may take place *in vacuo*. For example, Tinbergen (1951) has described the behaviour of a male stickleback when confined in an empty tank. It comprises a sequence of zigzag movements (termed the 'zigzag dance') that, under normal conditions, takes place only when the male stickleback perceives the characteristic appearance and movements of a pregnant female. This behaviour normally induces the female to follow the male to the nest, where the eggs are laid and fertilized. In the empty tank, however, the zigzag dances may be performed alone. Similarly, captive starlings have been observed to carry out the movements of fly-catching even when no flies are present (Lorenz, 1937). It is, of course, impossible to state dogmatically that these 'vacuum activities' are homologous with similar behaviour in human beings. All we can do is note with interest that, in many species, when 'seeking' behaviour is evoked at high intensity, 'finding' behaviour will often occur even in the absence of the object sought.

We have no means of knowing if the vacuum activities of social animals are accompanied by a sense of the presence of the sought for object, but it seems likely that they are. Tinbergen pointed out that in many species deprivation lowers the threshold for the perception of 'releasing stimuli' whereas satiation raises that threshold.

Could some such process explain the misperception of the newly bereaved woman who 'sees' her husband approaching in the street, only to find, when she goes to greet him, that it is somebody else, or the behaviour of a woman whose infant has died who goes into the child's room in order to rock an empty cradle?

In the newly bereaved widow the perceptual element is very strong: 'He's with me all the time. I hear him and see him although I know it's only imagination'; 'If I didn't take a strong hold on myself I'd get talking to him'. Occasionally hypnagogic (half-waking) 'hallucinations' occur. One widow was resting in her chair on a Sunday afternoon when she saw her husband, quite clearly, digging in the garden with only his trousers on; another saw her husband coming in through the garden gate; a third saw her dead father standing by her bed at night. These 'hallucinations' are very transient and disappear as soon as the bereaved person becomes fully aroused. It is this that distinguishes them from true hallucinations.

That 'searching' and 'finding' go together is not surprising. A 'sense of the continued presence of the deceased', 'a clear visual memory of him', and 'preoccupation with thoughts of him' were statistically associated (see Appendix 6; Table 4); that is to say, widows with a strong sense of their husband's presence also tended to recall him with great clarity and to be preoccupied with his memory. All these phenomena, which have been referred to as components of searching, are also components of finding.

THE SENSE OF PRESENCE

Confirmation of this evidence comes from Rees's (1971) well-conducted study of 227 widows and sixty-six widowers of all ages. He found that 39 per cent had a sense of the presence of the dead spouse and 14 per cent experienced illusions of his or her presence from time to time.

Those who experienced such illusions or a sense of their spouse's presence reported significantly more loneliness than those who reported no such phenomena; and they also missed the dead person more, and thought and dreamt of him or her more often. But

69 per cent of those with a sense of the presence of the dead spouse felt helped by their illusions and they had significantly less sleep disturbance than the rest. Although, like the clarity of memories, the sense of presence commonly persisted long after the distress of grief had declined, it did eventually decline and was less frequently reported after ten years had elapsed.

Less easy to explain was the association between the sense of presence and being over forty years of age, of 'hysteroid' personality type and higher social class. There was no relationship between the prevalence of illusions and religious faith, mode of death, social isolation, depression, appetite, or weight disturbance.

We conclude that, although these phenomena meet the definition of illusions, i.e. they are false perceptions, they are certainly not symptoms of psychosis and simply reflect a strong attachment to the person who has died.

It seems that while searching and finding cannot, logically, occur simultaneously, they are often so closely juxtaposed as to be inseparable. Thus a widow may be preoccupied with a clear visual memory of her husband: at one moment she is anxiously pining for him, and a moment later she experiences a comforting sense of his presence nearby; then something reminds her that this sense is only an illusion and she is pining again.

As time passes, if all goes well, the intensity of pining diminishes and the pain and pleasure of recollection are experienced as a bitter-sweet mixture of emotions, 'nostalgia'. By this time the two components seem to be experienced simultaneously.

> Mrs P. was the devoted, thirty-year-old daughter of an assertive and somewhat dominant woman. When her mother died Mrs P. consciously directed her search towards making contact with her mother's departed spirit. In company with her sister she improvised a planchette with which she 'received' messages, which she believed came from her mother.
>
> At this séance she noticed a Toby jug, which seemed to resemble her mother. She felt that her mother's spirit had entered into the jug and persuaded her sister to give it to her. For some weeks she kept the jug near at hand and had a strong sense of the presence of her mother. However, the jug proved a mixed blessing since she found that she was both attracted and frightened by it. Her husband was exasperated by this behaviour and eventually, against her

will, he smashed the jug. His wife noticed that the pieces, which she buried in the garden, 'felt hot' – presumably a sign of life.

Mrs P. did not give up her search. Shortly after the jug was broken she acquired a dog. Her mother had always said that if she was ever reincarnated it would be in the form of a dog. When interviewed three years later Mrs P. said of the dog: 'She's not like any other animal. She does anything. She'll only go for walks with my husband or me. She seems to eat all the things that mother used to eat. She doesn't like men'.

It is easy to dismiss the behaviour of Mrs P. as 'abnormal', but is it so remote from the behaviour of other bereaved people who build memorials to 'keep alive' the memory of the dead? They derive the same comfort, the same sense of having found the lost person, from such memorials as that which Mrs P. derived from her Toby jug and her dog. Moreover, as Gorer (1965) has pointed out, a majority of people in the world believe in reincarnation.

THE BEREAVEMENT DREAM

The recovery of the lost person may also be achieved in dreams. Half the London widows reported dreaming of their husband after his death, and half of these dreams had a peculiarly vivid and realistic quality.

It was just like everyday life – my husband coming in and getting his dinner. Very vivid so that when I woke up I was very annoyed [informant cried].

Most commonly these dreams were happy dreams of interaction with the dead husband. Less frequently he was dying or going away, but even in the happy dreams there was usually something to indicate that all was not well.

The third week after he died I dreamt I was lying in bed and he came up and sat on the bed. I frowned up at him and he said, 'Take care of the children, because I'm going back home'. He wanted to take J. and I said, 'No, you can't have him because there's no one to look after him at home [in the West Indies]'. He banged the door and went off. I had a feeling that he's no more, he shouldn't be around here.

He was trying to comfort me and putting his arms round me. I kept turning away and crying and crying. Even in the dream I know he's dead . . . But I felt so happy and I cried and he couldn't do anything about it . . . When I touched his face it was as if he was really there – quite real and vivid.

He was in bed. I was saying, 'Come on P., you're going to be all right'. Then I woke up and it wasn't. It was quite a shock.

Such dreams are not just wish-fulfilling fantasies; they all contain intimations of the husband's death. Even in a dream, reality insists upon asserting itself.

He was in the coffin with the lid off and all of a sudden he came to life and got out. And I was so overjoyed to think that he was here that when I woke up I wondered where I was. It was so clear I was crying and laughing. I looked at him and he opened his mouth. I said, 'He's alive. He's alive'. I thought 'Thank God, I'll have him to talk to'.

These examples typify the bereavement dreams originally described by Waller (1951). As in waking life the imagery is vivid, dead people are thought of as if they are alive, but the shadow of their death falls over all. Hadfield (1954) has spoken of dreaming as a form of problem-solving behaviour, and it is no surprise to find that bereaved dreamers continue to go over in their minds the vivid mental images that preoccupy their waking hours and, out of them, create the action, setting and cast of their dreams. Unfortunately the 'problem' of bereavement, the recovery of the lost object, is one that cannot be solved (even in dreams). No matter how happy the dream, there must always be a 'sad awakening'.

DISBELIEF

But there are other ways of mitigating the pain of grieving. These enable the bereaved person to avoid, consciously or unconsciously, the thoughts that are so painful, or to dissociate the pain from the thoughts.

One of these ways, perhaps the most frequently encountered, is to disbelieve that the loss has occurred. 'I can't believe it's true' was a sentiment expressed, in some form, by most widows in the London Study, and even a year after bereavement half of them still said that there were times when they could not believe what had happened: 'It's like a dream. I feel I'm going to wake up and it'll be all right. He'll be back again'. Others felt that they were waiting for their husband to come back after a temporary absence.

Disbelief in the fact of loss was seldom complete. As one man whose wife had died said: 'I just didn't want them to talk about it, because the more they talked the more they'd make me believe she was dead'.

Joan Didion, while rejecting the comforts of religion, has to admit the illogicality of her own thoughts:

> Of course I knew John was dead. Of course I had already delivered the definitive news to his brother . . . Yet I was myself in no way prepared to accept this news as final: there was a level on which I believed that what had happened remained reversible . . . This was the beginning of my year of magical thinking.
>
> (Didion, 2005, pp. 32–33)

She goes on to describe the several ways in which she both believed and disbelieved that he was dead:

> I could not give away the rest of his shoes . . . He would need the shoes if he was to return.
>
> (p. 37)

She found it very difficult to read his obituaries, seeing a photograph of him in a journal:

> . . . I realized for the first time why the obituaries had so disturbed me. I had allowed people to think he was dead. I had allowed him to be buried alive.
>
> (p. 35)

She delayed making a decision to donate his organs because:

> How could he come back if they took his organs?
>
> (p. 41)

This tendency to disbelieve the true situation is evident in many bereaved people prior to the death, during the terminal illness. Indeed there were some doctors who colluded with their unrealistic optimism. Even so, nineteen of the twenty-two London widows had been warned of the seriousness of their husband's illness before his death; twelve of them later admitted that they had not believed what they had been told. Either they did not believe that the doctor had diagnosed their husband's illness correctly or they accepted the diagnosis but thought that their husband was not as seriously ill as they were told, and among the seven who said that they had believed what they were told there were three who subsequently distorted the information or 'pushed it to the back of their minds'.

Whereas, in the normal course of events, a person who has reason to doubt the correctness of a doctor's diagnosis will ask for a second opinion, this was not the case when the disbelief was an attempt to avoid realization of incipient loss. At one level of awareness these women knew very well that their husbands were dying and they dealt with that knowledge by splitting it off and continuing to think, and to some extent act, as if he was not. But, while they continued to pretend to their husband and to themselves that he would recover, they did not fail to inform other relatives of the seriousness of the situation or to make essential plans for the contingency of his death. This capacity to hold in the mind two contradictory beliefs has been termed 'double knowledge' (Weisman, 1972). It is commonly seen in patients with terminal illness whose insight into their prognosis seems to vary in a bewildering way.

The fact that the wives of seriously ill men regularly minimized the gravity of their husband's illness does not mean, therefore, that they were completely unprepared for the death when it occurred. After they had been informed of the seriousness of their husband's condition, each woman came to terms with the illness in her own time and in her own way. Some, whose husbands had been ill for a long time, had observed a gradual deterioration and the doctor's words simply confirmed their own fears. But nearly all of them were unrealistically optimistic and continued to hope for recovery long after the medical authorities had given up.

NUMBNESS

If there are advantages to be obtained from denying the true situation during the terminal illness one would think that the death itself would put an end to all self-deception. But, as we have said, this is not the case. In half the London widows a feeling of 'numbness' or 'blunting' followed the actual bereavement. This experience is so common that it has been regarded (as described on page 7) as the first phase of bereavement. It did not necessarily come on at once, but usually within a few minutes; it then lasted for a few hours to a few days. During the period of numbness outbursts of extreme distress may 'break through' or the bereaved person may feel 'ill' or 'solid'.

One widow whose husband died alone during an attack of a rare form of asthma had found his body hanging over the banisters. Her first thought was to get the children out of the house. As the door closed behind them, 'I suddenly burst. I was aware of a horrible wailing and I knew it was me. I was saying I loved him and all that. I knew he'd gone but I kept on talking to him'. She went into the bathroom and retched. Then the feeling of numbness came over her. 'I felt numb and solid for a week. It's a blessing . . . everything goes hard inside you . . . like a heavy weight'. She felt that the numbness enabled her to cope with the children and arrange the funeral and family gathering without crying.

Even in cases when the death came as a relief, numbness and difficulty in accepting the fact of its occurrence were likely. One woman, who had felt as if she were living on the edge of a precipice during the long series of coronary thromboses suffered by her husband, had an immediate sense of relief when he died. At the same time, however, 'It didn't register at all. It didn't seem real'. She shut her mind to the idea that he would not be coming back from the hospital and carried on automatically.

Outright disbelief was rare, but some widows tried to convince themselves that there had been a mistake and it was not until they saw their husband's lifeless body that they were forced to believe him dead. 'I wouldn't believe it till I saw him on the Monday (four days after his death).'

For several widows it was the funeral service that 'brought home' the reality of what had happened. This was particularly so when the remains were cremated, since this seemed somehow 'more final' than burial. Two widows described fantasies of their husband being alive inside his coffin and one had to be restrained as the coffin was moved away.

PHYSICAL SYMPTOMS

The incompleteness of the defensive numbness is indicated in the sense of impending disaster and tension that hangs over the bereaved person at this time. 'It's like walking on the edge of a black pit', said one. Others felt pent up, 'As if my head was going to burst . . . I was in a dream . . . just couldn't take it all in . . . I couldn't believe it'.

Despite the lack of overt emotion, several developed physical symptoms at this stage. Thus one widow felt 'ill and shivery' and took to her bed for two days. Another felt 'as if my inside had been torn out'. But they were usually able to carry on and behave in a controlled and automatic manner, 'There was so much to do, but I didn't feel like I was doing it for anyone – not for him, if you see', or, 'It didn't seem real'.

DEPERSONALIZATION AND DEREALIZATION

Depersonalization occurs when bereaved people feel as if they are themselves unreal, derealization implies that it is the world that seems unreal. Either or both of these phenomena can occur following bereavement. These feelings of unreality were transient and seldom severe except in two of the London widows. In both of these cases derealization persisted throughout much of the first year of bereavement.

A woman fifty years of age lost her husband after nursing him at home for over six months. During this time she kept her knowledge of his condition from him. She was, she said, fully prepared for his death, which came after he had been unconscious for two days. Nevertheless, she cried profusely and was in 'utter despair' for the next two days. She then experienced a sense of unreality and emptiness, all her reactions seemed blunted, and she was unable to feel anything for her children although she described their behaviour as 'marvellous'. When first seen, a month after bereavement, she spoke in a hushed voice and often seemed distant, mishearing the doctor's questions and seeming dazed. 'I feel I'm waiting for something to happen, for the unreal feeling to pass', she said. 'I feel this as a different life . . . as if there's another life going on somewhere else and I'll waken up.' In this 'other life' her husband was alive and well.

She kept her mind occupied as much as possible to avoid thoughts of her loss. When forced to think of her husband, she was aware of a sense of dread, almost panic. Because of this she tried to avoid people who would remind her of his death and she found interviews with the researcher an ordeal. But she continued to take part in the study. By the sixth month the real world was beginning to re-establish itself, and at the end of a year she no longer felt the need to avoid people who reminded her of the past. The feeling of unreality had almost gone and returned only occasionally when she was on her own.

AVOIDING THOUGHTS OF LOSS

As seen in this case, another way of mitigating the pain of grief is to avoid all thoughts of the lost person and to avoid people and situations that will act as reminders. Two-thirds of the London widows said that they attempted to avoid reminders from time to time during the first month of bereavement, and six were still avoiding them a year later, though to a marked degree in only one case. In some cases avoidance may have been a symptom of PTSD, in which anything that triggers recall of a horrific death and the circumstances surrounding it are avoided. But more common in bereaved people is avoidance of anything that might bring home the reality of the fact of loss itself.

Thoughts of loss can be avoided by filling one's life with activities, and several widows deliberately kept themselves busy and worked until late at night for this purpose. Others put away photographs or personal effects that they found particularly evocative of their husband and many went through a period during which they were unable to pluck up courage to sort out or dispose of their husband's clothing. They usually remained at home because they feared that if they went out they would meet sympathetic people and they were afraid of showing their distress in public. On the other hand, a few moved away from the home which held so many reminders of the past and stayed, for a while, with relatives.

These conscious attempts to escape the pain of grief contrasted strangely with the way in which the bereaved were preoccupied, at the same time, with thoughts of their loss. They felt drawn back again and again to thoughts and situations associated with the lost person. For example, one widow who left home to escape painful memories returned there after only two days in order to be closer to her husband. Activities that were taken up in order to keep the mind occupied were often abandoned because of the difficulty of concentrating upon them.

That is not to say that attempts to avoid the pain of grief were uniformly unsuccessful. One woman of fifty-eight lost her husband suddenly and unexpectedly from a cerebral haemorrhage. She found it very difficult to believe him dead and kept breaking down and crying during the first week. She then discovered that she could stop crying by deliberately keeping her thoughts occupied with other things. She avoided going into her husband's room and persuaded her son to dispose of most of his possessions. Interviewed a month after bereavement she broke off several times, unable to talk for fear that she would cry. A year later her overall state was much calmer but she still avoided possessions that would remind her of her husband and disliked visiting his grave. 'If he comes in my mind I try to get – to think of something else', she said.

As time passed, and the intensity of grief diminished, those who had been avoiding things found it less necessary to do so and those who had been preoccupied with thoughts of the death found it easier to think of other things. Going through the husband's clothes or sorting out his belongings was viewed as a turning-point by some widows; others felt that their turning-point was reached when they redecorated the house and rearranged the furniture for the first time. Thus while searching and avoidance of searching occupied much of the widow's time during the early months of her bereavement, both became less intense with the passage of time, and other interests returned.

SELECTIVE FORGETTING

One other means of mitigating the pain of grieving was 'selective forgetting'. Lindemann (1960) has described how 'the image of the deceased disappears from consciousness'. In Parkes' studies this was a very rare occurrence and the opposite was the rule. That is to say, the image of the deceased was retained with great clarity. The one exception was a widow of twenty-six who was unable to recall the face of her husband during the first month after his death. She complained bitterly of this and by the time of the second interview, three months after bereavement, she had recovered her memory and now had a clear visual picture of him. Unlike most of the other psychological features of grieving, the memory of the dead person tends, if anything, to increase in clarity in the course of the first year of bereavement.

CHANGES OVER TIME

In talking to widows about their memories of their husband we have the impression that it takes time to order these and to see him as a whole person; the harder they tried to recall him the more difficult it was. C. S. Lewis, shortly after his wife's death, wrote in his diary of his fear of forgetting her and angrily denounced as 'pitiable cant' the idea that 'she will live forever in my memory'. Later, he described an experience that was not uncommon among widows:

> Something quite unexpected has happened. It came this morning early. For various reasons, not in themselves at all mysterious, my heart was lighter than it had been for many weeks. For one thing, I suppose I am recovering physically from a good deal of mere exhaustion . . . and after ten days of low-hung grey skies and motionless warm dampness, the sun was shining and there was a light breeze. And suddenly at the very moment when, so far, I mourned H. least, I remembered her best. Indeed it was something (almost) better than memory; an instantaneous, unanswerable impression. To say it was like a meeting would go too far. Yet there was that in it which tempts one to use those words. It was as if the lifting of the sorrow removed a barrier.
>
> Why has no one told me these things? How easily I might have misjudged another man in the same situation? I might have said, 'He's got over it. He's forgotten his wife', when the truth was, 'He remembers her better because he has partly got over it'.
>
> (1961)

Does this contradict our notion that the clarity of visual memories of lost people is related to the need to search for and to find them? We think not. Two factors seem to contribute to the gradual increase in the clarity of memories as reported by widows and widowers.

First, there is the reduction, over time, of conscious monitoring of the search. Just as it is often hard to remember names if we are trying too hard to recall them, so it seems that too intense a conscious wish to recall the features of a lost person inhibits the recollection. It is impossible to search when we are preoccupied with thinking how impossible it is to search. 'Is it', says Lewis, 'the very intensity of the longing that draws the iron curtain, that makes us feel we are staring into a vacuum when we think about our dead?'

Often, when we stop striving to remember, memories come back to us unbidden.

Second, it seems to take time for us to begin to recall 'as a whole' people whose lives have been so close to our own that we have experienced them in a thousand fragmented parts. Parkes again, 'I have a clear memory of Mr Harold Wilson, whom I have never met, looking at me out of my television set and talking in a serious, weighty voice. But my wife has become so complex and so familiar a person that I cannot view her as a whole at all. I suspect that it would take a long period of absence for me to fit together my numerous fragmentary recollections of her to make anything like a consistent picture. I am too close to see the wood for the trees'.

BUILDING A NEW IMAGE OF THE DEAD PERSON

Viewed in this light the work of grieving becomes a creative activity. A gradual piecing together of the pieces of a jig-saw that, eventually, will enable us to find an image and a place in our lives for the people we have loved and lost. One aspect of this task is the re-evaluation of the dead person, an activity sometimes termed '**idealization**' since it is the happy memories and valued aspects of the relationship that we treasure and wish to perpetuate.

Memories of the negative aspects of the dead are lost and idealization is carried out by most bereaved people and encouraged by society. Attempts to establish the reliability of the widow's view of her marriage by interviewing other members of her family had to be abandoned early in the London Study because it was clear that questions on so charged a matter were likely to be resented and that the information obtainable from other relatives would be just as distorted as that obtainable from the widow. It is not possible, therefore, to make any reliable estimate of the degree of idealization that was usual.

A woman of fifty-nine had quarrelled frequently with her husband and left him on several occasions during their married life. She blamed his alcoholism and gambling for their poor relationship and was rather surprised to find that she missed him at all. When first seen by Parkes she admitted, 'I shouldn't really say so, but it's more peaceful now that he's gone'. In the course of her first year as a widow her two youngest daughters got married and left home. She was left alone in her flat and became increasingly lonely and depressed. She spoke nostalgically of the old days and at the last interview, a year after bereavement, was hoping to marry again – 'to someone kind like my husband'.

As long as her husband had been alive this lady had been caught up in a long series of quarrels, which had coloured her view of him. If 'idealization' implies a rose-tinted view of reality the opposite is also possible. This lady seemed to have 'monsterized' her husband and, at the time of his death, she could see little good in him. Later she came to regret this alienation and the new image of her husband may have been no more distorted in a positive direction than her previous memories had been distorted in a negative way. Since nobody can be all good or all bad the opportunity for monsterization and idealization is always present and it may be that one of the things we need to do when somebody dies is to redress the balance in a positive direction. Most of the time this does no harm.

FINDING A BALANCE – APPROACH AND AVOIDANCE

To the psychiatrist it is all too easy to see the mental processes by which the bereaved reduce some of the pain of grief as 'defences'. Freud's concept of defence arose from his studies of neuroses and he first used the term in an article entitled 'The Neuro-Psychoses of Defence', published in 1894. Because repression and other defensive processes play a large part in neurotic illness and because psychoanalysis was developed as a means of helping patients to abandon their defences, a somewhat negative view of defence prevails today. A subtle ethic has crept into much of our thinking that seems to imply that ego defences are a 'bad thing' and that we would all be much better off without them.

Studies of bereavement throw doubt on this assumption. In short, it seems to me that most of the phenomena we lump together as defences have an important function in helping to regulate the quantity of novel, unorganized, or in other respects disabling information an individual is handling at a given time. We see this most clearly in the nursery when young children are scanning, manipulating, and exploring an environment whose complexity varies greatly. In the face of new, large or threatening stimuli they withdraw or hide, or call upon their mother for support; then, gradually and warily, they begin to make familiar those very stimuli they at first found alarming.

In a similar way the widow, whose world has suddenly changed very radically, withdraws from a situation of overwhelming complexity and potential danger. Lacking her accustomed source of reassurance and support, she may shut herself up at home and admit only those members of her family with whom she feels most secure. She avoids stimuli that will remind her of her loss and attempts, in the ways described, to regain some part of her lost spouse. At the same time, and to an increasing extent as time passes, she begins, little by little, to examine the implications of what has happened and in this way to make familiar and controllable the numerous areas of uncertainty that now exist in her world.

Thus we have two opposing tendencies: an inhibitory tendency, which by repression, avoidance, postponement, etc., holds back or limits the perception of disturbing stimuli, and a facilitative or reality-testing tendency, which enhances perception and thought about disturbing stimuli. At any given time an individual may respond more to one of these tendencies than to the other, and over time, he or she will often oscillate between them, so that a period of intense pining will alternate with a period of conscious or unconscious avoidance of the circumstances that trigger pining.

Viewed thus, 'defence' can be seen as part of the process of coping with a problem, of coming to grips with it in a relatively safe and effective way. That it may not always enable the individual to succeed in mastering the problem, and may at times become distorted or pathological, does not detract from its proper function, which is, presumably, the restoration of control by distancing an individual from a situation that threatens to become overwhelming.

The term 'coping' is nowadays preferred to that of 'defence' but there are also problems in the use of this term. 'Coping' implies an element of choice, we choose to cope in a particular way. Yet bereaved people who experience a sense of numbness or unreality in the face of overwhelming grief are not consciously choosing to cope with their grief by shutting it out. Their reaction is automatic and outside conscious control.

Psychotherapists sometimes speak of a person as being 'highly defended' or 'poorly defended'. The underlying assumption is that there is a general 'defensiveness', akin, perhaps, to the 'g' factor of intelligence. This would lead us to suppose that people who defend themselves against the pain of grieving by intense numbness during the early stage of grief would also have greater difficulty than most in accepting the fact that loss had occurred and a greater tendency to avoid reminders of loss; hence measures of 'numbness', 'difficulty in accepting the fact of loss', and 'avoidance of reminders' would inter-correlate. In the London Study, however, there was no significant correlation between quantitative assessments of these three defences (see Appendix 6; Table 4).

Another hypothesis would be that these defences or 'coping strategies' are alternatives, for instance, that a person who disbelieves in the reality of the loss does not need also to avoid reminders. If this was the case, however, one would expect to find a negative correlation between the defences: widows who scored high on 'disbelief' would score low on 'avoidance', and vice versa. But again there was no significant negative correlation between the three defences.

It may be that both these hypotheses are partially correct and that the effect is to cancel out any correlation, positive or negative, that might have occurred were only one of them applicable. The only justifiable conclusion would seem to be that defences are not simply an additive matter and that assessments based on one do not permit us to make assumptions about other defences or about 'defended-ness' in general.

OSCILLATION

The problem is that the lost are gone and the bereaved want them back. Reality-testing tells them that this is impossible. But immediate acceptance of this would involve an instant and major change in their identity or rather a host of major changes in their identity, which cannot take place in a moment, they take time. In order to buy time the mind has its own ways of limiting the input of disorganizing information. If this limitation was complete individuals could not begin to adjust to the problem (achieve a fresh identity). Most of the time, therefore, defences are partial blocks, which alternate or coexist with painful realization. The 'Dual Process' of oscillation, which was described on page 59, is, therefore, a part of a gradual process of realization. In this context the searching that follows bereavement is a form of facilitative behaviour whose function is the recovery of the lost object. It is not itself a defence although it depends upon a defence (partial denial of the permanence of the loss) for its occurrence.

It is clear that in this instance the behaviour does not eliminate pain or anxiety. It may reduce it but it also prolongs it. Provided that the balance of facilitation and defence is right, however, the grief work will continue, patterns of thought and behaviour that have been recognized as redundant will be habituated, and new, more appropriate patterns will be developed.

In like manner, repeated reviewing of the events leading up to the loss, which is described below, is an attempt to attack the problem of loss that would be inappropriate if the individuals had fully accepted the fact of loss. In denying the full reality of the loss they provide themselves with the opportunity to prepare for it.

REVIEWING AND WORRYING

For bereaved people, time is out of joint. They may know, from the calendar, that a year has passed since their bereavement, but their memories of the lost person are so clear that it seems like 'only yesterday'. Of the twenty-two London widows, eighteen said that time had passed quickly, and the first year of bereavement was looked back upon as a limbo of meaningless activity.

Much more real was the memory of the period leading up to the bereavement, and bereaved people found themselves repeatedly reviewing, going over in their minds, the events leading up to the death, as if by so doing they could undo or alter the events that had occurred. 'I go through that last week in the hospital again and again', said one widow, 'it seems photographed on my mind'.

These reminiscences obtrude upon the mind much as anticipatory worrying preoccupies people who fear a possible misfortune. And since, as we have seen, the newly bereaved are rarely able to accept, in full, the reality of what has happened, it may be that they have the same need to prepare themselves for disaster as those who have not yet experienced one. This type of anticipation has been called 'worry work' (Janis, 1958), and when it occurs before a misfortune it has the effect of focusing the attention on possible dangers and providing an opportunity for appropriate planning. It also enables individuals to begin to alter their views of the world and to give up some of the assumptions and expectations that have been established; this, of course, is a painful process.

Human beings are seldom surprised. Their ability to anticipate important changes in their lives enables them to make the necessary changes in expectations in advance and to experience a part of the emotion appropriate to the disaster before it occurs. When it occurs they are to some extent prepared for it both intellectually and emotionally; their behaviour is correct and emotion adequately controlled. It is the capacity for worry work that makes this possible.

REALIZATION

The change having taken place, one might think that the need to worry about it had come to an end, and in respect of minor changes this is probably the case. But we have seen that a major change such as bereavement cannot be fully realized at one time. The bereaved people continue to act, in many ways, as if the lost person were still recoverable and to worry about the loss by going over it in their mind. This activity has been termed 'grief work' by Freud (1917), and it can be assumed to have the same function as worry work in preparing the bereaved individuals for a full acceptance of their loss. An important difference between worry work and grief work is that worry work is based on anticipation whereas grief work is based on memory. People who anticipate an event may get it wrong; they may pretend to themselves that a particular outcome cannot occur; or they may worry unnecessarily about dangers that never arrive. Grief work, on the other hand, arises largely from memory, although bereaved people may use their imagination to fill in the gaps – to provide pictures of events that they have forgotten or have never witnessed.

At such a time there is a conscious need to 'get it right', and getting it right is not just a matter of recalling the traumatic event correctly; it includes the need to 'make sense' of what has happened, to explain it, to classify it along with other comparable events, to make it fit into one's expectations of the world. 'I think, if only I'd woken up early, perhaps I could have saved him.' Trying out new solutions, searching for clues to explain 'Why did it happen to me?', and repeatedly, monotonously, remembering the sequence of events leading up to the death – these are what make up the process of grief work.

These painful reminiscences should not be confused with the haunting memories of traumatic events that characterize PTSD. These, as we saw on pages 44–6, involve a type of memory that is quite different from, and affects different parts of the brain from, the memories that take time to integrate. In normal circumstances the transformation of SAM to VAM is carried out automatically during sleep. Finding meaning in bereavement is a conscious process and takes very much longer.

Freud has described how, in grief work, each memory that bound the survivor to the lost object must be brought up and 'hyper-cathected'. By this he means that 'energy' must be used to sever the link with the lost object and thereby set free the energy that is bound up with it (cathexis). It is important to bear in mind that Freud is not here speaking of real physical energy but of a hypothetical psychic energy (libido), which obeys similar laws. His libido theory, of which this is a part, is a cybernetic model that is useful insofar as it fits the observed data, but it should not be taken too far.

In recent years energy models of this type have come under scrutiny (see, for instance, Bowlby's, 1969, critique of libido theory) and it seems to us that they add little to our understanding of bereavement. No one would deny that real physical energy is involved in all mental processes, but the concept of mental energy begs too many questions. It seems very reasonable that when an event occurs that threatens our life or produces a major change in our assumptions about the world we need to devote time and physical energy to appraisal of the event and its consequences. If the event takes place suddenly or unexpectedly, then the appraisal can take place only after the event.

We suspect that the repeated recollection of traumatic experiences has some such function and the extent to which it persists may well reflect the extent to which the individual has failed to complete the painful process of replanning that such experiences necessitate. Presumably appraisal of a trauma normally enables people to establish in their minds, as realistically as possible, the true external situation so that they can make appropriate plans to cope with it. If they find themselves with no suitable plans for dealing with the fresh situation it may be that they will be unable to complete the process of appraisal. They may then find themselves repeating the chain of memories again and again rather than giving way to the depression that would arise if they admitted to themselves their own helplessness. Looked at in this way reminiscences are similar to obsessions, ruminations, and compulsions; these recurrent patterns of thought or activity seem to enable people to ward off anxiety while at the same time attempting to grapple with the problem.

COMPONENTS OF GRIEF WORK

It seems, then, that several components go to make up the process of grief work:

1   There is preoccupation with thoughts of the lost person, which, we suggest, derives from the urge to search for that person.
2   There is painful repetitious recollection of the loss experience,

which is the equivalent of worry work and which must occur if the loss is not fully accepted as irrevocable.

3   And there is the attempt to make sense of the loss, to fit it into one's set of assumptions about the world (one's 'assumptive world') or to modify those assumptions if need be.

These are not three different explanations of the same phenomenon but three interdependent components of a larger picture. Attempts to make sense of what has happened would seem to be one way of restoring what is lost by fitting its absence into some superordinate pattern. These attempts may succeed or they may not. If they do not then the preoccupation will increase and may indeed become obsessive.

DOES ANTICIPATORY GRIEF TAKE PLACE?

It is this that has caused some writers to question the validity of the concepts of anticipatory grief and of grief work. Thus, Levy (1992) has shown that people with high scores on a measure of 'Anticipatory Grief' were more depressed after bereavement than were those with lower scores. He concluded that 'Anticipatory Grief may be a risk factor for early bereavement adjustment'. This finding has been confirmed in another recent study of the relatives of patients with cancer (Prigerson *et al.*, 2009, unpublished data). But these studies were confined to the relatives of patients with cancer who normally have every opportunity to anticipate the death of the patient and, even if this were not the case, we should not be surprised to find that those who were most distressed before bereavement were also the most distressed afterwards.

In similar vein Wortman and Silver (1989) quote figures from Parkes' work, as well as their own, which indicated that intense yearning for a lost person and preoccupation with thoughts of the loss, during the early period after a bereavement, predicts later problems in adjustment to loss. This they see as casting doubt on the value of 'grief work'. In fact our own studies suggest that high degrees of pining and preoccupation often reflect a type of dependent attachment which overrides and interferes with the working through of grief and leads to a form of chronic grieving, which will be described in more detail in Chapter 8. Conversely people who showed little or no evidence of having expressed grief also do badly. It is the moderate grievers who seem to cope best and who can be said to be carrying out the 'grief work' successfully. (Further details of these findings are given on page 86 and in Appendix 13; Figure 10.)

LOSS AND CREATIVITY

Rochlin (1965) has written at length on the hypothesis that much creative activity and philosophico-religious thought has the purpose of restoring, in some form, the love objects we fear to lose or have lost. 'We shall meet again in the after life'; 'He will survive in the works he created'; 'They died so that the world might become a better place for those who come after them'. Each of these sentiments reflects a wish to preserve or restore some part of the person who is lost. To what extent this is in fact possible is matter for debate and we would certainly not suggest that such activity is meaningless. On the contrary, there may be very real ways in which a person can survive physical dissolution, and the manner in which the survivors carry out their grief work may influence this outcome. In a study of 121 people bereaved by accident, suicide, homicide or natural death Smith, Range, and Ulmer (1992) found that belief in an after life was associated with more recovery, greater well-being and less avoidance of grief than was lack of belief.

'A sense of immortality', says Lifton (Lifton, Kato, and Reich, 1979), 'is not simply a denial of death. Rather it reflects a compelling and universal inner quest for a continuous symbolic relationship between our finite individual lives, what has gone before and what will come after. It is a search for symbolizing continuities, despite the discontinuities of death'. Lifton goes on to describe five general modes in which this striving can be expressed – biological, theological, creative, natural and experiential transcendence. Any or all of these modes is likely to become part of the attempt to find meaning in bereavement.

But for most people in the early stages of bereavement the world is in chaos. Because they are striving to find what cannot be found they ignore what can be found. They feel as if the most central, important aspect of themselves is gone and all that is left is meaningless and irrelevant – hence the world itself has become meaningless and irrelevant. In their heart of hearts they often believe that the dead do not return, yet they are committed to the task of recovering one who is dead. It is no wonder that they feel that the world has lost its purpose, and no longer makes sense.

6

ANGER AND GUILT

Blow, winds, and crack your cheeks; rage, blow.
You cataracts and hurricanoes, spout
Till you have drench'd our steeples, drown'd the cocks.
You sulph'rous and thought-executing fires,
Vaunt-couriers of oak-cleaving thunderbolts,
Singe my white head. And thou, all-shaking thunder,
Strike flat the thick rotundity o' the world;
Crack nature's moulds, all germens spill at once,
That makes ingrateful man.

King Lear, Act III, Scene 2

The expression of irritability and anger in bereavement varies from one person to another, one family to another and one time to another. Sometimes it is directed against others and sometimes against the bereaved themselves as self-reproaches or guilt.

PROTEST

On the basis of his observations of young children separated from their mother through admission to hospital or residential nursery, Robertson (1953) coined the term 'protest' for the first phase of their response. And in a study comparing children aged sixteen to twenty-six months in a residential and a day nursery, those in the residential nursery showed violent hostility of a type hardly seen in the day nursery (Heinicke and Westheimer, 1966). Examples of aggressive behaviour in animals as a reaction to separation are included in a paper by Bowlby (1961) exploring the psychological processes engaged in mourning and their biological roots. He quotes from the literature the case of Stasi, a mongrel bitch described by Lorenz (1954), who after being separated from her master for the second time became disobedient, unruly, and increasingly ferocious. He also cites the raging and screaming of Yerkes's apes when taken forcibly from their companions (Yerkes, 1943).

Bowlby saw protest as the means whereby the child punishes its mother for desertion and he claimed that the experience may be so unpleasant for the mother that the likelihood of her deserting the child again is greatly reduced. But anger, as we saw on page 40, is also a likely reaction to any situation of danger, particularly among people who expect to be able to master that danger. Hence the phase of protest has survival value and effectively strengthens the bond between mother and child. As an integral part of the normal reaction to separation it is also to be expected following bereavement in adult life.

From both the London Study and The Yale Bereavement Study (Maciejewski *et al.*, 2007), it would appear that, in human adults, irritability and anger peak at about five months after bereavement. It was, however, not a regular feature of grief in older bereaved people. By contrast, all save four of the younger widows from the London Study reported excessive anger at some time during the first year of bereavement. But both the London and the Yale studies also showed that anger is not inevitable and that bereaved people often became less aggressive as time passed. Anger should not, therefore, be regarded as a necessary component of grief or a continuous state.

BITTERNESS

The most frequent form, described by over half the widows in the London Study, was a general irritability and bitterness. This was commonly associated with a feeling that the world had become an insecure or dangerous place, an attitude that often persisted throughout the first year of bereavement.

Anger was closely associated with restlessness and tension and, as noted in Chapter 2, those widows who felt most irritable and bitter commonly regarded themselves as physically unwell even though they reported no more overt physical symptoms than the rest.

The general impression was one of an intense impulse to action, generally aggressive, which was being rigidly controlled. Restless widows were likely to 'flare up' at any time and to fill their lives with activities. 'I feel all in a turmoil inside'; 'I'm at the end of my tether';

'Stupid little things upset me'; 'My nerves are on edge'. These remarks illustrate the generally irritable mood. When tension was severe, an irregular fine tremor was often present and sometimes a stammer.

These features are a part of the general, non-specific reaction to stress described in Chapter 3 and are a regular feature of PTSD. Indeed the increase in abuse of partners found by Prigerson, Macie-jewski, and Rosenheck (2002) in troops after combat were regularly found to be associated with PTSD.

We can conclude from these studies that the bereaved individuals are behaving as if they are in a situation of danger. But what is the danger? It will be clear from the preceding chapters that, until the reality of the loss has been fully accepted, one danger is the danger of the loss itself. The bereaved person still feels that the dead person is recoverable and anything that brings home the loss is reacted to as a major threat.

RESISTANCE

Relatives and friends who try to induce a widow to stop grieving before she is ready to do so, or even those who indicate that grief will pass, are surprised at her indignant response. It is as if they are obstructing the search for the one who is lost. Marris (1958) mentioned one widow who beat the doctor who brought news of her husband's death. While such incidents are rare, the impulse to resist the bearers of evil tidings is strong, and anyone the bereaved person meets is likely to make real the fact of the loss. Those who come to console the widow recognize her antipathy and are deterred by it: 'What can one say?' In such circumstances there is a tacit agreement not to utter the word 'dead' but to speak of the dead person in hushed tones as if he were sleeping near at hand. Funeral directors learn to treat the dead as if they were asleep and the Anglican funeral service refers to the dead as resting or asleep in the Lord pending eventual resurrection (rest is mentioned three times and resurrection thirteen).

To speak of the goodness of the dead person and to ignore nega-tive attributes diminishes the risk that the comforter will be seen as an enemy. It also reassures the bereaved that the dead person is worth mourning for, that loved ones were not deserted as an act of hostility. 'Why did he do this to me?' said one widow; and another, reminded that her husband really was dead, nine months after bereavement, burst out, 'Oh Fred, why did you leave me?' and, later, 'If he'd known what it was like you'd [*sic*] never have left me'.

BLAMING

One can detect in these remarks some of the reproach and protest to which Bowlby refers, and it is true that widows often seem to regard the pain of grieving as an unjust punishment and to feel angry with the presumed author. The death is personalized as something that has been done to them and they seek for someone to blame. The blame is directed against anyone who might have contributed to the suffering or death of the husband and the husband may himself be reproached. Thus, one widow blamed her husband for not telling his general practitioner about his headaches; another felt angry with the hospital authorities for sending her husband home by bus when he was not fit to travel; she also expressed great anger towards a nurse who had hurt her husband by ripping off an adhesive dressing, and towards God for taking her husband away. God and the doctors came in for a lot of angry criticism since both were seen as having power over life and death. 'I still go over in my mind the way those doctors behaved', said one widow who accused them of ignoring significant symptoms. Such accusations sometimes give rise to formal complaints against health-care staff and may even result in malpractice suits.

Failure or delay in diagnosis was a common cause of complaint. While some of this anger may have been justified much of it seemed as irrational as its opposite, an uncritical adulation of the medical profession. Adulation seemed to be a means of appeasing these powerful people and was, if anything, commoner than its opposite, punishment by denigration. One widow who was very angry with the hospital staff at the time of her bereavement later retracted her accusations and added ruefully, 'I wish there was something I could blame'.

Seeking for someone to blame was often associated with going over memories of events leading up to the loss, as described in Chapter 5. Presumably there was still a feeling that, if the person responsible could be found, the loss could somehow be prevented or undone. This feeling was vaguely expressed in terms of finding out what went wrong, as if life had suddenly been diverted from its orderly course and needed to be put back on the right track.

Anger is an emotion that is not always directed towards the object that gives rise to it. It was expressed over a wide variety of matters, many of them quite trivial. Quarrels arose with old friends who 'did not understand' or who failed to give support; one widow was constantly bickering with her teenage daughter, who had had a particularly close relationship with her father; another quarrelled with her mother over the disposal of a jointly owned car and provoked a series of quarrels with her employer, which she later regretted.

THE SPREAD OF ANGER

What distinguished such behaviour from the quarrelling and angry feelings that any of us might experience at times was the frequency of the quarrels and the atmosphere of bitterness and irritability in which they took place; one could only regard them as part of the reaction to bereavement. It was sad that the other members of the family, who might have been able to help the widow to get things in perspective, were so often unable to be any more objective than the widow herself. They too were bereaved and found it hard to contain feelings of irritability and anger. Thus a mother-in-law, who had had a long-standing antipathy to her son's wife, accused her of being responsible for his death. The widow was badly hurt and reacted by telling the mother-in-law what she thought of her. The two then refused to see each other and split the family. The husband's relatives sided with the mother-in-law and the wife's with the wife. A series of angry altercations broke out over the rights and wrongs of the situation and the widow was left without the support and friendship of people she had previously liked. This example illustrates the way in which splits can occur, reputations can be damaged, and sources of support withdrawn.

There is clear evidence from the London Study that the widows who expressed the most anger became more socially withdrawn than those whose anger was less severe (see Appendix 6, Table 4, and Appendix 8). Whether they drove their friends and relatives away or whether they dealt with their angry feelings by shutting themselves up at home, the result was loneliness and insecurity.

SELF-BLAME

Anger, in the early phase of bereavement, was often associated with self-reproach. Many widows, who felt guilty at the way they behaved, recognized the irrational component in their anger. 'I get furious with myself', said one. Another reproached herself, 'You tend to magnify, look for trouble'.

Thirteen of the twenty-two London widows expressed self-reproachful ideas at some time in the course of the year. In its mildest form this was no more than a tendency to go over the events of the death in order, apparently, to seek reassurance that all was done that could have been done. 'I think "What could I have done?" ' 'I think to myself, "Did I do right?" My friend said, "You couldn't have done more." ' 'I wonder whether we could have done any more.' 'Is there anything I could have seen early on?' Again, one finds the widow retrospectively trying to get things right, to find a reason for the catastrophe that will somehow bring order out of chaos and restore her faith in the meaning of life.

Seven widows expressed self-reproachful ideas centred on some act or omission that might have harmed the dying spouse or in some way have disturbed his peace of mind. In agonizing over events that were often quite trivial, they seemed to be looking for a chance to castigate themselves, as if by accepting blame they could somehow reverse the course of events and get back the missing spouse. One widow attributed her husband's illness to over-tiredness and blamed herself for not learning to drive: 'If I'd have drove [sic]', she said, 'he'd probably be here today'. Another had had a hysterectomy shortly before her husband developed a cancer of the colon – she thought that his illness might have been caused by worry over her and blamed herself for this. Several reproached themselves for failing to stand the strain of the terminal illness. One had nursed her husband at home for a year before his death. Eventually she had lost her temper with him after he had awakened her during the night. Although she apologized and her husband forgave her he died a few days later. 'I felt as if God had given him to me to look after and when I couldn't cope he took him away.'

Regret at failure to satisfy expectations was a source of self-reproach in another widow who felt guilty because she had never made her husband a bread pudding. Another blamed herself for failing to encourage her husband's artistic talents during his lifetime. She endeavoured to make restitution after his death by finding a market for his paintings. Regarding their relationship she said: 'We were both always on the defensive. Now I can see how often he was right'.

INSECURITY

The death of a loved person is so important an event that it is difficult to shrug it off as the result of an accident or ill luck. To accept the fact that death can strike anywhere and that illness is no respecter of persons or deserts undermines one's faith in the world as an ordered and secure place.

All the widows in the London Study were under the age of sixty-five and their husbands were not much older. This meant that most of the deaths that occurred were untimely; they occurred before the usual life-span was complete. Untimely deaths cast doubt upon the 'reasonable expectations' upon which all of us base our lives. We know that disasters happen, but we cannot afford to worry about possibilities that are statistically unlikely. We continue to cross the road despite the danger that we might be run over; we travel in cars, trains, and aeroplanes knowing full well that they may crash. To worry about the possibilities would make life intolerable and most people rely upon the knowledge that accidents are statistically rare and feel that they are protected from disaster.

A major bereavement shakes confidence in this sense of security. The tendency to go over the events leading up to the loss and to find someone to blame even if it means accepting blame oneself is a less disturbing alternative than accepting that life is uncertain. If we can find someone to blame or some explanation that will enable death to be evaded, then we have a chance of controlling things. It is easier to believe that fate is malevolent than to acknowledge our helplessness in the face of events. God is not subject to the laws of statistical probability, he is a 'cosmic sadist' who punishes unjustly (C. S. Lewis, 1961). Railing against God or Fate is, of course, another way of trying to control the order of things. It is not so much an expression of helplessness as an attempt to influence events by browbeating their author. The thought that the loved person's death was accidental is unacceptable because it makes us feel so impotent.

PSYCHOANALYTIC THEORIES

In *Mourning and Melancholia* (1917), Freud pointed to the sadistic impulses present in all ambivalent relationships. In melancholia, which he regarded as a pathological form of grief, these sadistic impulses are commonly turned against the self. As evidence of this Freud claims that the terms of abuse the patient uses about her- or

96

himself 'always' fit the love object rather than the patient. Ambivalence, says Freud, gives rise to a wish for the other's death, but it is not so very unusual for the ego to tolerate a wish as harmless so long as this exists in fantasy alone and seems remote from fulfilment, while it will defend itself hotly against such a wish as soon as it approaches fulfilment and threatens to become an actuality.

In order to defend themselves against what Melanie Klein (1940) has called the 'triumph' over the dead, bereaved people turn their anger against themselves or direct it outwards towards others who are to hand. Hence guilt and anger are thought particularly likely to follow the dissolution of an ambivalent relationship and, because of their destructive nature, to lead to pathological forms of grief.

Whether or not the self-reproaches of the London widows also reflected a dim awareness of death wishes towards an ambivalently loved husband is uncertain. Parkes' interviews seldom permitted the analysis, in depth, of unconscious motivation. It did appear, however, that at least one woman in the London Study, and a large proportion of those in the Bethlem Study, expressed intense feelings of guilt that could be explained in this way. In fact it was the frequency and intensity of feelings of guilt that most clearly distinguished the bereaved psychiatric patients of the Bethlem Study from the unselected widows of the London Study. We return to this issue again in Chapters 8 and 9.

PASSIVITY AND DEPRESSION, AN ETHOLOGICAL THEORY

In contrast to these feelings of anger and guilt we turn now to a consideration of the opposite phenomenon, loss of aggressiveness, which seems to occur along with feelings of apathy and despair once the intense pangs of grief are past their peak.

Lorenz continues his description of the behaviour of a greylag goose who has lost its mate (p. 50):

> From the moment [the partner is missed] ... it loses all courage and flees from even the weakest geese. Sinking rapidly in the ranking order of the flock, the bereaved goose becomes shy, fearful, and panicky.

John Price (1967) provides an explanation, in ethological terms, for this behaviour, which he assumes also takes place in man. He points

out that man is a social animal whose place in the dominance hierarchy is maintained by means of alliances with his mate and other
loved persons. Loss of such a person can be expected to lead to a fall
in status, and decline in status produces loss of courage and depression. To be effective a dominance hierarchy must be stable. Leadership must be clear and members of the social group must be aware of
their own place in the hierarchy. This makes unnecessary the
determination of a new precedence every time the interests of two
members conflict. A strong dominance hierarchy is found, according
to Price, in practically all species that do not limit their aggression by
the strict division of territory. Attitudes of, on the one hand, submis-
siveness to and anxious withdrawal from individuals higher than
oneself in status and, on the other, of irritability and threat towards
those lower than oneself, ensure that the hierarchy is maintained and
that, when conflicts do break out, the lower-status individual will
usually be defeated without bloodshed.

Changes in social structure, however, are bound to occur when age
or sickness reduces the powers of the higher-status members or when
alliances are dissolved, as in bereavement. In such circumstances,
says Price, those whose status is declining are overcome by a depressive mood, which counteracts their normal tendency to fight to
defend their position and allows them to decline in status without the
danger of combat with each individual in the group who attempts to
supersede them. The advantages of this peaceful solution to the
problem of status change are obvious and in the long run would tend
to operate to maximize the chances of survival of individuals and of
the social group of which they are members.

No attempt has yet been made to assess systematically the extent
to which bereaved people 'lose heart' and adopt a submissive,
defeated attitude, but experience suggests that they usually do this
during the periods of apathetic withdrawal that follow the pangs of
grief. Between these episodes, and after the phase of intense pining is
past, depression and an attitude of defeat intervene. 'I don't want to
fight it any more', said one widow nine months after bereavement.
She was clinging to a friend of her former husband: 'I just let Bob
lead me'. But from time to time she would feel aggressive and attack
him, 'because he's not Jim'. Other widows who are depressed have
described feelings of panic when they would like to run away if only
they had somewhere to go.

IS THERE A DEPRESSIVE PHASE OF GRIEF?

The suggestion that yearning and protest peak before anger and that depression and disorganization peak after both states was first postulated by Bowlby and Parkes (1970), but it has only recently been established by quantitative research (Appendix 1; and Maciejewski *et al.*, 2007). There is no sharp end-point to yearning, and pangs of grief can be re-evoked even years after a bereavement. It does seem true, however, that as time passes anger and pining grow less, while episodes of apathy and depression remain. In Maciejewski *et al.*'s study their measure of depression peaked about six months after bereavement. The situation is complicated by the wide range of variation in the readiness with which individuals express both aggression and depressive withdrawal. Dominance/submission is closely related to personality and there are some individuals who habitually express aggressive attitudes while others are more submissive. Individuals are also extremely sensitive to the attitudes and expectations of others, consequently there are many interacting factors that influence both depression and the expression of aggression after bereavement.

Finally, there is the problem of measurement. In the London Study every effort was made to assess the intensity of expressed anger and it was usually possible to find out when this exceeded the norm for the individual. But no attempt was made to measure anger or assertiveness that was *less* than normal. The fact that anger and guilt are common components of grief does not, of course, mean that they may not also have a special significance in pathological developments.

In conclusion, it is important to remember that, although there is probably a depressive phase of grief, depression has so many other causes that it cannot be regarded as peculiar to grief or bereavement. As we saw on pages 26–8, depression and anxiety, both in their common and their psychiatric forms, can be triggered by a variety of life situations and traumas in addition to losses. They remain a common consequence of bereavement and, for that reason, we shall return to examine depression more closely in the next chapter.

7

CHANGING THE
ASSUMPTIVE WORLD

> You that are she and you, that's double shee,
> In her dead face, half of yourself shall see;
> Shee was the other part, for so they doe
> Which build them friendships, become one of two.
> * * *
> For, such a friendship who would not adore
> In you, who are all what both were before,
> Not all, as if some perished by this,
> But so, as all in you contracted is.
> As of this all, though many parts decay,
> The pure which elemented them shall stay ...
>
> John Donne, 'To the Lady Bedford', 1609

It comes as rather a shock to hear an unsophisticated London widow (Mrs J.) describing her feeling of identification with her dead husband in the following words:

> My husband's in me, right through and through. I can feel him in me doing everything. He used to say, 'You'll do this when I'm gone, won't you?' ... I enjoy the things my husband used to do ... It's like a thought in my head – what he would say or do.

She cited watching the Cup Final and Goodwood racing on television as examples of activities deriving from him.

> I quite enjoy it because he liked it. It's a most queer feeling ... My young sister said, 'You're getting like Fred in all your ways ...' She said something about food. I said, 'I

couldn't touch that', and she said, 'Don't be stupid, you're getting just like Fred' . . . There's lots of things I do that I wouldn't think of doing [before Fred's death] . . . I suppose he's guiding me the whole of the time.

Much has been written, in the psychoanalytic literature and elsewhere, about the way in which people who have suffered a loss sometimes seem to take into themselves certain aspects of the lost person. Freud at one time regarded identification as 'the sole condition under which the id will give up its objects' (Freud, 1923). But ten years later he said, 'If one has lost a love object or has had to give it up, one *often* compensates oneself by identifying oneself with it . . .' (Freud, 1933, our italics).

These statements describe but they do not explain the phenomenon of identification with a lost person, which remains as mystifying to us today as it was to John Donne. How can my husband be part of me? What does a widow mean when she says, 'My husband's in me, right through and through'? How can her husband be guiding her the whole of the time?

Equally mystifying is the experience of loss of self that is reported by many widows. 'I feel as if half of myself was missing', said one widow, and another spoke of 'a great emptiness'. What do these statements mean? How can a person be 'full' or 'empty'? Why should the loss of someone 'out there' give rise to an experience of the loss of something 'in here'?

It would seem that the experience of bereavement may throw light on some fundamental questions concerning the nature of identity. It is our purpose in this chapter to present some of the data and to formulate some hypotheses that seem to begin to make sense of such phenomena.

PSYCHO-SOCIAL TRANSITIONS

Before discussing the change of identity that follows bereavement, let us look at what it is that changes. When somebody dies a whole set of assumptions about the world that relied upon the other person for their validity are suddenly invalidated. Habits of thought that have been built up over many years must be reviewed and modified, a person's view of the world must change. This transition has been termed a Psycho-Social Transition (PST) and it inevitably takes time and effort (Parkes, 1971; 1993b).

PSTs are not confined to bereavement, they take place whenever we are faced with the need to make major changes in our lives; the amputee has to learn to stop trying to use a leg that is no longer there before he can learn to use the artificial limb that is now provided for him; the blind person must learn new ways of perceiving the world and the cancer patient can no longer take for granted a whole series of assumptions. Each of these situations faces the sufferer with the need to give up one set of habits of thought and behaviour, and to develop another.

The loss of a loved person inevitably creates a host of discrepancies between our internal world and the world that now exists for us. This is true not only at the superficial level (Who will be there when I get in from work in the evening?), but also at the deeper level of basic assumptions (If I am no longer a married man or woman, what am I? Is there a just God?). Bereaved people are repeatedly surprised at the number of habits of thought which involve the other person and the extent to which things take their meaning from the presence of another person. (Often the person who has died is the one we would have turned to at times of trouble and here we are, in the biggest trouble we have ever experienced, constantly turning to someone who is not there.) Small wonder that bereaved people often feel as if life itself has lost its meaning.

CONSTRUCTIVISM AND THE ASSUMPTIVE WORLD

In recent years attention has been drawn to the extent to which each person constructs their own unique view of the world. Although we may live in the same external environment and with the same workmates and friends as others, our view of everything and everybody that we know, or think we know, is coloured by our previous experience of the world and its meanings.

Each one of us, from the moment of our birth, has been building inside ourselves a model of the world, a set of assumptions on the basis of which we recognize the world that we meet and plan our behaviour accordingly (Piaget, 1955). Because this model is based on reality it is, most of the time, a valid and useful basis for thought and behaviour. We rely on the accuracy of these assumptions to maintain our orientation in the world and to control our lives. Anything that challenges the model incapacitates us. Yet discrepancies between the world that is and the world that should be (on the basis of our internal model) do arise and cannot be ignored. Our assumptive world must be constantly monitored and updated.

Minor changes in the model do not challenge basic assumptions and are relatively easy to make. They may even be pleasurable and give us the feeling of increasing our knowledge and extending our repertoire of ways of coping with the world. Hence the popularity of overseas holidays and participation in sports and pastimes that extend us.

Only if the change is very great or challenges deeply held assumptions is it likely to be difficult and to be resisted. Not only does a major PST require us to revise a great number of assumptions about the world, but most of those assumptions have become habits of thought and behaviour that are now virtually automatic. A widow will come down for breakfast in the morning and find that she has laid the table for two when there is now only one person to eat it. Faced with a problem she will catch herself thinking, 'I must ask my husband about that'. In either case she has continued to operate a set of assumptions that are now obsolete. For a long time she will have to watch what she thinks and what she says; nothing can be taken for granted any more.

Since we rely on the possession of an accurate internal model of the world to keep us safe, people who have lost confidence in that model feel very unsafe. And because anxiety and fear cloud our judgement and impair our concentration and memory, our attempts to make sense of what has happened are likely to be slow and inefficient. The familiar world suddenly seems to have become unfamiliar, habits of thought can let us down, we have lost confidence in our most essential possession, our internal model of the world, and because of this we may lose confidence in ourselves.

Not that bereavement affects all aspects of our world. Those who have invested themselves in jobs and other activities that did *not* involve their partner will find that they can continue to manage these worlds relatively easily. In fact they may feel that, when they are working, they are able to escape, for a time, from the problems of bereavement. Similarly, a mother who has lost her husband may find that the care of the children who survive him provides her with a sense of purpose and meaning in her life that contrasts with the desolation that emerges after they have gone to bed at night.

In the circumstances it is not surprising if, as we saw in Chapter 5, people attempt to avoid reminders as a means of mitigating some of the pains of grief. By the same token too much avoidance means that we are not tackling the problem of relearning that is necessary if we are to adapt our model of the world to fit the world that now exists. Freud called this process of reviewing the internal world 'the work of mourning' (1917) and, in many ways, each PST is a job of work that needs to be done. But *the mind that is doing the reviewing is also the object that is being reviewed.* A person is literally lost in their own assumptive world, and the more disorganized one's thinking the more difficult it is to step aside from the disorganization and to see clearly what it is that is lost and what remains.

RESISTANCE TO CHANGE

Because we can only bring to new situations assumptions that arose out of the old, we cannot easily abandon the past. For this reason major changes are usually resisted and this is not necessarily a bad thing. Our old assumptive world may be imperfect but it is the best we have and if we abandon it we have nothing left. Our first effort, therefore, in the face of change, must be to interpret the change in the light of our old assumptions. 'I can't believe it's true' is an understandable reaction to massive change and we should not be surprised if newly bereaved people find it hard to accept the facts of the situation. At such times the bereaved are disorganized and disabled by loss. They may need the protection and support of others, whose world has not been similarly shattered, to provide the security that will enable them, little by little, to take in the reality of what has happened and make it real. It then becomes possible for them to modify their assumptions and with them their sense of identity.

Newly bereaved people may cling to long-established habits and patterns of social interaction in an attempt to retain what little stability remains in their lives. Prigerson *et al.* (1994) have shown that disruption of such social rhythms is associated with an increased risk of depression and other research suggests that this depression may even result from the disruption of biological rhythms (Monk *et al.*, 1994).

THE EMPIRICAL SELF

What is this identity, this self that can be invaded, changed, or lost? William James (1892) distinguished the 'empirical self', the self that can be the object of one's own scrutiny, from the 'conscious self', the self that does the scrutinizing. The latter, that-which-experiences, can never, paradoxically, itself be experienced. We can experience the world that strikes or impinges upon us and we can experience the memories and thoughts deriving from that world (thoughts too can 'strike' us), but we can only infer the 'I' that experiences these phenomena. When we speak of changes in the self, therefore, we must be speaking of changes in James's 'empirical self'. How does someone come to recognize this self, see themselves as an individual separate and different from their fellow human beings?

Human beings are multicellular organisms. That is to say, they are groups of individual living organisms, body cells, which are more or less closely linked together to form a single structure. Within that structure, and part of it, is a subgroup of nerve cells, the brain, organized in such a way that it receives signals from the rest of the organism and from the outside world that enable it to make predictions about that world and to direct the organism to act appropriately. Among the signals it receives from the world are some that indicate the presence of other multicellular organisms similar to itself. The similarity is so great that the brain in one person finds itself able to see the world through the eyes of others. It also becomes able to see itself through the same eyes. The being that each of us infers from observing our own organism and behaviour and comparing it with that of others is what we call the 'self'.

COMPONENTS OF THE SELF

Parkes speaking:

> I see myself as a psychiatrist, husband, and writer – each of these aspects of my identity stems from my roles. I am also identified by my bodily characteristics – tall, white, male, etc. – and by my behaviour – even-tempered, cat-loving, etc. Finally, I have the attributes of my social group – I am middle class and English.
>
> Each of these characteristics defines both similarities to and differences from other people. They enable me to be identified and they indicate to the world and to me that I have a certain status, certain powers and responsibilities, and certain possessions that are essentially my own.

Nearly all of these roles, bodily characteristics, powers, and possessions may be affected by a major loss such as a bereavement. Let us consider first how the thirty-year-old wife of an estate agent coped with the changes that followed her husband's sudden death:

In Mrs B.'s case it was the changes in role that were seen as the major problem. She had been left with two children, a boy aged eight and a girl of five. After her husband's death she grieved deeply and lost two stone in weight. She had a strong sense of his presence near at hand and could not get the thought of his dead body out of her mind. Her grief reached its peak about two weeks after the death and a marked improvement set in during the fourth week when she went to stay with friends on the coast.

At this stage and during the next six months she felt 'totally inadequate', tense, physically tired, and irritable. She remained at home most of this time and became very reliant upon a man much older than herself who had been a friend for many years. At the same time she resented her dependence, she quarrelled with her mother-in-law and with several other members of her husband's family, and seemed to regard the world as dangerous and potentially hostile.

About the middle of the year she began to realize that she was tougher than she had thought. She took a part-time job as a shop assistant and enjoyed the work. She redecorated the house and started judo classes 'for a bit of a giggle' (also because she wanted to be able to defend herself if any man should 'get fresh'). Episodes of grieving became less frequent and her pleasure in her new-found independence increased. This reduced her reliance on the old friend who had done so much for her during the early months, and although he had always insisted that there was nothing 'romantic' about their relationship he became very upset when he found her drinking with another man and he terminated the relationship.

A year after her husband's death Mrs B. said, 'I think most of the time I've got over it. But if I go over it in detail ... I get panicky again'. Her weight was steady and her health good although she still had 'blinding headaches' from time to time and had thought of asking her doctor for a tonic. She rated her overall happiness as 'up and down' but was optimistic about the future. Although she had many problems to work out she felt she could master them and enjoyed doing so. She took every opportunity to go out and said that if the right man came along she would consider remarrying.

One can see from this account the sequence of stages by which a new set of roles began to be established for Mrs B. At first her preoccupation with pining for her husband drove all but the most urgent problems from her mind. After a brief retreat to the care of her friends she returned to an insecure and dangerous world feeling 'totally inadequate'. For a while she remained reliant on her man friend while taking stock and planning her life afresh. Her decision to take up judo seemed to reflect both her fear of the dangers of the world and her determination to master it. As her confidence increased her need to rely upon her man friend diminished and she experienced a sense of achievement and a relaxation, which were visibly different from the restlessness and tension witnessed at earlier interviews.

ROLES AND SOLUTIONS

The roles that a person performs in life are made up of a complex series of focal action patterns that constitute a repertoire of problem solutions. This repertoire, because it is based on experience, assumes that reasonable expectations of the world will be fulfilled. As time goes by, the individual's stock of 'solutions for all eventualities' grows greater, and novel situations requiring novel solutions become rarer.

However, a major change in life, such as that produced by the death of a spouse, not only alters expectations at the level of the focal action patterns (How many teaspoons to lay on the breakfast table?) but also alters the overall plans and roles of which these form a part. A widow is no longer a wife; she is a widow. Suddenly, and always in some degree unexpectedly, 'we' has become 'I', 'ours' has become 'mine'; the partnership is dissolved and decisions must be made alone and not by a committee of two. Even when words remain appropriate, their meaning changes – 'the family' is no longer the same object it was, neither is 'home' or 'marriage'; even 'old age' now has a new meaning.

In large measure the newly bereaved widow confronts the same problems as the adolescent school-leaver. A new set of expectations and roles faces her and she must learn a new model of the world and a new repertoire of problem solutions before she can again feel safe and at ease. Like the adolescent she may feel that too much is being expected of her and she may react with anxiety, insecurity, and irrit-ability. She may attempt to hold on to the idea that she is still the cherished wife, protected from the world by a loving husband. Even when this assumption is given up, there will be other aspects of the new situation that she cannot accept. 'I hate it when people use the word widow', said one widow. The very word implied an identity she was not willing to assume.

DISORGANIZATION AND DEPRESSION

Besides assuming a new identity, it is necessary to give up the old, and, as we have seen, this can be a long and painful business and one that is never complete. But as pining diminishes and each role or focal action pattern is recognized as inappropriate, there seems to follow a period of uncertainty, aimlessness, and apathy that, as we saw in the last chapter, has been termed the phase or state of dis-organization and despair. The characteristic emotion is depression, and the widow is likely to remain withdrawn from contact with those who will make demands upon her and to rely upon relatives and close friends who can be expected to protect her. Only when circum-stances force her to do so or when depression is minimal will she venture out to find a job, meet people, or attempt to re-establish her place in the hierarchical society to which all social animals belong.

This period of disorganization is not a clear-cut phase of grief but occurs again and again in one context or another. Once habituation has taken place and the old assumptions and ways of thinking have been given up, the individual is free to take stock and to make a fresh start. Making a fresh start means learning new solutions and finding new ways to predict and control happenings within the life-space. It also means seeking a fresh place in the hierarchy, reassessing one's powers and possessions, and finding out how one is viewed by the rest of the world.

THE SOCIAL SELF

Cooley (1909) defined the self as those things that individuals con-ceive as belonging peculiarly to them. To some extent we choose where we place the boundaries around ourselves. In a similar way we choose where to place our territorial boundaries and how permeable we make them. It is in accord with the view presented here to regard territory as an extension of the self. It is easier to share territory, however, than it is to share more intimate parts of the self.

William James's 'social self' (my view of the world's view of me) he termed 'the looking-glass self'. Clearly these two views are closely allied since many of the possessions, attributions, and characteristics we term 'ours' are ours only by consent. The work of Lifton and others who have studied 'thought reform' or 'brain-washing' has revealed the extent to which individuals' views of themselves are dependent upon the confirmation of others. Writing of circumstances before the cultural revolution in China he noted:

> In thought reform, as in Chinese Communist practice generally, the world is divided into the 'people' . . . and the 'reactionaries' . . . The thought reform process is one means by which non-people are permitted, through a change in attitude and personal character, to make themselves over into people. The most literal example of such dispersing of existence and non-existence is to be found in the sentence given to certain political criminals: execution in two years' time, unless during that two-year period they have demonstrated genuine progress in their reform. . . .
>
> For the individual, the polar conflict is the ultimate existential one of 'being versus nothingness'. He is likely to be drawn to a conversion experience, which he sees as the only means of attaining a path of existence for the future.
>
> (Lifton, 1961)

While the extent, pervasiveness, and duration of the subjective changes in the individuals' views of themselves vary greatly according to their life circumstances and previous experience, the powerful influence of extreme social pressures such as these cannot be denied. It comes, therefore, as no surprise to find that changes in the world's view of us are likely to be associated with changes in our views of ourselves. This is particularly likely when changes take place in those things we view as most intimately ours.

While there are grounds for preserving the distinction between my view of the world and my view of myself, the tools by which I act upon that world, 'my hands', 'my language', 'my motorcar', span the boundary between me and the world and blur the distinction between my 'self' and 'others'. Since I can share many of these 'possessions', what is the boundary of me? Is my little finger a part of me? Is my spouse a part of me? Am I a part of him or her?

At once it is apparent that although I think I know myself there is a hinterland between 'self' and 'other' that is not clear-cut and which may change. If my little finger is cut off it ceases to be a part of me; if I lose my job I cease to be employed; if I lose my temper I cease to be even-tempered; if my wife or husband dies I cease to be a spouse and she/he ceases to be my spouse.

Such changes may be forced upon me or I may choose to bring them about. I may dissociate myself from my government, I may divorce my spouse, or I may give away my money. Conversely, I may refuse to acknowledge in myself changes that should alter me. I may live above my income, pretend to be a better golfer than I am, or refuse to regard myself as a widow or widower. Who is the real me? Am I the person I believe myself to be or the person the world believes me to be? Is there an essential, unalterable me?

Carl Rogers (1961) makes it the aim of psychotherapy to help the patient to discover his 'real self' by stripping away the masks that hide it. His account of this psychological fiction, however, suggests that for him the 'real' person is that identity which is most appropriate to the potentialities of the individual. The awareness of a 'fit' between form and function reassures people and strengthens them in their belief that they have discovered the authentic, the 'real' self. Conversely, a lack of 'fit' is experienced as 'unreal' or false.

My body is constantly changing. Old cells die and new ones are born to replace them. Only a minority of the living beings that make up my multicellular organism were alive five years ago. Within my brain the changes are more slow. As I grow older nerve cells die but none replace them. The part of me that perceives, directs, and remembers is gradually dwindling. Age is carrying out a series of minute lobotomy operations on me, and my personality is slowly being altered. Fortunately the change is gradual and it is possible for me to maintain the illusion that I am the person I thought I was five years ago. Unless, that is, something occurs that suddenly proves to me that I am not.

If the possessions and the roles by which we control, order, and predict the world can be shared, changed, or dissolved, then it may be that the self that depends so much upon these tools and tasks to provide an image is also capable of experiencing change. If I lose my ability to predict and to act appropriately, my world begins to crumble, and since my view of myself is inextricably bound up with my view of the world, that too will begin to crumble. If I have relied on another person to predict and act in many ways as an extension to myself then the loss of that person can be expected to have the same effect upon my view of the world and my view of myself as if I had lost a part of myself.

MUTILATION OF THE SELF AND THE PAIN OF GRIEF

From this standpoint, we can begin to understand why widows speak as if they had lost a part of themselves. When the loss has been sudden, large, and forced upon the attention, words implying mutilation and outrage tend to be used. One widow described her feelings on viewing the body of her husband: 'It's as if my inside had been torn out and left a horrible wound there'. A comparison is sometimes made to amputation: widows say that their husband has been 'cut off', 'as if half of myself was missing'.

In less-violent terms the loss of self is often referred to as a 'gap', 'it's a great emptiness', 'an unhappy void'. These words illustrate how the people we love seem to become part of our self, a view that is often held by poets but one that others may find hard to accept – perhaps because it makes us so much more vulnerable. It is more comfortable to think of the self as a separate, independent, and therefore safe, entity than to accept, with John Donne, that 'any man's death diminishes me' (1624). To some extent we choose where we place the boundaries around ourselves. In a similar way we choose where to place our territorial boundaries and how permeable we make them. It is in accord with the view presented here to regard territory as an extension of the self. It is easier to share territory, however, than it is to share more intimate parts of the self.

Apart from this conjecture we do not yet have any satisfactory explanation of why widows sometimes refer to the experience of bereavement in physical terms. 'It's a horrible feeling here [pointing to her chest]', said a sixty-five-year-old widow. Another described a pain in her throat: 'Like something was pulling . . . I think it was because I wouldn't let myself cry . . . if I could cry it did relieve it'. One can only guess why some should locate the 'pain' in one place and some in another. In most cases the pain of grief is viewed as psychological and seems to have no clear physical location. On the face of it there appears to be empirical justification for Grinberg's (1964) belief that the pain of grief, like physical pain, is the experience of damage to the self.

REORGANIZATION

As will be clear from the foregoing chapters, it takes time for individuals to realize and accept the change in themselves that follows a major loss. External objects may change rapidly but it will be many weeks before corresponding changes have taken place in the plans and assumptions which are their internal equivalents and the changes that do occur may never be complete. Widows continue to think of their husbands as if they were still alive although they know, at the same time, that they are really dead. The corresponding feeling in the self was expressed by one: 'I don't feel that I am a widow'.

But the illusion that nothing has changed can be retained only as long as the widow avoids placing herself in situations in which the 'gap' will show. She looks backwards to the past and makes no plans for the future; in a sense she may try to stop living, to arrest time. Emergence from this state was described by the widow who spoke of her inside as being torn out: 'I think I'm beginning to wake up now', she said, a year after bereavement. 'I'm starting living instead of just existing. It's the first time I've had a positive thought. I feel I ought to plan to do something. I feel as if I was recovering from a major illness or a major operation – you suddenly wake up. It's physical – I felt I was hollow inside, as if my heart had been torn out and left a ragged hole. Now I feel more like a person.'

Kuhn (1958) pointed out that mourners have the feeling that it is not the dead person but they themselves who have been ejected from the world hitherto familiar to them. The 'real' world seems 'unreal', desolate, or empty, and they behave in a careful, muffled way, just as people do at night: 'The mourner has turned away from the real world of everyday life towards the past'. In point of fact the mourner really has been ejected from the assumptive world that existed before bereavement, and the careful movements and the hushed voice sometimes adopted by newly bereaved people could be the same phenomenon as the timorous behaviour of a person who is physically ill. In both cases relatives and friends are afraid of damaging the sufferer by impinging too directly or strongly upon them, by making too real the painful thing that has happened and the consequences of it for their identity. Doctors, aware of the psychological injury they are inflicting, normally disclose bad news in hushed tones as if they can thereby minimize the mutilation. As one widow put it, 'I feel terribly fragile. If somebody gave me a good tap I'd shatter into a thousand pieces'.

MEANING MAKING

The human brain is a meaning-making machine. That is to say, much mental functioning is taken up with screening the huge number of stimuli reaching every nerve ending in our bodies, at every moment of our lives, in order to identify those patterns of sensory input that make sense. Most of these stimuli reflect a world that is familiar and contain little or no new or useful information, they can safely be screened out; indeed the brain devotes more activity to tuning out than tuning in. The remaining stimuli need to be integrated with other stimuli and with the memories of previous stimuli. The patterns that emerge are called perceptions and are themselves assigned varying degrees of salience according to their assumed meaning. Much of this information processing takes place outside consciousness and in an automatic way.

Some perceptions (including all unfamiliar perceptions) are danger signals and immediately take priority over perceptions lower in the hierarchy. These are the ones most likely to receive conscious attention. They must be matched with similar patterns in the memory in order to decide what action must be taken.

Other perceptions are salient because they enable us to meet one or more of the fundamental needs that we share with other animal species (physiological needs for air, warmth, excretion and internal homeostasis, food, drink, attachment, sex, affiliation, status, and territory). These, in the end, increase the chances that our genes will survive.

Problems arise when basic assumptions are invalidated at the same time that large amounts of unfamiliar information is being received. This is often the case following a major bereavement. We saw, in Chapter 3, how the whole brain becomes aroused and may even become disorganized, and, in Chapter 5, we saw how large amounts of information processing can be postponed or avoided.

More difficult to explain are the peculiarly human moral, social, and spiritual needs. Many of these seem to be elaborations of the needs for social approval, affiliation, attachment and status that we share with other species, others may arise from the awareness, peculiar to humans, of our own mortality. The fact that we are programmed for survival, but are aware that, in the long run, none of us will survive, faces us with an existential dilemma that has preoccupied man from time immemorial and given rise to a wide range of 'solutions'. The death of a loved person brings home, in the most incontrovertible manner, the inevitability of death.

In the day-to-day flux of our lives we learn to meet our essential and immediate needs. Even those needs that remain unmet become tolerable because we have a feeling that we are making progress, we have hope. However imperfect our world may be, most of us, most of the time, have a feeling that we know where we stand. 'I know where I'm going and I know who's going with me'; our lives seem to be 'on course', part of a narrative that makes sense. An overall sense of life as meaningful arises out of the countless small assumptions that contribute to this trajectory.

Bereavements, particularly those that we are not prepared for, challenge many of these assumptions (or 'constructs'), undermine the assumed meaning of our lives and take away our hope. One way or another we become aware of the fact that many of our needs are unmet and may never be met. Joan Didion (2005, p. 189) described the experience as '. . . the void, the very opposite of meaning, the relentless succession of moments during which we will confront the experience of meaninglessness itself'.

Much research in recent years has focused on the ways in which bereaved people reconstruct meaning in their lives, for good or ill (see, for instance, the multi-contributor book edited by Robert Neimeyer, *Meaning Reconstruction and the Experience of Loss*, 2001). This is an important task to which we shall return in later chapters.

CHANGES IN THE SOCIAL SYSTEM OF THE FAMILY

Let us return from these difficult psychological problems to look more closely at some of the sociological problems. Sociologists have paid much attention to each person's place in society and the roles that they perform. If one regards the bereaved family as a social system, which has lost one of its members, then there are four possible outcomes:

1   The roles and functions previously performed by the missing member may remain unperformed.
2   A substitute for the missing member may be obtained from outside the family.
3   The roles of the missing member may be taken over by other members of the family.
4   The social system may break up.

Any of these events may take place, or a combination of them.

Consider the effects of loss of a family leader. Although it would be possible, though time consuming, to look at this from the point of view of the whole family we confine attention to the ways in which the loss of the husband's roles affects the widow herself.

1 Roles of deceased person unperformed

Among the roles that are likely to remain unperformed are sexual and companion–protector roles. It is likely that the widow's sexual needs will remain unmet because her persisting attachment to the dead husband will make sexual liaisons with other men almost as strictly forbidden after his death as they were before it. More consciously missed is the companionship of the husband and the emotional security and opportunities for interaction that this previously provided. This is what most people mean by 'loneliness'. Loneliness was complained of by most of the twenty-two London widows and it was most pronounced at night. A year after bereavement nine were still sleeping badly and five of these were taking sedatives.

2 Substitutes from outside the family

Substitutes for a missing husband are not readily acceptable. Only one widow in the London Study became engaged within the first year of bereavement; three others said that they had hopes of remarrying. Reasons such as age and the difficulty of finding an eligible suitor were given for this lack of interest in remarriage, but many of the widows seemed to regard themselves as still married to their dead husband and remarriage would have been a form of infidelity. Children often resented any male who seemed to be usurping the place of their dead father. By contrast, widowers often remarry, and Helsing, Szklo, and Comstock (1981) found that at least half of the widowers whom they studied had remarried within twelve years of bereavement.

Only three of the twenty-two widows moved out of the home they had shared with their husband, and the number living alone increased from five to seven in the course of the first year of bereavement (owing to the marriage of children). Despite their loneliness only four widows now spent more time in social contact with friends and relatives than they had done before bereavement, and seven of them said that they now spent less time in social contact. Thus it seems that they did not seek social relations as a substitute for the companionship of their husband. It may be, however, that a follow-up of these widows over their second and third years of bereavement would have revealed a change in this pattern.

3 Substitutes from within the family

The role of principal wage-earner was often taken over by the widow. Over half (thirteen) of the bereaved London families suffered a drop in income after the death of the wage-earner and in four cases this was severe and caused great anxiety. Most widows, in consequence, took a job, and fourteen were going out to work by the end of the year (five more than before bereavement); in addition, two of those who remained at home took in paying guests. Half of the widows had children under fifteen living at home and these constituted an additional burden. Responsibility for family affairs, finances, house, and children weighed heavily on a similar proportion a year after bereavement.

Roles that were, of necessity, taken over by the widow herself thus included: principal wage-earner, family administrator and planner, and disciplinarian of the children. The overall responsibility for the future of the family rested squarely on her shoulders and opportunities for discussion and joint decision making with her husband no longer existed.

The increase in self-esteem that might have resulted from taking over a leadership role often seemed to be cancelled out by the widow's own feelings of personal inadequacy in this role and by the decline in status of the family as a whole which resulted from the loss of the principal male.

4 Family disintegration

The fourth outcome that can follow loss of the family leader, disintegration of the family as a close-knit social unit, occurred immediately in five cases, where the children had already left home before the father's death, and shortly afterwards in three cases, where the children got married and left home soon after the death. In a further five cases it seemed probable, a year after the death, that the children would leave within the next two to three years. Thus, over half the families were broken up or about to be broken up after the death of the father even though, in all cases, the surviving widow was under sixty-five years of age. In the case of older widows and widowers the social isolation caused by bereavement is a common problem and loneliness is often described as the besetting problem of old age.

Whether the family broke up or stayed together, a gap was left by the death of the father. If the family stayed together it was usually the widow who eventually came to fill the gap. If the family disintegrated the sense of a gap remained, but many of the roles formerly carried out by husband and wife were no longer required. In such a situation the widow was likely to feel unneeded and unwanted. Although it has not been possible to follow up such functionless widows for more than a year, experience in Cruse: Bereavement Care suggests that for some this aspect remains a problem, which may continue unsolved for many years.

IDENTIFICATION

In those cases in which it was necessary for the widow herself to fill the gap left by her husband's death the responsibilities involved often constituted a great strain. Several widows deliberately modelled themselves on their husband and went out of their way to take over his interests and carry out activities in the way in which he would have carried them out. Their efforts were accompanied by a feeling of satisfaction and closeness to the husband.

The practical necessity for the widow to take over roles and activities previously carried out by the husband may coincide with her own wishes and provide her with an opportunity to maintain a sense of proximity to her lost husband, but is there more to it than this? Ever since Freud put forward the notion in 'The Ego and the Id' (1923) that withdrawal of the libido that attaches one person to another can take place only when the lost person is 'reinstated' within the ego, some psychoanalysts have regarded identification with the lost object as a necessary component of mourning. Abraham, writing a year later, saw the object as 'hiding in the ego' – 'The loved object is not gone, for now I carry it within myself and can never lose it'.

Krupp (1963) regarded identification as deriving from the repeated frustrations and losses of early infancy: 'The infant tries to become the loved one to prevent further loss . . . Out of bits of the personalities of others [the growing child creates] the unique mosaic of the self'. In this view, identification with the lost person is not just another way of postponing the realization of loss; it is the necessary condition without which grief cannot end and a new identity be developed. The object is never truly given up; it is made into a part of the self. In this way 'figures who appear to be given up or lost are

permanently held with bonds that are impervious to being severed'
(Rochlin, 1965).

What, then, are the forms of identification that have been found
among the widows studied? In the London Study one of the questions regularly asked was: 'Do you feel that you have got more like
your husband in any way?' The usual response was for the widow
to admit that she had come to resemble her husband during their
marriage but that there had been no increase in resemblance since
his death.

This reply is borne out by the work of Kreitman (1964, 1968), who
has shown that married people tend to develop the same neuroses,
what is more, the longer they have been married, the more similar
their symptoms will be. The most likely explanation seems to be that
married people learn from each other; they gradually come to see the
other's point of view and to make it their own. Attitudes, preferences
for certain television programmes, taste in food, fears and hopes of
the world, all these tend to be shared by husband and wife so that it
becomes possible for either one to use the word 'we' and speak for
both. Thus the identification of husband and wife goes on throughout
married life and grows stronger as time passes. It is not something
that occurs only after the dissolution of the relationship. Nevertheless,
there were in the London Study two widows who showed quite
clearly an increased tendency to behave and think like the dead person, and a further eight in whom there was inconclusive evidence of
such a tendency at some time during the year. One, Mrs J., was
referred to at the beginning of the chapter; and evidence concerning
two others is given below. At no time did more than four of the
twenty-two widows admit to this type of identification.

Mrs D.'s husband was a gardener and a very practical man whose
main interest was the care of his house and garden. After his death
his wife remained at home with her daughter and son-in-law. Within
three months, however, her mother-in-law, of whom she was very
fond, died and the daughter and son-in-law moved away leaving her
alone in the house. During the next nine months Mrs D. spent most
of her time repairing and decorating her house: 'Dad done [sic] it
well', she said. 'I've got to do it the same as him'. Her lawyer remon-
strated with her because she could not afford to spend so much on
the house, but she remarked, 'If I do what my husband wanted I
don't mind if I spend every penny I've got'. 'I've become more like
him; I have to now he's not here to do things'. She learnt to drive,
'because I don't want to sell the van, he prided it so much'.

Another widow, Mrs T., also enjoyed decorating the house. 'I can see him doing it', she remarked. 'I find myself doing jobs around the house the way he would have done them' – she found this comforting.

Another phenomenon, which was very striking when it did occur, was a sense of the husband's presence inside the surviving widow. Mrs D., whose attempts to make restitution to her dead husband were described above (page 118), had been at odds with him throughout their married life and had felt her security threatened by behaviour which she regarded as irresponsible. Her husband had sometimes sacrificed his family's interests in order to satisfy his artistic inclinations and his wife had repeatedly pressed him to settle down. 'At dawn', she said, 'four days after my husband's death, something suddenly moved in on me – invaded me – a presence, almost pushed me out of bed – terribly overwhelming'. Thereafter she had a strong sense of her husband's presence near her and sometimes inside her. She adopted his sense of values, accepted his criticisms of her bourgeois attitudes, and planned to try to market his paintings. At the end of the year she now saw many things 'through his eyes'.

The sense of the presence of the dead husband is a common phenomenon, which was discussed in Chapter 5. Sometimes it consisted of a general feeling that the husband was somewhere near at hand; at other times he would be located in a specific place, a particular chair, a bedroom, or the grave in which his body was buried. Occasionally, however, the husband was sensed to be within the widow herself.

This was a pleasant feeling that seemed to minimize grief. 'It's not a sense of his presence', said one widow when asked if she felt that her husband was nearly at hand. 'He is here inside me. That's why I'm happy all the time. It's as if two people were one . . . although I'm alone, we're sort of together if you see what I mean . . . I don't think I've got the willpower to carry on on my own, so he must be'.

This widow solved the problem of locating her dead husband in space by finding him in herself. Five others found him in somebody else. For instance, one widow had been married to a black West Indian man. She had two children: the first, a boy, was dark skinned, but the second, a girl, was fair. The girl was born shortly before her father's death and 'was meant to replace him'. After the death, Mrs L. was disturbed to find herself identifying the girl with her husband: 'She has his hands – it gives me the creeps'.

The respondent who married eight months after the death of her de facto husband, Bill, soon became pregnant. She was 'dead keen' on having a baby and identified her unborn child with Bill. 'Giving birth', she said, 'will be like getting Bill out of me'. She seemed in this statement to express her wish both to have and to get rid of Bill.

Another type of identification phenomenon, the development of symptoms resembling those of the husband's last illness, is obviously pathological. It is considered in the next chapter.

THE NEW PERSON

In sum, it appears that the ways of identifying with the husband that have been described achieve two ends: they enable the widow to get back, in some sense, the man she has lost, and they help her to take over the roles he has vacated. But, however attractive these ends may appear to be, it was only a minority of widows who, at any time during the first year of bereavement, were conscious of coming to resemble or contain the dead spouse. These widows got through their grief no faster than the widows who reported no evidence of identification, and there was nothing to suggest that identification is a necessary part of the process of recovery. It seems, rather, that identification with the lost person is one of the methods that bereaved people adopt to avoid the painful reality of loss; as such it may delay acceptance of the true situation, but, like most other coping mechanisms, it is only intermittently effective. The sense of the husband 'inside' is a transient phenomenon, and those who experience it are likely to locate him in some other person or place on other occasions. Similarly, the adoption of roles or attitudes of the dead person is seldom permanent and never complete; episodes of comfortable 'closeness' are followed by periods of grieving and loneliness, and it is only intermittently that identification occurs.

Golan (1975) spoke of the process as a progression from 'being a wife to being a widow to being a woman' – growth is completed as she gives up her view of herself as being a 'partnerless half' and becomes an autonomous individual. This progression is aided by the gradual return of bodily appetites. The appetite for food is often the first to reassert itself, perhaps because starvation begets hunger. Sexual and other interests come later and lead eventually to a resurgence of interest in the world and a willingness to plan for a new future.

The London widows seemed at last to find their new identity emerging from the altered life situations that they had to face. New friends and new workmates provided role models and several widows remarked that they had been much helped by talking to other widows with whom it was easy for them to identify.

This does not mean that the identification with the husband, which had grown up during the years of marriage, was altogether lost. Clearly, the points of view, values, and modes of problem solving that had been established over the years did not all cease to be appropriate, and the first thought of many a widow when faced with a new problem was often, 'What would my husband have done about this?' But the answer to this question is not always apparent and the use of the remembered husband as an ever-present referee tends to diminish with time. As the old assumptions about the world prove ineffective and a fresh set of assumptions is built up so the old identity dissolves and is replaced by a new and different one.

8

COMPLICATIONS OF GRIEF

The grief hath craz'd my wits.
King Lear, Act III, Scene 4

We know that a proportion, albeit a small one, of bereaved people are referred for psychiatric help with problems that result from their bereavement. In this chapter the forms that such problems may take are described, and in the succeeding chapters we consider why it is that some people react in these ways while the majority come through the stress of bereavement without seeking psychiatric help. The fact that someone seeks psychiatric help does not necessarily mean that they are suffering from a psychiatric disorder. Like many physical illnesses such disorders do not fall neatly into 'all or nothing' categories. The point at which a sneeze is diagnosable as a cold or an aching back as arthritis is arbitrary and, while doctors need to define disorders and set criteria for their diagnosis in order to justify their work and provide 'patients' with the privileges of treatment, there is a grey area between health and illness. Despite this, the majority of the people who sought help from Parkes in his role as a psychiatrist with a special interest in bereavement, did meet criteria for psychiatric disorders.

As indicated on page 27, their diagnoses fell into two categories, non-specific and specific. The non-specific problems are not special to bereavement and include a wide range of psychiatric conditions that can be caused by a variety of stressors in addition to bereavement. The specific conditions are types of complicated grief and it is this group that is the main focus of this chapter. However, the study of reactions to bereavement also throws light on the non-specific disorders, so we shall also refer to these while bearing in mind that there is a great deal of research into the psychiatry of depression, anxiety and other psychiatric disorders that cannot be covered here.

The situation is further complicated by the fact that many of the people whose presenting symptoms were of a non-specific type also showed evidence of pathological grief and many of those presenting with pathological grief also had evidence of non-specific reactions. Mixed pictures, as we have seen, are not uncommon in psychiatry.

Be that as it may, it is clearly necessary to study more closely the types of symptom that follow bereavement if we are to find out which ones are indicative of pathology. Let us, therefore, look at the constellation of psychological symptoms experienced by a group of patients who came into psychiatric care after bereavement and compare them with the symptoms shown by unselected widows.

HOW DO WIDOWS WITH PSYCHIATRIC PROBLEMS DIFFER FROM OTHER WIDOWS?

Much recent research by Prigerson, Horowitz and others now confirms and extends the findings of Parkes' early studies. These indicate, first of all, that the widowed psychiatric patients had experienced many of the same grief symptoms as the widows in the non-psychiatric samples studied (Horowitz, Bonanno, and Holen, 1993). Indeed there is no sharp dichotomy between complicated and uncomplicated grief, it is largely a matter of degree. For instance Holland *et al.* (2009) used sophisticated taxometric methods to discover whether the Prolonged Grief Disorder described below lies at the extreme end of a continuum with 'normal', uncomplicated, grief or whether there is a clear distinction between the two. They conclude that the evidence points to a continuum.

However, it is not only the intensity and duration of the grief that distinguishes people at the psychiatric end of the continuum from the non-psychiatric groups. Two main categories of reaction have been described, Prolonged Grief Disorder and Delayed or Distorted forms of grief. The first are now well-established, the last remain controversial.

PROLONGED GRIEF DISORDER (PGD)

Out of twenty-one bereaved psychiatric patients (four male, seventeen female) interviewed in the Bethlem Study (see page 30 above) there were fifteen whose grief seemed more prolonged than expected. Indeed, six of the twenty-one had been bereaved for two years or more and their grief was unabated. These patients suffered from what Anderson (1949) termed 'chronic grief'. Years after bereavement many of them were still preoccupied with memories of the dead person, pining intensely and severely distressed by any reminder that brought him or her to mind. Eight patients cried uncontrollably and several others said that they felt 'too hurt to cry'. Agitated and aggressive outbursts occurred in four cases and four admitted to having suicidal preoccupations. The intensity of grief impaired working capacity in eight cases and caused most to shut themselves up at home or withdraw in some way from contact with their friends and relatives.

'I miss him every moment of the day'; 'I want my husband every minute of the day but neither you nor anybody else can give him to me' – these statements would be normal enough if made a few weeks after bereavement but in fact they were made one and a half and nine and a half years later. Even allowing for exaggeration they reflect a sad state of affairs and one that is not very uncommon.

> Mrs S. lived for eleven years with a man twenty years older than herself. She described their relationship as 'ideal – everything – it was so right – he was so fine . . . I'd absolutely found myself'. Even during his life she was intolerant of any separation from him and when he died after a long illness she 'never stopped crying for months'. 'For years I couldn't believe it, I can hardly believe it now. Every minute of the day and night I couldn't accept it or believe it'. She stayed in her room with the curtains drawn: 'For weeks and weeks I couldn't bear the light'. (One is reminded of the widow who spoke in a whisper for fear of making reality too real.)
>
> She tried to avoid things and places that would remind her of her loss: 'Everywhere, walking along the street I couldn't look out at places where we were happy together . . . I never entered the bedroom again . . . can't look at animals because we both loved them so much. Couldn't listen to the wireless'. But she retained a very clear picture of her partner in her mind which she was unable to shut out: 'It goes into everything in life – everything reminds me of him'. For a long time she went over and over in her mind the events leading up to his death.
>
> At first she used to agonize over minor omissions and ways in which she had failed him, but gradually these

preoccupations lessened and she tried to make a new life for herself. However, she found it difficult to concentrate on her work and hard to get on with other people: 'They've got homes, husbands and children. I'm alone and they're not. I'm so unhappy, they're not'. She tried to escape by listening to recorded music and reading a great deal, but this only increased her isolation.

A friendly chaplain advised her to seek psychiatric help but, 'I had the idea that psychiatrists can't help with real-life problems'. Her general practitioner treated her for bowel symptoms (spastic colon) but, 'You only get three minutes and you can't talk about psychological problems in that time'. Eventually she sought help from a voluntary organization, and it was the people she met there who finally persuaded her to seek psychiatric help.

It will be clear from this example that there is more to PGD than severe and prolonged grief alone. Prigerson and Horowitz, with their separate teams, each carried out systematic studies and came up with very similar criteria. Recently they have reached agreement that, in addition to the presence of prolonged and severe grief, there is a cluster of other phenomena that are commonly reported by people with PGD. The reader will note that most of these 'real-life problems' were reported by Mrs S.:

1 Sense of self as empty or confused since the loss, or feeling that a part of oneself has died as a result of the loss.
2 Trouble accepting the loss as real.
3 Avoidance of reminders of the loss.
4 Inability to trust others since the loss.
5 Extreme bitterness or anger related to the loss.
6 Extreme difficulty moving on with life (e.g. making new friends, pursuing interests).
7 Pervasive numbness (absence of emotion) or detachment (social withdrawal) since the loss.
8 Feeling life is empty and the future bleak without the deceased.
9 Feeling stunned, dazed or shocked by the loss.

The findings of The Yale Bereavement Study indicate that anyone with more than five of these symptoms, along with the other criteria to be discussed below, should be regarded as suffering from PGD. The research justifying these claims is summarized in Appendix 5.

For the reasons discussed on page 5, the formal diagnosis of a psychiatric disorder should not be made lightly. In addition to the above criteria the researchers propose that a diagnosis of PGD should only be made if (a) these symptoms cause clinically significant distress or impairment in social, occupational, or other important areas of functioning (e.g. domestic responsibilities), and (b) they have continued for at least six months from their onset (further justification for this time period is given in Appendix 5). This implies that the condition has impaired the functions that make life worthwhile over a long period of time. It does not mean that people who do not meet all of these criteria do not need help, but it does ensure that they will not be given a psychiatric diagnosis unless it is likely to be to their benefit to do so.

This research has shown that people meeting these criteria regularly have high scores on the Index of Complicated Grief (ICG) and this has enabled the ICG, and it's more recent revised and shorter version, the PG-13, to be used instead of formal psychiatric diagnosis for research purposes, although they lack the precision necessary for clinical use. Research also shows that, although people with PGD sometimes also suffer from major depressive disorder (Barry, Kasl, and Prigerson, 2002), depression and prolonged grief are two quite different things (Boelen and Prigerson, 2009; Boelen, van den Bout, and de Keijser, 2003; Prigerson et al., 1995a, 1995b, 1996, 1997). Likewise, PGD may co-exist with PTSD, but is a quite different disorder (Barry et al., 2002; Bonanno et al., 2007). These three diagnoses follow different courses and require different treatments.

In several respects PGD is a more serious disorder than major depression and PTSD. In a study of 149 bereaved persons with ICG scores over 25, two-thirds reported thoughts of wanting to die following the death of a loved one, 29 per cent engaged in indirect suicidal behaviour and 9 per cent made a suicidal attempt (Szanto et al., 2006). In another study Latham and Prigerson (2004) found an increased risk of suicidality in bereaved people with high ICG scores, which remained after controlling for major depressive disorder and PTSD. In addition, PGD has been shown to be associated with an increased risk of cancer, hypertension, and cardiac events (Prigerson et al., 1997; and Appendix 5, page 285).

In later chapters we shall see that PGD is preceded, and in all probability caused, by very different circumstances from those that precede other psychiatric diagnoses. For the same reasons it requires very different approaches to treatment.

INHIBITED AND/OR DELAYED GRIEF

As we saw above persistent numbness, avoidance of reminders, and difficulty in accepting the fact of loss are common features of PGD. In these cases the avoidance seems to reflect the magnitude of the distress and the need to avoid being overwhelmed.

In addition, the diagnostic criteria for PGD allow for the fact that some bereaved people do not develop PGD immediately after bereavement, only after a delay do they become severely and lastingly disturbed. Prigerson *et al.* noted that, during the period of delay, these people suffered an eleven-fold increase in sleep disturbance (see Appendix 5, page 285). It seems that it is more difficult to avoid thinking about distressing subjects as we relax control of our thoughts at night.

Because people vary greatly in their resilience, their capacity for emotional control, and the intensity of their attachments, failure to express grief cannot be taken to mean that something has necessarily gone wrong. Furthermore, the longer time elapses after a bereavement the more difficult it is to prove that subsequent symptoms are the result of the earlier bereavement; other traumatic life events may have occurred and it is difficult to establish clear cause and effect. In these circumstances it is not surprising that the claims made in previous editions of this and other publications, for the existence of inhibited or delayed grief as a psychological problem for which help is needed, have not gone unchallenged (Wortman and Silver, 1989). For this reason we need to look closely at the evidence.

There were eight patients in the Bethlem Study whose grief seems to have been delayed for more than two weeks after bereavement. In three cases this seemed to be a prolongation of the numbness described in Chapter 5, but the remaining five behaved as if nothing had happened – not even numbness was acknowledged.

> When told of the death of her husband, Mrs K. remarked, 'Oh, would you give me a cigarette?' She went about her household tasks automatically and her sister thought, 'It hasn't penetrated; how awful when it does and she realizes'. Mrs K. said, 'I just couldn't believe it. I didn't realize he was not coming back'. About two weeks later she became more subdued and depressed, but she was still unable to cry: 'Tears came to my eyes but I was unable to let them go'. Her depression gradually got worse and she became socially withdrawn and preoccupied with self-reproachful ideas

centring on another widow to whom she had been unkind during her husband's illness. It was in this state that she was admitted to a psychiatric unit six months after bereavement.

In this case it was depression and suicidal thoughts that brought the patient into the care of the psychiatrist and in fact all the patients with delayed reactions whom Parkes saw in that study eventually developed depression. It is not surprising that some psychiatrists prefer to regard this as a depressive illness caused by bereavement rather than a delayed grief (Osterweis *et al.*, 1984, pp. 18–20).

In his classic paper 'The Symptomatology and Management of Acute Grief' Lindemann (1944) described various *formes fruste* of grief that may occur during the period of delay, and in the Bethlem Study the forms of atypical grieving shown by the bereaved patients were often associated with panic attacks, persisting and intense guilt, or a peculiar kind of hypochondriacal condition in which the patient developed symptoms closely resembling the symptoms suffered by the dead person during the last illness.

In the Love and Loss study, which linked complicated grief to earlier attachment problems, Parkes identified 25 bereaved psychiatric patients suffering from what could be termed an Avoidant Attachment Disorder. All of them had been emotionally inhibited, distrustful of others and controlling of others by aggression or assertion rather than by affection before their bereavement (see pages 172–3 for more about avoidant attachments). They had reacted to bereavement in a variety of ways, which had prevented them from leading functionally effective lives and had caused them to seek psychiatric help. Parkes writes:

At first, some people with avoidant attachment disorders appeared to cope well with bereavement. Their lack of overt grief and their reluctance to ask for help led others to assume that they did not need support. Only later did it become apparent that their compulsive independence was a cover up. At this point some experienced a break-through of delayed grief or turned in on themselves and became depressed. Some developed psychosomatic symptoms reflecting chronic anxiety and tension, others became irritable and subject to outbursts of anger or rage. Yet others reacted immediately to the bereavement but found the break-through of emotions extremely distressing and did their best to inhibit or conceal it, and some experienced severe anxiety and panic but were quite unable to cry. Expressions of grief and anger, which others would see as appropriate, gave rise to fear and were seen as a sign of incipient mental collapse. People often feared, that if they 'broke down' and showed feelings they would indeed have a 'nervous breakdown'.

(Parkes, 2006, p. 239)

While some cases of delayed grief go on to meet the criteria for PGD, it seems that inhibition of grief can give rise to a number of different patterns of response. More systematic work will be needed to enable us to decide which other patterns of response, if any, should be diagnosed as psychiatric disorders in their own right.

ANXIETY, PANIC ATTACKS AND PHOBIAS

Panic attacks were described by six of the twenty-one patients in the Bethlem Study. They were brought on by reminders of death and by loneliness at loss of support, and included 'choking sensations', breathless attacks, and other somatic expressions of fear.

Mrs C. was fifty-six when her husband died from lung cancer. Her mother had died the previous year and her only daughter had left home to get married at about the same time. Consequently, when her husband died she was left alone in the house. 'I tried to go on as before. I said "Goodnight mate" just as if he was there.' After a few weeks she got a job as a kitchen-maid to get herself out of the house during the daytime. She began to sleep badly and to dread returning to the empty house. She experienced attacks of trembling, with sweating, palpitations, and pains in the stomach. These were brought on by thinking about the empty house and by reminders of her loss. She became increasingly depressed, tense, and agitated, feeling that she had let people down by getting depressed and blaming herself for her illness.

It was in this state that she was admitted to hospital five months after bereavement. 'It's definitely connected with his death', she told me. 'I love too hard, I love so much, that's why I get hurt. I think, "There's no good going in the kitchen – he'll never come back".' She still found her memories so painful that she tried to avoid them, but she felt that there was something wrong about this. 'I can't think about him now as I should . . . I don't talk about him. I avoid thinking about him. It's easier to die than to keep on like this.'

Loneliness and social isolation seemed to make it more difficult for this widow to tolerate the pain of grief. She tried to go on as if nothing had happened and to avoid thinking or talking of her husband but it became difficult for her to control her thoughts in this way and the attacks of severe anxiety from which she suffered seemed to reveal the intensity of her fear of being overwhelmed by grief.

These two features, intense separation anxiety and strong but only partially successful attempts to avoid grieving, were evident in all the forms of atypical grief that we have come across. The degree of disbelief and avoidance varied considerably, but whatever its degree there was always an impression that the underlying separation anxiety was severe.

The DSM makes a distinction between Panic Disorders, Phobias and Generalized Anxiety Disorder. Panic Disorders are attacks that seem to come out of the blue while people with phobias tend to panic in particular situations. In bereaved people panic attacks seldom justify a psychiatric diagnosis of either condition, but when they are so severe that they cause people to avoid going out of the house or interfere with other important life tasks and responsibilities they justify the term phobia. The commonest form of phobia is agoraphobia, a fear of going out. Generalized Anxiety Disorder is characterized by lasting feelings of pervasive anxiety and tension, short of panic, but nevertheless sufficiently debilitating to prevent people from enjoying life or carrying out important social, occupational or other functions. This, too, can arise after bereavement.

Although these conditions can be distinguished from each other, they seldom occur in isolation and, after bereavement, anxiety disorders, depression and prolonged grief often coexist.

SELF-BLAME

Ideas of guilt or self-blame in relation to the deceased were expressed by two-thirds (fourteen) of the bereaved psychiatric patients. Sometimes this consisted of mild self-reproach as when a widow felt that she could have done more for her dying husband. Other patients were convinced that they were directly responsible for the death.

Over half (eight out of fourteen) of the patients who expressed ideas of self-reproach also expressed marked hostility towards other individuals, usually doctors, nurses, or clergy, who had attended the dying person during his last illness. This had sometimes caused problems, since it had led to immoderate outbursts. Fortunately, social controls in Western society seem strong enough to prevent the more extreme outbursts of anger that can be a danger in other cultures. Thus Westermeyer (1973) has described eighteen Laotian men who ran amok and exploded grenades in public places. Sixteen of these cases had followed recent losses (five the death of a wife). There was no great difference between the forms of guilt and anger expressed by these bereaved psychiatric patients whom Parkes studied and those shown by the unselected widows, as previously described. But both guilt and, to a lesser extent, anger were reported more commonly in the psychiatric group and were more often seen as a major problem. As we shall see below, irrational or excessive guilt is often a symptom of major depressive disorder.

> Mr M. was sixty-eight when his wife died. They had been married for forty-one years and according to a member of the family he had 'coaxed and coddled her' throughout their married life. She died, unexpectedly, after a brief illness. For several days he was 'stunned'. He made all the funeral arrangements, then shut himself up at home and refused to see anyone. He slept badly, ate little, and lost interest in all his customary pursuits. He was preoccupied with self-reproachful thoughts and had fits of crying during which he blamed himself for failing her. He blamed himself for sending his wife into hospital (fearing that she had picked up a cross-infection on the ward), and was filled with remorse for not having been a better husband and for having caused his wife anxiety by himself becoming ill.
>
> At the same time he was generally irritable, blaming his children for hurting their mother in the past and blaming the hospital for his wife's death. When he went to meetings of a local committee he lost his temper and upset his fellow members.
>
> His son took him on a trip abroad in the hope of getting him out of his depression but he became more disturbed than ever and broke off the holiday to return to the home that he had cared for fastidiously since his wife's death.
>
> Ten months after bereavement he was admitted to a psychiatric hospital where, after spending some time in

psychotherapy talking about his loss, he improved considerably. It was at this time that he was seen by Parkes who was struck by the way in which he talked of the deficiencies of his wife while denying any feeling of resentment. 'I looked forward so much to when I retired – that was one of the things that cracked it. I wanted to go on holiday abroad but I couldn't get her to see eye to eye with that. She had been brought up to believe that to go without was essential. I never cured her of that.' He bought her a home but 'she regarded it as a millstone' – nevertheless she became very attached to her home, 'happier there than anywhere'. Her timorous attitude was reflected in numerous fears. 'She was afraid of the sea – I never pressed her to go abroad. The children would ask her to do things and automatically she'd say "No". No man could have wished for a better wife.'

One might expect that this man would now feel free of the restraints placed upon him by forty-one years of marriage to a difficult woman, but his conscious attitude can be summed up in his own words. 'Supporting my wife gave me a purpose in life. I've always been able to exert my will through her. Now I don't need to any more.' We can speculate that the anger, which formed so marked a part of his reaction to bereavement, may have been displaced from the wife herself onto others, including himself. The trip abroad with his son may have been a bid for freedom, but it was defeated because this man was still influenced in some degree by the assumptions and expectations that had become 'built in' throughout his married life. To take advantage of his wife's death to do the things that he had failed to persuade her to do in life would have been an insult to the part of her that still survived in his mind.

SOMATIC SYMPTOMS AND
IDENTIFICATION

Bodily symptoms that arise without a physical cause are usually referred to as 'hypochondriacal' and psychiatrists use the term 'hypochondriasis' for people who believe that they have a physical illness where there is none. Sadly, these terms are often used in a pejorative way as if the sufferer was malingering.

If the anger and guilt expressed by Mr M. have their counterpart in the recriminations expressed by the unselected widows (see

Chapter 6), the bodily symptoms that are considered next seem likely to be related to the identification phenomena discussed in Chapter 7. We use the term 'identification phenomena' for those features of the reaction to bereavement which, rightly or wrongly, seem to indicate identification with the deceased. 'Identification symptoms' we reserve for hypochondriacal symptoms such as are described above. Thus 'identification symptoms' are a type of 'identification phenomenon'.

Such symptoms were found among five of the twenty-one patients in the Bethlem Study and Parkes has since encountered six other cases in which there seemed to be a relationship between bodily symptoms and the symptoms experienced by a dying relative during his last illness. They were usually aches and pains at the site of a pain that had been prominent during the illness of the relative whose death preceded their onset.

Six of these eleven patients complained of chest pain, and in four of these cases the pain resembled the pain of coronary thrombosis, one patient had pain simulating lung cancer, and another the supposed pain suffered by a son who had died in a car accident. A further three showed the apparent effects of a stroke, and there was one case of recurrent vomiting.

In a few cases it seemed that the identification symptom was an exaggeration of symptoms that are common enough after bereavement. Thus palpitations frequently accompany anxiety and a woman whose husband had just died from heart disease may easily imagine that she is suffering from the same condition. Mrs I., for instance, became very panicky after the death of her husband from a coronary thrombosis. She thought that the palpitations and gasping she experienced at the time, and the sense that her heart was bursting, indicated that she too had a coronary thrombosis.

When a bodily symptom involves loss of sensations or movement it falls onto the category of a dissociative symptom (formerly such symptoms were referred to as 'hysterical' but this term, too, is so often used in a judgemental way that it is better avoided). Mrs H., for example, when told of her husband's death, immediately lost the use of her voice for ten days. Her husband had died from the second of two strokes, the first of which had left him unable to speak.

The link between the terminal illness and the identification symptom appeared most clearly in a woman who was in psychotherapy at the time when her father died from a stroke that had paralysed the left side of his body. She had nursed him at home for several weeks before his death. The day after this event she related to her psychotherapist a dream, which had occurred the previous night. In it she saw her father lying in his coffin; he had reached up at her from the coffin and 'stroked' the left side of her body whereupon she woke up to find that the left side of her body was paralysed. The paralysis wore off over the course of the next hour and she had no further symptoms of this nature.

This example shows clearly how the struggle to realize, to make real, the father's sickness and death was expressed in a bereavement dream. The father, neither alive nor dead, reaches out and, in a gesture that contains and expresses the ambivalence of their relationship, strokes his daughter and passes on to her the stroke that killed him. It is perhaps no coincidence that a recurring problem for this woman, which came up repeatedly in psychotherapy before and after her bereavement, was her feeling of having been harmed by her father.

In one bereaved psychiatric patient a dissociative symptom itself resembled a similar dissociative symptom suffered by a close relative:

> Miss O., an American spinster of middle age, had lived with her sister for many years. After her sister's death her grief was delayed for three months and then broke through with great severity. She had not recovered from this when, seven months later, she became paralysed and anaesthetic from the waist down. These dramatic symptoms bore no resemblance to the symptoms of her sister's last illness but they did closely resemble an illness her mother had suffered, apparently as a reaction to bereavement. This illness had greatly affected the patient's life. Her mother had developed a paralysis of both legs after the death of the patient's two brothers. She had become a cripple, in the care of the family, and had thereby succeeded in dominating them. Whether or not the mother's illness was in fact a reaction to bereavement, it was believed by the family to have been so, and the patient shared this belief. After the mother's death her place had been taken by the patient's sister, who resembled her mother in many respects. Miss O.'s illness perpetuated the pattern and caused great concern in the family.

In another case a hypochondriacal illness occurred in a woman whose father was said to have vomited every morning for thirty years. When seen seven months after his death she claimed that she had taken over the habit. She was preoccupied with his memory and said, 'I do exactly the same things as my father'.

These examples illustrate some of the forms that identification symptoms may take. As with the other symptoms commonly experienced by bereaved psychiatric patients, they bear a close resemblance to similar phenomena reported by unselected widows in the London Study. In fact, one of the London widows had a hypochondriacal illness described by her GP as 'mimicking her husband's illness', and four others, at one time or another, complained of symptoms suspiciously similar to those of their husbands. Four of these five also showed other identification phenomena of the types described in the last chapter.

These identification phenomena go some way to explain the hypochondriacal and dissociative symptoms to which they give rise but they have received little attention in their own right. As previously noted, psychiatric diagnosis is firmly locked into a diagnostic system focused on symptoms and emotions rather than causes.

DEPRESSION

Depression, as we have seen, commonly arises following bereavement and may even meet criteria for psychiatric disorder. As such it does not differ from the major depressive disorders (MDD) that occur for a variety of reasons other than bereavements. It is, however, a different phenomenon from both uncomplicated and complicated grief (see Appendix 5).

The classical symptom of MDD is a continuously depressed mood, with feelings of helplessness and hopelessness, most of the day and every day. If this has lasted for over a week the diagnosis is very likely. In addition the following features are present in most cases:

- loss of interest in all or most activities that normally give pleasure and meaning to life;
- major loss or gain in weight;
- insomnia (particularly with early morning waking) or hypersomnia (excessive sleep);
- extreme slowing of thoughts and/or movements or agitation;
- fatigue and loss of energy, feelings of worthlessness and inappropriate guilt;
- difficulty in concentrating and making decisions; and, most significant,
- preoccupation with thoughts of death or suicide (the risk of which should always be considered).

Bereavement is a well-recognized cause of depression, particularly in people with a previous history of depression or a gloomy, pessimistic view of the world. Sometimes entire families have a tendency to depression and, in the Love and Loss study, a history of depression in parents was associated with unhappiness in childhood and a disorganized attachment pattern that was itself associated, after bereavement, with an increased risk of depression, anxiety and a tendency to use alcohol to excess. Alcohol abuse, because it reduces self-control, can increase the risk of suicide in depressed people.

Apart from the risk of suicide, MDD probably causes more misery than any other psychiatric problem. Sufferers often feel that nothing can possibly help them and may not seek for the help that they need. It follows that all who reach out to bereaved people should be familiar with these symptoms and accept responsibility for ensuring that appropriate help is given. We shall return to consider how on pages 226–9.

Another factor that may increase the risk of MDD is the nature of the bereavement. Traumatic bereavements, particularly those for which the bereaved feel responsible, increase the risk of depression. But the Love and Loss study showed that this was mainly in conjunction with a previous problem in attachment to parents. It seems that the resilience that results from secure parenting can enable us to cope with the most traumatic losses. We shall return to this issue in Chapter 11, in which we show how one particular pattern of attachment predisposes people to become depressed and anxious after traumatic bereavements.

In this chapter we have identified some of the psychological problems that cause people to seek help after bereavement. In the chapters that follow we look more deeply at circumstances that make for vulnerability or resilience. As we begin to see how certain situations increase the risk while others reduce it we shall also begin to see why this is so. As each piece of the jig-saw of bereavement fits into place we begin to understand the whole, to understand why problems arise, and what we can do about them.

9

DETERMINANTS OF GRIEF – I

Kinship, gender and age

No different, I said, from rat's or chicken's,
That ten-week protoplasmic blob. But you
Cried as if you knew all that was nonsense
And knew that I did, too.

Well, I had to say something. And there
Seemed so little anyone could say.
That life had been in women's womb before
And gone away?

This was our life. And yet, when the dead
Are mourned a little, then become unreal,
How should the never born be long remembered?
So this in time will heal

Though now I cannot comfort. As I go
The doctor reassures: 'Straightforward case.
You'll find, of course, it leaves her rather low.'
Something is gone from your face.
David Sutton (b. 1944), Not to be Born

Those who are concerned with the effects of bereavement have to take into consideration many possible factors when trying to explain the differences between individuals in their response to this event. It is not enough to say that the loss of a love object causes grief, and leave it at that. Grief may be strong or weak, brief or prolonged, immediate or delayed; particular aspects of it may be distorted and symptoms that usually cause little trouble may become major sources of distress. These points have been illustrated in previous chapters and the cases cited will already have indicated a few of the antecedent influences that seem to play a part in determining people's reactions to bereavement.

In some cases a particular response is the consequence of a number of circumstances each of which contributes to the outcome; in others, one factor may appear to be the chief determinant. For example, in the case of a young woman with a previous history of psychiatric illness whose husband dies suddenly and unexpectedly, there are several factors – her youth, her predisposition to mental illness, and her lack of opportunity to prepare herself for bereavement – that would be likely to have a determining influence on her reaction to his death.

On the other hand a unitary cause is exemplified by Queen Victoria. Her strong, dependent attachment to Prince Albert was such that she became upset by the briefest of separations throughout their married life (Longford, 1964). This fact alone is sufficient to explain the severity of her reaction to his death although cultural and other considerations have to be taken into account if we are to explain the form this took. We also have to explain why she established this type of attachment to the prince in the first place.

A complete explanation for any psychosocial event would be possible only if we knew everything that had preceded it – which clearly can never be the case. We shall never be able fully to understand any piece of human behaviour, nor can we expect to identify major factors that are important to outcome in every case of bereavement. But we can learn something of the factors that play a part in most cases and a major part in some.

Relevant data can be obtained from detailed studies of a few people or from statistical studies of larger samples. Ideally, the two types of study should complement each other, for it is only by studying large numbers of people that we can generalize, and only by intensively studying a few that we can evaluate the significance of the mathematics of many. Reference will be made in this chapter to a number of other studies that have been carried out in recent years. Taken together these studies point to certain of the major determinants of outcome after bereavement.

It was indicated in the last chapter that many of the patients who come for psychiatric help after bereavement are suffering from intense and prolonged forms of grief. It seems reasonable, therefore, to consider first what factors affect the overall magnitude of grief before going on to try to explain more specific variables.

ATTACHMENT

It would seem, on the face of it, a truism to say that the intensity of grief is determined by the intensity of love. But this is easier to state than to prove. In our society 'love' is so much a virtue that you will seldom find a widower or widow willing to admit that he or she did not love his or her spouse. Besides, what do we mean by 'love'? The meaning is imprecise.

Since love is a tie and the strength of a tie is its resistance to severance, one might suppose that intolerance of separation could be taken as a measure of love. But this would be to equate love with the particular type of clinging we see in young children who will not allow their mothers out of their sight. As Bowlby has pointed out (1953), a well-established love relationship is one in which separation can be tolerated because the loved one can be trusted to return when needed. Ainsworth refers to this as 'security of attachment' (Ainsworth and Wittig, 1969).

The situation is further confused by the ambiguity of the term 'dependent', which is used sometimes to mean 'intolerance of separation' and sometimes to indicate 'reliance on someone for the performance of particular roles or functions'. Thus a man may be 'dependent' on his wife because he cannot bear to be parted from her or because he needs her to help him into his wheel chair.

Finally, there is the question of 'involvement'. By this we mean the extent to which one person's roles, plans, and repertoire of problem solutions depend upon the presence of the other person for their relevance and practicality. Thus the greater the area occupied by A in the life-space of B, the greater the disruption that will result from A's departure.

We return to consider these factors in the light of the particular circumstances that have been found to influence them and the reaction to bereavement. These have emerged from a large number of follow-up studies of bereaved people. Initially these were simple, empirical, studies to examine the extent to which particular variables, selected on grounds of common sense, predicted good and bad outcomes. More recently the chain of causation between particular factors and particular types of outcome has become clearer and, as we shall see in Chapters 13 and 14, has given rise to particular action to prevent or treat particular problems.

Determinants of the outcome of bereavement

ANTECEDENT
Relationship with the deceased
  Kinship (spouse, child, parent, etc.)
  Strength of attachment
  Security of attachment
  Degree of reliance
  Involvement
  Intensity of ambivalence (love/hate)
Childhood experiences (especially insecure parenting and losses of significant persons)
Later experiences (especially losses of significant persons)
Previous mental illness (especially depressive illness)
Life crises prior to the bereavement
Mode of death
  Timeliness
  Multiple deaths
  Previous warnings
  Preparation for bereavement
  Violent or horrific deaths
  Disenfranchised deaths
  Culpable deaths

CONCURRENT
Gender
Age
Personality
  Grief proneness
  Inhibition of feelings
Socioeconomic status (social class)
Nationality
Religion (faith and rituals)
Cultural and familial factors influencing expression of grief

SUBSEQUENT
Social support or isolation
Secondary stresses
Emergent life opportunities (options open)

RISK ASSESSMENT

Knowledge of the determinants of grief enables us to identify widows and other bereaved people who are at 'high risk' of getting into difficulties; that is to say, people to whom it may be appropriate to offer counselling or other forms of help after bereavement. This is already being done in many hospices where nurses and others who get to know a family before bereavement can ensure that relatives who are thought to be at risk get the help that they need. Some are using predictive questionnaires based on the findings of research in order to quantify the risk. Such screening methods not only enable us to focus help where it is most needed but they also tell us who will respond best to the help that is given.

Of course our ability to predict the course of grief will never be perfect. Too many unpredictable events and circumstances render such attempts very approximate. Even so the results already obtained indicate that systematic methods of prediction using a questionnaire are more reliable than an 'informed guess'. They also show that people who need and will benefit from counselling cannot be relied upon to seek help; it is necessary for helpers to offer their services. A detailed account of one such predictive measure is given in *Recovery from Bereavement* (Parkes and Weiss, 1983) and its value has since been confirmed by Beckwith *et al.* (1990) and Robinson *et al.* (1995). The research that has been carried out in recent years has advanced our understanding of these risks. It encourages us to believe that the time is ripe for others to develop more sophisticated measures that will enable us to spot particular problems before, or as soon as, they become evident, and to develop appropriate preventive and thera- peutic services. The next three chapters review the principle determinants and the two that follow explore implications for prevention and treatment.

RELATIONSHIP WITH THE DECEASED

It would be hard to tease out the contribution of the four components of human relationships – strength of attachment, security of attach- ment, reliance, and involvement – to a particular relationship, and all we can hope to do is to examine instances where it seems that one or other component predominates.

In the developed world partners, be they married or unmarried, tend to form small close-knit family units with their children, and to have a lesser degree of involvement with their parents and siblings than they did in the past. The woman's roles, plans, and problems tend to be family and husband centred and she is usually more reliant on her partner for money, status, and company than he is on her. It comes as no surprise, therefore, to find that **loss of a spouse** is one of the commonest types of relationship loss to cause people to seek psychiatric help after a bereavement. Among 151 people who have been referred to the writer for the treatment of psychiatric problems following bereavement (and took part in the Love and Loss Study), 22 per cent had lost a spouse (18 per cent a husband, 4 per cent a wife), 21 per cent had lost a parent, 19 per cent a child and 16 per cent other people. The remaining 22 per cent had multiple bereavements. In The Yale Bereavement Study it was the loss of spouses and children that were more likely to lead to PGD than loss of siblings or other bereavements.

In the earlier Case-note Study the number of women psychiatric patients whose illness had come on following the death of their husband (twenty-five) was seven times greater than would have been expected had the bereavement not been a causal factor in determining illness. On the other hand, the number of men whose illness had followed the death of their wife (six) was only four times greater than expected; and the illnesses that followed the death of a parent showed hardly any excess over expectation.

Those, in the Love and Loss Study, who sought psychiatric help after the death of a spouse differed from those with other types of loss in having had mutually dependent relationships with the spouse and a similarly close relationship with their father during childhood. Their reaction to bereavement was one of intense loneliness, which was not assuaged by the presence of others (Parkes, 2006, Chapter 13). We shall return to look more closely at these issues in Chapter 11.

Loss of a child

Losses of children are particularly hard to tolerate and Gorer (1965) described the loss of a child at any age as, 'the most distressing and long-lasting of all griefs'. This observation was confirmed by Neidig and Dalgas (1991), who found that bereaved parents obtained higher scores on the Texas Inventory of Grief than are found after other types of bereavement. Barrera *et al.* (2007) reported that 25 per cent of parents who had lost a child by cancer, congenital heart disease, meningitis, or drowning in the last 19 months, were 'consumed by grief', their loss of hope and control made it hard for them to carry out their daily activities.

The loss of a child is associated with an increased risk to physical and mental health. We saw in Chapter 2 (page 17) that parents suffer an increased mortality rate. Clayton (1980) found that a surprisingly high proportion of people developing a depressive illness had suffered the death of a child within the preceding six months, and Mann (1987) reported that 8 per cent of women who had lost a child attempted or committed suicide.

On the whole, women seem to be more vulnerable to the loss of a child than men (Wretmark, 1959). In the Love and Loss Study, among 29 parents who sought psychiatric help after the loss of a child, 25 (86 per cent) were women and in two recent studies, of parents who had lost a child, mothers suffered a greater increase in mortality rates than fathers (Li *et al.*, 2003; Wijngaards-de Meij *et al.*, 2008). But the loss of a child is not sufficient in itself to cause parents to seek psychiatric help, none of the parents in the Love and Loss Study were secure people who had lost a child by a predicted death. All showed evidence of prior vulnerability and/or they had suffered particularly traumatic bereavements (further details of which will be given in Chapter 10).

These researchers also found that the intensity of grief and depression increased with the age of the child until the age of about 17, when it declined. Archer (1999) has reported similar findings, which he attributes to the influence of parental investment on the survival of their genes. A woman has a greater chance of having another child if she is still young.

It is only in the present century that the loss of a child has become a rare event, and what evidence there is suggests that during earlier days, when most parents would expect to lose up to half of their children in infancy or early childhood, they accepted their losses more readily than we do today. Hence Montaigne can write: 'I have lost two or three children in their infancy, not without regret, but without great sorrow'. To this day, those who lose young children in parts of the world where mortality is high have been observed to show little grief (Scheper-Hughes, 1992).

Granted that there has been a change in the reaction to the death of children, how can it be explained? Since we have fewer children to a family today than in the past, it may be that the tie between each child and mother is correspondingly greater. Could it be that each mother has a total amount of potential for attachment and that it is therefore easier to lose one child out of a family of ten (10 per cent of one's children) than it is to lose one child in a family of two (50 per cent of one's children)? Another important factor is likely to concern the expectation of loss. In a society in which deaths of children are statistically rare we are particularly likely to be unprepared for those that do occur. Even less likely is the death of grandchildren, and one study has found an increased mortality rate among Israeli Jews who had lost a grandchild (Roskin, 1984).

An important finding in the Love and Loss Study, was the discovery of high rates of separation from or rejection by their own mothers, in mothers seeking psychiatric help after the loss of a child (Parkes, 2006, Chapter 12). It seems reasonable to conclude that, if our own experience of attachment has been deficient, and particularly if we lack the memory of warmth and nurture, either because of separation from or rejection by our parents, we grow up in dread of the possibility that love and security will not last. The love that we share with a child may be our strongest experience of a love that is unqualified and unconditional. It may help to redress the balance of our own deprivation. If we then lose that child we are doubly bereaved and our dreaded world becomes our assumptive world.

The loss of a child in the womb or at birth will be considered in the next chapter.

Loss of a parent in adult life

By comparison, the loss of a parent in adult life seems, as a rule, to cause much less distress than loss of a child but it is, of course, much more common. Moss and Moss (1995), reviewing the literature on this subject, state that the loss of a parent in adult life is 'rarely pathological'. Even so, psychiatric problems can be triggered in adults by the death of a parent, and they constitute the second commonest reason for people to seek help from a psychiatrist, or suffer PGD after a bereavement, and the most frequent loss among people seeking help from Cruse Bereavement Care.

What distinguishes the minority who need help after the loss of a parent from the majority who do not? Once again problems in attachment to the parent turn out to be crucial. In Bunch et al.'s (1971) study of suicide, among married people who committed suicide few had followed the loss of a parent; but among single men who committed suicide 60 per cent had suffered a maternal bereavement during the preceding three years. This compares with only 6 per cent of single men who had not committed suicide. It would seem that adult men who remain unmarried and continue to live with their mother are particularly vulnerable to suicide when she dies.

On the other hand, those who have happy marriages are less likely than others to need psychiatric help after the death of parents. In the Love and Loss Study 17 women and 5 men had been referred for psychiatric treatment after the death of a mother (Parkes, 1995a). A third (7) had never married, 7 were now separated or divorced, and of the 8 who remained, only one had a marriage that was satisfactory.

Fewer (9) had sought help after the death of a father and, although most of these had partners, they too reported unsatisfactory marriages. Their relationship with their father had been insecure, and in 4 cases had been complicated by the father's alcoholism.

Adult orphans, more than any others, reveal the lasting influence of the attachments that we make in childhood. Most of the parent-bereaved psychiatric patients had been unusually close or dependent on the parent who died and it was often this that had caused both their psychiatric and their marital problems. Seventy per cent were lacking in self-confidence and, without a supportive marital relationship, they had found the death of their parent particularly hard to tolerate. On the other hand, the parent's death did present them with a chance to discover that they were not in fact as weak and helpless as they had feared and most of them eventually did well, a finding that is in keeping with the Moss's conclusion that the death of a parent in adult life is often an opportunity for personal growth.

Loss of a sibling

Most studies do not indicate that the loss of a sibling in old age (which is when most of us lose siblings) is a major loss for most people and only 8 per cent of bereaved people in the Love and Loss Study had sought psychiatric help after the loss of a sibling. One exception seems to be the death of a twin and, more particularly, the death of an identical twin. Segal and Bouchard (1993) compared the intensity of grieving in 49 identical (monozygotic) and 19 non-identical (dizygotic) twins after bereavement. The intensity of grief following the death of the twin significantly exceeded that for mothers, fathers, grandfathers, grandmothers and other relatives. Identical twins grieved more intensely for the death of their twin than non-identical. The authors argued that this shows that grief intensity increases with genetic relatedness and confirms Archer's (1999) theory that grief has evolved as a Darwinian adaptive mechanism. This may not be as far fetched as it sounds if we accept

145

the theory proposed in Chapter 3 of this volume that the essence of grief is the cry for a lost person and has its roots in the attachments that enable our genes to survive.

Although the loss of a sibling was only reported by 8 per cent of people seeking psychiatric help in the Love and Loss Study, it can have a 'considerable impact' (Perkins and Harris, 1990). Even in the elderly there are some families in which siblings play an important role in preserving the meaning and identity of the family, their death may have distressing consequences for the surviving siblings (Moss and Moss, 1995).

Loss of a grandchild

Loss of a grandchild is rare but can be traumatic when it occurs. Ponzetti and Johnson (1991) indicated that grandparents grieve not only for the child who has died but also for their own child, the grandchild's parent, and Roskin (1984) has reported that Israeli grandparents suffer an increased risk of mortality in the special circumstances of the loss of a grandchild in war.

GENDER

Men and women differ in the ways they grieve and the problems that follow bereavement. One way and another women show more distress and report more symptoms during the first year of bereavement than men. Seventy-seven per cent of 171 bereaved psychiatric patients in the Love and Loss Study were women and a study of forty relatives of patients who died in a St Louis hospital showed significantly more crying and a greater consumption of sedatives and tranquillizers among women than men (Clayton, Desmarais, and Winokur, 1968). Furthermore women are much less likely than men to remarry (Schneider *et al.*, 1996).

By contrast it is men whose level of distress declines more slowly over the years than does the distress of women. In the Harvard Study, which comprised forty-nine widows and nineteen widowers under the age of forty-five living in Boston, Massachusetts, it was clear that the women showed more overt distress after bereavement than the men and their psychological and social adjustment a year later was less good than that of the widowers. However, measures of psychological and social adjustment also revealed large differences between married men and women in a matched control group of married people. When this is taken into account it seems that the widowed women showed no greater decrement in adjustment after bereavement than the widowed men; moreover, at follow-up two to four years after bereavement, it was the men who were found to have taken longer to recover than the women. This suggests that a large part of the difference reported above is attributable to the tendency of men to hide their feelings and to their reluctance to seek help, a finding that is confirmed by Brabant, Forsyth, and Melancon (1992) and by Tudiver, Hilditch, and Permaul (1991), both of whom have carried out studies focused on widowers.

Widowers are more likely than widows to die of a heart attack after the loss of their spouse (see pages 16–17). Why this should be is not known. It is possible that men repress their grief more rigorously than women and that the increased mortality reflects some psychosomatic effect of this repression on the heart. Support for this hypothesis comes from Bonnano's (1994) study of conjugal bereavement, which showed that bereaved people with *low* scores on grief-related symptoms had more rapid heart rates than people with high scores.

Other gender differences were found in a study of 92 widows and 58 widowers who were followed up over two years (Chen *et al.*, 1999). Not only did the widows have higher rates of PGD, Anxiety and Depression, but those widows with high levels of PGD at six months after bereavement had significantly more physical health problems (e.g. cancer and heart attacks) than widowers. On the other hand, men with high anxiety at six months were more likely than women to report suicidal thoughts. Unfortunately this study did not have a sample of married controls so it is unwise to draw firm conclusions about the bereavement effect.

Men are less likely than women to seek psychiatric help following all types of bereavement and they often see themselves as having responsibility to contain their own grief in order to look after their wives. This is particularly likely following the death of a child. Thomas and Striegel (1995), who studied 26 couples who had lost a baby by stillbirth, concluded that: 'Mothers and fathers grieve differently, mothers grieve for their babies, fathers grieve for their wives'.

These findings have important implications for the provision of support for men and for women. We examine these on page 230.

OLD AGE

Other factors that might be expected to affect the magnitude of the reaction to bereavement are the **timeliness** or untimeliness of the loss and the opportunities for anticipatory preparation that precede it. This is most obvious in old age. There is a great difference between the quiet slipping away of an old person and the tragic cutting off of a young one 'in his (or her) prime'.

This is reflected in the reactions to bereavement of those who survive. In a study of 141 elderly bereaved spouses five out of every six adjusted well over time, and about a third showed considerable resilience without negative consequences (Ott *et al.*, 2007). Similarly, in Parkes' study of the consultations that forty-four London widows had with their general practitioners (see page 23 above) he found that, whereas widows under the age of sixty-five frequently consulted their GP for help with emotional problems during the first six months after bereavement, this was not the case with older widows. Furthermore, the consumption of sedative drugs was no higher among the older widows after bereavement than it had been before-hand, whereas there was a seven-fold increase in sedative consumption in the under-sixty-five age group during the first six months of bereavement, which declined only slightly over the following year (see Appendix 9 for statistical details).

Among the one in six in Ott's study who did less well, the commonest problems were loneliness, chronic grief, and depression, which tended to go together. Likewise, in the London Study, bereaved psychiatric patients over the age of 55 showed less distress than younger patients unless they now lived alone, in which case they were more likely to report loneliness and persisting grief. Sudden deaths, which are so traumatic for the young, are less so in old age, probably because most of them are less unexpected and more timely (Carr *et al.*, 2001).

It seems, then, that while young age may be associated with greater intensity of grief, pathological reactions are not confined to the young. Among 71 patients admitted to a psycho-geriatric ward, 22 (31 per cent) had suffered one or more bereavements and an additional 10 (making 45 per cent in all) had suffered other losses such as loss of health or roles (Clegg, 1988). Bereavement is certainly a cause of depression in old age and several studies have demonstrated that between 10 and 17 per cent of elderly widows can expect to experience levels of depression equivalent to those found in psychiatric clinics at some time during the first year of bereavement (Clayton,

Halikas, and Maurice, 1972; Duran, Turner, and Lund, 1989; Lund, Caserta, and Dimond, 1989). Similar problems have been found in elderly people after the loss of a twin (Lichtenstein *et al.*, 1996).

Gender differences exist among elderly bereaved people as they do in younger. A study in Australia (Byrne and Raphael, 1999) indicated that although elderly widowers were more anxious and slept less well than married men of the same age, they differ from elderly widows in having lower scores of depression. But it is elderly widowers who are at the greatest risk of both successful and attempted suicide (Erlangsen *et al.*, 2004; Li, 1995).

One possible explanation for psychological problems following bereavement in old age is the multiplicity of losses that often occur at this time. The loss of a spouse in this age group commonly sets in train other losses (e.g. of income, home or friends) and these may prove as traumatic as the bereavement itself. Gass (1989) has shown that widows who, in addition to the loss of their spouse, face other threats are at greater risk of psychological difficulties than those for whom the spouse's death was the only loss.

There is also evidence that older people may be more vulnerable to the effects of bereavement on physical health. This is evident in the increased mortality rate and the diminished nutrient intake that has been demonstrated in elderly widows after bereavement (Rosenbloom, 1993). An important study in Japan, in which 184 elderly persons who had lost a spouse were followed up for 16 years, showed that those with high scores of depression in the first year of bereavement were more likely to suffer sickness and/or death in the next 8 years. If the depression had diminished at the 8-year interview health improved, but if it had increased so did the level of sickness (Kawai and Sasaki, 2004). Of course, it may be that old people who are physically infirm are more vulnerable to depression after bereavement than those who are physically healthy (Schoevers *et al.*, 2006). The most likely explanation for these findings would seem to be that both factors interact with each other. Grief and loneliness cause depression, which increases the risk of physical ailments, which then increase the depression.

Social support is claimed to be a buffer against poor health. In an ingenious large-scale study of 1369 women over the age of 69 in the USA, Laditka and Laditka (2003) found that widows who lacked social support (as indicated by low telephone usage) had poorer health and increased hospital admissions during the first year of bereavement. Social support after bereavement also emerged as associated with better mental health in a large-scale study in Tokyo

(Okabayashi *et al.* 1997). This said, several studies bring home the fact that there can be no substitute for a loved person, indeed, the presence of friends can increase emotional loneliness (van Baarsen, 2002).

Gender differences are found in religious faith, observance and support from a religious community, with elderly widows scoring higher than elderly widowers on all of these. These religious factors in turn are found to correlate with scores of optimism, personal meaning, psychological well-being, and fewer health problems (Fry, 2004).

Clearly the alleviation of grief, loneliness and depression together with social and spiritual support, are important objectives in this age group, as is the maintenance of good physical health. We shall look at these issues again in Chapters 13 and 14.

YOUNG AGE

At the other extreme of age we have children who may also suffer bereavements. Separations and losses of parents in childhood have long been recognized as contributing to a variety of psychological problems many of which persist into adult life. These problems have received a great deal of attention in recent years and special services have been set up for bereaved children (Monroe and Kraus, 2005). The topic is a complex one and has lifelong implications for the children.

Despite the amount of interest in the field, well-conducted research studies are still few. Perhaps the most systematic, and useful, is the Harvard Child Bereavement Study, which was carried out by William Worden and Phyllis Silverman (Worden, 2002). Worden concluded: 'Most bereaved children do not need special counseling. However, a third of the children have emotional/behavioral problems sufficient to warrant some type of counseling intervention during the first two years of bereavement'.

He identified ten 'red flags', which should alert us to the need for professional evaluation:

1 persisting difficulty in talking about the dead person;
2 persistent or destructive aggressive behaviour;
3 persisting anxiety, clinging or fears;
4 somatic complaints (stomach aches, headaches, etc.);
5 sleeping difficulties;
6 eating disturbance;

7   marked social withdrawal;
8   school difficulties or serious academic reversal;
9   persistent self-blame or guilt; and
10   self-destructive behaviour.

Like the 'risk factors' that help us to assess the need for special help after bereavement in adult life, these are useful indicators rather than psychiatric disorders in their own right.

It lies outside the experience and expertise of the authors of this volume to examine more closely these consequences of bereavement in childhood; this is reflected in the subtitle of this book *Studies of grief in adult life*. Rather we pass on now to consider the influence of the way people die on the reactions of those who survive them.

10

DETERMINANTS OF GRIEF – II

Mode of death

There is no comfort for those who are grieving
For faith is not enough
To assuage the tearing wound of sudden death.
O let me not drown in the flood of grief
For all young men who died before their time
And for this one so newly dead.
O let me catch the raft of life again
And not be swept away
In the darkest depths of grief and loss.

Marjorie Pizer, *Lament for Glen*
(killed in a motor cycle accident,
aged nineteen)

Among the bereaved people who seek psychiatric help after bereavement *nearly all* are found to have suffered unusually traumatic forms of bereavement and/or to show evidence of prior vulnerability. Sudden unexpected deaths, multiple deaths, violent deaths and deaths involving human agency (murders, suicides, etc.) represent a special risk to mental health even in the absence of other vulnerability. By comparison natural deaths are relatively untraumatic (Weinberg, 1994).

Some communities have high rates of traumatic loss and one study found this to be the strongest factor contributing to an increased incidence of Prolonged Grief Disorder in bereaved African Americans, 21 per cent of whom met criteria for this condition compared with only 12 per cent of whites (Goldsmith *et al.*, 2008). Of course, other communal stresses may also be playing a part in these differences and we should not assume that all black communities are alike. We look more closely at these issues in Chapter 12.

UNEXPECTED DEATH

But first we need to examine the various types of traumatic death that have been listed above, we start with unexpected deaths. The young widowers and widows in the Harvard Study were quite clearly more emotionally disturbed following deaths for which they had had little time to prepare, and their disturbance persisted throughout the first year of bereavement (see Appendix 10). 'Short duration of terminal illness' came first among fifty-five antecedent variables as a predictor of poor outcome thirteen months after bereavement. Other studies in Britain, the USA, and Sweden have come up with similar findings (Duke, 1980; Lundin, 1984a; Vachon *et al.*, 1980; Wijngaards-de Meij *et al.*, 2008).

When Lundin followed up his group of 130 first-degree relatives eight years after bereavement he found that the unexpectedly bereaved were still more tearful, self-reproachful, and numb, and that they missed the dead person and mourned for them more than other people (Lundin, 1984b). In young widows and widowers, the increased mortality that follows bereavement has been found to be greater if the death was sudden and unexpected than if it was expected. This remains true to a lesser extent in older widowers but not in older widows, they show no difference in mortality after sudden as opposed to expected deaths (Smith, 1990).

The death of a spouse in old age may be sudden, but it is not untimely or entirely unexpected, and those studies that contain a substantial proportion of older widows show no significant association between sudden death and poor outcome (Clayton *et al.*, 1972; Fulton and Gottesman, 1980). Furthermore, in one study of older men and women (Gerber, Rusalem, and Hannon, 1975), those whose spouse had suffered a very long illness had a poorer outcome after bereavement than did others with short histories. This suggests that very long illnesses, in which the life of the spouse becomes centred on the partner, may give rise to special problems after the partner dies.

Another category of death that has received close examination in recent years is the sudden death of a newborn infant, or 'cot death'. Reviewing the growing literature on this topic, Osterweis *et al.* (1984) conclude: 'The suddenness of SIDS (Sudden Infant Death Syndrome) in seemingly healthy babies may lead to extra difficulties in the bereavement process . . .'. Misunderstandings commonly arise in the course of police inquiries, parents may blame each other, and some engage in a relentless search for a cause (Raphael, 1984). 'Shadow grief' may continue to plague some mothers from time to time for the rest of their lives (Peppers and Knapp, 1989).

Shanfield and his colleagues (Shanfield and Swain, 1984a; Shanfield, Benjamin, and Swain, 1984b; Shanfield, Swain, and Benjamin, 1985) found that deaths of adult children in road traffic accidents were associated with more intense grief in the surviving parents, more symptoms from a health check list, more depression, and more guilt than deaths of older adult children from cancer that had been treated in a hospice. Among the parents who had lost a child in a road traffic accident, mothers had worse outcomes than fathers. The deaths of younger unmarried children who were still living at home and of children who died in single-car, single-driver accidents or who had alcohol or relationship problems were predictive of poor outcome in the parents.

But even if there is ample warning of an incipient death, it is not easy to prepare adequately for bereavement. Part of the difficulty resides in the fact that even though people may know that a person is dying they are likely to suppress their own anticipatory grief for fear of upsetting the dying person.

> Typical was Mrs I., who said: 'My husband could read me like a book, so I couldn't show any sign of being upset. When the doctor told me it was cancer, I was upset for half a day, and pretended to him it was because he was likely to have to go into hospital. It was such a terrible thought I pushed it to the back of my mind'. The lack of communication got worse as his disease progressed: 'I seemed to go away from him. He wasn't the person I'd been married to. When I tried to share his pain it was so terrible I couldn't'. Her dissociation from the patient, her husband, was such that when he eventually died she felt: 'It wasn't really him . . . I wondered where he was'. When seen, three weeks later, she was still dazed and numb: 'I'm waiting for him to come back from somewhere', she said.

Experience in hospices suggests that it is sometimes possible for a husband and wife to work together towards an acceptance of the approaching death of one of them. If the circumstances are right (as discussed in the next chapter), they can share some of the anticipatory grief, which each needs to feel. The striking thing about such cases is that, despite the sadness, which is an inevitable component of anticipatory grieving, couples who choose to face the future in this way often seem to win through to a period of contentment and calm that persists to the end. After bereavement has occurred, the surviving spouse is likely to look back on this period with a satisfaction that contrasts with the dissatisfaction expressed by many who have chosen to hide the truth.

In the Harvard Study unexpected and untimely deaths were found to give rise to a characteristic type of response to bereavement. The initial reactions of numbness and disbelief persisted for a considerable time and were associated with social withdrawal and a continuing sense of the presence of the dead person near at hand. This did not prevent the bereaved from becoming lonely, anxious and depressed, a reaction that was still present in over half the group two to four years later.

Those who have suffered unexpected and untimely bereavements are often preoccupied with memories of the lost person and, if the death was of a particularly painful type and was witnessed by the bereaved person, the memories themselves will be painful and meet the criteria for PTSD. Indeed Schut *et al.* (1991) found higher rates of PTSD following unanticipated deaths than other types of bereavement. Intrusive and painful memories seem to prevent happier memories from emerging and in this way interfere with the work of grieving. It is not unreasonable to assume that this is one of the reasons for the long duration of some of these traumatic grief reactions (Kaltman and Bonanno, 2003).

Pynoos *et al.* (1987a, 1987b), who used their own check lists to measure both grief and PTSD in children who had been subjected to a sniper attack, found, as one would expect, that the magnitude of grief correlated with the intensity of attachment to a friend who had died while the magnitude of the symptoms of PTSD correlated with the extent to which the child had been in personal danger. When both grief and PTSD occurred together the PTSD tended to take priority.

DEATHS BY VIOLENCE

Deaths by **violence** (Dillenberger, 1992; Horowitz, 1976), murder or manslaughter (Parkes, 1993a), suicide (Cain, 1966; Silverman, Range, and Overholser, 1994), civil disaster (Raphael, 1986; Tyhurst, 1957), and military action (Sanua, 1974) have been the topic of a number of studies. All show an increased risk to mental health. Thus Dillenberger, who used a variety of standard methods of assessing mental health to assess several groups of violently bereaved widows in Northern Ireland, showed high scores on most measures of psychological problems and Murphy *et al.* (1999) found that two years after bereavement about 20 per cent of parents of adolescents who had died by accident, suicide or murder, suffered psychiatric levels of all ten symptoms in a check list of psychiatric symptoms (the Brief Symptoms Inventory).

In many of these cases grief is complicated by intense feelings of anger and guilt. If the danger persists, as in the case of an unsolved murder or a civil or military disaster, disillusionment with the power of the authorities to maintain a secure environment may generate a host of fears. Yet times of war are not associated with dramatic increases in neurosis and the social supports that focus on the families of those who have died 'for their country' may help to mitigate their grief. Thus Rubin (1992), who followed up parents who had lost a son in the Yom Kippur War, reported that 13 years later bereaved parents had no more psychological symptoms than non-bereaved controls. On the other hand, they continued to remember and to relate to vivid memories of the lost child who remained an important part of the family. Indeed Malkinson and Bar-Tur (2004–5) reported that, even in old age, the memories of a child lost by violence remain ever present, 'It seems that the deceased child's position becomes more and more crucial as the other children leave home' (p. 115). Grief has become a link with the dead and elderly parents may fear that, when they die, the memory of the lost child will die with them.

Murder and manslaughter

Some, but not all, violent deaths are the result of human agency in which case reactions of anger and guilt are very understandable. In an attempt to focus on the issue of blame, Weinberg (1994) carried out a postal study of 200 people who reported a bereavement as their most distressing experience. Forty-seven per cent blamed someone else for the death, but blaming others was only associated with poor outcome if it was associated with a persisting desire for revenge. It seemed that a 'desire for revenge can keep survivors focused on the loss . . .'.

This was certainly the case among many of the seventeen patients who were referred to Parkes' psychiatric clinic following bereavements by murder or manslaughter (1993b). Many of the risk factors associated with poor outcome after bereavement are to be found in such cases, which must represent one of the most traumatic kinds of bereavement. Thus the combination of sudden, unexpected, horrific and untimely death, with all the rage and suspicions that followed, and the long, drawn-out legal proceedings (which often led to a sentence that seemed trivial by comparison with the magnitude of the loss), can be expected to overwhelm the family as a support for its members and lead to lasting psychological problems. It does this in several ways – by inducing PTSD, by evoking intense rage, by undermining trust in others (including the police and legal systems that are expected to protect us), and by evoking guilt at failing to protect the deceased. These consequences easily set in train vicious circles, which perpetuate the problems. Avoidance of reminders and depressive withdrawal can lead to social isolation, which aggravates the depression; lack of trust may cause people to turn away from sources of help; angry outbursts may further alienate others; and feelings of guilt may lead to self-punitive behaviour. It can be no surprise that most of the families bereaved by murder who attended Parkes' clinic saw themselves as stuck in a rut from which they could not escape. By the same token it was important for him, as therapist, not to be so drawn into this maelstrom to the extent that he too felt overwhelmed. By adopting a slow and gentle approach, insisting on dealing with only one problem at a time, maintaining a calm but caring attitude, and by allowing the bereaved to choose their own agenda, it was usually possible to create a safe place in which they could gradually begin the process of reviewing and rebuilding their lives. We shall return to further consideration of these issues in later chapters.

Suicide

The families of suicides often blame themselves and may feel socially stigmatized. A recent study of parents of children who died by suicide found extremely high scores on the Inventory of Prolonged Grief (Rynearson and Prigerson, unreported data). On the other hand, according to Cleiren (1992) 50 per cent of suicides have been antici-pated so we should not expect them all to be equally traumatic. His comparison of people bereaved by suicide, road traffic accidents and long illnesses indicated that road traffic accidents caused the most severe depression with suicide second and long-term illness third. Those bereaved by suicide were most likely to feel guilty and to wonder what more they could have done but this was seldom a major problem. On the whole, parents of suicides suffered more than spouses (who tended to become depressed and to withdraw during the first four months but recovered sooner than the bereaved parents).

One group at special risk after suicide are identical twins. They are at even greater risk than non-identical twins to attempt suicide (Pompili *et al.*, 2006).

Psychiatrists and other health-care staff are usually at hand when someone commits suicide, indeed they may blame themselves or be blamed by the family for failing to prevent the death. Because of this few take the opportunity to offer help to families bereaved by suicide. In a study by Brownstein (1992) eleven out of twelve families of psychiatric patients who had committed suicide said that they would have liked some contact with the psychiatrist who had cared for the person who died, but only one psychiatrist had initiated any such contact. This may well have compounded any problems that existed rather than resolving them.

MULTIPLE LOSSES

Multiple concurrent losses are more traumatic than single losses. They are particularly common in disaster areas and will be considered in Chapter 17.

DISENFRANCHISED GRIEF

A category of loss that creates special problems has been termed by Doka (1989) '**disenfranchised grief**'. By this he means losses that cannot be openly acknowledged, socially validated or publicly mourned. The most obvious example is death from AIDS but there are many others. Doka divided them into:

1   *Unrecognized relationships* (e.g. extramarital attachments, homosexual relationships, ex-spouses or lovers, true parents of adopted children and doctors or nurses who have become attached to their patients).
2   *Unrecognized losses* (e.g. perinatal deaths, abortions, returning foster children to their parents, giving up children for adoption, loss of a pet and social or psychological loss without death as when a partner develops Alzheimer's disease).
3   *Unrecognized grief* (e.g. children who are thought to be too young to grieve, elderly or brain damaged, as when a death

occurs in an old people's home, mental hospital or an institution or those with learning difficulties).

In all of these groups problems can arise in the expression of grief, which may be intensified by being ignored or repressed, anger and guilt, which are very likely to arise and which then complicate the course of grieving, exclusion of the griever from helpful rituals of mourning, and lack of social support or sanction for grieving.

AIDS is an example of a type of loss that is often concealed, unrecognized or ignored and Schneider *et al.* (1991) have shown that gay men who suffered the death of a partner (usually from AIDS) are more likely to express suicidal intentions than those who have not. Working in a hospital in which many HIV-positive patients are seen Parkes has been struck by the number who have experienced multiple bereavements. Such patients are typically more distressed by the loss of friends and partners than they are by the threat to their own life. The hospital provides them with doctors, nurses and counsellors who can see them through the bad times and it is not surprising that they often turn to these staff for support at times of bereavement. For a review of fifty-four papers on the complex problems of AIDS see Bergeron and Handley (1992).

Unrecognized losses such as the death of a foetus also come to the attention of medical and nursing staff and it is important for staff to give sensitive support. This said, the death of a foetus rarely causes people to seek psychiatric help, only 2 per cent of the bereaved patients referred to Parkes had suffered a miscarriage and 0.7 per cent a stillbirth. A good account of the problems that can arise and their implications for the organization of support is given by Kowalski (1991).

When Joan's baby was born dead she asked the nurse what would become of the body. The nurse replied that, technically this wasn't a baby but a foetus, an abortion. It's body would be consigned to the rubbish bin and incinerated along with the other detritus from the ward. Joan, who had grown attached to her unborn child, could not accept this, she asked to see the baby and, when the nurse demurred became very upset. Eventually the nurse gave in and produced the foetus wrapped in a towel. Joan could see that it had fingers and toes and was very much a human being. She asked if she could see the hospital chaplain and was told, incorrectly, that there was nothing that the chaplain could do, there could be no funeral or other ritual for an abortion.

At this point Joan's distress became greater than ever. She discharged herself from the hospital and arrived home clutching her dead baby and in a distraught state. Her husband did not help by telling her that she had been very foolish and should return to the hospital. He refused to look at the baby.

Joan, on her own, took her baby to the crematorium where a surprised attendant showed her the first understanding that she had received. He provided her with a shoe box and accompanied her to the chapel where he turned on some recorded music and stayed with her while she prayed for her baby. Eventually he pressed the switch, which transferred the shoe box with its sad contents to the cremation oven.

Followed up two years later, Joan was still seething with anger at what had happened and wanted to know if it was she or the world that was mad. Parkes reassured her that she was certainly not mad and encouraged her to share her thoughts and feelings about what had happened. Her marriage was now threatened and it was important to see her husband and explain to him the normality of her reaction. A complaint to the hospital caused them to revise their instructions to staff regarding the handling of miscarriages and terminations of pregnancy.

Joan's case is not unusual and hospital chaplains are now recognizing the need for ritual and emotional support to mothers who need it. Peppers and Knapp (1980), who carried out a systematic study of 80 mothers who had abortions, found that most of the mothers complained that they had nobody to whom they could talk about what had happened. Most had showed little grief but there were many exceptions. Persisting grief was most likely the later in the pregnancy the death had occurred, Roman Catholics were more likely to grieve than Protestants, the importance of the pregnancy in terms of the age and fertility of the mother, lack of education and a history of previous miscarriages all contributed to aggravate grief.

Since these early studies more systematic research has been carried out into the factors that determine why some women cope with the miscarriage of a foetus without great distress while others become clinically depressed. Length of pregnancy has emerged as a predictive factor (Keefe-Cooperman, 2004) and Benkendorf et al. (1990)

have suggested that it is in the second trimester of pregnancy that mothers may become attached to their babies. Stillbirths, the birth of a dead baby after the 24th week of pregnancy, is obviously likely to be more traumatic than an abortion or termination before that time.

Other determinants include previous depression, a lack of social resources, an ambivalent attitude to the lost foetus (Beutel *et al.*, 1995), and marital and family disharmony (Stirtzinger *et al.*, 1999).

Another type of unrecognized loss occurs when somebody develops Alzheimer's disease or some other type of dementia. Here the spouse or other caregiver not only suffers grief in anticipation of the coming death of the patient but also grieves for the loss of the person they knew, who is now radically changed by the disease. A systematic study of this phenomenon using an 'Anticipatory Grief Scale' has been conducted by Theut *et al.* (1991).

Grief can go unrecognized if the person who suffers it is unable to communicate or belongs to a group who are not expected to understand the loss. Recent studies of people with learning difficulties have shown that they have as much need to express grief as others (Bonell-Pascual *et al.*, 1999). Sadly they are seldom invited to funerals or provided with opportunities to share their thoughts and feelings about the death of a friend or family member.

OTHER STRESSFUL EVENTS

Other stressful events occurring prior to bereavement can influence the nature of the reaction to it (Maddison, Viola, and Walker, 1969). In the London Study there was a significant association between the occurrence of major stresses during the two years preceding the bereavement and a poor overall adjustment afterwards (see Appendix 11). Stresses reported by the London widows were: losses of people (four); family discord (four); threats of loss (three); change of domicile (one); and poor housing conditions (one). When we add to these the secondary stresses that resulted from the bereavement itself – loss of income (for thirteen out of twenty-two widows), problems concerning work (twelve), worry about the future (five), and problems with children (uncounted but numerous) – the surprising thing is that nearly half of these widows seemed to have made a satisfactory adjustment a year after bereavement.

Although incidental stresses may contribute to a poorer outcome, their effect upon the intensity of the grief itself is by no means clear. In the London Study those widows who reported most stress prior to

161

bereavement showed slightly (but not significantly) more grief symptoms than the rest.

An exception to the general rule that natural deaths give rise to less severe grief than unnatural can occur when survivors have centred their lives on caring for a sick person. One might have expected that the death of a person whose care the survivor had found stressful would lead to a relief of stress but some studies have found that caregivers who found their caring stressful suffered *more* difficulties in bereavement and more continuing strain than those who found their caring less stressful (Bass and Bowman, 1990; Schulz, Boerner, and Hebert, 2008). Likewise the burden of caring for someone with Alzheimer's disease can be considerable and, although the death itself can come as a relief, those with high scores of 'caregiver burden', less family support, and lower income, have been found to suffer more depression, persisting after bereavement, than other caregivers (Zhang *et al.*, 2008).

Extreme deprivation

The effects of extreme deprivation is evident in studies of the Nazi holocaust. In Kval's (1951) study of life in Theresienstadt internment camp, where the Nazis kept 140,000 Jews: 'It was characteristic that serious matters like the death of relatives or close friends often met with only superficial sympathy, whereas trifles or small quarrels . . . would lead to severe temper outbursts'. In this situation unjust imprisonment, hopelessness, sexual segregation, lack of privacy, forced labour, semi-starvation, and the constant threat of being sent to an extermination camp were ever present stresses. Grief and depression in such circumstances could well have tipped the scales against survival, and it may be that psychic defences come into operation to protect people in extreme conditions such as these. After the liberation a number of the survivors had severe depressive reactions: 'A strong feeling of guilt for having survived where relatives and friends succumbed was one of the outstanding features'. The grief was sometimes expressed in a prolonged search for the graves of beloved persons, as if it was possible in this way to get them back.

Kaminer and Lavie (1991), in a well-conducted study of concentration-camp survivors showed that those who were most successful in finding a balance between recalling and repressing their memories and emotions were better adjusted than those who continued to be preoccupied by them both waking and sleeping. This finding has been cited by Stroebe *et al.* (1994) in support of their dual process model of bereavement (see pages 59 and 84).

All-in-all, traumatic losses can be seen to disrupt the underlying meanings of our lives. Faced with the shocking trauma of the concentration camps, Viktor Frankl wrote *Man's Search for Meaning* (1946/1963), an inspiring document that has given rise to a corpus of work focused on the ways in which we can create new meanings in our lives, and a way of helping termed 'logotherapy'. We shall return to consider this, and other therapies, in Chapter 14.

11

DETERMINANTS
OF GRIEF – III

Personal vulnerability

Care draws on care, woe comforts woe again,
Sorrow breeds sorrow, one grief brings forth twain.
Michael Drayton, *England's Heroic Epistles*.
Henry Howard, Earl of Surrey to the Lady Geraldine, l. 87

If the magnitude and number of the stressors can influence the magnitude of the reaction to stress, what of the strength or weakness of the stressed person? The global term 'resilience' is sometimes applied as an indication of capacity to cope with stress. Its usage is not altogether satisfactory, since there is always a danger of circularity in the argument – they cannot cope with stress, therefore they lack resilience. The next step is to assume that we have explained the inability to cope with stress by attributing it to lack of resilience whereas all we have done is to define resilience in terms of coping ability. Similar circular arguments arise in the use of the term 'ego-strength' and the obsolete terms 'lack of moral fibre' and 'psychopathic inferiority' – they tended to be used as value judgements to imply a global incapacity to cope with stress. The exercise of such global judgements, which ignore the nature of the stress, the situation in which it occurs, and the events that lead up to it can hardly be justified.

This said, it is useful to recognize the particular characteristics that make a person more or less vulnerable to the stress of bereavement. In doing so we should beware of making value judgements about characteristics that, in other circumstances, may be admired. Only those who lack the capacity to love are completely invulnerable to bereavement.

One indicator of vulnerability is, of course, a prior history of mental illness and this has been shown to be associated with increased risk after bereavement (Nuss and Zubenko, 1992). While such a history may alert us to the existence of vulnerability we need to know much more about the nature of the illness if we are to be of use to the bereaved person. Indeed, the study of the roots of problematic grief has thrown much light on the lasting assumptions and patterns of behaviour that often contribute to the causation and character of mental disorders.

It seems, from this work, that some people are 'grief prone'. What constitutes a 'grief-prone' person? One can answer this question empirically by saying that it is anyone who tends to react strongly to separations, but this does not take us much further. We also need to discover the causes of such excessive reactions. To answer this question we need to look more closely at the roots of our attachments to others.

The early, empirical studies that were described in the first edition of this book identified three types of relationship that were commonly associated with poor outcomes after bereavement, dependent, avoidant and conflicted relationships. More recent research indicates that these problematic relationships are themselves often the result of lasting problematic attachments to parents early in life. These are explained in detail in Parkes' (2006) book *Love and Loss* but will be summarized here.

DEPENDENCY

When one person greatly relies on or has a strong but insecure attachment to another the severance of the relationship is likely to give rise to difficulties. In the Case-note Study bereaved persons who still had grief symptoms at the time of their referral for psychiatric assessment were significantly more likely to describe themselves as 'dependent' on their lost relative than those whose grief was less evident. On the other hand, they were also more likely to describe the dead person as having been 'dependent' on them. This points to the reciprocal aspect of relationships: A is useful to B because he does things for her that she cannot or will not do for herself but B is also useful to A in making him feel useful. In some senses people who lose a relative who relies on them are in a similar position to the mother who loses a child.

The Harvard Study found that intense yearning for the dead person in the early weeks of bereavement predicted prolonged grieving later. A strong association was also found between the intensity of yearning three weeks after bereavement and assessments made by the coders (who listened to our tape-recorded interviews) of the extent to which the person had been 'dependent' on the dead person.

Although both of these studies were carried out many years ago and were confined to young widows and widowers, similar results have been found by Johnson *et al.* (2000) who made use of Prigerson Index of Complicated Grief and a well-founded measure of various aspects of marital relationship. Their scale of marital dependency was quite the most powerful predictor of Prolonged Grief Disorder. Johnson's study also showed that dependency increased the risk of Major Depressive Disorder, General Anxiety Disorder, and suicidal ideas.

At the age of twenty-eight Mrs S., whose severe and lasting reaction to her bereavement was described above (pages 124–5), met a man twenty years older than herself who was separated from his wife. He had been invalided out of the Navy and was having difficulty in settling down in civilian life.

'From the first our relationship was absolutely ideal – everything – was so right – he was so fine.' There was never any need for explanations, he accepted everything. She found she could do lots of things she'd never done before: 'I never feared anything with him. I could do new dishes. It was such a joy. I didn't get that feeling of incompetence . . . I'd absolutely found myself'.

They lived together and she changed her name by deed poll to that of her de facto husband. To her great regret, she did not conceive a child, but despite this and despite the fact that they were very poor Mrs S. described this period as the best in her life.

Mr S. had a 'smoker's cough', which caused some anxiety to his wife, but she did not become seriously alarmed until 1959 when they had been together for eleven years. Then he had a haemorrhage from the lung and had to be admitted to hospital for six weeks. Shortly after returning home he lapsed into a coma. His doctor said that he had had a stroke and that his kidneys and lungs were failing. He was unable to move his limbs but made signs to her with his eyes. That same night the nurse roused her to tell her that he had died.

She was still grieving deeply nine and a half years later and had quite lost confidence in her ability to lead a worthwhile life in a world which she perceived as dangerous and insecure: 'I don't have much faith in the goodness of things', she said.

Parkes' early studies led him to look more closely at the roots of dependency, which are found in the attachments that children make to their mothers early in life. The scientific study of attachment and loss has received much attention thanks to the work of one of John Bowlby's former trainees, the American psychologist, Mary Ainsworth. She initiated a series of studies of the patterns of attachment between infants and parents that arise and become established during the first two years of life. Ainsworth used a standard 'Strange Situation', a room containing a chair and some toys, in which observations could be made through a one-way mirror. Typically the parent was instructed to stay with the child for five minutes, leave the room for two minutes, then return for another five. In essence Ainsworth was studying the effects of a brief period of separation. The behaviour of child and mother during the experiment enabled the observers to distinguish four patterns of reaction to separation, which Ainsworth termed 'patterns of attachment'. Subsequent research demonstrated that these patterns remained consistent throughout later childhood and predicted subsequent relationships and much else. These studies have revolutionized our understanding of child development and provided a scientific basis for attachment theory. The Love and Loss Study (which was described on page 31) made use of people's recollections of their own childhoods to identify the patterns of attachment that they had with their parents and to examine how these influenced subsequent attachments and their reactions when the attachments were interrupted by bereavement (details are given in Appendix 12 and will be summarized here).

Ainsworth had found that the first, and most frequent, pattern was found in infants whose mothers were relaxed, protective when protection was needed, but also sensitively responsive to the child's needs to explore and play. These infants tolerated the standard separation reasonably well and needed no more than a brief cuddle after mother returned to the room. This pattern Ainsworth termed 'Secure Attachment'. In the Love and Loss Study Parkes found that, in both psychiatric and non-psychiatric samples, secure attachments in childhood were associated with significantly less distress after bereavement in adult life than were insecure attachments (see Figure 4 in Appendix 12).

The three other patterns were termed Insecure and were sub-divided into Anxious/Ambivalent, Avoidant, and Disorganized categories.

'Anxious/Ambivalent attachment' is the term used to describe a pattern of anxious, angry, clinging to parents, during the Strange Situation Test (Ainsworth and Wittig, 1969). These infants have mothers who are anxiously over-protective, controlling, and insensitive to the child's need for autonomy. This has the effect of causing the child to increase its demands (Main, 1991).

In the Love and Loss Study people who scored highly on Anxious/Ambivalent attachment in their childhood reacted to bereavement in adult life by prolonged grief and loneliness along with a continued tendency to cling. Parkes had predicted that they would also be found to have highly dependent relationships with their spouses and, although this was sometimes the case, it was much more common for their relationships to be highly conflicted. Two things explained this finding. On the one hand, there were some who had never succeeded in separating themselves from their parents, when things went wrong, instead of turning to their partner, they went home to Mum or Dad. On the other hand, those who did attempt to cling to their partner commonly found that their partner could not tolerate their clinging. It takes two to make a dependent relationship. Either way the relationship with the spouse was spoiled.

As we saw above Mrs S. did find a spouse who reciprocated her clinging. She had been brought up abroad, and had been a sickly child. Perhaps because of this her mother dominated and fussed over her. She grew up nervous and timid, with the conviction that she was incompetent at any practical task. Like many children who are intolerant of separation from their parents, she was unhappy at school and was tutored by her father for much of the time.

Leaving school at seventeen she remained at home with her mother, taking the dogs for a walk and (with great satis-faction) helping to care for a sick child. She left home at twenty, but continued to be supported by her mother. Her principal occupation at this time appears to have been that of professional child minder and babysitter.

Does the evidence available allow us to speculate why Mrs S. should have continued to grieve so intensely and for so long? One possibility that must be considered is the secondary gain to be derived from

mourning. Did she use her grief as an excuse to avoid facing up
to the responsibilities and dangers of a new life? Was she clinging to
a Loss Orientation to avoid the challenge of the Restoration Orientation? It would not be surprising if this were so, for her mother
had long ago made it clear to her that her physical and mental weaknesses justified her attitude of reliance. But perpetual grief is a high
price to pay for self-esteem, particularly as other people are seldom
convinced by it for long. The friends and relatives of a bereaved
person always start by being sympathetic, but their sympathy will
pass if the grief does not abate, and before long the chronic griever
is likely to be left alone, often complaining bitterly that 'nobody
understands'. Mrs S. had a lonely life, because she succeeded in
alienating many of the people with whom she came into contact. Her
grief did not, as far as we know, cause others to support her
although she certainly gave it as the explanation, and, by implication, the justification, for her failure to cope. It may be that it was
more important for her to justify her failure in her own eyes than
in those of other people.

But such secondary gains do not, in our opinion, constitute a
satisfactory explanation for more than a part of the pathological
reaction to bereavement. In talking to patients such as Mrs S. one is
repeatedly impressed by the sheer intensity of feeling that is still
bound up with the lost person; it seems to be the magnitude of the
total psychological investment in the relationship that makes it hard
for the survivor to realize the possibility of continued existence
without them. 'He was everything', said Mrs S., and, by contrast, the
rest of the world was 'nothing'.

Another way of viewing this kind of problem has been put forward
by Horowitz *et al.* (1980). They suggested that current relationships
often hold in check earlier self-images and models of relationships,
which re-emerge when the subject is bereaved. Her marriage enabled
Mrs S. to believe in her own competence, but once the marriage
came to an end her earlier image of herself as incompetent reas-
serted itself.

The important thing about Mrs S.'s relationship with her husband
would appear to be not her reliance on him but her relative competence in this setting. For the first time in her life she felt a useful,
competent person. By her account he seems to have accepted her
uncritically and, perhaps because she no longer felt criticized, she
discovered new competencies she had not believed she possessed.
She literally 'found herself' – that is to say, she found a new and more
satisfactory self-model. But in another sense she relied on her

husband for the maintenance of this new self and when he died she not only grieved deeply but also regressed to the earlier view of herself as incompetent, which had been implanted in her in childhood. All the problems of her childhood and early adult life returned, and her grief, instead of being a gradual relinquishment of one state of organization followed by disorganization and then the establishment of a fresh state, became stuck.

Independent confirmation of these findings comes from two other studies of attachments to parents in childhood. The first, by Vanderwerker *et al.* (2006), showed that among those who suffered prolonged and complicated grief a significant proportion had high scores on a measure of separation anxiety in childhood. Thus, many of them had refused to go to school and showed other evidence of fear of separating from their mother and/or father. Throughout their lives they had remained anxious and intolerant of separations. In The Yale Bereavement Study those who reported high levels of parental control, also reported dependent relationships with their partner or spouse and high scores on the Index of Complicated Grief, which, as we have seen, can be taken as a measure of Prolonged Grief Disorder (Van Doorn *et al.*, 1998).

Bowlby's early work focused on the harmful consequences of separating children from their mothers. In the Love and Loss Study, Parkes found that bereaved psychiatric patients who reported many or prolonged separations from their parents in childhood reported more insecure attachments than others, more vulnerability in childhood, and more lasting distress and clinging after bereavement in adult life. In a similar study, Birtchnell (1975) found that female psychiatric patients who had lost a mother before the age of eleven had high scores on 'dependency'. Many of them had become chronic worriers and vulnerable to depression later in life. Similar findings have been confirmed in four other studies (Barry, Barry, and Lindemann, 1965; Feeney and Noller, 1990; Mireault, Bearor, and Thomas, 2002; Silverman, Johnson, and Prigerson, 2001).

Previous experience of loss can be helpful or harmful depending on the success with which it has been handled. There is some evidence that people can learn from experience how to cope with loss (Bornstein *et al.*, 1973). On the other hand, psychiatrists often see patients who have been referred after a loss that may be quite trivial but has triggered off a reaction that properly belongs to an earlier loss. Thus, Barnes (1988) found that 48 per cent of the 105 patients who sought help from his service for 'Bereaved in Trouble' had unresolved previous losses.

In the Love and Loss Study a comparison was made between those bereaved people with and without psychiatric illness. To the investigator's surprise, this showed similar scores of separation in both groups. It was the combination of separations and insecure attachment that predicted lasting distress after bereavement in the people whose bereavement was followed by psychiatric illness whereas those in the non-psychiatric, control group, whose parental attachments were more secure, seemed to cope well with their loss. Their experience of separations in childhood had left them better prepared for bereavement in adult life.

AVOIDANCE OF GRIEF

As indicated in Chapter 5, the mitigation of the overwhelming emotions of grief by avoidance of the full reality of the loss is a necessary part of 'distancing', of keeping the implications of disaster at a distance so that they can be dealt with little by little. Grief work is the process of learning by which each change resulting from the bereavement is progressively realized (made real) and a fresh set of assumptions about the world established. Nobody can 'take in' at one blow the reality of so massive a psychic event as a major bereavement.

As we have explained, there are many ways of avoiding the reality of loss. There is also wide variation in the duration and degree of avoidance. Some people express their feelings relatively freely and openly after the death of their spouse, whereas others inhibit their feelings but may only succeed in postponing them: few get through the first three months of bereavement without expressing distress at some time.

In the London Study an attempt was made to assess, from self-reports and from observations, the severity of emotional upset during the early months (see Appendix 13). It was found that the widows showed three patterns in the expression of their grief.

One group became severely disturbed within a week of bereavement; they remained disturbed throughout the first and much of the second month; but by the third month most of them were only mildly disturbed. A second group showed moderate emotion within the first week; a week later most of them were severely disturbed, but their grief soon passed and they recovered more rapidly than the others. The remaining widows showed little or no emotion during the first week of bereavement, they succeeded in avoiding their grief;

but by the fourth week most were moderately disturbed and at three months they were all moderately or severely disturbed and certainly more disturbed than either of the other two groups. It seems, then, that the widows in this last group were not able to avoid emotion but only to postpone it. Subsequent to the third month they began to improve, but as the anniversary of the death approached they again became more disturbed than either of the other two groups (see Appendix 13, Figure 10).

Even during the first month this group of widows complained of more physical symptoms than those who had 'broken down' in the first week; headaches, insomnia, palpitations, and various aches and pains were common, and three of them suffered loss of hair (alopecia) in the first month. Thirteen months later the overall outcome was rated as good in only one of these cases and the rest all had psychological symptoms of one kind or another.

Why was it that this group initially failed to react emotionally to their bereavement? Several of the factors that have already been described seemed to play a part. Thus, these widows were, on average, nine years younger than the other widows studied; only one of them was over the age of fifty. Also, their husbands tended to have died suddenly and unexpectedly, these deaths, therefore, were both unexpected and untimely. Moreover, a majority of these widows (five out of seven) had a history of previous psychiatric illness compared with only a third of the other widows. After bereavement it appeared that they had managed to avoid the early expression of their grief in a variety of ways: for instance, they engaged in little formal mourning (only one wore dark clothing) and none visited the grave or crematorium except on the occasion of the funeral. Several deliberately kept themselves extremely busy in order to avoid feelings: 'I had so much to do I was geared at a tremendous tempo'. They found themselves unable to cry although a few expressed a wish to do so: 'I think that if I had a good outburst I might feel better'. Were they clinging to the Restoration Orientation in order to avoid the pains of the Loss Orientation?

Again, the roots of problematic avoidance can be found in the childhood attachments of our bereaved psychiatric patients. The second pattern of insecure attachment described by Ainsworth and Wittig (1969) is Avoidant Attachment. They found that young children who cling to their mothers in the Strange Situation and cry a great deal during separation can be contrasted with others who take little notice when mother leaves and avoid or ignore her when she returns. Despite their apparent indifference, the avoiders have

172

surprisingly high heart rates throughout the period of separation (Sroufe and Waters, 1977). They have mothers who are intolerant of bids for attention or closeness and it seems that they learn how to cope with these mothers by keeping a safe distance from them and inhibiting, or repressing, their natural inclinations to cling and to cry. In later childhood the anxious/ambivalent remained excessively reliant on others, with little confidence in themselves, whereas the avoidant became compulsively self-reliant and distrustful of others.

The Love and Loss Study showed that those who recalled their parents as intolerant of cuddles and other closeness, themselves became intolerant of closeness. They found it difficult to acknowledge and express both affection and grief. This often persisted into adult life, and increased the risk of interpersonal conflict with partners. The fact that these people had difficulty in expressing grief should not be taken to indicate that they did not care. Among 39 people with high scores on Avoidant attachment in childhood 37 agreed that they were now 'filled with regret about something which you did or said, but cannot now put right'.

These studies may explain the personality categories described by Horowitz, Bonanno, and Holen (1993) as either 'repressers' or 'anxious'. Repressers habitually avoid situations that will cause anxiety and deny that they feel anxious even when their bodily reactions suggest the opposite. Anxious people, on the other hand, are oversensitive to danger and tend to seek it out and obsess about it. When faced with major traumas repressers avoid reminders of loss and minimize their distress while anxious people are haunted by intrusive thoughts and are overtly fearful. These people reflect the two main categories of pathological grief, avoidance and chronic grieving that have been described and explained above.

It would be misleading to suggest that avoidant strategies never work. In a world in which independence is prized above attachment avoiders may achieve a great deal and may indeed tolerate minor separations and losses because they have learned to 'stand on my own two feet from an early age'. This said, their independence is often more apparent than real and bereavements may bring home the extent of their need for others.

From the research point of view it is not easy to distinguish avoidance from autonomy. Those who do not seek help may not need it, they are not necessarily denying their needs. Likewise, those who fail to show grief may not be strongly attached or they may already have grieved quietly in anticipation of a loss. But it would be unwise to conclude from this that the repression of grief never gives rise to problems and those who work in clinical settings often become aware of the clinical consequences of avoidance either because the grief erupts unbidden or in distorted or partial form.

AMBIVALENCE

It is clear from what has been said thus far that both anxious/ambivalent (clinging) and avoidant patterns of attachment can give rise to conflicted, or ambivalent relationships in adult life. Ambivalent relationships can also arise for a variety of other reasons. What happens when these relationships are interrupted by death? Much has been written in the psychiatric literature about the effects of the dissolution of relationships in which feelings of love and hate were mixed. Fenichel (1948), for example, regards ambivalence as a cause of intense mourning. In such relationships the wish to drive out or hurt the other is often present and even the death of the other person may, from time to time, be consciously desired. When that death wish is gratified, it is claimed, survivors are left with a burden of guilt that is hard to bear. They may attempt to expiate their guilt by intense and prolonged mourning.

The study of bereaved psychiatric patients provides evidence to suggest that ambivalence does indeed contribute to pathological reactions, but research in this area is not easy. Retrospective distortion, particularly idealization of the dead person, is so common after bereavement that it is hard to know how much reliance to place on reports of the interpersonal relationship with that person. Furthermore, the fact that a woman who has difficulty in relating to her husband during their marriage also has difficulty making fresh relationships after his death is not in itself convincing evidence that one causes the other – both may result from a pre-existing difficulty in making relationships.

Nevertheless, anyone who has worked clinically with bereaved psychiatric patients is likely to be impressed by the frequency with which ambivalence towards the dead person is seen by the patient as an important problem, and Parkes' evidence tends to confirm this impression. We might expect that the death of a parent who has been physically and/or sexually abusive would be a cause for celebration rather than distress, but that is seldom the case. Such deaths re-arouse feelings of anger and bitterness that may have been held at bay for many years. They may even give rise to feelings of guilt if the child was repeatedly told that the abuse was a punishment for his or her faults.

As was shown in the last chapter, guilt is more commonly reported by women who develop a mental illness after bereavement than by unselected widows. Even so, it was reported by half the widows in the (non-psychiatric) London Study, and it is hardly surprising that those who reported the largest amount of guilt over the course of the first year of bereavement also admitted the most quarrelling (see Appendix 8). Furthermore, they reported significantly more physical symptoms, showed more general tension than the other widows, and were less likely to have a comforting sense of their dead husband's presence near at hand. A year after bereavement they tended to be socially isolated, to be seeing little of their friends and relatives, and to be less happy than those whose relationship with their husbands had been satisfactory.

In the Harvard Study widows and widowers who reported two or more areas of conflict in their marriage were more likely to have poor scores on our outcome measures than those who had fewer or no areas of conflict. This was particularly the case when there had been warning of coming bereavement. In such cases the existence of a conflict-free relationship with the dying person seems to have allowed the partner to come to terms with the death. The death of a partner with whom the survivor had been in conflict gave rise to less distress during the first few weeks of bereavement than did unconflicted deaths. The survivors were laughing more and were more likely to be visiting others; on the surface they did not appear to be unduly upset by their bereavement. Yet this apparent recovery was short lived. A year later this same group were showing signs of lasting tension and anxiety and at follow-up two to four years after bereavement, 82 per cent of them were still anxious, 45 per cent depressed and 61 per cent having difficulty in coping with their roles and responsibilities. More remarkable still, nearly two-thirds were yearning for the return of the partner with whom they had been in conflict (compared with less than a third of the rest).

> One person who had great difficulty in coping with con-flicted grief was Mrs Q. She was forty-five when her husband died. They had been married for twenty-six years, but their relationship had never been good. Mrs Q. said that she had always been very fond of her husband but felt that he had never appreciated her or expressed very much real affection. This may have been due to his jealousy of her close relationship with the children but, according to a

friend who knew them both well, her 'terrible temper' may also have contributed. At all events there were frequent quarrels. As Mrs Q. put it, 'We were a passionate couple'.

Several years before his death Mr Q. had a stroke. He had been an energetic, meticulous, and practical man and he found it particularly frustrating to be partially paralysed and dependent on his wife. He became querulous, complaining, and resentful, 'taking it out' on her and criticizing her unjustly. She 'pushed him' to do more and made plans for their future together but 'all he gave me was criticism and abuse'. Most painful of all, he frequently said that he hoped she would have a stroke too. She worried a great deal and complained of headaches that, she feared, might indicate that she had indeed had a stroke.

Mr Q. died unexpectedly one night. When told that it was useless to continue mouth-to-mouth resuscitation since he was dead, Mrs Q. would not believe it: 'I just couldn't take it in'.

Matters were made worse when the will was read and she discovered that most of his property had been left in trust. She became very bitter and resentful, saying, 'What have I done to deserve this?', and spent a great deal of time trying to persuade doctors and lawyers to contest the will on the grounds of her husband's mental incapacity. When they refused to support her in this she became angry with them and, when interviewed, recited a long list of the people who, she felt, had rejected her.

Alongside this deep anger were strong feelings of guilt, but she was unable to explain these and spent much time justifying every aspect of her conduct towards her husband. She was restless and fearful, fidgeting and going from one task to another, unable to concentrate on any.

During the course of the following year she remained agitated and inclined to panic attacks. On several occasions she complained of symptoms resembling those her husband had suffered. She alienated friends and professional helpers by her aggressive attitude and demands for help.

She was given a variety of drugs by a psychiatrist and these helped a little, but thirteen months after bereavement she declared that she was no better than she had been a year previously. 'If only I was an ordinary widow – it's the bitterness and the will – the dreadful words. I go over it again and again thinking there must be a loophole.' Yet, 'If he could come back tomorrow I'd love him just the same'.

One gets the impression that if this woman had been able to write off her husband as a 'bad lot' or as 'mad' it would have been easier for her to forget him. But she was not able to do this. Her protestations served only to raise more doubts in her own mind. In condemning her during life and after death (in his will) her husband threatened to destroy her self-esteem. 'I feel', she said, 'if I ever accepted what he has done to me I'd be destroyed – trampled underfoot.' Her attitude to the world betrayed her fear of just this eventuality, and because hostility provokes hostility she created a situation in which she was, in fact, repeatedly rejected by others. Thus, her anger, instead of enabling her to overcome real external dangers, perpetuated the situation it was intended to relieve.

Why was it so difficult for this woman to allow herself to accept the guilt and loss of self-esteem that threatened to emerge? Some guesses can be made. Perhaps the newly bereaved need every bit of confidence in themselves that they can muster: the sense of internal desolation is so great following a major bereavement that a sense of personal worth must be maintained at all costs. Alternatively, the answer in this case may be found in the long-term attitudes of this woman. She seemed to lack trust in life and to regard others as bad and dangerous people from whom she could get nothing without a fight. If, as I suspect, this was a lifelong attitude, stemming, perhaps, from experiences in her early childhood, then it becomes easier to see why her self-esteem had to be maintained all the time. In such a world who else but yourself can you rely on?

A contrast with Mrs Q. is Mrs D., whose reaction to the death of her 'artistic' husband was described above (pages 118–19). Whereas Mrs Q. had tried to combat the real and implied criticisms her husband had made of her and in so doing had taken arms against the world, Mrs D. accepted her husband's criticisms and attempted to make restitution to him and to tolerate the guilt she freely admitted. Nevertheless, a year after bereavement she was still socially isolated and preoccupied with self-reproachful ideas – 'I feel criminal', she said, 'terribly guilty'.

Further confirmation of the effects of marital dysfunction on the bereaved family comes from a study by Shanfield (1979). Among the predictors of poor outcome were 'skewed decision making, constricted expression of affect, lack of resolution of conflict and insensitivity to feelings'.

HELPLESSNESS

Thus far we have treated the insecure attachment patterns as if they were opposite or mutually exclusive. Yet both clinging and avoidance reflect insecurity of attachment and differ only in the person's strategies for coping with that insecurity. The anxious/ambivalent babies learn to cope with their parents by clinging when close and crying when separated. The avoidant learn to cope with their parents by keeping their distance and inhibiting any temptation to cling or to cry. But what if neither of these strategies is successful?

In Ainsworth's early studies she noted the existence of a group of infants whose behaviour in the Strange Situation was inconsistent, unpredictable and difficult to classify. Sometimes they would run towards their parent when (s)he returned after separation, then stop suddenly and turn back, others would sit rocking back and forth for no apparent reason. She termed them 'Disorganized'. On follow-up these children seemed quite the most disturbed category with a high propensity to emotional and behavioural problems (Carlson, 1998; Lewis et al., 1984).

It was Mary Main, one of Ainsworth's trainees, who carried out further research that threw light on this disorganized attachment pattern (Main and Weston, 1982). She and her colleagues found that the birth of these babies had taken place at a time of high emotional stress on the parents. Often the mother had suffered a major loss or trauma at or around the birth. Her ability to provide consistent parenting to this infant had been severely disrupted. Sometimes her own needs were so great that she was unable to respond to the child's bids for attention or affection, at other times she might become immoderately anxious or 'smother' the child with unwarranted affection. Other research demonstrated that disorganized attachments are sometimes associated with outright rejection and abuse of the infant (Carlson et al., 1989). It seems that the child's sole source of security has become a source of pain and punishment. In all of these cases there is no strategy that this child can discover that will enable him or her to cope effectively with this parent, neither closeness nor distancing will solve the dilemma, and the child is literally helpless.

This state of learned helplessness has been identified by Seligman (1975) as a major cause of the negative assumptions about the world that are now widely recognized as contributing to both anxiety and depression later in life. Fortunately they are not irreversible, as we shall see in Chapter 14.

In the Love and Loss Study, bereaved people with high scores on Disorganized attachment, in the psychiatric groups, were found to react to stress by turning in on themselves rather than seeking help from others. This tendency to 'turn in', which seems to be a measure of helplessness, was, in turn, predictive of anxiety, depression and alcohol abuse following bereavement (Appendix 12, Figure 8). Although many members of the non-psychiatric bereaved control group also reported Disorganized attachments in their childhoods, they differed from the psychiatric patients in adult life in their inclination to turn to others when at the end of their tether and they were much more likely to have someone in whom they could confide. It seems that they had succeeded in revising any negative view of others that might have resulted from their childhood experience. Clearly we are not all doomed by our childhood attachments.

DO THESE FINDINGS EXPLAIN
PROLONGED GRIEF DISORDER (PGD)?

We saw, in Chapter 8, that PGD may come on immediately after bereavement or following a lapse of time. The research reported above suggests that both forms may result from insecure attachment patterns established in childhood. It also indicates that these insecure patterns of attachment commonly give rise to conflicted relationships in adult life and that these, too, may complicate the course of grief. In addition it shows that insecure attachments, which profoundly influence people's sense of security, leave them vulnerable to traumas of all kinds. This may explain why PGD is more frequent after traumatic types of bereavement than it is after other types of loss.

None of these findings conflict with the possibility that genetic factors may also play a part, perhaps by influencing the sensitivity of parts of the brain that are involved in the process of grieving. Some recent research begins to throw light on this possibilitys further details of which are given in Appendix 7 (pages 288–9).

CONCLUSION

It would seem from these studies that two of the most important lessons to be learned in childhood are a reasonable degree of trust in oneself and a reasonable degree of trust in others. Lack of self-confidence may cause people to become over reliant on others and vulnerable to their loss. Lack of trust in others may cause people to form ambivalent or 'controlling' relationships, but they are no less 'dependent' on these others for their security, which may crumble in the face of losses. Finally, those who lack trust in themselves and others are in double jeopardy.

While insecure attachment patterns established in infancy tend to remain stable, those who experience them are not doomed, nor are those whose early attachments were secure guaranteed a stress-free life. In the chapters that follow we shall see how an understanding of attachment patterns throughout our lives helps us to prevent or treat the problems that arise when these attachments are severed by bereavement.

12

DETERMINANTS
OF GRIEF – IV
Social and cultural influences

> If we treat the dead as if they were wholly dead it shows
> want of affection; if we treat them as wholly alive it shows
> want of sense. Neither should be done.
>
> Confucius

The extent to which human behaviour is determined by society has
long been debated. Does a widow grieve because of involuntary psychological forces, emotions that well-up within her and demand
expression, or because she is fulfilling the social role of mourner,
meeting the expectations of a society which sees the expression of
grief as a duty to the dead? Even in societies that encourage religious
freedom and tolerate dissent, many bereaved people want to be told
what they should do or feel. Children are taught how to think and
behave from an early age and, even in adult life, we prepare ourselves
for the occupational and other major roles that we fulfil. Small
wonder that the reaction to a major bereavement is often: 'What
am I supposed to do now? What am I supposed to feel, are the
unaccustomed feelings that I experience normal or do they reflect
some mental illness or deviance?'

Inevitably, bereaved people will take their cue from others, from
their friends and families, and from the professionals, the doctors,
nurses, and funeral directors, each of whom brings their own set
of expectations. The extent of such influences was brought home
by one woman, whose grief and depression had persisted for over
two years following the death of her husband. Somewhat reluc-
tantly she was persuaded to join a local art group. A few weeks
later she remarked, 'You know, they don't think of me as being a
widow'. Clearly her family and friends, when they visited, put on
their 'visiting the poor widow' expression. This behaviour then

aggravated her fear that she would remain a 'broken reed' for the rest of her life.

Many of these influences are enshrined in cultural and religious beliefs. It would take us beyond the confines of this book to describe the wide variety of behaviours and beliefs about death and the similar variety of mourning customs that are found across the globe. These have been outlined in *Death and Bereavement Across Cultures* (edited by Parkes, Laungani, and Young, 1997) and their possible benefits will be considered in Chapter 13. Here we shall focus on the main social and cultural differences that influence the responses of bereaved people within 'developed' countries and the few studies that enable systematic comparisons to be made between these countries and others. The differences include influences on the continuing relationship with the dead as well as influences on the overt expression of grief, and other emotions, within the family, and in the wider community.

RELOCATING THE DEAD

Most religions offer solutions to Confucius' dilemma (quoted above), unseen places where the dead live on, and ways in which the living can communicate with them. The rituals, prayers and declarations of faith that are expected of the living may be offered as a service to the dead, but they often seem more like repetitive attempts to reassure ourselves of their continuing existence. Either way, as we saw in Chapter 4, there is likely to remain a conflict between the urge to search for the dead and the assumption that this is illogical and antisocial. The dead cannot be left out of the equation.

This is most obvious at the funeral. Some see the function of the funeral as a way to dispose of a dead body, others see it as a support to the bereaved, but bereaved people see it as a support to the dead, a chance to say 'Goodbye', and to give gifts in the form of flowers and tributes. The dead are always assumed to be present to some degree.

Most funerals and similar rituals end by indicating a location for the dead, a grave, shrine, columbarium or similar place where bereaved people can visit them, communicate with them and, to some degree, continue to care for them. While such places are a poor substitute for the physical presence of the lost person, they often give comfort and are seen as mitigating some of the pain of separation (Yamamoto *et al.*, 1969).

CULTURAL INFLUENCES ON THE
EXPRESSION OF GRIEF

Gorer concluded from a survey, back in 1965, that 'the majority of contemporary Britons . . . have in effect neither help nor guidance in the crises of misery and loneliness which are likely to occur in every person's life'. He was of the opinion that the decline in formal religious belief and ritual has itself removed an important form of guidance. Since that time, the need to communicate thoughts and feelings at times of stress seems to have become more widely accepted and Walter concluded that: 'The dead live on not only in private memory and experience, but also in conversation among the living. In the absence of ancestor cults and formal religious rites of remembrance, everyday conversation is probably the primary means by which the dead live on in modern society' (1999, p. 82). Be that as it may, there still remain some families where no such conversation takes place.

Support for the view that societies that encourage the expression of grief are likely to have fewer problems following bereavement comes from Burgoine's (1988) comparative study in which she made use of the interview schedule used in the London Study to interview a comparison group of newly bereaved widows in the Bahamas. Bahamian widows, who live in a culture in which overt and public expressions of grief are expected and encouraged, had better health and fewer psychological problems than widows living in London. Similarly a comparison of women in Scotland and the Swaziland, who reported their reactions to the death of a close relative, showed that, although the Swazis showed more initial tearfulness and distress, they were less troubled by feelings of guilt a year later than the Scottish widows (Lovell, Hemmings, and Hill, 1993).

These studies contrast with a report from Norbert Mintz (personal communication) who worked in a mental health clinic serving Navajo Indians in the USA, he found that Navajo regularly 'repress and suppress death and grief'. The names of the dead are no longer mentioned when three days have elapsed after a death and several elderly, traditional, Navajos whom he interviewed, denied recalling the names of their dead parents. He found that 'about one third of all patients attending the mental health clinic had a history of the death of a close person within the past year'. He claims excellent results for psychotherapy aimed at helping these patients to express their grief and says that the results of therapy 'matched or exceeded the improvement in health for all [other] patients'.

Mrs F. was an English woman aged forty-five, and her husband ten years older, when he died suddenly and unexpectedly. He had worked for many years to build up his own business and this had absorbed much of his time and interest. With his wife he had maintained a somewhat distant relationship, but they had never quarrelled. Mrs F. was an intelligent, socially ambitious woman of working-class extraction.

Her husband had died while at work in his garden in South London. Although it was known that he had a heart condition, it was a complete surprise to his wife to find him dead when she returned from shopping. She felt very 'shocked', but experienced no other emotion for three weeks. As an avowed atheist she felt that her beliefs could be of no help to her children or to herself and she found the burial service quite 'horrible'. She had a large number of responsibilities in relation to her husband's business and these kept her fully occupied. She took drugs in order to sleep but, even so, found herself waking early; when this happened she occupied herself writing letters. Constantly restless and irritable, she complained of tension headaches, weakness, and loss of appetite.

Towards the end of the third week she began to tire. She became increasingly anxious and depressed, missed her husband's guidance, and felt fearful of the future. For the first time and to her great annoyance she began to have episodes of uncontrollable crying.

During this time she lived at home with her three children aged seventeen, twelve, and ten. She found herself unable to discuss their father's death with them and her own irritability widened the gap she felt between herself and them. The only relative with whom she had much contact was her mother, but, as Mrs F. said, 'I'm fond of her but she worries about me so much that I'm afraid to tell her anything'.

She remained tense, anxious, and often depressed throughout the year. Her tension headaches continued and she developed chronic indigestion. In order to maintain her standard of living she took over the direction of her husband's business although she hated the work and the responsibility. Her relationship with one of her daughters deteriorated to the point where the daughter, whose standard of school work had dropped off, refused to do anything that her mother suggested. It was this girl's hostile attitude that was blamed for the break-up of an attachment between Mrs F. and a man friend.

Although Mrs F. expressed little need to grieve for her husband, she did grieve intensely for the security of the life she had lost and for the hopes and expectations she could no longer entertain. She gave the impression of engaging in a continual battle to maintain her status and possessions. Although she was now financially very much poorer than she had been before her husband's death, she was quite unable to accept any change in her way of life and seemed to be placing all her hopes on the prospect of remarriage.

It would take too long to discuss all the nuances of this sad situation, but it is worth reiterating, at this point, the four principal factors that seem to explain why Mrs F. avoided the expression of her distress after her husband's death. First, the fact that she had not had a close love relationship with her husband enabled her to pretend that she had nothing to grieve for and that life could go on in much the same way as it had before his death. Second, her view of herself as an intelligent, poised, sophisticated woman, well able to control her destiny, implied that she must suppress any signs of weakness. She hated crying because of the damage such behaviour inflicted upon her own self-image. Third, lacking any religious faith she was unable to take advantage of traditional mourning rituals, which might have given social support to the expression of despair. Finally, she had no close relative with whom she could share her grief and her inability to communicate effectively with her own children served only to increase her sense of helplessness and isolation.

Enough has been said to indicate our agreement with Gorer's hypothesis that the absence of social expectations and rituals facilitating mourning is likely to contribute to the occurrence of problematic reactions to bereavement, although we would not go so far as he does in suggesting that this may be the chief cause of maladaptive behaviour.

FAMILIAL INFLUENCES

Although it is usually assumed that families support their members, the fact that all are bereaved and grieving may make this difficult. In addition there are some families that cope better with bereavement than others. Difficulty in expressing feelings sometimes reflects a family style. 'I've always been brought up to bottle up my feelings', said one widow. Another described how her sister would not let her cry: 'At the funeral she said, "People can hear you". The undertaker told her to leave me alone . . . My sister says, "He's gone and there's an end to it" '.

In a study of the difficulties experienced by 57 adults in Minnesota in giving support to the bereaved (Rosenblatt *et al.*, 1991) many family members reported conflicts with other family members. These concerned lack of support, intrusion, accusations of grieving too little or too much, conflicting perceptions of the dead person, attitudes and behaviour towards the dead person when alive and reassignment of family roles and responsibilities.

A systematic study of family functioning was carried out in Texas by Traylor *et al.* (2003). They used postal questionnaires to study 61 adults who had lost a parent or spouse. Those who scored highly on measures of family cohesion, open communication and the sharing of feelings at 4–5 weeks after bereavement, showed less grief six months later. A similar study, carried out in Australia by Kissane and Bloch (2002), drew much the same conclusions and showed family functioning to be the most consistent predictor of bereavement outcome.

These findings are consistent with the findings on attachment patterns reported in the last chapter. Thus people who have experienced secure attachments in their childhood, tend to form secure and cohesive relationships in adult life and are likely to share thoughts and feelings more easily than those from insecure attachments. These findings have important implications for assessing and reducing bereavement risk.

One might think that the presence of young children in the home would be a godsend to the widow, providing her with roles and rewards she would otherwise lack. This may be true in the long run, but it is also true that the responsibility of providing for the physical and emotional needs of children at a time when, because of her own grief, the widow is least able to do so represents a considerable burden. Thus, in the Love and Loss Study, bereaved people with children under the age of 16 at home had higher scores of Anxiety/Panic and their scores of Grief/Loneliness were no lower than those without children at home. The numerous practical tasks and unfamiliar responsibilities that face the family leader are onerous enough, in addition to the special tasks consequent upon the bereavement itself, including, frequently, the need to earn a living, the widow with

children at home has to continue most of her household and maternal duties, it is not surprising that in this situation she often finds it
hard to cope.

Contrast the ways in which two widows, Mrs G. and Mrs H., dealt
with the problem of children at home.

Mrs G., an immigrant from Poland, aged twenty-seven at
the time of her husband's death, was left with two pre-
school children, Peter, aged two, and a baby, Mary, just a
year old. Mrs G. had herself been sent to an orphanage at
the age of four, when her mother was killed. As a consequence of her own childhood experience she was determined on no account to be separated from her children: 'I
always had the feeling that my mother was the only one who
wanted us', she said. She had been married for five years to a
labourer who had brought her to England where jobs were
easier to obtain. Three years after the marriage he had
developed a tumour, which resulted in severe headaches and
irritability. He was in hospital for seven months before dying
in a coma.

Because he had not worked in Britain for very long and
had failed to stamp his national insurance card, Mrs G. was
not entitled to a widow's pension. Her husband left no
money and she had no job of her own which would have
enabled her to earn a living. Consequently, she was totally
dependent on National Assistance payments. She lived in a
one-room flat in a decayed Victorian house in East London.
Fuel, lighting, food, and clothing for herself and her family
had to come out of the small allowance she received from
the Assistance Board. It is hardly surprising that she was
constantly depressed and anxious about her ability to survive and bring up her children in this situation.

Her family were all abroad and although they paid for her
husband's body to be shipped home for burial, it was clear
that her own financial situation would have been even more
hazardous if she had decided to return home. During the
first three weeks of bereavement she was so preoccupied
with practical matters that she had little time to grieve.
Towards the end of the first month, however, she became
increasingly depressed and slept badly. Having little appetite
she economized by living mainly on tea and giving the food
to the children. She was one and a half stones under weight

187

when seen six weeks after bereavement and was suffering fits of giddiness, dyspepsia, and loss of hair. Her GP prescribed a vitamin mixture but she was still in a very similar state five months later and had developed a skin condition, which was probably caused by malnutrition. In the course of the year she had a host of problems: threats of eviction, sickness in the children, misunderstandings with the Assistance Board, and, greatest danger of all, sickness in herself. Parkes writes, 'As a thoroughly partial investigator I found myself persuading landlords, jogging the Assistance Board, and consulting doctors on her behalf, and it was in this capacity that I discovered that she was far from helpless, and indeed talented in the arts of persuasion. The children were always clean, happy, and well looked after'.

Nine months after her husband's death Mrs G. spent a month with her family in Poland and returned looking better nourished and with none of the physical symptoms that had previously given rise to anxiety. When interviewed four months later it was clear that she was still preoccupied with her many problems; she had episodes of depression – and confined her attention solely to her children. She had only one friend and said that she had talked with no adult for over a week before the interview. She was planning to send the children to a day nursery school as soon as they were old enough, and said that she would then find herself a job. She had no intention of remarrying; nobody else could possibly match up to her husband; and he, being rather jealous, had made her promise, on his deathbed, never to take another husband.

Parkes' work took him overseas for a year at this point and when he returned Mrs G. had left her flat and he was unable to trace her whereabouts. He guesses that she continued to make ends meet and would be very surprised if, after all she had been through, she did not continue to provide the love and most of the material things that her children needed.

The situation of Mrs H. was similar in many respects to that of Mrs G. She too was an immigrant with no relatives in Britain; she was the same age as Mrs G., and her husband had also died from cancer. Like Mrs G., she was left with young children and had to choose whether to stay at home and look after them or to separate from them. She too lived in a decayed part of London and had difficulty in making ends meet. She had the same matter-of-fact approach to life and was not lacking in intelligence.

Here the resemblance ends. Mrs H. had been brought up in a township in South Africa. Her father had died when she was two years old and her mother had left her in the care of her aunt for long periods while she travelled about the country selling rugs. Despite these periods of separation Mrs H. had a happy childhood. She developed close ties to her mother and her aunt and had numerous friends. At school she was an academic success and on leaving at the age of fifteen she spent a year at home and then took a job as a primary school teacher until her marriage two years later.

She accompanied her husband to England and they lived in a part of London where many of their childhood friends had come to live. Her husband worked in an office while taking evening classes with the aim of becoming a dental mechanic. He had been working hard for this qualification for two years when he developed a lump on his left leg, which was found to be malignant. The disease progressed gradually, but Mrs H. succeeded in nursing her husband at home until three weeks before his death. At this point he became confused and incontinent and it was clear that she could cope no longer. She was well prepared for his death but she still grieved severely over the first three weeks. She found herself preoccupied with her husband's memory and commonly misidentified people around her as being her husband.

Mrs H. was left with four children ranging in age from nine to two. During her husband's last illness they had been a great burden to her and after his death she decided that the best plan was to find homes for them for long enough to enable her to learn a trade; she could then return to her home town with every prospect of earning a good living. She sent the two eldest children to live with her mother in Africa, and the two youngest, aged four and two, were admitted to a children's home, which was close enough for her to visit weekly.

It took six weeks to find places for the children but once her plans were made her anxiety about them and her grief diminished. She had numerous friends living in the same house and shared a communal kitchen. Also, she wrote weekly letters to her mother and her aunt and visited the children's home where she was relieved to find her youngest children happy and very fond of the house mother. She took a job as a cook while taking evening classes as well. The work was hard and she suffered from insomnia and occasional troublesome headaches. In all other respects, however, she remained very well and when seen thirteen months after bereavement she was well and happy. She estimated that she had talked with twenty-four friends and one relative in the course of the previous week but, although she had gone out with men, she did not think she would remarry until she had finished her studies. She passed her first annual examination easily and expressed surprise and some pride at her own competence. It was this sense of increased competence, as much as anything else, that made her reluctant to remarry at once.

These two cases illustrate rather well the difference that dependent children can make to the life of a widow. On the one hand we have Mrs G., courageously struggling to retain her children at great cost to herself. Her adjustment could not be described as anything but tenuous, she had almost no social life, and her physical health was constantly threatened but her children were obviously thriving. Mrs H., on the other hand, was healthy and more successful than she had ever been before. It is not possible to determine the cost of her success, however, since we know little of the effect upon her young children of three years of separation from their mother. The observations of Bowlby and others indicate that such separations are potentially pathogenic, but much depends upon circumstances and upon the extent to which a satisfactory substitute for the missing mother can be found.

SOCIAL NETWORKS

The wider **social networks** that surround the bereaved person may be particularly influential in the case of the widow, when they may or may not provide her with support, with new roles, and with a start in her new 'career' as a widow. Systematic study of the effectiveness of social support is complicated by the fact that distressed people may attract more social support than those who are less upset, and the presence of other people may increase loneliness rather than reducing it. This may explain why several studies show negative correlations between social support and distress (Stroebe and Schut, 2001; Zettel and Rook, 2004). There can be no substitute for a loved person.

In the Love and Loss Study both living alone and lack of social support were associated with increased grief and loneliness among the bereaved psychiatric patients, and this influence was greatest in the older age group (Appendix 12, Figure 9). Ninety per cent of bereaved people in the control group (who did not seek psychiatric help), answered 'Yes' to the question 'Do you have anyone in whom you can confide your inmost thoughts and feelings?' compared with only 55 per cent of those who sought psychiatric help. These findings confirm the value of social support from adults in whom the bereaved person can confide.

POVERTY AND DEPRIVATION

Economic factors are seldom a major problem in wealthy communities but they can be very important in poor communities. Thus Ide *et al.* (1992), comparing 64 Anglo-American widows with 53 Mexican-American widows at six month intervals after the death of their husbands found that the Mexican Americans were poorer and less educated than the Anglo Americans, they also suffered worse health after bereavement.

While some poor families have a cohesiveness that may compensate for some of the stresses of life, this is not necessarily so. A comparison of 50 bereaved black Caribbeans living in the UK and 50 bereaved white people showed significantly more clinical depression and anxiety in the black group. Further analysis indicated that the most powerful contributing factors were housing problems and legal issues (Koffman *et al.*, 2005). By contrast, the high rate of PGD in African Americans in the USA seems to be more closely linked to an increased incidence of traumatic deaths (page 179) and those black communities who remain in the Caribbean have lower rates of long-term distress after bereavement than white communities, as we saw in Burgoine's study (page 183).

CONCLUSIONS

The last four chapters will have provided readers with a great deal of information about the many factors that explain why some people cope well with bereavement while others have lasting difficulties. They will have dispelled any idea that there is a single cause for problematic bereavements. This, of course, means that we are unlikely to find a single solution to the problems that arise. There is no one form of counselling or therapy that is likely to provide a magical solution to complicated grief.

In the chapters that follow we shall see how each of the major risk factors carries with it a different set of problems and each problem had different implications for prevention or cure.

13

HELPING THE BEREAVED – I

Bereavement support: History and evaluation

Your logic, my friend, is perfect,
Your moral most drearily true;
But, since the earth clashed on her coffin,
I keep hearing that, and not you.

Console if you will, I can bear it;
'Tis a well-meant alms of breath;
But not all the preaching since Adam
Has made death other than Death.
James Russell Lowell (1819–91)
After the Burial

If bereavement can have detrimental effects upon physical and mental health, what can be done to prevent these effects from occurring and by whom should this help be given? A wide range of services for bereaved people have been developed over the years but their quality varies greatly and we must look to research to decide between them. A large number of systematic studies of the outcome of bereavement interventions have now been carried out and we no longer need to start from scratch in our attempts to provide bereavement services. Unfortunately the sheer number of studies make it impractical to review them all here.

Currier, Neimeyer, and Berman (2008) report the result of a meta-analysis that lumped together the results of 61 outcome studies, all of which met reasonable scientific standards. The results of these studies, which are outlined in Appendix 14, have disappointed any expectation that we may have had that all, or even most, bereaved people need or will benefit from the general run of bereavement services. Other meta-analyses have been carried out by several other reliable researchers with similar results (Forte *et al.*, 2004; Schut *et al.*, 2001), yet this flies in the face of the feedback that is regularly received from the bereaved recipients of services, who regularly report their improvement over time and their satisfaction with the help they have been given. This has encouraged service providers to disregard research that contradicts this feedback. However, grief does abate over time in most cases, even without help from outside the family, and what people like is not necessarily what they need. Even help that is needed in the early stages of bereavement may do more harm than good if it is continued for too long.

The good news is that Currier *et al.* found significant benefits from interventions offered to people with symptoms of psychiatric disorder (e.g. Prolonged Grief Disorder, Major Depression and Anxiety/ Panic Disorder) or to others 'manifesting problems adapting to loss or with clinically significant difficulties' (e.g. loss-related intrusions, anxiety and guilt feelings). These benefits were apparent immediately after the intervention and on follow-up. Also beneficial, but only in the short term, were interventions offered to people selected on the basis of risk assessment. As a general rule most bereaved people find that grief and its associated 'symptoms' improve with time and the effect of interventions aimed at high-risk groups have the effect of bringing forward an improvement that would eventually have taken place sooner or later. There were no significant differences between benefits of group interventions, individual interventions or family interventions, nor was gender, age, the relationship to the deceased (e.g. spouse, parent or child), or mode of death (e.g. violent or unexpected) associated with special benefit.

It seems that problems in adapting to bereavement, and the various manifestations of severe and lasting distress, are the risk factors that now deserve closer attention if we are to prevent or minimize the impact of the psychological complications of bereavement. As to the other determinants of outcome outlined in previous chapters, these may not have given rise to effective treatments in the past, perhaps because of the fallacious assumption that a single model of bereavement support is appropriate for all; but they remain import- ant indicators of the underlying causes of problems in adaptation to loss and the psychiatric disorders that arise following bereavement.

There is, of course, a danger that such block-buster research methods will blur the distinction between individual interventions. A lack of overall benefit across studies might mean that none of them had any effect *or* that the benefits conferred by some interventions were cancelled out by the harm done by others. Indeed it is quite possible that the same intervention may do good to one person and harm to another or good in some circumstances after the bereavement and harm in others.

CAN BEREAVEMENT SERVICES DO HARM?

Possible harmful effects of bereavement intervention have been claimed in over a third of cases (Fortner, 1999; Neimeyer, 2000). If, as we have seen, the overall influence is zero, it follows that a similar third must benefit from the intervention. Clearly it is important to discover why some do well and some badly. Although Fortner and Neimeyer's statistical method has been challenged (Larson and Hoyt, 2007), and many researchers agree that a substantial minority of bereaved persons does benefit from intervention, few have paid serious attention to those who may be harmed.

To answer this type of question more detailed examination of particular studies is needed. This has been carried out by Schut *et al.* (2001) who concluded, 'The more complicated the grief process . . . the better the chances of intervention leading to positive results'. This unexpected finding implies that most people will come through bereavement without the need for specialist help and that specialist help should be reserved for the minority who have complex problems. It also challenges us to question the one-size-fits-all approach to bereavement support. Complex problems are unlikely to respond to simple solutions.

If bereaved people with complex problems benefit from special help what of those whose bereavement is relatively uncomplicated? The statistics imply that referral for counselling or other interventions may do more harm than good to them. Why should this be? Possible explanations include:

1   The intervention may interfere with the support given by family and friends, whose love and understanding may be of more value to bereaved people than that of outsiders, and who may back off when faced with the 'experts'. This said, those who are truly 'expert' in the care of bereaved people will foster support from the family and either, when appropriate, alert them to the seriousness of the situation, or reassure them when it is not. The attribution of a psychiatric diagnosis is more likely to result in an increase in family support than a decrease.

2   By treating people with uncomplicated bereavements as fragile, sick, or damaged, (as 'victims') we may encourage them to see

themselves as damaged and encourage their families to think of them as damaged. Mourning can then become a sick identity, an excuse to retire from previous and emerging responsibilities and challenges. This is sometimes termed 'medicalization' of grief, but it can be encouraged by non-medical persons just as easily as doctors. In fact enthusiastic volunteers may, by their very sympathy and pity for the bereaved people whom they want to help, fan the flames of self-pity that are a natural response to any shattering life event. Doctors, on the other hand, tend to be more tough minded, reserving a psychiatric diagnosis for the minority who are genuinely in need of help from outside the family. In like vein, support groups may foster a powerful group identity that is difficult to relinquish. Loyalty to the group may make it difficult for people to leave the group and move on. Some may even find satisfaction in their new role as a 'mourner' or 'victim'.

3   Anger, which, as we have seen, is a frequent response to losses of all kinds, may be channelled into destructive revenge seeking by counsellors who fail to recognize the danger and collude out of sympathy for their client. Splits within the family may then occur removing the most important source of support to the bereaved. Likewise 'support' groups may turn into 'grumble groups' or 'pity parties' in which leadership roles are taken by the most aggrieved members. This does not contradict the possibility that anger may also be justified and channelled in worthwhile directions.

4   The reader will recall that, according to the dual process model (see page 59), most bereaved people oscillate between the backward-looking Loss Orientation of the pang of grief and the forward-looking Restoration Orientation. Problems arise if either one of these orientations predominates. That being so it seems likely that interventions with the sole aim of facilitating one but not the other orientation will be of limited value and may indeed be harmful to some. In the past, bereavement support has emphasized the importance of helping people to express their grief, but an exclusive focus on the Loss Orientation will not help people who are already preoccupied with grief, indeed it may magnify the problem. Likewise, cognitive interventions aimed at facilitating the Restoration Orientation may not help those whose grief is delayed or inhibited, and they may do harm by colluding with the person's attempts to avoid grief.

5   Interventions that have been developed for bereaved people of one culture, religion, gender, age, or type of bereavement, may be inappropriate and even harmful when applied to others. For instance, Murphy *et al.* (1999) found that a service for parents who had lost a child by violence benefited women who had previously expressed high levels of distress, but the same treatment given to men increased their distress. We need to recognize and respect the different coping strategies and nurturant attachments of men and women.

Does that mean we should all pack up and go home? Certainly not, there is no reason to believe that we cannot help bereaved people, provided that we are clear in our minds about these dangers.

Bereaved people are faced with many possible sources of help, these include:

- their families;
- their friends and acquaintances;
- specialist or non-specialist help;

   - individual or group help;
   - from professionals or volunteers;
   - medical or non-medical;
   - religious or secular;

- face to face or via telephone or other media of communication.

WHAT HELPS? SOME GENERAL CONSIDERATIONS

The first source of help for most of us is, or should be, our family; that is, after all, what families are for. The very attachments that keep a family together usually become stronger at times of trouble and members draw together to support each other. As we saw in Chapter 4, the function of the family has evolved to increase the security, not only of the children, but of all its members. Outsiders, however good our intentions or sophisticated our knowledge, seldom know or understand a family as well as its members, and it is a good policy to start with the assumption that outsiders are not much needed. This said, there are, as we saw in the last chapter, some circumstances in which an entire family is overwhelmed, there are some families that are dysfunctional, and some individuals whose attachments to their families make them less not more secure. They may need help from outside the family. But even then, we should not assume that the family can or should be ignored. A little help, or the passage of time, may enable family function to be restored. We return to consider family-focused therapy in the next chapter.

After the family, friends are likely to be the next source of support. We cannot choose our families but we can our friends. Again we saw in the last chapter how important social supports can be, but we also saw that some people are socially isolated and others feel unsupported by those they had regarded as friends. Bereavement can be a test of friendship, and at such times bereaved people often say, 'You find out who your friends are'. By this, they mean that there are some friends who stay close and can be relied upon to be there when needed while others back off.

Most doctors and clergy would regard it as one of their roles to give support and advice to the dying and the bereaved, and, while they cannot be regarded as therapists, they are well placed to provide factual information and psychological first aid. So too are the nurses, social workers and other professional carers who are in attendance at times of death and bereavement. Unfortunately few are adequately trained in these skills.

Here we examine the kind of help that can be given by families, friends, and caring professionals and volunteers and in Chapter 14 the special problems that require special types of intervention. The fact that most bereaved people, with uncomplicated bereavements, will eventually come through without the help of non-specialists, does not mean that volunteers have nothing to offer. Appropriate support before and after bereavement is usually much appreciated and enables them to spot the minority of bereaved people for whom special help may be needed.

PREPARING FOR BEREAVEMENT

From the data presented in the last chapter it would seem that a timely death is less likely to upset the psychological adjustment of those who survive than an untimely one. This may be because, when death is considered timely, the bereaved person is better prepared psychologically than when death is untimely. But how can one prepare for bereavement?

Even when a death occurs long before the age when it would normally be expected to occur there is usually some advance warning.

This may take the form of an event, such as an attack of coronary ischaemia or a stroke, which increases the probability of premature death but gives no definite indication when it may occur; or it may comprise a progressive illness such as an inoperable cancer, which provides a definite expectation of death within a certain time span. It is, of course, excessively rare for anyone to know precisely the hour of their death and the predictions of doctors and nurses are demonstrably unreliable (Glare *et al.*, 2003; Parkes, 1972a).

The difference between these two types of warning is that while cancers allow plans to be made the outcome of coronary attacks and strokes is so uncertain that only contingency plans are possible. The woman whose husband has had a single coronary attack can only say, 'If he has another attack he may die'. In such circumstances two plans are necessary, a plan for survival and a plan for demise. In practice we suspect that it is very hard to make adequate psychological preparation in such uncertain circumstances and unless the husband insists on facing up to the danger himself and talking it through with his wife, she is likely to brush the whole thing aside and act, as most of us do, on the assumption that there is no need to prepare for a future that is uncertain and about which she would prefer not to think – we don't look forward to the things we don't look forward to.

Even when the death is confidently predicted by medical authorities there is, as was shown in Chapter 5, a tendency to disbelieve, ignore, or distort the truth. The extent to which this is done often depends on the extent to which it is thought necessary to hide the true situation from the dying patient, and it is unusual for husband and wife to talk openly to each other about this subject. The tendency is for the healthy relative to hide the truth in an attempt to protect the dying person. That this pretence seldom succeeds completely was shown by Hinton in his 1967 study of dying patients. Hinton visited patients in a general hospital at intervals throughout the course of their illness and took particular note of the comments they made about their expectation of recovery. Some were known to have fatal illnesses, others did not have such illnesses. His experience led him to two important conclusions. One was that, regardless of what they had been told, the majority of terminally-ill patients realized that they were going to die at some time before the end. The other was that the opportunity to talk about such disturbing possibilities was viewed very positively by the patients. Far from stirring up discontent on the ward by upsetting the patients with his questions, Hinton found that most patients were glad to discuss their fears with a sympathetic listener who did not insist upon jollying them along.

This study is not isolated. Several other investigations have been carried out in this field and they tend to confirm the overall finding that nurses, doctors, and relatives often have great difficulty in communicating with dying patients. Their reticence reflects their own inability to cope with the whole concept of death: 'What can one say?'

One of the consequences of this is the tendency to continue active treatment, including aggressive methods, long after they can reasonably be expected to relieve distress and prolong life. That this can impact on caregivers before and after bereavement as well as causing unnecessary suffering to patients has been amply demonstrated in a recent study by Wright *et al.* (2008). They found that physicians who communicated with their patients and families about the prospect of death did not trigger severe depression. These physicians were less likely to engage in aggressive treatments and patients experienced a better quality of their remaining life as did their caregivers. This continued, in the caregivers, after the patient's death and was associated with lower rates of Major Depressive Disorder.

During recent years hospices and similar palliative care services have been set up all over the world in which importance is attached to the physical, psychological, social, and spiritual needs of dying patients and their families. The aim is to provide a setting, either at home or in a special in-patient unit, in which it is 'safe' to die. This may sound like a paradox, but experience does seem to show that it is often possible to help patients and their relatives towards a calm acceptance of the true situation.

Research into the benefits of these types of care for bereaved families is complicated by possible selection bias. If referral to a hospice results from distressing symptoms in the patient or high levels of anxiety in the family, these circumstances may increase the probability of complicated bereavements and make it less likely that a simple comparison between hospice and non-hospice bereaved will find fewer problems in the hospice group. On the other hand those who opt for a hospice may be better adjusted than those who take no such initiative, in which case a better outcome might be expected.

One study that attempted to overcome this bias was a comparison of 29 former caregivers of patients who had died within 3 days of referral, who could not have been expected to benefit much from the support they received, with 149 caregivers of those who had survived for longer periods. This showed significantly less Major Depressive Disorder, six months after bereavement, in the group who received more sustained support (Bradley *et al.*, 2004). But this, too, may be fallacious if the better adjusted are more likely to plan ahead.

It is less a question of 'Should the doctor tell?' than of 'How much should the doctor tell? When should he tell it? And how should he tell it?' Patients on admission are often frightened and depressed. They have come through a long and sometimes painful illness and have seen themselves deteriorating in health despite the drastic operations and treatments to which they have been subjected. In such a situation the long-suspected truth can come as a relief: 'At last I know where I stand'. But only sometimes. There are other patients who, when they ask for the truth, are desperately asking for reassurance: 'It's not cancer, is it, doctor? If I thought it was cancer I'd kill myself'. Clearly, in a case like this, we need first to find out what this person means by the word 'Cancer' for it is very likely that their image of the condition bears little resemblance to the illness they face.

In trying to help patients through their terminal illness, doctors and nurses are taking part in a process of psychological transition that requires time, empathy, and trust. A ward in which the spiritual and psychological resources of the medical staff enable them to accept death as a meaningful event, and in which the psychological as well as the physical needs of the patients are the central concern of everyone, can enable many patients, in time, to talk about the various fears and griefs that trouble them.

A busy intensive care unit is not always a good place in which to die, because the staff are preoccupied with heroic efforts to save life and the patient who cannot be saved is a failure for all. If, however, the inevitable progression of a disease can be accepted, a hospital ward can become a peaceful place. In such a setting the disease is seen as one factor among many that influence the patient's peace of mind; attention is paid to the social climate of the ward, and physical and drug treatment is directed towards the relief of distressing symptoms. Measures for the prolongation of life are considered alongside the quality of the life that remains and in full awareness that fruitless attempts to prolong life can result in very bitter endings.

Here patients soon discover that the staff want to know them as people. 'The lung cancer in the end bed' has become 'Chris Jones who is depressed because his wife is on her own at home', and nurses know that they can sit and talk to patients without being told to get on with their work – talking to patients is work.

The wife who has shared her thoughts and plans with her dying husband and with others, who has begun to anticipate what life without him will be like, and who has made adequate preparation for managing practical affairs, is in a far better position to cope with bereavement than one who has pretended that her husband is going to survive until it is too late for her to prepare for anything. When both know that there are others around who will help her through the period of adjustment, it is easier for them to face the situation and, having faced it, to enjoy what remains of their time together.

The opportunity to care for the person before and at the time of death is of special importance when it is a child who is dying. Wijngaards-de Meij *et al.* (2008) followed up 219 couples over the first 20 months after the death of a child. Those parents who had expected the death, said farewell to the child, been present at the time of death, and spent time with the body of the child at home, suffered less lasting and severe grief than those who had been unprepared and lacked these opportunities.

Not that anticipatory grieving can ever be complete. No matter how well people may think they have prepared themselves for bereavement there are still things that cannot be anticipated. Partly this results from the similarity between a plan and a wish. The truth of this can be seen in our reluctance to buy a coffin before death has occurred. The very act would seem to be a dangerous thing to do.

Consideration was given on page 86 to the distinction between grief work and worry work and there is no need to repeat the argument here. Suffice it to say that, if they are given time and support from those around, it is often possible for dying patients and their relatives to 'worry' to good effect. When the death occurs it is then seen as one more step in a process of psychosocial transition which all are prepared for and in which all the family have a share.

THE IMPACT OF BEREAVEMENT

Let us turn now to the newly bereaved person and consider what forms of help she needs at this time. (Because most research has been with widows we shall refer to the bereaved person as a woman, but much of what is said here could apply equally to widowers, and to men and women after other types of bereavement.) If she is in a dazed or numbed condition the bereaved person is likely to need help with the simplest decisions. She also needs time: time in which to sit back and begin to organize her ideas, to take in what has happened. The first task of close relatives and friends, therefore, is to help her with what must be done – e.g. the final visit to the hospital, the notification of other relatives – and then to bring her home and to look after her.

When she is ready to do so they should assist with the registration of the death and the funeral arrangements. They may need to protect a widow from the well-meaning attention of neighbours and friends, but even at this time they should not be too possessive – the widow needs her friends and it is important not to alienate them. It is a good idea to draw in friends and neighbours by asking for their help with practical matters while waiting until the initial shock of bereavement has passed before encouraging the widow to accept the sympathy and assistance that they want to offer. This advice need not contradict the more general advice to do nothing that will inhibit the expression of appropriate grief, but it is particularly hard during the first few hours for those around to 'tune in' to the real psychological needs of the widow. Until she has 'taken in' the fact of her bereavement she seems, in the phase of numbness or shock, to be confused and disorganized. She has no plans that will enable her to cope with the situation and needs time and protection from intruders.

It was to protect them from excessive distress that Benjamin Rush, the famous American physician and signatory of the Declaration of Independence, wrote: 'Persons afflicted with grief should be carried from the room in which their relatives have died, nor should they ever see their bodies afterwards. They should by no means be permitted to follow them to the grave'. Few would agree that such overprotection is appropriate today; nor would we accept the advisability of prescribing Dr Rush's panacea for grief – 'liberal doses of opium'. But his statement does serve to emphasize the peculiar helplessness of the bereaved during the first day or so of a major bereavement. A little help given at this time is often recalled with special gratitude later.

One setting in which much can be done to minimize the impact of bereavement is the Emergency Room. Here medical and nursing staff have the unpleasant duty to inform families of sudden and unexpected death. If they do this in a sensitive and supportive way, taking time and trouble to make sure that people are not kept waiting for information and that the experience is as untraumatic as possible, they will have done much to mitigate the horror that can cause intrusive post-traumatic memories. An evaluation of the introduction of a special programme aimed at improving such care came up with very positive results (Adamowski *et al.*, 1993).

The death of a child, as we have seen, is likely to be very hard for parents to tolerate and particular care is needed when breaking the news. Even an abortion or termination of pregnancy is traumatic for some, but not all, mothers. In each case we need to take the time and trouble to discover how the parent feels before offering advice.

THE RITUALS OF MOURNING

In the United States funeral directors play a very much larger role in counselling the bereaved than they do in the United Kingdom. Most people take out life insurance to pay for their funeral and funeral directors normally attempt to assess the bereaved person's financial position before deciding what type of funeral to recommend. They are thus in a good position to advise the bereaved on financial matters. Several books have been written criticizing the activities of unscrupulous American funeral directors who are said to take advantage of their position to persuade bereaved people to pay large sums of money for unnecessarily elaborate funerals. Expensive padded coffins, embalmment, special clothing, and facial restoration by means of cosmetics, have been lampooned in Evelyn Waugh's (1948) novel *The Loved One*, and more seriously criticized by Jessica Mitford (1963) and Leroy Bowman (1959). Much of this expenditure is attributable to the tradition of displaying the corpse for inspection in an elegantly furnished 'funeral parlour' prior to burial.

As a result of these criticisms a movement towards simpler funerals with closed coffins sprang up, led by the Continental Association of Funeral and Memorial Societies. This has now been superseded by the Funeral Consumer's Association (www.funerals.org).

What is the cash value of a funeral? This is a question easier to ask than to answer. The funeral is usually regarded as a last gift to the dead and there is no doubt that many of those who come to 'pay their respects' are treating the dead person as if they were still alive and about to leave on a journey – they come in order to say, 'Goodbye'.

The funeral reformers point out the irrational component in such attitudes; they emphasize the fruitlessness of attempting to make a corpse look 'life-like' or to produce an illusion of sleep when death has nothing to do with sleep. By their matter-of-fact approach they make funeral directors look like tricksters and the public like gullible fools.

VIEWING THE DEAD

But even if we believe that the rituals attending bereavement can have no value to the dead, may they not have a value to the living? It has been repeatedly shown in previous chapters that physical death and social death do not take place simultaneously. Grief is a process of realization, of 'making real' the fact of loss. This process takes time and, while it can be assisted, anything that forces reality-testing in the early period of bereavement is likely to give rise to difficulties. Panic reactions, the massive shutting off of emotion, and/or the repetitious reliving of the traumatic experiences seem to be common consequences of premature confrontation. A painful death or a mutilated or distorted corpse may haunt the memory of the griever and shut out happier memories of the dead person, it may even give rise to PTSD. 'I keep seeing his mutilated face – as if someone suddenly puts a slide on', said one woman after the death of her brother in a car smash. But this memory was somewhat mitigated by the memory of the funeral, which was 'awfully pretty'. She carried photographs of the cortege in her handbag, which she showed to others as if to demonstrate how she had tried to repair the damage.

In the London Study eight widows spoke of viewing the body after bereavement. Three were horrified by what they saw and the horror remained with them as an unpleasant memory; four, on the other hand, were pleased and referred to the peaceful appearance of the corpse, which seemed to imply that their spouse was at rest. 'He looked just like a little boy. I felt he'd died in a contented frame of mind.' 'I like to think of him like that. He was smiling and looked so peaceful. You could see he was all right. The last few weeks he was suffering and he'd showed it – but afterwards . . . .'

Unlike those in London, a much larger proportion of the Boston widows and widowers had viewed the body of their spouse. Despite the efforts of the funeral directors feelings were mixed, and half the women and a quarter of the men were upset by the experience. Nevertheless there was very little criticism of the work of the funeral directors and most of the widows and widowers seemed grateful for the help they had been given At such times it is important to avoid horrific surprises and bereaved people should be told what to expect when viewing or touching the dead. Warning someone that, 'He'll feel very cold', will give people permission to touch but prevent the shock of kissing a spouse who, in life, was always warm.

SHOULD MOTHERS BE ENCOURAGED TO
SEE AND HOLD THEIR DEAD BABY?

Much has been written about the importance for a mother whose baby has died to see, touch and hold their dead baby. Indeed some see this as an issue of women's rights and pour scorn on the (male) doctors who seek to prevent them (Robinson, Baker, and Nackerud, 1999). As a result most mothers are now advised to hold their baby and a photograph is taken and placed in the case notes in case any mother who does not wish to see the baby should change her mind. A study in Sweden showed that 59 per cent of nurses tried to persuade or in other ways influence the parents to change their mind, and 60 per cent were of the opinion that the parents mourning process is always facilitated when they touch or hold their dead baby.

The evidence from research is less convincing. Indeed, two follow-up studies have shown that mothers who opt not to see their dead baby tend to become less depressed and to have a better overall outcome than mothers who see and hold their dead baby (Brabin, 2004; Hughes *et al.*, 2002). This finding raises an important question. Is it possible to become firmly attached to someone you have never seen or held? In many animal species there is good evidence that mothers do not become attached to their babies until they have seen and smelled them after the birth. Farmers know that, if a cow loses a calf it will accept an alternative only if the adoptive calf has been smeared with the scent of the dead one. In human beings, difficulties in attachment may arise if mothers are separated from their new born babies at birth (Reynolds, 2004).

Human beings are more complicated than other species and our capacity for imagining and relating to our unborn baby is greater. The advent of scans have now made it possible for mothers to 'see' their babies before birth and even without this help many mothers have a close relationship with their unborn child. Consequently it seems that some mothers do become firmly attached and resent any suggestion that they should not see or hold their dead baby. On the other hand, there are some mothers whose experience of seeing a dead baby is so traumatic that it can give rise to PTSD. It would seem that the approach most likely to succeed is one that respects the mother's wishes and does not push her either to see and hold or to avoid the dead baby. If the mother should opt to see the baby, it is important that she be warned in advance of any deformity or other potentially shocking circumstance.

FUNERALS – ORDEAL OR THERAPY?

The funeral itself is also likely to give rise to both positive and negative feelings. It is, of course, distressing to most bereaved people, but the overall attitude among about half the London widows and two-thirds of the Boston widows was favourable. 'It was such a lovely service.' 'I still like to think of the words.' 'Fifty of his workmates came; it was an ordeal, but I was very proud – they respected him.' 'It makes you feel you're not alone . . . You've got something to hang on to.' These remarks seem to imply that it is the beliefs expressed in the funeral service and the sense of social support that are viewed positively.

In contrast, negative or mixed feelings were expressed by some people who were clearly unprepared for the forceful way in which the funeral, and particularly the committal, brought home the reality of their bereavement. 'When the coffin went into the flames I thought, "Suppose he isn't dead?" It was as if I'd been hit or something.' 'I still can't get the memory [of the service] out of my head.' 'It was horrible – I don't want to talk about it.' 'It was terrible. We were the last cremation of the day. There didn't seem to be any meaning in it whatsoever. Seeing the coffin go through the door – for a few minutes it made me realize I'd never see him again.' Cremation, chosen by over half the London widows (but still rare in the USA), was more often seen as upsetting, mechanistic, and alienating than was burial. On the other hand it was praised on grounds of hygiene and simplicity: 'It's so much tidier. The grave doesn't get over-grown, they look after them so nicely'.

It is not possible, on the anecdotal evidence of the widows in the London Study who gave their opinion of the ritual aspects of bereavement, to make definitive judgements of the relative merits of burial and cremation. The preference of the spouse and other cultural and personal expectations, which together determined the choice, also provided the frame of reference by which the decision was justified in retrospect.

Although some widows in the London Study subsequently visited the crematorium, entered their husband's name in the Book of Remembrance, and attended memorial services, there was less tendency to feel close to the dead person at the crematorium than there was at the cemetery. This was regarded by several widows as a distinct disadvantage of cremation.

On the whole we have the impression that for many of these young widows the funeral service took place too early after the death to be of great positive psychological value. It was too soon, in the first week of bereavement, for the service to constitute a successful *rite de passage*. Nevertheless, the funeral did have the effect of drawing the family and friends close to the widow, and the support that was offered was mentioned as a source of satisfaction and help by over half the widows in the London Study.

In many parts of the world, but particularly in Australia and, more recently, the USA, funeral directors employ counsellors for the bereaved people whom they serve. Parkes first became aware of this in Boston, Massachusetts, where the administrators of a Jewish cemetery employed the services of a public relations officer, herself a widow, who offered support and practical advice to the widows of men buried in the cemetery. She organized annual conferences for these widows at which invited speakers gave expert information on careers for women, the education of young people, the psychology of bereavement, and other relevant topics. A surprisingly large proportion of the widows who were invited to these conferences attended them, and they certainly seemed to appreciate the service provided.

The unusual feature of this service is that it was part of the contract when a husband bought a grave in the cemetery. It thus gave him an opportunity to buy support for his wife during a period when she was likely to be in need of it. Like other forms of insurance this method can be expected to satisfy the dying man's wish to continue to 'look after' his wife after his death and can therefore help to remove one possible source of anxiety.

RELIGION AND RITUAL

As we saw in Chapter 12, most studies of bereaved people have been carried out in the English-speaking world where Christianity is the dominant religion. In order to address this defect and to provide readers from Christian countries with information that will help them to understand to help people from other cultures, Parkes, Laungani, and Young invited authorities from many of the major religious and ethnic backgrounds to contribute chapters to their book *Death and Bereavement Across Cultures* (1997). This proved to be a fascinating endeavour that confirmed what we had always suspected, that one of the major functions of religion is to provide ways of thinking about and coping with death. While it would take us beyond the remit of this book to repeat that exercise here it is worth summarizing our main conclusions.

When meeting people from other cultures than our own there are two myths that need to be exposed. On the one hand, is the assumption that all people are alike, grief is grief, and my grief is the same as your grief. Cross-cultural studies indicate that there are large differences between, and even within, cultures. On the other hand, the assumption that these differences are so great that we have nothing to offer to people from other worlds is also fallacious. It may take longer to communicate across cultural divides but that does not mean that we should not try.

Most of those who have emigrated from one land and culture to another need to spend time trying to explore and integrate the differences between their country of origin and their country of adoption. They are glad of any opportunity to do that, particularly at times of death and bereavement. Rather than assuming that we understand their point of view it helps to invite people to explain it to us. While they are explaining themselves to us they are explaining themselves to themselves. This is a very rewarding activity from which we may benefit as much as the people whom we have set out to help.

Even for those of us who remain in our country of origin the death of those we love presents us with existential and religious dilemmas for which we may feel unprepared. This is, perhaps, the acid test of faith. A month after bereavement thirteen widows out of eighteen in the London Study who expressed belief in God said that their faith had helped them. But these issues are not simple. A recent review of 73 empirical studies concludes that '. . . results suggest relations between religion and adjustment to bereavement are generally positive but inconsistent and vary depending, in part, on how religion/spirituality is measured' (Wortmann and Park, 2008). They found no evidence that affiliation to one particular faith helps more than any other, but those with stronger commitment to any faith usually fared better than those without.

There was some evidence in the London Study that those whose religious beliefs helped them to place the bereavement in a meaningful perspective, coped better with bereavement than those who had no such faith, but it was also true that several of the regular church attenders did not make out well. Again the evidence from other studies is confusing and Wortmann and Park found that, although ten studies reported a positive association between church attendance and adjustment to bereavement, another six did not.

The view of God as a protecting, loving father is hard to maintain in the face of untimely bereavement, and the possibility of reunion in days to come does not help the widow to tolerate the absence of her

husband now. On the other hand a study by Bohannon (1991) indicated that, after the death of a child, mothers, but not fathers, who
were church attenders showed less rumination, depersonalization
and loss of control than mothers who were not.

In general, Parkes got the impression, and it is no more than an
impression, that several of the more religious widows were insecure
women who tried to find, in their relationship to God, the same kind
of support they had sought from their parents and husbands. Since
such women tend to do badly after bereavement it is not surprising
that 'faith in God' and 'regular church attendance' were not necessarily related to good outcome following bereavement. This observation is supported by Kirkpatrick (Kirkpatrick, 1999; Kirkpatrick
and Shaver, 1990), who showed that the pattern of people's attachment to God resembled their attachment to their parents, those with
secure attachments to parents were more likely than others to see
God as personally loving, the avoidant were likely to doubt God's
existence and the 'ambivalent' more often saw God as punitive
(reviewed by Parkes in *Love and Loss*, 2006, pp. 184–185). It seems
that, like the memory of a long-gone parent, God may or may not be
an 'invisible means of support'.

Beliefs and rituals, which provide an explanation for death and
social support for the expression of grief, should reduce the confusion felt by the newly bereaved and might even be of psychological
value in helping them to express their grief.

But it is not enough to prescribe a ritual; faith is also necessary. In
his study of mourning customs in contemporary Britain, Gorer
praises the Orthodox Jewish shivah as an example of a custom that
seems to provide ritual support for grief. The three Orthodox Jews
whom he interviewed had found the 'very concentrated and overt
mourning' that took place during the first seven days of bereavement
to be of therapeutic value. During this period, prayers are said for
the dead and the mourners are expected to spend much of their time
talking to visitors about the dead person. Parkes' impression, from
talking to a number of intelligent middle-class Jews, is less favourable than Gorer's. They have pointed out that while it is true that the
shivah still serves its traditional function of drawing the family
together at a time of bereavement there is a tendency for it to be used
as a distraction from grief rather than as an occasion for its expression. Conversation with the bereaved person often takes the form of
neutral chat and the expression of overt emotion is avoided, as it is in
other 'public' situations. The 'successful' mourner is thought to be
the one who shows a proper control of his feelings on all occasions.

In such circumstances the funeral, wake, or shivah becomes an ordeal that is likely to be viewed with mixed feelings.

After the rituals associated with the disposal of the body are at an end, there normally follows a period of mourning, which gives social recognition to the fact that those most affected by the bereavement are in a vulnerable state. In the 1950s, when Parkes was carrying out his initial studies in Britain, the wearing of tokens of mourning, a black armband or a dark-coloured dress, used to provide an indication that certain individuals were to be treated differently from others. Such people were not expected to take part in 'light-hearted' activities. Insofar as they felt heavy hearted it helped them if society recognized this. It also, presumably, encouraged the mourner to accept their grief rather than to avoid it.

But customs are changing. The black armband and the dark dress, themselves a diluted version of the black mourning and widow's weeds of the Victorian era, are now abandoned altogether. By 1965 Gorer found that: 'The customs of mourning dress, which were general when I was a boy, are now predominantly maintained by the old, the poor and the unskilled'. Today mourning dress has almost disappeared.

When there is a prescribed period for mourning, a time is prescribed for its ending. (The term quarantine comes from 'quarantina', the Italian for 'forty', which was the number of days of sequestration expected of the widow.) Thus, an accepted mourning period provides social sanction for beginning and ending grief, and it is clearly likely to have psychological value for the bereaved. While it is true that social expectations concerning the duration of mourning cannot correspond closely to all individual psychological needs to express grief, which vary considerably, the absence of any social expectations, as is common in Western cultures today, leaves bereaved people confused and insecure in their grief. Hunter refers to this paucity of ritual as 'An incomplete rite of passage' (Hunter, 2007–8).

While ritual is generally assumed to be the province of the church there is no reason why it cannot be used in other settings. It is interesting to note the emergence of new rituals outside the authority of the churches. Thus, roadside memorials commonly spring up near the site of fatal road traffic accidents. Clark and Franzmann (2006) suggest that '. . . the strength of grief, the power of presence, and the importance of place, allows ordinary people to assume and, therefore, challenge the authority of the church and the government as official purveyors and regulators of mourning ritual'. They may also be a creative response, warning surviving motorists to take special care.

Another new ritual is the creation of quilts in memory of those who have died of AIDS. These are a creative memorial in which each panel commemorates an individual, a political statement of Gay Rights and a symbol of warmth and security. 'The dead are pressed into the service of creating solidarity both within the gay community, and between it and the straight community' (Walter, 1999, p. 53). To this we can add the websites such as http://www.mydeathspace.com/ where people can add their own tributes, comments and criticisms on deaths that are in the news.

Many of the procedures performed by doctors have the character of rituals, they are often rites of passage or ordeals through which a person must pass on their way to the next chapter of their life. If they have beneficial effects these may well result from their ritual qualities. The use of drugs with dangerous or unpleasant side effects is an example and may account for the success of some antidepressants, despite the fact that recent research has shown them to be associated with equal improvement when replaced by placebos. Only when used for the treatment of the most severe forms of clinical depression do their benefits exceed the placebo effect (Kirsch *et al.*, 2008).

One person who makes deliberate use of ritual in therapy with the bereaved is Van der Hart (1988). He regards preparation for the ritual as an important part of the process and spends time helping the bereaved to undertake tasks that will allow them to review the implications of the death. Tasks are set to stimulate the working through of grief by writing poems or stories for the dead person. Only 'when it is clear that reorganization has come to an end' can the final leave-taking ritual begin. This enables the bereaved to bid a 'solemn and stately farewell' to the dead, to bury or otherwise dispose of symbols of the dead person and, finally, to take a cleansing bath followed by a meal or other ritual, which includes the person's family and symbolizes the relationships that will continue to matter in the next phase of the person's life.

AFTER THE FUNERAL

The funeral often precedes the peak of the pangs of grief, which tends to be reached during the second week of bereavement. The 'bold face' put on for the funeral can then no longer be maintained and there may be a need for some close relative or friend to take over some of the accustomed roles and responsibilities of the bereaved person, thereby setting him or her free to grieve. The person who is most valued at this time is not the one who expresses the most sympathy but the person who 'sticks around', quietly gets on with day-to-day household tasks and makes few demands upon the bereaved. Such a person must be prepared to accept without reproach the tendency of the bereaved person to pour out feelings of anguish and anger, some of which may be directed against the helper. In fact it may be necessary for the helper to indicate to the bereaved that he or she expects such feelings to emerge and that there is no need for them to be 'bottled up'. The helper should not 'pluck at the heartstrings' of the bereaved person until breakdown occurs any more than he or she should connive with the bereaved in endless attempts to avoid the grief work. Both probing and 'jollying along' are unhelpful. The bereaved person has a painful and difficult task to perform, which cannot be avoided and should not be rushed. True help consists in recognizing this fact and in helping the bereaved person to arrange things in whatever way is necessary to set him or her free for the task of grieving. This attitude was supported by Pope Pius XII who, in 1957, delivered an encyclical that pointed out that there is nothing ignoble in tears and that widows should withdraw from activities of the world for 'a reasonable period of mourning' (Miller, 1961).

To what extent is it appropriate for the helper to 'share' grief? 'Dry your eyes', says Shakespeare's Richard II. 'Tears show their love, but want their remedies.' Nevertheless it is often seen as reassuring by a bereaved person when those who are nearest show that they are not afraid to allow feelings of sadness to emerge. Such communal expressions of sorrow make the bereaved person feel understood and reduce the sense of isolation he or she is likely to experience. This was clearly illustrated to me by a widower in the Boston study who said that he had succeeded in rigorously suppressing his own feelings until he saw his father weeping at the funeral. He had always regarded his father as 'tough' and his first reaction was one of shocked surprise. Then it dawned on him that perhaps there was nothing wrong with weeping at a funeral and he too began to cry. Subsequently he viewed this event as a valuable lesson, which had helped him over a difficult hurdle.

Much research has been carried out into the question of whether or not it helps bereaved people to express or 'disclose' thoughts and feelings about their loss and doubt has been cast on the value of spontaneous disclosure on the grounds that people who show feelings do less well after bereavement than those who do not (Bonanno,

2004; Wortman and Silver, 1989). Much of this is vitiated by the fact that those people who obtain high scores on 'disclosure' are usually the most disturbed and grief-stricken. We should not, therefore, be surprised to find that their distress continues after bereavement. Even when the 'disclosure' has been prescribed in the form of written exercises no benefit has been demonstrated except among those bereaved by suicide (Range, Kovac, and Marion, 1999).

There is an optimal 'level of grieving', which varies from one person to another. Some will cry and sob, others will betray their feelings in other ways. The important thing is for thoughts and feelings to be permitted to emerge into consciousness and to contribute to a new and meaningful view of the world. (This has been termed 'cognitive restructuring' and it is not much different from the earlier concept of 'grief work'; Archer, 2008, p. 56). How the process appears on the surface may be of secondary importance.

Helpers should show, by their willingness to reveal their own feelings, that they are not ashamed of them or rendered useless by them. If they are ashamed or feel destroyed by them, they will not help the newly bereaved and had better stay out of the way. It is not unknown for people who have been unable to master feelings of grief after a loss to attempt to do so by offering help to other bereaved people. Clearly these helpers are not to blame for their own difficulties, but it seems unlikely that they will succeed in reassuring the newly bereaved that it is 'safe' to grieve.

In a similar way the bereaved parent who is succeeding in coping with his or her own grief can help the children to cope with theirs. But if, as is likely in early days, the parent feels overwhelmed by grief, it may be advisable to draw upon the support of others to help with the children. Conversely, adult or near-adult children can give a great deal of support to a grieving parent. Who is the caregiver and who the cared for in this situation is an open question, but in most cases the sharing of grief is more likely to do good than harm.

People entering a household that contains a newly bereaved person are often enjoined not to say anything that will 'upset' the bereaved. Since conversation about trivialities is irrelevant at such a time, this makes communication difficult. Usually such an attitude reflects a mistaken notion that grief can somehow be avoided. Even when no explicit prohibition is made the visitor may have the impression that his presence is embarrassing – others do not know how to react to him any more than he knows how to react to them. While a conventional expression of sympathy can probably not be avoided, pity is the last thing the bereaved wants. Pity makes one into an object; in being pitied, the bereaved person becomes pitiful. Pity puts the bereaved person at a distance from, and in an inferior position to, the would-be comforter. So, it is best to get conventional verbal expressions of sympathy over as quickly as possible and to speak from the heart or not at all. This is not a situation in which there is a proper thing to say: trite formulae serve only to widen the gap between bereaved and non-bereaved.

Pain is inevitable in such a case and cannot be avoided. It stems from the awareness of both parties that neither can give the other what they want. The helper cannot bring back the person who is dead and the bereaved person cannot gratify the helper by seeming helped. No wonder that both feel dissatisfied with the encounter.

And yet bereaved people do appreciate the visits and expressions of sympathy paid to them by others. These are seen as a tribute to the dead, thereby confirming the mourner in the belief that the dead person is worth all the pain. They also reassure the bereaved that they are not alone in the world and so reduce feelings of insecurity. The world may seem dangerous and alien but they have some allies.

Since pain is inevitable, helpers must be prepared to share the pain, to accept it as their contribution to friendship, while assisting the bereaved quietly with the small tasks and responsibilities that still have to be carried out even though they may have lost much of their value. Help derives, therefore, from the quiet communication of affectionate understanding and this can be conveyed as well by a squeeze of the hand as by speech. Into such a warm silence the bereaved may choose to pour the worries and fears that are pre-occupying them. It is not necessarily a bad thing if they become upset, for they may be glad of an opportunity to express their feelings. 'Give sorrow words', says Malcolm to Macduff. 'The grief that does not speak, knits up the o'erwrought heart and bids it break.'

A person from outside the family who offers help at this early stage of grief may find himself or herself occupying a role that is not open to family members. The family are seen as 'too involved', too easily hurt by each other's grief. Also, they may be in competition with each other to show a brave face or retain a position of respect in the family. All families have their own hierarchy, and elements of rivalry and competition frequently distort the natural expression of feeling. If one member cries more, or less, than another, this is noticed and conclusions are drawn about the nature of their rela-tionship with the dead member. Several widows have told me how they felt obliged to curtail the expression of their own feelings after witnessing what they took to be insincere grief in in-laws. Others put on a bold face for the sake of children or elderly relatives who were seen as weaker than themselves. It may, therefore, be easier to talk to outsiders about problems that threaten self-esteem, and those families whose traditions provide no acceptable means of expressing grief are in particular need of an outsider who is not ruled by such inhibitions.

Many bereaved people are surprised and frightened by the sheer intensity of their emotions and imaginings after bereavement. Reassurance that they are not going mad, that such feelings are perfectly natural, and that crying does not mean a 'nervous breakdown' can be given explicitly, and especially by an attitude that shows that the helper is not alarmed, frightened, or even surprised.

It is important for those who attempt to help the bereaved to know what is normal, and the reader will already have a good idea of this from what has been said in foregoing chapters. Bereaved people are so surprised by the unaccustomed feelings of grief that they often ask, 'Am I going mad?', or 'Is it normal to be like this?' Such fears are particularly felt when intense feelings of anger or bitterness erupt, but they may also arise in relation to disturbances of perception. Hallucinations are so well known as a sign of madness that it can be most alarming to experience the hypnagogic hallucination of a dead husband. Fortunately it is easy to reassure people of the normality of such phenomena. Vivid nightmares are another occasional source of alarm, as are nocturnal orgasms occurring during sleep or in a half-waking state. Distractibility, difficulty in remembering everyday matters, and a slight sense of unreality are other features of the typical reaction to bereavement that may worry the bereaved. There is no reason to regard any of these as signs of mental illness.

On the other hand, absence of grief in a situation in which it would have been expected, episodes of panic, lasting physical symptoms, excessive consumption of alcohol or drugs, excessive guilt feelings, excessive anger, or the persistence of intense grief beyond the normally expected period – these should be taken as signs that all is not going as it should. Not that the bereaved person is going mad, psychosis as such seems to be a very rare consequence of bereavement; but bereaved people who show these features may require special help. When, despite our efforts, it is clear that the bereaved person is 'stuck', or if, for any reason, the caregiver is uncertain about the course of events, he or she should not hesitate to advise the bereaved person to get additional help. Possible sources of such help will be considered in the next chapter.

LATER BEREAVEMENT

Our discussion so far has focused upon the early stage of bereavement, which is the time when most people first seek help. Let us go on, now, to consider what kinds of assistance and support are most appropriate at a later stage.

The early stage of bereavement is a time when family, friends, and others usually rally round, give emotional support and relieve newly bereaved people of some of their roles and obligations. This may last for one or two months after which many people find that they are on their own. A study by Kaunonen *et al.* (2000) showed that bereaved people who received a supportive telephone call at about four months after bereavement suffered less despair and experienced improved personal growth by comparison with people who received no such call.

The later stage is one when bereaved people should be helped to establish their own autonomy. It may be important for them to grieve, but it is also important for them to stop grieving, to give up their withdrawal from life, and to start building a new life for themselves.

In a situation in which well-established norms are absent, the expectations of those around are potent determinants of behaviour. Thus friends or relatives can indicate, implicitly or explicitly, that grief is expected and permitted, but they can also indicate that it has gone on long enough. To some extent grieving is seen as a duty to the dead and it may take an outsider to point out that that duty is now done, or at least that the mourner can be permitted to let up a little.

Although there is no clear ending to grief, it is common for widows to describe one or several 'turning-points' – that is, events associated with a major revision of their feelings, attitudes, and behaviour. Such turning-points may occur, for instance, when a widow goes away on holiday, takes a job of work, goes out with a man for the first time since her bereavement, or redecorates the house. They both reflect and engender an abandonment of the old modes of thinking and living. The widow shows that she is no longer doomed to centre her life upon the search for the dead husband, and, in proving this to herself as well as to others, she seems to open up the possibility of numerous other changes. Returning to the old home after a week with her sister, one widow said to herself: 'I'm not going to let all that start again'. She moved the furniture around, started redecorating the house, and found herself a job of work outside the home – all within a short space of time. Similar turning-points occur in the lives of widowers.

The timing of such turning-points is important. They tend to occur at the expiry of a set period of time, for instance at an anniversary. A memorial service or a visit to the cemetery carried out at this time can have the significance of a *rite de passage*, setting the bereaved people free from the past and allowing them to undertake fresh commitments. Friends, relatives, and others can often help to initiate such turning-points and to enhance the change in attitude that should accompany them. Problems can be talked through and practical arrangements made.

Frances Beck in her *Diary of a Widow* (1966) described a series of turning-points. The first occurred two months after bereavement, when she started attending evening classes: 'Perhaps I am coming out of my shell', she wrote, 'I won't cry tonight'. Nevertheless she continued to grieve deeply until six months after her husband's death, when she wrote a long 'letter' to him reviewing both positive and negative aspects of their relationship. From here on she referred to herself as a widow and took seriously the process of her own re-education. Jobs, homes, and children became major issues and she moved to a different city. But she was lonely and friendless, and after a while her 'letters' to her dead husband again became more frequent and pathetic.

Another turning-point occurred when she went on vacation eleven months after the death: 'For the first time I have the feeling that I can make it', she wrote. The anniversary itself was painful, but within three weeks she went to a dance for the first time.

It was the second new year after her husband's death, however, that constituted the decisive turning-point. Here she met, at a party, a fellow 'orphan of the storm' and henceforth she saw him regularly. A year later she became formally engaged, but only on the eve of her second wedding did she start to refer, in her diary, to her first husband in the past tense.

Frances Beck's diary illustrates clearly the point that 'full realization comes in steps'. Other people are involved in these steps and without others it is hard to give up habits of withdrawal and mourning. Part of the function of counselling services and clubs that provide special help for bereaved people must be to act as a bridge between the socially withdrawn widow and the community. Social activities with other widows should be seen as steps towards other forms of activity rather than as ends in themselves. Otherwise there is a danger that inward-looking cliques will develop whose members succeed only in reinforcing one another's fears of the outside world as a hostile and dangerous place.

CONCLUSIONS

In conclusion, it is clear from the results of recent research that time heals most grief and that well-meaning advisers can do harm as well as good. Furthermore, there is no single intervention or magic bullet that will alleviate or prevent all problems. Apart from the kind of concern and care that can be, and normally is, given by family and friends, professionals and volunteers can do much to help. But, just as parental love can harm children as well as helping them, so the caring professions must take care that their caring is well informed. This is why training and supervision are needed.

In the next chapter we identify the main issues that require consideration if we are to match the care to the problems.

14

HELPING THE
BEREAVED – II

Types of help for types of problem

> Without any warning, the tears rose up and broke out of her,
> and Potter sat on his chair saying nothing, and yet being a
> comfort to her, taking some of her grief on to himself. She
> wept as she had never wept before in front of another
> human being, and it was a good thing to do; it was more
> value than all the months of solitary mourning. It brought
> something to an end.
>
> *The Springtime of the Year* by Susan Hill , published by
> Long Barn Books. Copyright © Susan Hill 1974.
> Reproduced by permission of Sheil Land Associates Ltd.

Specialist help is now available to bereaved people from trained professionals but we should not decry the help that can be given by volunteers who have been carefully selected, trained and supervised in their work. They can often achieve higher levels of expertise than professionals whose training in bereavement may be minimal.

The following circumstances have been identified in previous chapters as likely to give rise to special problems after bereavement:

1 Traumatic losses.
2 Vulnerable people.
3 Lack of social and family support.

These do not necessarily occur in isolation. Vulnerable people are likely to be particularly vulnerable to losses that are also traumatic and the effects of both trauma and vulnerability are affected by lack of social supports. It follows that all three may need to be taken into account when deciding what help is needed. Nevertheless it is useful to consider the implications of each in turn.

TRAUMATIC LOSSES

We identified the special problems likely to be associated with traumatic losses as fear and its consequences, post-traumatic stress disorder (PTSD), and shattered assumptions. Each has implications for intervention.

Management of fear and it's consequences

We saw in Chapter 2 that the high levels of anxiety and fear that commonly follow trauma of all kinds easily give rise to a vicious circle in which the bodily changes caused by fear are misinterpreted as symptoms of physical or mental illness. This then increases the fear, which, in turn, increases the symptoms.

It follows that anything that decreases fear, and provides the sufferer with things to do that will enable them to control it, is likely to break the vicious circle and stop, or at least minimize, the fear. In attempting this we need to pay attention to anything that may be adding to the client's anxiety; the physical surroundings (hospitals can be frightening places), the people who are present (doctors and other authorities are themselves often a source of fear), the absence of family or trusted others, any misconceptions about the nature of symptoms, other sources of fear.

So we should attempt to address each of these issues by:

- Choosing a venue that is unthreatening (home is usually the place where most people feel safe).
- Encouraging them to bring a friend or family member with them; taking time to introduce ourselves in a friendly and reassuring way (don't loom over people or frown at them).
- Listening carefully and respectfully to their account of their 'symptoms'; providing them with an explanation for these reactions (in language that they will understand).
- Reassuring them of their normality.
- Showing them how they can control or minimize their own symptoms in ways that make sense to them and put them in control. (There is a wide range of ways of doing this ranging from relaxation exercises, to aromatherapy. They all help but for best results it is wise to choose the intervention that is viewed most positively by the client.)
- Checking that they have understood and accepted our reassurance.

Using these methods it is often possible to 'cure' people of anxiety symptoms at a single session, but they also need to be warned that, because of the persistence of adrenaline (epinephrine) and other chemical messengers in the blood, the symptoms of fear often persist after the fear is at an end. In any event a follow-up visit will enable the carer to monitor progress and give any further reassurance that is necessary.

Two other sources of help for anxiety and/or panic disorders are books and guidance on the Internet. A random-allocation study has shown that these are just as successful as an interview with a psychiatrist (Ghosh, Marks, and Carr, 1988), the only problem being the relatively high drop-out rates from the Internet self-help groups (Eysenbach, 2005). Two of the best validated are Marks' book *Living with Fear* (2001) and self-help Internet guidance from Fear Fighter (www.fearfighter.com). Craske and Barlow's book, *Mastery of your Anxiety and Panic* (2007), is also recommended.

Post-Traumatic Stress Disorder

It is important not to miss this diagnosis because not only is PTSD a very distressing condition, but it responds well to treatment. It follows that all who are involved at times of traumatic bereavement must be familiar with the diagnostic criteria as described on page 4. The sooner it is treated the less likely PTSD is to become chronic. Even so, the diagnosis cannot be made until a month after bereavement and many partial forms resolve themselves or respond well to support and reassurance during the first month.

Because effective treatments require special training they should not be attempted by untrained persons. This said, the training required is not particularly difficult to master and can even be learned from the Internet. The recommendations that follow are those that have been approved by the National Institute for Clinical Excellence (NICE) in 2005 following a detailed review of the research evidence.

The simplest, and usually the most effective treatment is Eye Movement Desensitization and Reprocessing (EMDR). This involves several sessions in which the client focuses attention on a painful memory or image of the traumatic event while watching an oscillating object. Repeated exposure in this way eventually results in a diminution of the pain evoked by the memory to the point where clients are no longer seriously distressed by it. They do not forget the event but learn to live with it, rather than being ruled by it, or needing to go to great lengths to avoid reminders of it.

Explanations for the success of this therapy vary but the important thing is that it works and without side effects. Because there are often a number of painful memories, it may be necessary to repeat the treatment for each one of them.

Good results can also be obtained by other techniques of trauma-focused cognitive behaviour therapy (CBT) including thought stopping, distraction and cognitive restructuring. These therapies require the help of well-trained psychologists.

If given during the first two to three months after a traumatic bereavement good results may be obtained in no more than five sessions. Once the condition has continued for over three months rather more sessions are likely to be needed. In Britain it is now government policy to make these facilities available, free of charge, under the National Health Service.

As described on page 78, PTSD sometimes interferes with the process of grieving. For this reason the support of someone trained in assisting with such problems is often needed and bereavement support should not be delayed until after the psychological treatment has been carried out.

On the other hand symptoms of depression often improve when PTSD is treated and specific treatments for depression may not be needed unless there is a suicidal risk or the person is very deeply depressed.

Drug treatments for PTSD are not recommended by NICE, although it is recognized that short-term night sedation may be helpful in some cases.

Shattered assumptions

These arise whenever someone is faced with a massive change in their lives for which they are quite unprepared (see page 155). The problem is, how we can help them to prepare for something that has already happened? How can people begin the slow and painful process of psychosocial change when their thought processes are disorganized by anxiety and their trust in themselves, their world and other people (including God and other protective powers) has been shattered?

Obviously the first step must be to manage the anxiety, to create a safe place and a safe therapeutic relationship in which it begins to be possible for people to think about the things that make them feel very unsafe. The techniques of anxiety management described above are all important. Likewise it is often necessary to treat any PTSD

223

that may be present as a result of the haunting memories and images evoked by the traumatic death.

Once this has been achieved, and even while it is in process, it becomes possible for the client to think about and 'make real' the events and assumptions that have been shattered.

John T. was 42 years of age when he was referred to Parkes. He had taken an overdose of paracetamol two months after the death of his mother and appeared very anxious and depressed.

John was the only child of a father who died when he was only two years old. As a child he was very close to his mother and fearful that she too would die. Always shy he became a loner and throughout his life was fearful of hospitals. He left school at fourteen to become a clerk, but at 25 had an illness and lost the use of his right arm. He had not worked since that illness. He never read a book and saw himself as a dummy, but he had a great love for music, which he shared with his mother and with a few friends.

His mother's death, three days after suffering a stroke, was quite unexpected. It shattered his precarious sense of security and he did not believe that he could survive without her. He said, 'It took a long time to sink in', but when the reality hit him he became depressed, anxious and panicky. He missed his mother a great deal and found himself unable to listen to music as it upset him too much. He seldom left the house and was sleeping very badly. By attempting suicide he seemed to be both calling for help, and trying to take control of his own inevitable death.

Seen in the clinic he walked with his shoulders hunched and appeared very shy. He recognized that he had been very dependent on his mother. Asked if he still wanted to kill himself. He replied, 'I don't think so, I don't feel so desperate and my mother would want me to go on'.

Parkes writes, 'Over the next year he kept his appointments with me, indeed he was eager for all the time I could give him and I realized that there was a real danger that he would become dependent on me. I prescribed a course of amitriptyline, which has both antidepressant and tranquillizing effects, and I saw him regularly, but not too frequently, with the aim of reassuring him about the nature of his symptoms and fostering his self-confidence. I believed that his intelligence was higher than he said and arranged for him to take an IQ test. He was amazed when told that this was average or above and that, although his verbal IQ was only 100, that would improve if he started reading. This stimulated him to start doing puzzles, listening to music and going out of the house. Before long he had resumed friend-ships that he had dropped including one with a former girl friend.

When I last saw him he was planning his first holiday abroad, to visit a friend in Spain, and was much less anxious and more confident in himself and others. He remarked that, "Bereavement does get better" '.

Solomon and Shapiro (1997) have developed an extension of EMDR and applied it to the treatment of shattered assumptions of one's core beliefs. While this technique has not yet been evaluated, other forms of EMDR have been.

Solomon claims that negative images of being let down by God, or of one's world falling apart, can be held in the mind, desensitized and reprocessed in much the same way that haunting memories are treated. Rather than challenging these assumptions, clients gradually get used to them and lose the feeling of being overwhelmed and destroyed. Little by little, they achieve a sense of being again in control. It is this sense of empowerment that enables them to begin to rebuild their assumptive world.

VULNERABLE PEOPLE

As we saw in Chapter 1, bereavement can act as a trigger for a wide range of psychological disorders in those who are vulnerable. Thus, those with a propensity to drink too much may develop alcohol-related problems and those of obsessive personality may develop an obsessional neurosis. It would take a psychiatric textbook to describe the treatment of all these conditions, the diagnosis and treatment of which is no different after bereavement than in other circumstances.

The two most common types of vulnerability that give rise to psychiatric problems after bereavement are tendencies to anxiety and depression. These are often present before the bereavement takes place and evident to medical staff who observe excessive reactions in family members before a patient's death.

Anxiety and panic disorders

John T. is a good example of a man who was vulnerable to anxiety. Since these problems commonly follow traumatic bereavements their diagnosis and treatment has already been covered under anxiety management above. But such treatment is unlikely to completely solve the problem. Anxious people will remain anxious people and it may be necessary to refer them for psychiatric care if they do not respond to the methods described.

Depression

John also met criteria for clinical depression. People with a tendency to depression or suicidal attempts may well relapse under the stress of bereavement. Because feelings of helplessness and hopelessness are symptoms of depression they may not refer themselves for help. Indeed, some people commit suicide without asking for help because they cannot believe that anything can be done to help them.

This makes it all the more important for us to be proactive in assessing the risk and reaching out to those vulnerable to depression. As we saw on page 99 depression and grief are two quite different things and depression is much more likely to end fatally.

Having established that someone is clinically depressed (see pages 135–6), it is wise to draw upon all available sources of support. The family and friends may not have realized the seriousness of the situation and will often rally round to good effect. Bereavement volunteers can also be of use in helping depressed people to get out of the patterns of withdrawal that deter them from doing the very things that will get them out of their depression.

In recent years cognitive behaviour therapies have gradually replaced antidepressants as the treatment with the best chance of success in all but the most severe forms of depression. Another important review by NICE (2004) concludes that, for mild cases of depression, a guided self-help programme, based on cognitive behaviour therapies, is most cost-effective. For mild to moderate depression, counselling along the lines developed by Harris (Harris, 2006; Harris, Brown, and Robinson, 1999a, 1999b), problem-solving therapy and brief cognitive behaviour therapy are as effective as antidepressants and without side effects. These will be discussed in more detail below.

Several studies of the use of antidepressants for the treatment of depression arising after bereavement have shown positive benefits.

Thus Reynolds *et al.* (1999) found that people with major depression after bereavement responded better to nortriptyline than to a placebo and were more likely to comply with treatment if they were also given interpersonal psychotherapy. Psychotherapy alone was no more effective than a placebo but this does not, of course, mean that psychotherapy was useless, placebos can have powerful effects! Zisook *et al.* (2001) reported similar benefits from a newer antidepressant, bupropion. The improvement in depression scores was accompanied by a slight improvement in two measures of grief (the Texas Revised Inventory of Grief and the Index of Complicated Grief).

Returning to the psychological treatments, their benefits are well explained in terms of the theories of causation of depression considered in previous chapters (pages 178–9). These see much depression as a consequence of negative assumptions about the world ('cognitions') arising out of feelings of helplessness and hopelessness. The psychological therapies aim to identify these negative assumptions and counteract them in systematic ways.

There are numerous offers of help for depressed people on the web. Some are stand-alone programmes offered without feedback or supervision. Although they may get good results among those who complete the course (Proudfoot *et al.*, 2004); they have a high drop-out rate. Most successful are the programmes that provide individual assessment, support, and feedback. A recent meta-analysis of twelve randomized control studies showed that studies with therapist support had a large effect while those without therapist support showed only minor effects (Spek *et al.*, 2007). This is hardly surprising given the negative expectations of depressed people.

Self-help on the Internet has characteristics that are both advantages and disadvantages:

1   The Internet is **easy to access** but also easy to drop out from, hence the high drop-out rate among depressed people, who are easily discouraged.
2   It **ensures confidentiality** but reduces the possibility of family support for the therapy.
3   It **appeals more to men** than women, probably because they prefer not to share feelings, yet, as we see on page 230, it is women who may be most likely to benefit from cognitive and men from emotive therapies.
4   Finally, **it keeps control in the hands of the patient**, which may foster a sense of empowerment that is valuable to depressed

people, but also increases the chances of misdiagnoses, and failure to recognize problems for which the treatment is inappropriate.

To some extent these disadvantages can be minimized when a well-qualified therapist is involved in the therapy.

Typically these programmes will expect the depressed person to undertake a series of writing assignments aimed at identifying their negative assumptions about themselves and the world. They are then challenged to think of positive alternatives. As in other cognitive therapies, attempts to explain how they came to develop such negative views are not thought necessary, but our own experience suggests that people are more likely to collaborate with the therapy if they understand the problem, and feel supported by the therapist, than they are if expected to take everything on trust.

In those who have moderate levels of depression one-to-one or group cognitive behaviour therapy is the treatment of choice. Programmes can more easily be tailored to meet the particular needs of the client. NICE recommend a course of 6–8 sessions over 10–12 weeks. These programmes are more structured with careful monitoring of the success or failure of each intervention. A variety of techniques are now in use which overlap with other types of therapy.

The success of CBT has overshadowed other treatments and left counsellors feeling deskilled. It is, therefore, a relief to report studies in which trained volunteers achieved good results in treating mild to moderate depression. These were carried out by Harris and her colleagues (Harris, Brown, and Robinson, 1999a, 1999b) who made use of volunteer 'befrienders' to develop a relationship of trust, in one study, with women who had been depressed for a year and, in another, with women about to give birth, who were at risk of post-partum depression. Although few of these women had suffered a recent bereavement, previous studies by this team had showed that losses of one sort or another play a frequent part in triggering and maintaining depression.

Their previous work also showed that women who reported having a confiding relationship were less at risk of depression than those without this support (this confirms a similar finding reported by Parkes, 2006, in *Love and Loss*, and on page 191). The main objects of the befriending were two-fold, to provide a confiding relationship and to initiate 'fresh starts', by which they meant 'experiences that heralded new hope'. Befrienders were encouraged to take a more active role than is usual in counselling relationships, for instance, accompanying their client to the job centre or to visit the cemetery. They were also permitted to share with the client any relevant loss or similar experience of their own.

When those who had received befriending were compared with waiting list controls a year later, the depressed women were twice as likely to have recovered from their depression than the depressed controls, and among the pregnant women the rates of post-partum depression in those who had been befriended was half the rate in those who had not. Writing about this project for *Bereavement Care*, Harris remarked, 'What stood out about the befriending process in many of the follow-up interviews was how readily the women understood what they needed in terms of supportive listening. This is something which bereavement supporters, such as those from Cruse Bereavement Care in the UK, are already quite expert at giving' (Harris, 2006).

Depression is sometimes so severe that there is a risk of suicide. Supporters are sometimes reluctant to ask questions about suicide for fear of upsetting the person or making them worse. Yet recent research supports clinical impressions that such questions are more likely to reduce the risk than to increase it (Gould *et al.*, 2005). Caregivers should never be afraid to ask direct questions about suicide. It is common enough for a bereaved person to say, 'I wouldn't care if I died tomorrow', and such remarks need not cause alarm, but a person who has thought seriously of killing himself or herself should always see a psychiatrist. If the bereaved person refuses to agree to a consultation, the helper should at least take advice. It is rare for anyone to commit suicide without telling somebody of the intention and a direct question will usually evoke a direct answer from those who have seriously contemplated it. People are often afraid to mention suicide as if, by doing so, they could bring it about. But a simple question, 'Has it been so bad that you have thought of killing yourself?' is more likely to save a life than to take one.

An actual suicidal attempt must also, of course, be taken seriously. Even if it is thought that it was only a gesture, the plea for help that the gesture implies should not be ignored. Once again close collaboration between the family, GP, psychiatrist, and anyone else in a position to help is desirable if further danger is to be averted.

Complicated grief

The psychiatric problems that we have considered so far are not confined to situations of loss and the help required is much the same as the help that is needed in other circumstances. We turn now to the problems that are more peculiar to bereavement.

Although many kinds of complicated grief have been described and a wide range of treatments recommended, very few have undergone the test of systematic evaluation. As we have seen in past chapters, they fall into two main categories, reflecting the dual process model; problems in loss orientation, notably delay in or inhibition of grieving, and problems in restoration orientation, notably Prolonged Grief Disorder. Both types of problem have been shown to be associated with insecure attachments in childhood and adult life, the former with avoidant and the latter with anxious/ambivalent attachments. They can be viewed as Attachment Disorders.

In recent years a school of Attachment-based Psychoanalysis has sprung up having a much firmer theoretical basis than its Freudian precursor. In a large-scale study, Fonagy *et al.* (1996) found that people with Avoidant (Dismissing) attachments responded better to psychotherapy than those with other forms of attachment. This is not surprising given the focus, in psychoanalytically oriented therapies, on the expression of repressed ideas and emotions.

Given the fact that men are more inclined to avoid emotional expression than women (see pages 146–7), it is not unreasonable to guess that men are more likely than women to benefit from help aimed at the expression of grief. Support for this hunch comes from an important study by Schut *et al.* (1997b). They assigned widows and widowers seeking help for the treatment of complicated grief, at random, to three groups; one was given Emotion-focused therapy, based on Lindemann's method and aiming to foster the expression of grief, one was given a form of cognitive, problem-oriented therapy, focusing on future plans and problems in restoration, and a third was a waiting list control group. When all three groups were followed up the men had not benefited from the problem-focused approach but men who received emotion-focused therapy had improved significantly better than either of the other two groups. Among the women, however, it was the problem-oriented group that had improved. These findings came as a surprise to the investigators and we must guess that, given a free choice, the men would have chosen the more cognitive approach. (For further details of this study see Appendix 15, Figure 11.)

Gender differences were also found in Sikkema *et al.*'s (2004) study of bereaved HIV-positive men and women. Here men improved following both cognitive therapy in a group and traditional psychiatric help whereas women only improved after the cognitive therapy.

Prolonged Grief Disorder (PGD)

Although Schut's study probably included patients with PGD, it did not make use of a systematic set of criteria for diagnosis. We turn now to studies that have made use of such criteria.

The distress, self-neglect, and health impairments associated with PGD, that were described in Chapter 8, make it important for health-care professionals to be on the look out for symptoms of this condition. Unlike the research that has demonstrated the efficacy of nortriptyline and interpersonal psychotherapy for the reduction of bereavement-related depression, these treatments have not proven effective for the reduction of the symptoms of grief (Pasternak *et al.*, 1991; Reynolds *et al.*, 1999). These studies support the assertion that symptoms of grief are distinct from those of depression and suggest that more research is needed before we can recommend medications for PGD. Promising results have been obtained from open trials of newer antidepressants (selective serotonin reuptake inhibitors; SSRIs) but randomized placebo-controlled trials are needed before firm conclusions can be drawn about their efficacy for the treatment of PGD (Zygmont *et al.*, 1998).

With respect to psychotherapeutic interventions designed for the treatment of PGD, Shear *et al.* (2005) carried out a randomized, controlled trial comparing a new type of 'Complicated Grief Therapy' with Interpersonal Psychotherapy for PGD. The new therapy showed significantly greater benefits in reducing both the magnitude and duration of the symptoms of PGD (see Appendix 16). It involves four components:

1   the use of the dual process model to focus attention on the loss and restoration components of grieving;
2   the treatment of trauma symptoms by tape recorded 'revisiting exercises', including role played conversations with the deceased person;
3   a 'memory questionnaire' used to identify positive and negative memories; and
4   'Motivational Enhancement Therapy' to identify goals and monitor progress.

For a more extended account of Shear's view of PGD, which fits well with the account given here, see Shear and Shair (2005).

Other online interventions for PGD, which are in development, are expected to prove promising for the reduction of grief-specific distress (Wagner, Knaevelsrud, and Maercker, 2006).

LACK OF SOCIAL AND FAMILY SUPPORT

In this category we include problems arising out of family dysfunction, disenfranchised grief and the problems of social isolation that are most likely to arise in old age.

Dysfunctional families

Ideally support to the family should be given before as well as after the patient's death and this is an aim of most hospice programmes. But most random allocation studies of hospice care have shown no more benefit to supported than unsupported families (Greer and Mor, 1986; Higginson *et al.*, 2003). It seems that, like bereaved relatives in other settings, most families of people dying in a hospice do not need and will not benefit from routine bereavement support. When, however, family functioning is impaired intervention may be both needed and effective.

This conclusion is supported by studies of Family Focused Grief Therapy (FFGT), which was developed in the setting of an Australian hospice. At this time this is the only service of its kind to have passed the acid test of a random-allocation study, details of which are given in Appendix 17 (Kissane and Bloch, 2002; Kissane *et al.*, 2006). The aim is to improve family functioning in families who have difficulty in communicating thoughts and feelings, and who lack cohesiveness (the ability to work as a team and to resolve any conflicts they may have). 'Active problem solving, conflict resolution and the acknowledgement and sharing of grief are the mainstay of the focused treatment' (Kissane, Lichtenthal, and Zaider, 2007–8).

The studies show that, while cohesive and mutually supportive families do not need or benefit from FFGT, good results have been obtained among those families who, while finding it difficult to communicate with and support each other, are eager for help. On the other hand overtly hostile families often drop out and those that do not drop out do not benefit and may even become more depressed in the course of therapy. Once again it seems that a therapy that helps some clients can harm others.

Disenfranchised grief

We saw on pages 158–61 that there are several reasons why certain categories of bereaved people do not get the acknowledgement and social support that they need. Some are stigmatized or rejected, some isolate themselves for fear of rejection, some are unable to show their grief, which is then ignored, some are over-protected, and others fail to recognize their own needs. Each of these failures reflect misperceptions, either in the social environment, particularly family and friends, or in the bereaved persons themselves, often both are involved. Sometimes the misperceptions can be corrected, at other times they are intractable and have to be circumvented. Members of the health-care professions are usually around when people are bereaved and we may be the only ones to recognize the situation and either provide the information and social support that is needed or steer the bereaved person towards the help that they need.

Problems of stigma

Stigma has a double barb. On the one hand, it causes other people to reject or ignore the needs of the stigmatized, on the other hand, it causes the stigmatized to give up trying to obtain support, having suffered rejection they may even imagine rejection where it does not exist. This causes stigmatized persons to band together and to prefer mutual-help groups over other services. Bereaved people who join such groups soon become attached to them and most value them highly.

People with physical disadvantages, homosexuals, intravenous drug abusers, immigrants from lands with a high incidence of HIV, prostitutes and even sufferers from blood diseases such as haemophilia are all members of minority groups who are likely to be misunderstood and whose psychological needs are ignored by society. Among those at risk for HIV infection, the fact that the disease itself causes fear and rejection gives rise to a fresh lot of problems. Small wonder that members of these communities form their own support groups on the assumption that fellow sufferers are the only people who will understand. This may create a fresh lot of problems, for within such groups there may be so many afflicted by the disease that before long everyone is bereaved and there is a danger that they will 'burn out'.

Other problems that can arise in mutual-help groups include the way in which some groups become dominated by their most disturbed members. Unless they have the leadership of a well-trained group leader they are in danger of becoming anti-therapeutic. But it is often seen as contrary to the principle of self-help to accept leaders from outside the index group and there may be no suitably qualified or motivated person within the organization.

Mutual-help groups now exist for bereaved homosexuals, those with physical disabilities and people bereaved by suicide, murder and manslaughter. A contact list is given in Organizations Offering Help to the Bereaved. Unfortunately good evidence to support the use of these groups is lacking and, despite the enthusiasm with which they are recommended by many of their members, we need to be aware of the problems.

In recent years both individual and group services have been developed by professionals and trained bereavement volunteers and several of these have passed the test of systematic evaluation. Doka (2008) pointed out that: 'The very act of counselling is valued because it offers support and validation that might not be provided elsewhere' (p. 236).

The assumption that only a homosexual can understand a homosexual is fallacious and those who offer their support to such people regularly find that they have much to offer. Likewise counsellors should not be deterred from offering support to those bereaved by homicide or suicide or from reaching out to people in prison. As we have already noted, when people are explaining themselves to others they are explaining themselves to themselves, and that is a therapeutic thing to do.

Evidence for the success of such services is growing. Thus, in a series of studies, Goodkin *et al.* (1998, 1999, 2001) evaluated the effects of 10×90-minute bereavement support group sessions on homosexual men who had lost a friend or partner from AIDS during the preceding six months. When compared with a randomly selected control group who received no such therapy, they found that the supported group came through their grief more rapidly, suffered less overall distress and, in a subgroup who were themselves HIV positive, showed improvement in several indicators of improved resistance to the virus (further details are given in Appendix 18).

In a similar study, Sikkema *et al.* (2006) found that AIDS-bereaved persons who received a 12-week course of group therapy showed less grief than a comparison group with non-specialist psychotherapy. Followed up over the next 12 months these differences disappeared in all but the minority who had reported high levels of distress before undertaking the intervention. Once again high levels of distress after bereavement turns out to be a good indicator that people will respond to therapy.

Impairment of functioning of the brain can cause problems both for people with learning difficulties whose grief may not be recognized, and for the families of people with dementia whose relative may 'die' as a person long before their physical death. The latter will be discussed in Chapter 16.

People with learning difficulties have lasting impairment (usually from birth) in their intelligence, ability to understand complex information, and to cope independently with the modern world. Their language skills are poor or absent although their non-verbal skills may be considerable. Several studies of people with learning difficulties, in institutional care have shown that, although they grieve much like other people, their inability to talk coherently about their grief often results in it being ignored or misinterpreted as a symptom of their brain damage (reviewed by Dowling, Hubert, and Hollins, 2003, and confirmed in a recent study by Dodd *et al.*, 2008). Caring staff may over-protect them by not talking about their loss or inviting them to funerals. Dowling *et al.* carried out a random-allocation study to compare bereaved people with these disabilities, half of whom received bereavement support from trained volunteers and the other half the care of their usual staff, who had also received training aimed at increasing their skills with bereaved people. Despite this training, it was the group who received the counselling from volunteers who benefited the most. The counsellors came from Cruse Bereavement Care and from the Merton and Wandsworth Bereavement Service, whose training is based on the model of care common in the United Kingdom and embodied in this volume and in the work of Worden (2003). The volunteers had attended a two-day workshop on working with learning disabilities and found it relatively easy to apply their knowledge and experience of supporting bereaved people in this new field. On the other hand the professional staff were much less convinced of the value of the new approach. They complained that they were too busy to give clients the time that they needed and clearly felt undermined by the suggestion that communication might be more important than the excellent physical care that they were used to providing.

People with learning difficulties often behave like children and it is no coincidence that bereaved children are over-protected in a similar way. It would take us beyond our remit in this book to discuss this further, suffice it to say that the lessons learned from helping bereaved children have much in common with the lessons learned from helping people with brain impairment.

Social isolation

Loneliness, as we saw in Chapter 9, is the besetting problem of old age and is commonly a consequence of the death of a spouse or partner. In that circumstance it is intimately mixed with grief and, because bereaved people know that there can be no substitute for the person they have lost, they often assume that they are doomed to a life of misery. As a result they may not ask for help or accept the help that is on offer. They may refuse to go to clubs for older people ('senior centers' in the USA) or, if they are persuaded to go, they hide in a corner and then complain that nobody wants them. Yet, in the long run, it is human contact such as this that holds out the best hope of re-engagement.

Disengagement is sometimes seen as a normal part of ageing and it is true that old people often narrow their horizons, finding it difficult to cope with the complexities of travelling long distances, keeping up with their grandchildren's latest interests, or going to new places, meeting new people and adapting to new ideas. This may explain their tendency to become socially isolated, but it does not contradict the observation that those who remain engaged will be more contented than those who turn their faces to the wall.

Loneliness is associated with an increased risk of hospital admissions in elderly bereaved people (Laditka and Laditka, 2003) and these same researchers showed that recently widowed women who had not spoken on the telephone to a friend or family member during the two weeks prior to interview (a useful measure of social isolation) were 3.5 times more likely to be admitted to hospital than those who had telephone contacts. Given the high cost of hospital admissions these authors see this as a strong argument for primary care teams and social workers to monitor the needs for social support after bereavement.

Why should bereavement and social isolation lead to poor physical health? The most obvious answer is self-neglect. Bereaved old people may neglect their health by eating too much or too little, smoking or drinking to excess, or not bothering to take medication. A study in Ohio showed that self-neglect could be successfully counteracted by 'health reminders and health assistance received from others' (Williams, 2004). Whether it was the social contact or the specific advice that did the trick is not clear.

Those in a position to help will require patience and persistence. It is an art to recognize when it is a time for grief and when a time when elderly bereaved people need to be gently persuaded to emerge from seclusion.

We have also noted (pages 148–50) that old age is also a time when bereaved people, who are also physically disabled, are at increased risk of depression and suicide. It follows that prompt and effective treatment of the depression as described above is important.

15

HELPING THE
BEREAVED – III

Sources of help

Who cannot give good counsel? 'tis cheap, it costs them nothing.

Robert Burton (1621) *Anatomy of Melancholy*, pt. II,
3, memb. 3

Having identified the main problems and suggested some solutions we can draw together the findings of the last two chapters as they affect the practice of the main sources of help from outside the person's network of family and friends. Given our recognition that most bereaved people do not need this help we are now in a position to provide much more cost-effective services than was the case in the past, when it seemed that we should attempt to counsel every bereaved person.

Services range from group to individual, medical to social, psychiatric to psychological, religious to secular, and professional to voluntary, each has its place and none is right for everybody. Newly bereaved people and those who are shy seldom feel brave enough to join groups and will prefer someone they can meet on their own or with a family member. Clergy, GPs and many bereavement services such as **Cruse Bereavement Care** offer such support. On the other hand group support is a good way to meet others who are 'in the same boat' and groups have particular value to bereaved people who are in danger of becoming socially isolated.

We should not assume that, just because someone has a medical degree or a training in social work, they are necessarily well trained in the care of the bereaved and there are many professionals who refer bereaved people to bereavement services provided by volunteers because they feel that the latter have more understanding of bereavement than they do. In recent years professional counsellors who charge fees for their service have become more numerous and many of them provide excellent care but, again, unless they have had special training in working with the bereaved they may prove less helpful than a volunteer who has been carefully selected and trained for this one job and the cost of whose services may be minimal or free. The important thing is not to be afraid to ask for information on such matters. The services available vary widely from one country to another, and, within countries, from one district to another.

Medical care is obviously needed if people think that they are sick and, in Britain, it is GPs who are the first people to consult. They are often able to provide reassurance about the normality of many of the physical symptoms that can worry bereaved people. They are also in a good position to decide when or if the help of a psychiatrist or psychologist is needed and they are aware of the strengths and weaknesses of the existing services.

Clergy are, of course, the traditional source of succour for the bereaved and those who have made a religious commitment will usually find their religious community a good source of spiritual and social support, but there are few people today who seek their help. This is a pity because many clergy are well able to provide support and advice without putting pressure on people to 'return to the fold'. Again, in selecting a clergyman to confide in it may be wise to ask around, a lot will depend on the interest and training of the particular cleric.

Let us now examine, in more detail, the main alternatives.

THE INTERNET

This is an area in which major savings in costs can be achieved. It is rapidly becoming the first place where bereaved people will seek for help. In recent years the advent of the Internet has made available a large number of sources of help including information services, professional services (charging fees), mutual-help groups, general and personal advice (often provided free of charge), blogs, and much else. These are accessible from across the world but also include or provide links to local services. Few of them have been subjected to systematic evaluation and their sheer number makes it hard to decide between them.

The journal *Bereavement Care* publishes regular reviews of such sites and is a useful source of information about them. In choosing a site it is wise to look first at the organization sponsoring the site.

Universities and other reputable bodies are unlikely to lend their names to irresponsible websites. Contact information about organizations and websites for bereaved people and those who care for them are given in Organizations Offering Help to the Bereaved. There we have limited our recommendations to the small number of services that have undergone satisfactory evaluation and a few other sites of which the authors have personal knowledge.

MUTUAL HELP

People who have themselves experienced a major bereavement may be particularly well qualified to help the bereaved. They really do understand what the other person is going through and know that bereavement is not the end of life. In the Laboratory of Community Psychiatry in Boston, Massachusetts, a research social worker, Dr Phyllis Silverman (1967), started a **Widow-to-Widow** programme, which has been widely copied. Mature widows routinely call upon newly bereaved women living in their area. They offer friendship, help, and advice, but they do not present themselves as 'professionals' and in fact have no professional qualification although they are paid for the work. The one qualification they all have is to have grieved effectively. Parkes' impression from talking with these widows' aides was of great enthusiasm for the work and a strong positive conviction of its usefulness, but no adequate evaluations of its efficacy have been published and those few well-conducted studies of mutual help that have been undertaken have had equivocal results.

Thus Tudiver *et al.* (1992) assigned 113 widowers in their first year of bereavement, at random, to a mutual-help group or to a waiting list. After the mutual-help group had received nine semi-structured sessions, which focused on 'grief process, diet, new relationships, exercise and lifestyle issues', the two groups were compared but no significant differences were found between them.

A similar programme involving widows rather than widowers has been evaluated by Vachon *et al.* (1980). They compared a group of sixty-eight widows who had received support from **Widow Contacts** with another ninety-four who had no such support. Only a few results reached statistical levels of significance but there were consistent trends in favour of the supported group. As in many other studies of bereavement services, those widows who showed the greatest distress at the time of bereavement benefited most from counselling.

A mutual-help organization for the bereaved that has spread rapidly across the English-speaking world since its inception in 1969 is the **Compassionate Friends** (founder Rev. Simon Stephens). This is run by parents who have lost a child and provides comfort and support to others who are about to suffer or have already suffered such a loss. The organization enables parents in such a situation to feel less isolated and to meet others who understand their feelings because they have experienced them themselves.

In the United States and Canada another mutual-help organization that has reached out to many widows and widowers is **Parents without Partners**. It is open to widowed, separated, and divorced parents, who themselves organize a wide range of recreational and educational activities. Participation in the numerous committees that organize these activities helps to re-establish feelings of self-reliance and esteem. Although this is now an international organization, most of its chapters are in the USA and Canada.

BEREAVEMENT COUNSELLING AND SUPPORT BY TRAINED VOLUNTEERS

The term 'counselling' has evolved over the years from any advice given by volunteers to what is now a professional level of service. Organizations such as the British Association of Counselling (BAC) have set standards of training that have become so rigorous that they can seldom be met by volunteers. Organizations such as Cruse Bereavement Care have stopped using the word for most of the voluntary service that they provide. Nevertheless, many of their volunteers are every bit as competent as most professionals and Cruse has set its own standards of training and service. In this section we focus on the services provided by both kinds of provider. These are aimed at the minority of bereaved people who are at special risk following bereavement, and they range from individual or family support in the client's home, to office consultation, group meetings, and support by telephone and e-mail. As we saw above, several of them have passed the test of scientific evaluation.

Most hospices across the world now provide support for the families of patients who have died under their care. The first of these to have been set up, and still a good example, is the **Family Service at St Christopher's Hospice**, Sydenham, which makes use of volunteer counsellors who have been subjected to a rigorous programme of selection and training.

Parkes' evaluation by random assignment of people at 'high risk' of problems after bereavement to the service at St Christopher's or to a control group, showed that the provision of counselling can reduce the anxiety and tension levels in 'high-risk' widows and widowers to that of the 'low-risk' group (Parkes, 1981). The control 'high-risk' group, who received no special counselling, were found to have more persisting symptoms of anxiety and tension twenty months after bereavement and to be consuming more drugs (psychoactive medication), alcohol, and tobacco (see Appendix 19). In this study it was the males who benefited most significantly from the service. It may well be the case that the reason for this gender difference lies in the fact that, at that time, in the 1970s, bereavement services were still strongly influenced by Eric Lindemann's advice that the aim of counselling was to facilitate the expression of grief. Even then, it seems, women were less in need of that help than men. It is also worth noting that, whereas six successful suicides are known to have occurred within two years of bereavement among relatives of patients who died in the hospice during the two years before the Bereavement Service was started, only one further suicide is known in the ten years that followed.

A more recent evaluation by Relf (1994) of a similar service in Oxford, has shown that the provision of the help of bereavement volunteers to those at risk can not only significantly reduce levels of anxiety but also reduces the need for medical care from GPs. As in the social service to elderly bereaved people described above, low-cost support to bereaved people at risk may well give rise to major savings in the cost of health care. As a result many branches of Cruse have contractual arrangements to provide bereavement services on an 'item of service' basis, with local Primary Care Trusts who, under the NHS, administer funds for health care in the community.

Cruse Bereavement Care

This organization is a good example of the strengths and weaknesses of relying largely on volunteers for services to bereaved people. Over the near half century of its existence *Cruse* has evolved from *Cruse Clubs for Widows*, a small organization created by a social worker, Margaret Torrie, to empower widows, into a service for all people bereaved by death in the United Kingdom. Cruse Bereavement Care Scotland went independent in 2001 for administrative reasons but remains closely associated and organized on the same model as

Cruse in the rest of the UK. Cruse's most distinctive feature is its reliance on c. 6000 volunteers who have been carefully selected and trained to meet the wide variety of needs of the bereaved people who seek its help. Cruse also employs a number of professional administrators, trainers and supervisors. All services are provided free at the point of delivery. That is to say, as in Britain's National Health Service, the bereaved clients pay nothing.

The use of volunteers enables the service to be run on a shoestring, but it also makes it vulnerable to problems in recruitment. As a consequence Cruse never has quite enough financial or personal resources to provide an ideal service. Some areas of the UK still lack a branch of Cruse, others have waiting lists. Part of the waiting list problem results from the preference for an open-door service, which can easily lead to overload and may even do harm for the reasons discussed on pages 195–7. Despite these difficulties the Council of Cruse have insisted on maintaining a high standard of training and support. As a result the organization has an excellent public reputation, has been called upon by the government for support in disaster areas, and, since 1984, has had Her Majesty the Queen as its patron.

In addition to the provision of one-to-one support Cruse offers many other services. These include a nationwide helpline, which, despite understaffing, currently answers 1000 calls a month and a similar e-mail service responding to over 8000 e-mails a year and growing rapidly.

In addition, Cruse is extending its international influence through its website, publications department, the international journal *Bereavement Care*, which is a peer-reviewed journal, now available online, and its open-access service for bereaved young people which had 250,000 users from across the world during 2007 (www.RD4U). Cruse is already the main source of bereavement support in the British Isles.

In addition to Cruse there are many local bereavement services using volunteers in Britain, although some provide excellent services, they lack a central organization that can set standards and provide accreditation.

In the USA, Australia and New Zealand bereavement counselling by paid professionals plays a larger part than it does in the UK. **The Association for Death Education and Counselling** (ADEC) in the USA and the **National Association for Loss and Grief** in the Antipodes, provide training courses, set standards, and act as licensing authorities. As well as one-to-one counselling all of these organizations advocate group work when this is appropriate.

SUPPORT GROUPS

During the first few weeks or months of bereavement it is difficult to persuade bereaved people to join a group, but there are some who may benefit from group counselling when the first pangs of grief are over. This can range from the mutual support of a social group for widows who get together to help each other, to structured groups such as Weiss's programme in which formal seminars/discussions focus on specific topics of importance to bereaved people (Parkes and Weiss, 1983). Many of those who have run such groups have used models of 'therapy' derived from psychiatric settings and may be in danger of treating the bereaved as if they were sick.

This may explain the modest results of the few attempts that have been made to evaluate such groups.

There are, of course, numerous other organizations available to widows, and without the disadvantages of being limited to widows only, they can serve as a bridge to the wider community. However, the newly bereaved are not readily clubbable, and the organizations that offer personal help on an individual basis may be needed to enable them to take the first step. A list of national organizations for the bereaved is given at the end of this book and the **Hospice Information Service** publishes regular lists of training courses relating to death and bereavement.

Despite the existence of these resources, the day-to-day counselling of the bereaved will remain the responsibility of those members of the care-giving professions whose work brings them in close contact with bereaved people: clergy, doctors, district nurses, social workers, health visitors, and the like.

What special contributions can members of these care-giving professions give to the bereaved? Let us consider first the clergy.

THE CLERGY AND OTHER RELIGIOUS LEADERS AND THERAPISTS

In most churches, it has been traditional for the clergy to visit the sick and the bereaved, but the opportunity thus given to the clergy is often missed. Clergy, like everyone else, may be embarrassed and ineffectual when face to face with those who have been or are about to be bereaved. Many have now abandoned the tradition of routinely visiting bereaved parishioners they may never have met. This may explain some of the inconsistent benefits from religious observance discussed on pages 209–12.

Among the twenty-two London widows only seven had been visited by a clergyman at the time of the first interview a month after bereavement, yet five of those seven had enjoyed the visit and found it helpful. Several, who had an ongoing relationship with their local vicar, found him a 'tower of strength' and spoke very warmly of the encouragement and support he had given.

Clearly, parishioners who are already on friendly terms with their priest will be more likely to accept him than those who are complete strangers, or who believe that his only reason for calling is to take advantage of their bereaved state to get them back to church. And yet the majority of widows did express belief in God, although only a minority accepted, in full, the doctrines of a particular church. One gets the impression that a visit from the right clergyman at the right time would have been valued by all of them.

In general, the first twenty-four hours is too soon for strangers to call. The bereaved person is still in a state of numbness or shock and is not yet ready to come to grips with his or her confusion. At a guess we would say that the best time for clergy to visit is before the funeral, during the week that follows it and, when needed, later in the first year of bereavement.

It is when the funeral is over and the family have begun to disperse that the bereaved are likely to be left alone. At this time their grief is at its height and they are having to begin to try to deal with the painful, perplexing thoughts that beset them.

The role of the visiting clergyman is similar to that of any other friendly person who wishes the bereaved person well and would like to be of help. He, too, should be prepared to show by his manner acceptance of grief and particularly acceptance of the bitter anger against God and human beings that is likely to be expressed. He will not help matters by returning the anger, by meeting emotion with dogma or agony with glib assurance. He will help best by listening and, if invited to do so, by trying to collaborate with the bereaved person in an honest attempt to 'get things straight'. The clergyman who is 'in tune' with his parishioners may be able to find the right prayer or a helpful biblical quotation, but it is tempting to hide behind such 'easy' answers and avoid involvement by too readily prescribing 'magical' solutions to grief. Nobody can provide the one thing the bereaved person seeks – the lost person back again. But an honest acknowledgement of helplessness in this respect may make the visitor more acceptable than a spurious omniscience.

Members of other religious denominations will seek support from members of their own faith. For instance Azhar and Varma (1995) divided 30 Muslims who were clinically depressed after bereavement, at random, into two groups of 15, one received antidepressant medication and the other an antidepressant plus the addition of 'religious psychotherapy', by which they mean eliciting thoughts and ideas about their emotions and discussion of verses from the *Q'ran* and *Hadith*. This group were also encouraged to pray. Over the next year the group who received the Islamic therapy showed significantly less depression than those taking antidepressants alone. Which of the components of 'religious psychotherapy' explains this improvement it is not possible to say but the study raises important possibilities.

A person who goes to a clergyman or Imam probably expects to find a religious answer to problems. A person who goes to a doctor expects a medical answer. Because people are 'open' to the types of answer they seek, it is appropriate that doctors and clergy should attempt to provide the answers they feel qualified to give and not minimize the value of these answers. But members of both these professions must be sufficiently flexible to redefine their own roles so that they can act more effectively. The clergyman or doctor who can find the time to allow a bereaved person to talk about his or her feelings and fears will add a fresh dimension to counselling and a greater depth to their relationship with their parishioner or patient.

THE PRIMARY MEDICAL CARE TEAM

In Britain today, it is usually the family doctor to whom bereaved people most often turn for professional help. Thus in Parkes' study of the case records of forty-four unselected London widows (see Appendix 9) it was found that three-quarters (thirty-three) had consulted their GP at some time during the first six months of bereavement. In a more recent study a similar proportion (72 per cent) of first-degree relatives of patients who died in three London health districts had visited their family doctor during the first 10 months after bereavement (Koffman *et al.*, 2005).

Recognizing the key part that primary care teams are in a position to play, both in identifying problems before they become illnesses and in initiating and monitoring whatever intervention is needed, most general practices in the UK now keep a register of each death that occurs and the names of newly bereaved persons in their

practice. The fact that, in Britain, many family members are registered with the same primary care team makes this a practical possibility. Routine support was significantly more likely to be provided
by practices that kept a death register, discussed deaths together,
identified bereaved relatives, and had a special interest in palliative
care (Harris and Kendrick, 1998).

Primary care teams today provide a range of services themselves
and act as links to other special services. It is no longer the GP who
provides all of the service. Even so, the GP is the gate-keeper and
many still use medication as their first option despite its limited value
to bereaved people.

Nearly a half (twenty-one) of the widows in the London Study
obtained a drug for the relief of psychological symptoms from their
GP at some time during the first eighteen months of bereavement,
compared with only a fifth (nine) during a similar period before
bereavement.

Such medication was most common among the younger widows
even though, during the period preceding bereavement, it was the
older women who took rather more than the younger. But in our
society the commonest drugs taken are not those prescribed by
doctors but those we choose for ourselves – alcohol and tobacco.
Forty-one per cent of the young widows and 37 per cent of the
young widowers in the Harvard Study were smoking more a year
after bereavement than they had before it and 38 and 31 per cent,
respectively, were drinking more alcohol. Similar results have been
found by Umberson (1987).

These findings suggest that widespread use is made of drugs
to alleviate the stress of bereavement. Were their popularity any
indication of their value, drugs would be counted the principal
treatment for grief.

Drugs are, of course, taken for various reasons. Night sedatives
are popular (and alcohol is commonly taken for sleep), but tranquillizers are often given for anxiety by day and a great deal of use is now
made of antidepressive drugs, some of which also have sedative
effects.

Many widows and widowers complain of insomnia and subsequent
tiredness during the day, which adds to the difficulty of coping with
life. Night sedatives are prescribed in the hope that adequate sleep
will help them to deal more effectively with their problems in the
daytime. Some use alcohol as a sedative, but the level in the blood
wears off rapidly during the night and may cause the drinker to wake
up three to four hours later. Medical prescriptions provide better

drugs and control. Both forms of therapy are potentially habit forming and it is wiser not to take them regularly every night but to make use of them only intermittently. If a bereaved person has had one bad night and fears that the next will be equally bad, it makes sense to take something at bedtime. A dozen nitrazepam tablets can be made to last over two or three months if used judiciously, and they are more effective and less likely to be abused than a bottle of whisky.

Society permits the bereaved a greater measure of control over their alcohol intake than it does over other drugs, but it also provides a system whereby they can obtain some of the time of a highly trained professional, whose skills should include a greater understanding of psychosocial problems than is to be expected from the average barman. They are likely, therefore, to feel safer if their drugs are being prescribed by a doctor, who will tell them when they have had enough and who can supply a variety of medications to suit their special needs.

Dependence on alcohol is a real danger after bereavement, and thirteen of the 115 bereaved psychiatric patients in the combined Bethlem and Case-note Studies were suffering from chronic alcoholism. In the case of tobacco the dangers to health are, of course, now well established, and smoking may even account for a part of the increased mortality from coronary infarction that has been found following bereavement. The primary care team are in a position to provide health education on these issues and to monitor the consequences.

Drugs aside, family doctors, because they are likely to have cared for the dead person during the last illness and to have helped the relatives to prepare for bereavement, are in a very advantageous position to give psychological support after this event has occurred. Many widows have spoken of the great help afforded by GPs, who have come to be regarded as friends, and they are often thought of as the wisest and most understanding people available. Through their profession they are acquainted with the reality of death, and this should make it possible for the bereaved to talk to them about this taboo topic.

Their advice is treated with respect and their attitude to the situation is taken seriously. Unfortunately, it is all too easy for them to convey to the relatives their own sense of defeat when one of their patients dies. For example, they may see the widow as a survivor rather than as a person with a life of her own to lead, and this view will colour their attitude to her.

The GP who can recognize grief as the painful process through which a family must pass in becoming another kind of family is aware that the symptoms to which it gives rise must be seen in perspective. By showing willingness to accept their need to mourn, GPs may help them more positively than they would by taking the easier course of prescribing antidepressives and tranquillizers. It may be important, for instance, that they reassure a distressed woman that her feelings of anger and guilt or her hallucinations of her dead husband are a normal reaction to loss, and that physical symptoms resembling those suffered by her husband do not mean that she is dying of the same disease. They may need to remind her that she is not a bad mother if she finds that it is hard to cope with the demands of her children, and to assure her that it is right for her to call upon the support of others to help them and herself. And they may also need to sit patiently through outbursts of hostility towards themselves as one of the people who might have saved her husband and to show, by their attitude, that they understand such feelings and are not going to allow them to spoil their relationship with their patient.

In like manner community nurses, health visitors, and social workers who are in a position to help bereaved people will be able to find many opportunities to do so, and there is no need for me to reiterate, for each of them, the general principles that will have emerged from consideration of the roles of the clergy and the family doctor.

PSYCHIATRIC AND PSYCHOLOGICAL SERVICES

Since psychiatrists have, or should have, experience in recognizing the indirect ways of expressing conflict that are employed when grief becomes distorted, it may be easier for them than for others to help the bereaved person to deal with these problems; and since they are also likely to be well acquainted with the uses and side effects of the wide range of drugs that are available today, they can employ these, where appropriate, to tide the bereaved patient over a difficult period. Furthermore, they have access to a variety of forms of therapeutic community currently available – day hospitals, night hostels, in-patient psychiatric units – which can, in certain cases, provide the patient with a temporary retreat.

It should be emphasized, nevertheless, that the care of the bereaved is a communal responsibility, and family members and others should not withdraw their support simply because a person has been referred to a psychiatrist.

Under the National Health Service in Britain, community psychiatric nurses and psychiatric social workers play a part in the care of those who are referred for psychiatric treatment, they also liaise with the primary care team. Often they are the people who work most closely with the family and they constitute valuable additions to the therapeutic team. The way in which they are used varies greatly from one area to another, but since they often have more time and more opportunity than psychiatrists to visit patients' homes, they are uniquely placed to participate in family-centred service, they are also well placed to assist voluntary organizations.

In Australia Raphael (1977) carried out a random allocation study of the effects of her own intervention as a psychiatrist with bereaved people assessed as being at 'high risk'. This study closely resembled Parkes' study reported on pages 241–2, the main difference being that in Parkes' study the support was given by trained volunteers. Raphael's study showed significant benefits to the psychiatric intervention group that were somewhat greater than those reported by Parkes.

In recent years psychologists have become an important source of help and cognitive therapies are their own special contribution. Psychologists, more than social workers and counsellors, have the scientific training that will encourage research and, as has been shown, they are already paying dividends. It may well be that it is to this profession that we should look in the future for a lead in the establishment of well-founded services for the bereaved.

Many psychologists have taken a particular interest in the treatment of anxiety disorders, panic syndromes, depression and PTSD. They should be consulted when any of these problems are pronounced or a client fails to respond to traditional forms of support.

Claims have been made for a wide variety of other 'therapies' for bereavement, these include art therapy (Schut *et al.*, 1997a; Simon, 1982), Gestalt therapy (Parkes and Sills, 1994; Smith, 1985), hypnosis (Savage, 1993), imagery (Cerney, 1985), rational emotive therapy (van den Bout, 1994), and logotherapy (Giovinco and Monahan, 1994) but in the absence of well-conducted comparative studies it is not possible to evaluate their effectiveness.

It will be clear from what has been said, that there are a variety of people available to meet the variety of problems that can complicate bereavement. While there is no single therapy that solves all of these problems, the evidence from well-conducted research now enables us to match the problem to the therapy in a majority of cases. Those in the front line of care need to identify those who need help, to make themselves aware of the resources available in their areas, and to monitor the outcome of their attempts to match problems to solutions.

16

REACTIONS TO OTHER
TYPES OF LOSS

> Departure from this happy place, our sweet
> Recess, and onely consolation left
> Familiar to our eyes, all places else
> Inhospitable appeer and desolate,
> Nor knowing us nor known . . .
> John Milton, *Paradise Lost*

Thus far we have confined our attention to bereavement by death, we now move on to consider to what extent grief at the death of a loved person resembles reactions to other types of loss. Can the lessons we have learned in our studies of widowhood be of help, for instance, to the sick or the physically disabled? Conversely, can studies of other types of loss add to our understanding of reactions to bereavement? These are the themes of a multi-contributor book *Coping with Loss: Helping Patients and their Families* (Parkes and Markus, 1998), which looks at the many losses and changes that are met by members of the health-care professions. Other types of loss that have been studied using the same frame of reference include divorce (Kitson, 1982), unemployment (Fagin and Little, 1984), forced migration (Munoz, 1980), death of a domestic pet (Keddie, 1977; Morley and Fook, 2005; Rynearson, 1978), the recognition of serious and persistent mental illness in one's family (Solomon and Draine, 1996), similar recognition (by DNA testing) of hereditary risk of a life-threatening illness, Huntington's disease, (Sobel and Cowan, 2000), childlessness (Houghton and Houghton, 1977), relinquishing a baby to adoption (Askren and Bloom, 1999), and the losses involved in, of all things, recovery from cancer (Maher, 1982).

For the purposes of this chapter we draw on studies of the reactions to three types of loss: loss of a limb, loss of a home and dying from cancer (these are described in more detail in Parkes, 1972b, 1973, 1976). The field is a broad one, and these subjects have been chosen to illustrate it rather than to represent it.

We shall look, in turn, at the principal components of grief as they have emerged in bereavement studies and see what comparable features are discernible in the reactions to these three types of loss. Each of the main components of grief has had a chapter to itself in the present work, and it is not possible, in the space that remains, to give as thorough an appraisal of similar phenomena as they appear after these losses.

To recapitulate the features that are major aspects of many bereavement reactions:

I – The trauma response

1   *An alarm reaction* – anxiety, restlessness, and the physiological accompaniments of fear.
2   *Anger and self-reproaches*, which are often unjustified by the circumstances.
3   *Post-traumatic stress reactions*, including PTSD, the specific pathological response, and the less specific Anxiety States and Panic Syndromes.

II – The grief response

4   *Pining and an urge to search* for and to find the lost person in some form.
5   *A continuing bond* reflected in relocating the lost person, identification phenomena and a sense of that person's presence within the self.
6   *Pathological variants of grief*, i.e. the reaction may be excessive and prolonged or inhibited and inclined to emerge in delayed or distorted form.

III – The psycho-social transition

7   *A sense of dislocation* between the world that is and the world that should be, often expressed as a sense of mutilation or emptiness which reflects the individual's need to relearn their assumptive world.
8   *A process of realization*, i.e. the way in which the bereaved moves from denial or avoidance of recognition of the loss

253

towards acceptance and the adoption of a new model of the world.

9   This process may be impaired by the feelings of *helplessness and hopelessness*, which characterize depression.

LOSS OF A LIMB

In the amputation study referred to above Parkes obtained information from thirty-seven men and nine women under the age of seventy who were interviewed one month and thirteen months after the amputation of an arm or a leg. Loss of the limb was the main disability from which the majority of the subjects suffered. All were well enough to be fitted with an artificial limb. The interviews were all carried out by Parkes and followed a similar pattern to those of the London Study.

Loss of a limb does not, on the face of it, seem to bear much resemblance to loss of a spouse. People do not love their left leg, at least not in the same way that they love their spouse. Society does not expect us to mourn for the loss of a leg, and the soldier who insisted on placing his amputated leg in his tomb, to await the coming of the rest of his mortal frame, was clearly atypical. But those who have studied the psychological reaction to amputation repeatedly refer to the 'grief' they encounter. Thus Kessler (1951) wrote: 'The emotion most persons feel when told that they must lose a limb has been well compared with the emotion of grief at the death of a loved one'. Wittkower (1947) said: 'Mourning is the normal emotional reaction'; Dembo, Ladieu-Leviton, and Wright (1952): 'A person may mourn his loss'; and Fisher (1960): 'The reaction to loss of a limb, and for that matter to loss of function of a vital part, is grief and depression'. In none of these studies, however, is it clearly indicated just what it is that the amputee is mourning for or even just what is meant by 'mourning'.

Comparison with the components of the reaction to bereavement helps us to clarify the issues.

I – The trauma response

1. Alarm. The first component of the bereavement reaction, alarm, is to be expected in any situation of danger and it does, of course, occur in many people who are about to undergo or have just undergone major surgery. Feelings of anxiety, tension, and restlessness were common among the amputees and, during the year after amputation, 30 per cent complained of three or more symptoms that are attributable to the types of disturbance of the autonomic nervous system described in Chapter 3. Loss of appetite and weight were the rule during the immediate post-operative period, and 35 per cent of the amputees still required sedatives to help them to sleep at night a month after the operation. As pointed out in Chapter 3, there is nothing specific about the alarm reaction, but it is worth noting that amputees, because of their physical helplessness during and after the operation, are more reliant on others during the period of transition than are widows. They may, however, feel protected during this period. Only later do they begin to have to 'stand on their own feet' and give up the security arising from the role of 'patient'. Those who fail may be seen as 'cripples' but the stigma associated with this term is such that we prefer not to use it. Rather less negative is the term 'disabled' but this, too, should be reserved for the minority whose limitations necessitate a reduction in activities, and entitle them to special services.

2. Anger and self-reproaches Feelings of bitterness or *anger* are commonly expressed by amputees. Just as the widow says, 'I can't see a married couple without thinking – why should it happen to me?', so 35 per cent of the amputees admitted to feelings of envy towards healthy, intact people. Intense anger may be directed towards doctors or others whose actions might have helped to bring about the amputation, and, like the widow or widower, amputees often blame themselves.

3. Post-traumatic reactions Severe anxiety and panic syndromes were not uncommon among amputees and a number of them, who had suffered physical injuries when losing their limb, undoubtedly suffered from PTSD in which they were haunted by memories of the trauma.

II – The loss response

4. The urge to search The search for the lost object is less obvious in reactions to amputation than it is in bereavement reactions. An important question here seems to be, 'What is it that has been lost?' All the amputees interviewed answered 'Yes' to the question 'Do you miss your limb?', but when questioned further on this point it was clear that what they missed most was the functions that had formerly been performed by means of the limb. Leg-amputees described how they would lie in bed *pining* to go swimming or run through fields. The more athletic and active they had been in the past the more they seemed to suffer.

Some amputees did admit to missing the limb itself and 63 per cent admitted some concern over the disposal of the limb after it had been cut off. 'Outside the ward there's a great chimneystack. I used to look at the smoke and think, "They're having a burn-up" but I comforted myself by thinking that they might have kept my leg for medical research. I didn't ask them.'

Whereas the maintenance of contact with loved persons requires the use of searching, and following behaviour from early childhood, there is no need to develop such behaviour in relation to parts of the body. Nevertheless, like the widow or widower, amputees do tend to be preoccupied with thoughts of loss. They mourn for their lost intactness, particularly at times when this is forced on their attention.

Provided they are physically fit there is little that younger amputees cannot do with only one leg or one arm, once they have learned how. But many amputees are physically frail or old, and even in the case of a younger person it may take a long time for a well-fitting prosthesis to be achieved. In the meanwhile they must get about as best they can. For the new leg-amputee, going up and down stairs, carrying a cup of coffee across a room, or going to the toilet are difficult and dangerous manoeuvres. If it is an arm that has been lost, getting dressed, cutting up food, buying a bus ticket, or opening a letter are very hard. And either type of amputee is likely to be self-conscious about being seen in public in a mutilated state: 'Kids look at you – it's like the Lord Mayor's Show when I go out'.

Although 67 per cent of the amputees attempted to take their mind off their loss, they were constantly being reminded of it, and each frustration brought back a feeling of painful pining for the world that was no longer theirs.

5. A continuing bond   What of the identification phenomena that were apparent after bereavement? Do they too have their equivalent in the amputee?

From these studies it appears that amputees do experience a sense of the presence of the lost object, which is referred to in the medical literature as the 'phantom limb', indeed this is reported more frequently than the 'phantom husband'. A possible explanation for this may be that the phantom limb and the phantom husband are not strictly analogous. A wife, however close she may be to her husband, is not connected to him by nervous pathways that must be severed when he dies. It is reasonable to suppose that the phantom limb is, to some extent at any rate, attributable to the fact that a part of the nervous system, including nerves of the limb and all of their central connections, remains in existence after the removal of the limb.

Nevertheless, the phantom limb is influenced by psychological factors. Thus, one amputee described how, after the first weeks, his phantom limb seemed to grow shorter so that it was now a little foot situated where his shin would formerly have been. 'As soon as I put my artificial leg on it zips down to the foot again.' Clearly the location of the phantom in space was governed partially by this patient's psychological need to identify the residue of the lost limb with the substitute that had now been provided for it.

A phantom limb does seem to be treated as a part of the self. For example, one amputee described how he would lift his stump in the air if his wife was vacuuming the floor for fear that she would hurt his phantom foot.

Just as the widow may have symptoms resembling those of her husband, so the phantom limb may be perceived as suffering from the same disease that brought about the limb's removal. An ulcer on the heel, for instance, may still be felt to be present and even the pain that was suffered prior to surgery may persist. Among twelve patients who had experienced severe pain in a limb for eight weeks or more prior to amputation, nine continued to have severe pain in their phantom limb afterwards. Severe pain in the phantom limb was much less frequently reported by amputees whose pre-operative pain (and most had had some pre-operative pain) had been present for less than eight weeks (six out of thirty-four).

6. *Pathological responses*   Many of the complicated reactions to amputation resemble those to bereavement, they commonly reflect distortion or *prolongation* of the process of realizing the loss and, although additional research is needed to clarify the picture, it does appear that one of the main types of problematic reaction found among widows and widowers is also found in amputees – prolonged grief.

Like the identification symptoms of the bereaved, the pains in the phantom limb tended to disappear, but it is well recognized that in a minority of such cases pains persist or recur at some later date. The problem of the painful phantom limb has long been a matter of concern to surgeons and it is not possible here to review the literature on this subject. A wide variety of physical methods of treatment have been undertaken, but it seems that, whatever the treatment, there is a small minority of amputees who continue to complain. No physical cause is known for the majority of these pains but several studies have revealed their susceptibility to psychological influence: thus they have sometimes been aggravated by anger, tiredness, and frustration, and relieved by hypnosis and other forms of suggestion. Parkes found that complaints of pain are commoner in compulsively self-reliant individuals who find it difficult to accept helplessness and they often persist in the face of unsettled or inadequate settlement of compensation claims. It may be, then, that persistence of phantom pains sometimes represents one type of difficulty in accepting the loss of the limb.

By contrast there were sixteen patients who showed *little or no emotional reaction* to the loss of their limb. 'I had a feeling that I could kick the world about for quite a long time', said one patient; 'they told me they were going to write me up as their prize patient'. Later, however, he realized how restricted he was: 'I wept bitterly – the helplessness, being dependent on people, the humiliation'. Several amputees said that they had been told that the prosthesis would be a perfectly good substitute for the part that was being removed and they did not allow themselves to consider the possibility that they would be disabled in any way. This view of the situation was less easy to maintain when they left hospital and started trying to compete with intact others in the outside world. A man who earned his living as a roofer refused to accept that he would have to find alternative occupation. A few weeks after being discharged from hospital he was readmitted with a broken leg. He had fallen off a roof.

III – The psycho-social transition

7. *Dislocation* Feelings of internal loss of self, or *mutilation*, were also common and were well expressed by one man: 'You sometimes feel you've had part of your body taken away and you're no longer part of the world – they've taken part of your life away'. Another said: 'You feel mutilated, you know you'll never be the same again ... Underneath I feel badly damaged' – the 'underneath' reflects the injury to the self that lies within the body whose intactness has been shattered.

8. *A process of realization* Do amputees move from denial of the full meaning of amputation towards an acceptance of the true situation? We think they do. Just as the widow finds it hard at first to

believe that her husband is dead and often has a strong sense of his presence nearby, so the amputee has difficulty in accepting the loss of a limb and continues to feel that it is still present. Thus 39 per cent of the amputees described an initial period of 'numbness'; all forty-six had a feeling of the persisting presence of the lost limb, and 87 per cent related how they often forgot that the limb was missing and went to use it. The sense of numbness passed within a few days, but a year later 80 per cent still had some sense of the presence of the limb, 35 per cent still forgot it had gone from time to time, and 46 per cent said that they still found it hard to believe what had happened.

The modern prosthesis, despite intensive research and modification over the years, is a poor, cumbersome, and uncomfortable thing by comparison with a real limb. Lacking any sensation or muscle power of its own, it must be fitted to a stump of bone and tissue which was never meant to bear weight in the first place and which has an infuriating habit of shrinking or expanding whenever a decent fit has been obtained. The limb-fitters, who are great craftsmen in metal and leather, spend their lives patching, modifying, and remodelling the socket into which the stump must fit, and the amputees spend a lot of their time waiting hopefully for the perfect fit, which may never come. Patience and the acceptance of a modicum of discomfort are essential if the amputee is to make a good adjustment to the realities of a new life.

9. Helplessness and hopelessness Among the forty-six amputees interviewed by Parkes there were twelve who were still depressed and withdrawn a year after amputation. Most of them were making much less use of their artificial limb than their doctors had expected (bearing in mind their physical powers) and people were inclined to accuse them of 'giving up'. In fact several of these men and women seemed to believe that they were crippled for life and, because they believed it, they may well in fact be crippled for life.

Without placing too fine a point on it, it does seem that the psychosocial transition from being an intact person to being an amputee is a painful and time-consuming process which is, in many ways, similar to the transition from married person to widow or widower. It would seem justifiable, therefore, to regard these two situations as parts of the same field of study. Just what this implies for the organization of health care is spelled out elsewhere (Parkes and Markus, 1998), and there is no space to repeat it here. Instead, let us take a brief look at the findings of Fried's (1962) study concerning the effects of relocating 789 Boston slum dwellers. They were interviewed before compulsory rehousing took place and again two years later.

RELOCATION

Marc Fried (1962) carried out a study of the relocation of slum dwellers at the Center for Community Studies at Harvard Medical School, with Erich Lindemann as principal investigator. It is not surprising, therefore, that Fried should have attempted to find the same 'symptoms' in relocated slum dwellers that Lindemann had previously found in the bereaved (1944). The surprise, if surprise there be, is in the extent to which he succeeded. He writes:

> While there are wide variations in the success of post-relocation adjustment and considerable variability in the depth and quality of the loss experience, it seems quite precise to refer to the reactions of the majority as grief: These are manifest in the feelings of painful loss, the continued longing, the general depressive tone, frequent symptoms of psychological or social or somatic distress, the active work required in adapting to the altered situation, the sense of helplessness, the occasional expressions of both direct and displaced anger, and tendencies to idealize the lost place . . .
> 46% gave evidence of a fairly severe grief reaction or worse.

As in amputation reactions, each of the components of grief is present. Thus, Fried describes the way in which the relocated slum dweller attempts to minimize and postpone the realization of his loss by trying to avoid thinking about it, but, as in other forms of grief, the painful memories break through. Thus, one woman who had been brought up in the West End of Boston said: 'Home is where you hang your hat . . . Don't look back – try to go ahead'. But when asked how she felt when her old home was demolished she replied: 'It's just like a plant . . . when you tear up its roots, it dies. I didn't die, but I felt kind of bad. It was home . . .'.

Fried makes several references to 'somatic distress' and the physical accompaniments of the alarm reaction, but he gives rather more evidence for the urge to search. In this connection it is again relevant to ask, 'What is it that has been lost?' – for the answer to this question will determine what is missed. In the interviews carried out before relocation, an attempt was made to ascertain the 'focus of commitment' expressed by each respondent with regard to the neighbourhood. Their replies were grouped into 'Accessibility and financial', 'Interpersonal', 'Places', 'Interpersonal and Places', and 'Nothing'. When the respondents were reinterviewed after relocation, those who had expressed an *attachment* to people, places, or both showed much more grief than those who had valued the neighbourhood for its accessibility or financial aspects or those who had expressed no commitment at all. Intensity of grief was also found to be related to the amount of the surrounding neighbourhood that had been known to the respondent; in other words, intensity of grief correlated with the measured area of physical life-space that had been lost (in other types of loss we can seldom find so clear a measure of the magnitude of the loss).

Among respondents whose attachment was primarily to places it would seem to be places that were missed most, and we can see the urge to recover the lost object reflected in the wish expressed by some to return to the West End. For example, one person said: 'I always felt I had to go home to the West End and even now I feel like crying when I pass by'. And another: 'I used to stare at the spot where the building stood'. Those whose attachment was primarily to friends and neighbours were more likely to stress interpersonal loss: 'I lost all the friends I knew'. Attempts to retain as much as possible of the lost world were made by families who 'tried to remain physically close to the area they knew even though most of their close interpersonal relationships remained disrupted'.

Feelings of anger were expressed as denigration of the new environment by comparison with the *idealized memory* of the old, 'I felt cheated', said one respondent.

Most striking of all Fried's findings, however, is that many of his respondents expressed feelings of personal *mutilation* in a vivid way. 'I felt like my heart was taken out of me', said one. 'Something of me went with the West End.' 'It was like a piece being taken from me.' Like the widows described in Chapter 7 these people seem to have experienced a loss of self, a psychological mutilation, which was subjectively just as real as the mutilation experienced by the amputee. Once again we are forced to realize that the skin is not the only boundary around the self and that the home we live in and the people to whom we are attached are, in some sense, ours – they are parts of ourselves. Although Fried does not mention this point, there are several published accounts of the way in which people who have lost a home often try to build another in the same place and manner. Similarly, immigrants in an alien culture commonly attempt to recreate around them the culture they have lost. It is clearly not possible for a person to identify with a lost home in the same way that one can identify with a lost person. But the identification symptoms of widows and the efforts of relocated persons to re-create their lost environment seem to be two different ways of attempting to retain, in some measure, the world that has been lost.

Fried's assessments of the health and psychosocial adjustment of his respondents revealed two patterns of reaction that were associated with a high incidence of 'problems'. There were some individuals who overreacted to relocation: although they did not seem to be strongly committed to the neighbourhood before relocation they showed severe grief afterwards and required a lot of help from social and legal agencies. There were others who seemed strongly committed to the neighbourhood prior to relocation but who showed minimal grief afterwards: they were found to have a disproportionate frequency of physical and psychosomatic problems. It seems quite likely that these two patterns of 'overreaction' and 'denial' correspond to the 'prolonged' and 'avoided' forms of grief that have been found following bereavement.

It seems that attachment to home is similar to attachment to parent. Indeed, Lorenz referred to partners as having 'home valency' (1963, p. 186). Clearly both home and partner are sources of security to which we will turn when feeling insecure. The data from Parkes' studies suggest that loss of a home can give rise to grief that is similar to that experienced when losing a spouse.

THE GRIEFS OF THE DYING

In her influential studies of patients with late-stage cancer Elizabeth Kubler Ross formulated 'stages of dying' that are very similar to the stages of grief (1970). These were Denial, Anger, Bargaining, Depression and Acceptance and they correspond approximately to the phases of grieving described on page 7. This said, Ross's 'stages' have proved even more controversial than the phases of grief and most thanatologists now consider them simplistic. Indeed Parkes' own experience of working as a psychiatrist for 40 years in two hospices indicates that not only is the course of cancer, and other life-threatening illnesses, very variable, so that we should not expect a uniform pattern, but the losses that the patient suffers in the course of the illness are numerous and most grieve more for the physical limitations caused by the illness, and the suffering of their families, than they do for the loss of their own lives. This does not mean that loss and grief are not frequent problems but it does make it less likely that the reaction can be easily predicted. This said many patients, if they live long enough, seem to progress in fits and starts from relative incomprehension, avoidance and denial, towards some kind of acceptance of death. It is one of the merciful aspects of cancer that it gradually erodes all of the appetites and with them the *vis a tergo*, or drive for life.

This progression is very much influenced by previous experiences and attachment patterns, as are bereavements. A recent study of patients with advanced cancer uses the term 'demoralization' for a cluster of symptoms and assumptions that indicate a desperate clinging to life, a need to remain in control, and difficulty in accepting the prospect of death in people who believe that life can hold no meaning without their health (Jacobsen *et al.*, 2006). Feelings of helplessness and hopelessness are present but other symptoms of major depressive disorder are not and MDD constitutes a different condition. Perhaps the most revealing difference between these two conditions is the finding that, while patients with depression often express a wish to die, patients with 'demoralization' express a wish to live. This difficulty in accepting reality and letting go of life resembles the unrealistic pining of patients with prolonged grief disorder for the lost person and may, indeed, be a kind of PGD. Jacobsen *et al.* concluded that 'the individual may be grieving for the aspirations that he can no longer fulfill'. While it is common for patients to deny the prospect of death early in the illness most patients with late-stage cancers eventually accept reality and, in good conditions of care, die in a state of relative peace.

CONCLUSIONS AND IMPLICATIONS FOR CARE

We have tried to show, in this chapter, how some of the phenomena that have emerged in studies of the reaction to bereavement are found in similar form following other types of loss. Like stress, which was discussed in Chapter 3, loss can have many meanings and there is no reason to believe that all types and degrees of loss give rise to identical reactions. But, like stress, a loss tends to be a *post hoc* attribution. That is to say, we may not know, until after it has occurred, whether a given life-event is to be construed as a loss or a gain. 'You are not losing a daughter but gaining a son', says the optimistic wedding guest, but the truth of the matter is that the bride's mother is undergoing a major change in her life that, from her point of view, may be regarded as a net profit or a net loss. She may grieve or she may rejoice, or, with the typical human ability to split herself, she may oscillate between tears and delight. The hard-headed research worker may well find it difficult to classify such life-events as the marriage of a daughter as losses or gains but that need not deter us from studying both.

Similarly, there were a few amputees who were glad to lose a troublesome leg, and some of the slum dwellers interviewed by Fried regarded relocation as an unqualified blessing. Fried takes pains to point out that the grief that was expressed by the majority of his respondents might not be found among other populations in other places undergoing other experiences of relocation: the degree of attachment to a particular physical and social environment shown by the Boston working class, for instance, might not be found among nomads, sailors, soldiers, or ambitious young business executives for whom a change of city may be part of a desired pattern of adventurous progress.

Nevertheless, the similarities between bereavement, amputation, and the reactions to relocation, must lead us to expect that the main conclusions about problems and interventions also apply. Just as most bereaved people come through without the need for help from outside their network of friends and families, so too will most people faced with other types of loss.

Insofar as psychological difficulties do occur they are likely to reflect traumatic losses, personal vulnerability, and lack of effective social support. Since these difficulties can often be anticipated and/or treated it is important that those in a position to do so should be trained to recognize the difficulties and either provide the appropriate intervention or steer people to those who can. Finally, it is important that research be undertaken to test the theory that the methods of intervention that have and are still being developed to solve the problems of bereavement be developed and refined in other situations of loss and change.

Some of this work is already being carried out. Thus, the field of trauma and stress is already well developed and recent research indicates that changes in the assumptive world, that are inevitable after bereavement, are also likely to be necessary after other life-change events (Kauffman, 2002). Anticipatory preparation to enable a realistic picture of the new world to be built up before the destruction of the old can be useful, as can provision of support through the period of transition of such a kind that the necessary grief work is facilitated with eventual acceptance of the loss. Also, help can be given where necessary to introduce the individuals undergoing the transition to the new opportunities open to them, and to facilitate changes in their attitude by means of appropriate events (e.g. anniversary celebrations, holidays, training courses, or other 'rituals' that have the significance of rites of passage and act as turning-points in the process of realization).

The establishment of such methods of education and support on a sound scientific basis must be an important task of professionals in the field of public health in the years to come. We use the term 'public health' because we believe that 'preventive psychiatry' is too narrow a term for this field. We should not be concerned solely with attempting to reduce the prevalence of mental illness but should be seeking to improve the quality of living, the mental health of the community.

Times of transition are times of opportunity and any confrontation with an unfamiliar world is both an opportunity for autonomous mastery and a threat to one's established adjustment to life. Taken overall, the effect of such experiences is more likely to be beneficial than harmful. Education and upbringing have as their chief aim increased mastery of the unfamiliar, and mature people are the ones who have achieved a degree of autonomy that enables them to approach the unfamiliar with confidence. But there are some life changes that, because of their magnitude or because of a particular characteristic, carry a special risk of producing, not maturation, but dislocation.

This book, in focusing on bereavement, has attempted to illustrate and explain the consequences of one such change, and in this penultimate chapter brief reference has been made to three other types of change. No doubt, in time, the whole range of reactions to life changes (or PSTs) will be mapped out and we shall have a body of knowledge with implications for child care, education, medicine, and welfare services of all kinds.

But it is not enough to institute new ways of housing the homeless, rehabilitating the crippled, or counselling the bereaved. Any plan for change should include an attempt to anticipate and provide for the psychosocial effects of the change. Thus, the decision to remove a leg should be made in full awareness of the patient's prospects of making a successful adjustment to life as an amputee; plans for slum clearance should be made in full awareness of the probable effects of relocation upon the population to be resettled; the decision to send a person to prison should be made only after there has been an attempt to predict the probable effects of this action upon the individual and his family, and the likely influence of these on the probability of future offences.

We can extend this reasoning to include decisions in many areas: decisions concerning the admission of young children to nursery schools, and of old people to institutions; the introduction of new methods in industry and the redeployment of labour; the bombing of a city or the closure of a factory. Each of these situations imposes upon the planner the obligation to take full account of how the decisions taken will affect the populations or individuals concerned, and to do all that is possible to ensure that any planned change leads to growth and maturation rather than dislocation, dysfunction and cycles of violence.

17

DISASTERS

> Every night I would wake suddenly. I was there again in the
> crash. The confusion. The silence. The panic. The smell of
> blood and dust and faeces and fear. I used to dream it all the
> time. I don't now. But I will *never* forget it.
>
> Anon. Quoted in *When Disaster Strikes*,
> Beverley Raphael, 1986

We all spend much of our lives avoiding disasters and one of the functions of the state is to prevent them. Yet they continue to happen.

A disaster is an event that overwhelms our lives, outrages our expectations and disrupts our social systems. If people were prepared for disasters they would seldom happen. Disasters are times of massive loss for which we are nearly always unprepared. They concatenate many of the circumstances that increase bereavement risk: unexpectedness, terror, violence, multiplicity of losses, and the disruption of the families and other social systems on which we rely.

Those of us who have worked in disaster areas will find that the memories stay with us. Aberfan, Cheddar, Hillsborough, Bradford, Zeebrugge, Rwanda, 9/11; The Tsunami – each memory a wrenching shame, an abiding pity, a sense of personal inadequacy in the face of so much horror. What did we achieve? So little.

Disasters bring us face to face with mortality, much like a diagnosis of cancer. It is not only our body but our society that is threatened, desecrated, spoiled, mutilated. Can we trust God, the Government, the sources of our security and organizers of our lives, to save us? Certainly not.

One thing is for sure, disasters will continue to happen and this means that we must do our best to prepare ourselves to help those who are afflicted by them. These include the injured, traumatized survivors, anyone who thinks they are still under threat, bereaved people, and anyone who may be traumatized by the horrors that they have witnessed or imagined. It is not only people directly affected by the disaster who are at risk; rescuers, helpers, and bystanders are all caught up in the disaster and the power of the media of communication brings the catastrophe into the home of every citizen who owns a television set. Much of the world was traumatized by 9/11.

So, what can be done? It will not have escaped the reader that most of the factors that give rise to problems in bereavement are likely to arise following disasters and that many of the lessons that we have learned will be of value in our care of both bereaved people and others who are not bereaved. Just as there is no single intervention that will help all who are bereaved, so there is no single intervention, be it anxiety management, interpersonal psychotherapy, eye-movement desensitization or critical incident stress debriefing, that will meet the needs of those affected by disasters. We need a variety of skills to meet a variety of problems and we need a well-organized team to assess the risks, to identify individuals at special risk, and to ensure that they receive the kind of help they need.

This may sound a tall order, but there is little in the care of people affected by disasters that differs from the care that we are, or should be giving, in our day-to-day work with people who have suffered traumatic losses, deaths in road traffic accidents and the like. All bereavement services are disaster services, only the scale is different.

In this chapter we have no need to discuss the treatment of traumatized individuals, that has already been covered in earlier pages. Instead we will examine the organizational issues that make it possible to bring together teams of trained professionals and volunteers who can respond effectively, with minimum risk to themselves, and give them the small amount of additional training that will prepare them for working in a disaster area. For a more extended treatment of these issues see Parkes (2008) and Gibson (2006).

PREPARATION FOR DISASTERS

Every hospital has disaster plans, they ensure a rapid response that will save as many lives as possible and meet needs for medical care, food and shelter for survivors; but few of them take adequate account of the psychological consequences of the disaster or prepare us for those modern disasters when there are few or no survivors. It follows that those responsible for organizing disaster services should include psychosocial carers in their plans and their disaster exercises.

In the UK the Civil Contingencies Act (2004) made it the responsibility of Social Services to appoint a senior manager to plan for the provision of psychosocial help in emergencies. Crisis Response Teams are to be planned in advance of emergency situations including staff from both professional and voluntary agencies.

Cruse Bereavement Care, as the leading British national organization for bereaved people, has been involved in the aftermath of many disasters. Its staff have learned the value of working closely with the Family Liaison Officers (FLOs) of the police, whose roles include the short-term support of families affected by disasters. As a result Cruse now makes use of FLOs in training volunteers to work in disaster areas and the FLOs make use of experienced trainers from Cruse to train police officers.

In the USA the situation is more complex and, while there are many services for bereaved people, they often lack the central organization that is provided by Cruse Bereavement Care. This was very apparent in New York, after 9/11, when bereaved people visiting the Family Center were faced by a bewildering number of organizations each of which had been provided with a table and chairs and a placard on which to proclaim their identity. The **Federal Emergency Management Agency** (FEMA) coordinates disaster responses and set up **Project Liberty** to provide crisis counselling, but a subsequent investigation one year later concluded '. . . problems in service delivery urgently need attention. Funding for post-terrorist intervention must be usable to address inadequate and poorly distributed local resources. Local control of service delivery is necessary to ensure that actual needs are met' (Grant *et al.*, 2003).

People suitable to work in disaster areas need to be carefully selected for this work. They need training in the management of anxiety, trauma and bereavement, experience of supporting those who have suffered traumatic losses, and to be able to cope with stressful situations. Their training should include role play of disaster situations. This can itself be stressful and can help to select out those who are too fragile or too tough minded for this work. It is a tribute to the people who choose to undertake such training that most of them pass all these tests! Previous experience of personal disaster is neither a bar nor a necessary qualification to work in disaster areas. Those who put themselves forward for training should be invited to discuss any major losses in their lives with a sensitive and respectful interviewer who will soon be able to see whether or not they have come through their experience in a mature and appropriate way.

Disasters come in many shapes and sizes, small and large, local or widespread. These variables of size and scale are not one and the same. We can have small-, medium- or large-scale disasters that are local, national or international in their spread. Each combination has a different consequence for the organization of services (Parkes, 1991). Small-scale local disasters are the most frequent and may have no need to draw in services from outside their existing locality, provided that their existing services have been properly trained and are not already over-stretched. As the scale increases the greater the likelihood that help will be needed from outside the disaster area. Similarly, disasters affecting a widespread population need to set up appropriate liaison with local, national, and international services in the areas affected by the disaster.

Some disasters produce widespread loss of property but few deaths, others cause many deaths but little other damage; some are man-made, others 'acts of God'; some are soon over, others linger on. It follows that there is no single plan that will meet the needs of all disasters. A variety of scenarios must be considered. This said, the outline that follows has wide relevance and provides a basis for planning.

For these purposes it is useful to speak of a succession of phases from the moment of *Impact*, when Emergency Services take responsibility for bringing order out of chaos and saving lives is the top priority; through a phase of *Recoil*, when the extent of the damage becomes clear, Crisis Response Teams are mobilized and operational centres set up; to the *Aftermath* phase when the disaster is over but continuing care is needed for those who need it; and to the final *Long-term* phase, when the Crisis Teams can be withdrawn and the minority who need long-term care transferred to local specialist services.

IMPACT PHASE

Most human beings have a remarkable capacity to cope in the face of disasters. The most immediate response is often one of silent bewilderment and the image, beloved of novelists and film makers, of crowds of people rushing screaming in all directions, is very exceptional and only likely to occur if escape routes are thought to be blocked.

Lacking the information that would allow proper planning, the impact phase is often one of chaos. People on the periphery may believe themselves to be in the centre and this 'illusion of centrality' may cause emergency services to be diverted from those who are most in need. It is essential to set up proper 'triage' as soon as possible in order to identify those in urgent need of help, those who have little immediate need of help and those for whom no help is possible.

The dissociation that enables most people to remain calm in the emergency sometimes gives rise to the fugues states, amnesias or other dissociative syndromes described on page 133 and there is an increased risk of later PTSD (Steiner *et al.*, 2003). Most dissociation will resolve once order is restored and people begin to feel safe again.

Disasters are news, and news of disasters soon attracts offers of help from all and sundry. In 1966, in the linear village of Aberfan, the road in and out of the village was blocked by the cars of would-be helpers within a few hours of the avalanche of coal slurry that had destroyed the village school and killed 118 children and 18 adults. Ambulances and rescue vehicles were unable to get through until the roads were cleared.

Among those offering help there will be some who have the necessary experience and training to be useful, but the majority have no such qualifications and will do more harm than good. Disaster teams are well used to recording the names and contact details of the dead and injured but they seldom take the same care to register the qualifications and contact details of those who offer help. Yet these can be a valuable resource when local services are overwhelmed or financial resources are in short supply.

Although the Emergency Services take priority there is a place for Psychological First Aid. The provision of sympathetic people and a safe place where a familiar cup of tea is provided can work wonders. So can the provision of reliable information and reassurance from someone in authority. The provision of identifying labels on tabards or well-recognized uniforms enables people to orient themselves and find the help they need from the person best qualified to give it. It also creates a feeling that order has been restored, even if it has not.

Self-sacrifice is the order of the day and we need to monitor ourselves as well as keeping an eye on the front line of rescuers who will work until they drop or start making mistakes before they give up. Support for the supporters is essential and managers must insist that they take a rest from time to time. They, too, may need to cry on a comforting shoulder or give vent to feelings of frustration or rage before calming down and returning to the fray.

RECOIL

Once the disaster is under control, the dead have been counted, and resources of money and manpower assessed, a suitable place can be found for an office, which combines the role of an information centre and an operations room for the Crisis Response Team (CRT).

Where possible these will have been selected and trained in advance but further training will always be needed and it may be necessary to augment the team depending on the circumstances. For large-scale disasters Gibson recommends the creation of mobile teams who can be brought in from outside the locality. Whether this is necessary or not, meetings between all relevant persons, including leaders of non-governmental organizations, and one or two disaster specialists will ensure an appropriate response.

All of this costs money and, while money may pour into a Disaster Fund, it will take time to set this up and the fund managers may not realize the importance of using the funds to facilitate psychosocial care. In one disaster area the managers would only pay out moneys to those directly affected by the disaster and volunteers could not even obtain reimbursement of their expenses. Emergency Funds are normally obtained from local, and when needed, national government sources. Governments like to be seen to be doing good and make it appear that funds will be provided for all services in a disaster area. But NGOs are advised to obtain written Contracts of Service as soon as time allows.

Meanwhile continuing support will be needed to affected families. When many deaths have taken place an emergency mortuary will be set up and families seeking missing persons may need someone to sit with them, to assist with and, if necessary, carry out preliminary identification of the dead person, prepare the family for what they will see, stay with them during the formal identification of the dead, and support them afterwards. They will find this much easier if a visit to a mortuary has been included in their basic training.

AFTERMATH

Once a disaster control centre has been set up, the CRT mobilized, and the likely psychosocial consequences of the disaster assessed, the main support work can begin.

This mobilization can take a long time if the participants fail to recognize the need for a military style of leadership. This is no time for democratic decision making. Professional rivalry has to be put on hold and everyone in the team has to know their place and their responsibilities. People who have been first on the scene and who have taken control, should not assume that this gives them the right to go on running the show. Nor should volunteers, who are generously giving their time, assume that this gives them the right to make up their own rules. Only those who are prepared to accept this discipline have a place in a CRT.

Having said all this, the wise team leader should set up regular meetings with the team to brief them, debrief them, and provide them with all the support that they need. The term debriefing was coined during World War II when air crews were debriefed after a mission. This provided the authorities with important information about the success or failure of the mission. During the Vietnam War it came to be seen as an opportunity to provide emotional support to traumatized servicemen. Subsequently the term Critical Incident Stress Debriefing (CISD) was developed by Mitchell who provided detailed instructions on its use in a variety of situations with people who had been exposed to trauma (Mitchell, 1983). In recent years, several attempts to evaluate CISD by random-allocation studies have undermined confidence in Mitchell's methods, particularly when used in one-off, individual, debriefing sessions (Bisson *et al.*, 1997; Van Emmerick *et al.*, 2002). Like old-style bereavement counselling, CISD provided a single simplistic solution to complex problems, a kind of cookery-book psychiatry.

Our view is that regular team meetings are important to enable the team leader to monitor the work of the team and to provide the emotional support and reassurance that we all need at such times. This is best carried out as a group with the whole team present. This ensures that everyone knows what is going on and has a chance to contribute. Once the team get to know and trust each other it becomes safe for them to share feelings of fear, sadness, inadequacy, and anger, which are recognized as natural reactions to the situation they all share. Used in this way debriefing can play a positive role in creating a cohesive and mutually supportive team.

There is no need to repeat here the ways in which we can identify those individuals and families who are in need of support, or the methods of intervention that are required. These have been covered in the preceding chapters. Special problems may arise when an entire community, including members of the caring services, have been traumatized. Community leaders, GPs, and members of the CRT may have been bereaved or suffered other losses. Trained staff may be in short supply and finances unavailable. In such cases volunteers and professional support from outside the disaster area need to be recruited, trained, and properly organized.

Disasters today are very public affairs and representatives of the press and other media play significant and sometimes damaging roles. Traumatized individuals and families may need to be protected from intrusive reporters, sensationalist news may create alarm and community leaders may find themselves unfairly criticized. Anger, as we have seen, is a common response to traumatic bereavement. A traumatized community will be an angry community and news media can easily fan the flames of discontent. Caring staff are usually tolerant of irrational outbursts from their clients and see it for what it is. Newsmen, on the other hand, may aggravate communal anger by giving it undue publicity.

To minimize these dangers it is advisable for the team leader(s) to work with a press liaison officer who will help the press to find their material without adding to the problems of traumatized individuals and caring services. Responsible members of the media perform valuable services by counteracting rumours, giving accurate information about the disaster, its consequences, and the services available. They need the help of the caring team just as the caring team needs their help. The publicity generated by the media can provide the teams with recruits, publicity to requests for finance, and a link with the people whom they serve. In their turn the teams can provide the media with accurate information about the services they provide, and act as go-betweens in helping them to find well-motivated and articulate individuals who can speak for the traumatized and bereaved population without themselves being doubly traumatized.

Specialist services by psychologists, psychotherapists, and psychiatrists provide major sources of help for people with overt psychiatric illnesses, particularly major depression and PTSD. They can also play useful roles in helping to train others in communication skills and in the management of anxiety and trauma. Professionals are often suspicious of volunteers and vice versa. It is only by working together that they learn to value and trust each other.

Religious and secular rituals along with visits to the disaster area by important personages, play an important role in making sufferers feel that their suffering is acknowledged and justified. Disaster funds also empower the recipients and make everyone feel cared for.

LONG-TERM CARE

A rewarding aspect of disaster work, which eventually makes us feel less useless, is the gradual improvement that takes place over time in the great majority of clients. The first anniversary may renew grief but, once it is over, things often begin to get better. We may never know how much of the credit we should take for this but most of our clients are very grateful and the morale of the team, along with the morale of the community at large, grows gradually greater.

Communities, too, are changed by disasters. In Aberfan the birth rate began to rise in the second year after the disaster and over the next five years, when compared with births in the surrounding Welsh valleys, the number of births exceeded expectations by more than the number of children who died in the disaster (Parkes and Williams, 1975). When these results were published local citizens protested that, 'You cannot replace a dead child' and, of course, they were right, what this community seemed to be doing was to redress the balance by bringing something good out of the bad thing that had happened.

A new community spirit may emerge and can indeed be cultivated in public meetings that encourage the community to plan its future. 'This disaster was caused by apathy, and it is up to us to show that Aberfan will never become apathetic again', said the wife of the headmaster of the village school. Her words were repeated and became something of a mantra in the **Community Development Programme** that was launched at this time. A **Community Association** helped to plan a fine cemetery with spaces representing each classroom in the school. The **Disaster Fund** provided scholarships and other educational opportunities for the surviving children and contributed to the landscaping of the coal tips that had remained, hanging over the village throughout the year, a constant and menacing reminder of the disaster. As one woman said, 'Its like having the dead body of your child's murderer on your doorstep, you know its dead, but you can't be sure it won't come to life again'. Five years later Aberfan proudly acted as hosts to a conference on community development that was attended by authorities from many other parts of Wales (Ballard and Jones, 1975).

It would be wrong to suggest that those in Aberfan or other disaster areas, will all have recovered from the disaster by the end of the second year. There will always be a minority for whom continuing care is needed. Some may have fallen through the net of care for one reason or another, others may have delayed reactions, perhaps because the need to care for someone else has required them to put their own needs on hold, others may have rejected offers of care and then changed their minds, while yet others fall into the vulnerable categories described in earlier chapters.

The needs for care will taper off gradually over the years and there is no fixed end-point to grief. This makes it unwise for funding bodies to wind up the CRT on a particular date. A winding-down process, usually throughout the second and third years after the disaster, will meet the needs of staff as well as recipients of the service.

Eventually it is necessary to hand over any long-term care to existing services, who should, by now, have received any extra training that they need in the management of complicated grief and traumatic reactions.

It is not only bereaved and traumatized people who are changed by disasters. Caring staff, be they professionals or volunteers, are likely to undergo a major change in their view of the world and of themselves in it. Sometimes the responsibilities and stresses of the job may cause them to burn out, particularly if they have not received the support that they needed in their day-to-day work. More often the carers undergo an experience of maturation. They emerge older but wiser and may not wish to return to the mundane roles that formerly they occupied. Volunteers may consider joining a caring profession, professionals may seek for ways to make use of the special skills that they have developed. Either way it helps to discuss these issues with team leaders and career advisers.

ARMED CONFLICT AND THE CYCLE OF VIOLENCE

The greatest disasters that we face are, of course, the wars that have punctuated and marred the history of mankind from time immemorial. Is it possible that the understanding and skills that have brought hope to those with life-threatening illness, and to their families before and after bereavement, might also be applied to breaking the cycles of violence that give rise to war? People who have been traumatized by man-made violence are, quite naturally, enraged and their rage may spread, like ripples in a pond, to escalate the violence. For example, Prigerson *et al.* (2002) reported high levels of partner abuse and subsequent divorce among soldiers exposed to combat trauma. But anger and distress can have other consequences. Bereaved people have played important roles in fighting for peace in

Northern Ireland, Argentina, Israel and other places. If bereaved people can contribute to peace may not those who specialize in solving the problems of bereavement also have a role to play?

With this in mind, the members of the **International Work Group on Death, Dying and Bereavement** (IWG) have published the findings of workshops on 'Violent Death and Bereavement' (1997–8) and 'Breaking the Cycle of Violence' (2005, and online at http://www.iwgddb.org/). An ongoing workshop is now examining problems of 'Armed Conflict'.

It would take us beyond the scope of this book to attempt to summarize this work, which requires the consideration of a large number of issues. Suffice it to say that recent events and circumstances have made it more than ever important to face these issues and adopt new ways of resolving them.

In 1995 Parkes visited Rwanda to advise on the development of a programme of psychological rehabilitation for the victims of the genocide, which had swept that sad country only a year previously (Parkes, 1995c, 1996). The saddest aspect of his experience was the realization that the people who were most in need of help were the ones who were least likely to ask for or to get it – the refugees, soldiers and politicians who were themselves traumatized and who are already reacting to their trauma by repeating the pattern of violence in the Congo and other neighbouring countries. The harm caused by such cycles of violence across the world is incalculable and close study of the ways in which such cycles could be interrupted should be high on our list of priorities in the years to come.

CONCLUSION

In our present state of knowledge sociologists and psychologists are beginning to be able to meet the challenge of advising the planners and of helping those whose lives are most affected by loss and change. We can no longer ignore the fact that research into the effects of loss and change are an essential area of study. Willingness to look at the problems of grief and grieving instead of turning away from them is the key to successful grief work in the sufferer, the helper, the planner, and the research worker. Prisoners who remind us of the precariousness of our freedom, cancer patients who remind us of our own mortality, immigrants who encroach upon our territory, displaced persons who blame us for the loss of their homes, and widows and widowers who prove to us that at any moment we, too, may lose the people we love, are a source of anxiety and threat. We may choose to deal with our fear by turning away from its source, by condemning the prisoner, jollying the cancer patient along, excluding the immigrant, ignoring the displaced person, or avoiding contact with the widow and widower. But each time we do this we only add to the fear, perpetuate the problems, and miss an opportunity to prepare ourselves for the changes that are inevitable in a changing world.

APPENDICES

Many of the assertions made in the foregoing chapters are based on evidence that was referred to only briefly in the text. The detailed findings that constitute this evidence are presented and discussed below.

APPENDIX 1

The Yale Bereavement Study involved a community sample of over 200 persons in Connecticut, USA, who had lost a family member (84 per cent a spouse) by natural causes and who were not suffering from complicated grief. They were interviewed at c. 6, 11 and 20 months after bereavement. Questions aimed at identifying the phases of grief, (disbelief, yearning, anger, depression and acceptance of the death), were measured on a 5-point Likert scale where 1 = *less than once a month*; 2 = *monthly*; 3 = *weekly*; 4 = *daily*; and 5 = *several times a day*.

Figure 1 shows the changes in each of these variables over time since bereavement. It shows that each variable peaks at the expected time, as found by Bowlby and Parkes (1970) in young widows and widowers in London, UK. But there was no reason to believe that one 'phase' must end before the next could begin. In fact 'acceptance' was the most commonly reported feature from the outset and 'yearning' the most prominent negative feature throughout the first two years. The other variables were often absent or minimal. Features of all phases were often present at the same time (Maciejewski *et al.*, 2007; Prigerson and Maciejewski, 2008).

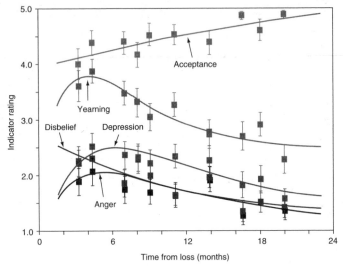

Figure 1 Changes in indicators of grief over two years post-bereavement.

APPENDIX 2

The assertion made in Chapter 2 that bereavement can increase the mortality rate, especially from heart disease, is supported by evidence for the increased death rate given by Young, Benjamin, and Wallis (1963), whose work was supplemented by Parkes, Benjamin, and Fitzgerald (1969). These papers contain data relating to all males over the age of fifty-four in England and Wales whose wives died during two months of 1957.

The National Health Service central register was tagged so that all deaths occurring in the sample of 4486 widowers would be reported. As Figure 2 shows, the mortality rate during the first six months of bereavement was found to be 40 per cent higher than the expected rate based on national figures for married men of the same age. The rate then drops to a plateau until the end of the third year; thereafter it drops again and becomes lower than the rate for married men of the same age.

The greatest proportional increase was in deaths from coronary thrombosis and other arteriosclerotic and degenerative heart disease, which group was 67 per cent above expectation ($p < .01$).

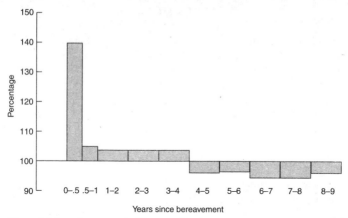

Figure 2 Mortality rate of widowers after bereavement as a percentage of rate for married men over ten years post-bereavement. $N = 4486$ widowers over age 54.

APPENDIX 3

The findings of Schmale and Iker (1966) concerning the diagnosis of cervical cancer by psychiatric interview can best be illustrated by reproducing one of their tables. Table 1 shows that when the psychiatrist predicted the diagnosis of cancer on the basis of the patient's report of having responded to a life event prior to the first cervical smear with feelings of hopelessness, he was more likely to be right than wrong. To be precise, he was right in thirty-six cases and wrong in fifteen, a finding that is significant at the .02 level. (The life events that preceded the illness were usually construed by the patient as being irrevocable losses.)

Table 1 Psychiatrist's predictions of cervical cancer and biopsy diagnosis in fifty-one women admitted for investigation of suspicious smear test

	Psychiatrist's predicted diagnosis	
	Cancer	Not cancer
Cancer	11 (61%)	8 (24%)
Not cancer	7 (39%)	25 (76%)

Source: Compiled from data in Schmale & Iker (1966).

Note: $\chi^2 = 5.29$; $p = .02$ (two-tailed).

APPENDIX 4

In the London Study (Parkes, 1970) twenty-two London widows were interviewed five times during the course of their first year of bereavement. The data collected at each interview included a subjective assessment by the widow of her 'general health' (scored as 'good', 'indifferent', or 'bad'), a count of the number of physical symptoms she had experienced since the previous interview (from a checklist), a count of the number of consultations she had had with her GP since the last interview, and an assessment of irritability or anger as observed at the current interview (scored as 'very marked', 'marked', 'moderate', 'mild', or 'absent').

Correlation coefficients between the mean scores on each of these variables are shown in Table 2. Only the correlation between general health and irritability and anger was statistically significant ($\sigma = .70$; $t = 4.28$; $p < .001$).

Table 2 London Study: Intercorrelation of health indices and anger in twenty-two widows

	Subjective assessment of general health	No. of symptoms from checklist over one year	No. of GP consultations in course of year	Irritability and anger observed at interviews
Subjective assessment of general health	–	.00	.23	.70*
No. of symptoms from checklist over one year	.00	–	.08	−.15
No. of GP consultations in course of year	.23	.08	–	.27
Irritability and anger observed at interviews	.70*	−.15	.27	–

Notes: Assessments represent sums of assessments made at five interviews during the first year of bereavement. *$p < .001$ (using t-test).

APPENDIX 5

In The Yale Bereavement Study (see above) criteria for diagnosing **Prolonged Grief Disorder** (PGD) were developed out of the recommendations of a panel of experts on psychiatric nosology and affective disorders who reviewed the existing evidence on complications of grief. They agreed that this justified further investigation and proposed a provisional list of diagnostic criteria. The Index of Complicated Grief (ICG) was developed out of this initial work in order to provide a systematic and replicable method of assessing the symptoms identified by the panel. After establishing the sensitivity and specificity of the instrument and refining the use of the diagnostic criteria (Prigerson *et al.*, 1995a; Prigerson and Jacobs, 2001) a field trial was carried out using a pool of 30 questions about symptoms on a community sample of 317 persons who were interviewed c. 6 and 20 months after bereavement. Techniques derived from item response theory were used to reduce bias arising from age, gender and kinship to the deceased, to evaluate the usefulness of the list of symptoms and to remove those that contributed less than 20 per cent of the information contributed by the most informative symptom (Prigerson, Vanderwerker, and Maciejewski, 2008). Twelve informative and unbiased symptoms emerged from this analysis for consideration in a diagnostic algorithm.

Although it was recognized from the outset, that there would be a continuum of scores, it was necessary to establish a cut-off point to establish 'caseness'. Trained diagnosticians decided which respondents met the clinical criteria for the diagnosis of PGD and this enabled the researchers to refine the revised list of ICG scores and to order the symptoms, on scales of 0–4 or 0–5, in terms of severity (Prigerson *et al.*, 2008).

From the outset 'yearning' had emerged as a mandatory symptom (Prigerson *et al.*, 1999) and the researchers used mathematical methods derived from 'combinatrics' to identify sets of symptoms that might be the basis for a diagnosis of PGD that would meet DSM standards. A total of 4785 possible algorithms were evaluated. The most efficient algorithm to emerge from this analysis included yearning and any five of the nine symptoms listed under section C below, to establish 'caseness'. Sensitivity, specificity and positive and negative predictive values were all greater than .94 (Prigerson *et al.*, 2008).

Further research demonstrated that those who now met diagnostic criteria for PGD at six or more months after bereavement were more likely to be unable to function effectively in occupational, social and other fields, and had a poorer quality of life, than those who did not meet these criteria; such impairment is considered a necessary criterion for most psychiatric diagnoses in the DSM and has, therefore, been added as an additional diagnostic criterion.

Although this research also showed that people meeting criteria for PGD at six months after bereavement were at increased risk of other psychiatric conditions, including PTSD, MDD and General Anxiety Disorder, over a half of them did not meet criteria for any of these disorders. Furthermore, even if we exclude all those who suffered from these other disorders, the half who remain were at increased risk of suicidal ideation, functional impairment and poorer quality of life at 13–24 months after bereavement than the non-PGD group. They would have been excluded from receiving help under existing psychiatric systems.

The decision to use a cut-off point of six months post-bereavement as a criterion for the diagnosis of PGD was reached by analysing the course of grief over time. During the first few months after bereavement many of the symptoms of normal, uncomplicated grief are the same as those of PGD. Only after six months have elapsed is it possible reliably to distinguish those whose future level of grief and quality of life will continue to improve from those who will remain severely impaired. PGD symptoms at six months predict continuing grief and more negative outcomes at 13–24 months than those assessed earlier (Prigerson *et al.*, 1995a, 1997, 2008).

Proposed criteria for the diagnosis of Prolonged Grief Disorder in the DSM (Prigerson *et al.*, 2008)

A   **Event Criterion:** Bereavement (loss of a loved person)
B   **Separation Distress:** The bereaved person experiences at least one of the three following symptoms which must be experienced daily or to a distressing or disruptive degree:
    1   Intrusive thoughts related to the lost relationship
    2   Intense feelings of emotional pain, sorrow, or pangs of grief related to the lost relationship
    3   Yearning for the lost person
C   **Cognitive, Emotional, and Behavioral Symptoms:** The bereaved person must have five (or more) of the following symptoms:
    1   Confusion about one's role in life or diminished sense of self (i.e. feeling that a part of oneself has died)
    2   Difficulty accepting the loss
    3   Avoidance of reminders of the reality of the loss
    4   Inability to trust others since the loss
    5   Bitterness or anger related to the loss

6 Difficulty moving on with life (e.g. making new friends, pursuing interests)
7 Numbness (absence of emotion) since the loss
8 Feeling that life is unfulfilling, empty, and meaningless since the loss
9 Feeling stunned, dazed or shocked by the loss

D **Duration:** Duration at least six months from the onset of separation distress

E **Impairment:** The above symptomatic disturbance causes clinically significant distress or impairment in social, occupational, or other important areas of functioning (e.g. domestic responsibilities)

F **Medical Exclusion:** The disturbance is not due to the physiological effects of a substance or a general medical condition

G **Relation to Other Mental Disorders:** Not better accounted for by Major Depressive Disorder, Generalized Anxiety Disorder, or PTSD

Table 3 The Yale Bereavement Study: Prolonged Grief Disorder (PGD) at six months predicts impairment at thirteen months

*Thirteen-month outcome**	*OR*
Hospitalization†	1.32
Major health event (heart attack, cancer, stroke)	1.16
Accidents	1.27
Altered sleep	8.39
Smoking	c. 16.7
Eating	7.02
High blood pressure	1.11

Notes: *At 25 months: cancer, cardiac problems, alcohol problems, suicidality. †Controlling for pre-loss levels of outcome measure, depression, anxiety, age and sex.

When those who met criteria for PGD at six months after bereavement were followed up at 13 and 25 months Table 3 shows how they compared with the rest of the sample who did not meet criteria for PGD.

When six bereaved persons with delayed onset of PGD were compared with twelve with early onset but persistent grief the most striking difference was a four-fold greater incidence of sleep disturbance in the delayed group ($p < .001$; Prigerson *et al.*, 1997).

APPENDIX 6

In the London Study the twenty-two young and middle-aged widows were assessed at each of the five interviews on a number of psychological measures. Assessments were based on information from the widow combined with Parkes' own direct observation at the interview, and each feature was rated on a 5-point scale as '*very marked*', '*marked*', '*moderate*', '*mild*', or '*absent*'. The meaning of the terms is usually self-evident, but note particularly: 'numbness' = reports of feeling 'numb', 'blunted', or 'cloudy'; 'difficulty in accepting the fact of loss' = difficulty in believing fully in the reality of the husband's death, statements such as 'I still can't believe it's true'; 'restlessness' = observable hyperactivity; 'tension' = observable increase in muscle tension.

The mean year scores (the mean of each measure over the whole year) were intercorrelated and the significance of all correlations was tested. This revealed certain clusters of associated variables.

Table 4 shows the correlation coefficients for each variable with each other variable (only those variables that intercorrelated are included). These results indicate that there are two main types of variable that go together and create two general trends of reaction to bereavement. The implications are: (a) that these variables are meaningfully related to one another; and (b) that individuals who show a feature of either cluster are also likely to show the other features of that cluster. It will be seen that the main clusters of variables are:

1   Preoccupation with thoughts of the deceased
    Clear visual memory of him
    Sense of his continued presence
    Tearfulness
    Illusions of the deceased (assessed only at the first interview)
2   Irritability and anger
    Restlessness
    Tension
    Social withdrawal (assessed only at the first interview)

These orientations provide evidence supporting the Dual Process model of bereavement (see page 9). The mode of response represented by the features in the first list is passive and oriented towards the dead husband. 'Preoccupation with thoughts of reunion' alternate with painful 'pining' and 'tearfulness'. One can characterize this as a Loss Orientation, a reaction of yearning for the past (see page 7 and Chapter 4). The second mode of response is more active and more aggressive. Here the survivor, instead of calling to the lost person to return, turns to contend with a potentially hostile world.

Table 4 London Study: Correlation (r) between mean year scores on psychological measures among twenty-two London widows

	Preoccupation with thoughts of deceased	Clear visual memory	Sense of his presence	Tearfulness	Illusions of deceased†	Irritability and anger	Restlessness	Tension	Social withdrawal†	Numbness	Difficulty in accepting
Clear visual memory of him	.73***	—									
Sense of his continued presence	.58**	.56**	—								
Tearfulness	.54**	.38	.42*	—							
Illusions of deceased†	-.13	.38	.52*	.34	—						
Irritability and anger	-.05	-.18	.02	.41	.04	—					
Restlessness	.18	-.04	.08	.32	.03	.65***	—				
Tension	.15	.18	.10	.43*	.09	.58**	.83***	—			
Social withdrawal†	.05	.17	-.13	20	-.19	.44*	.10	.12	—		
Numbness	-.11	.32	-.14	-.06	-.15	-.14	-.03	-.12	.35	—	
Difficulty in accepting fact of loss	.24	.21	.08	.29	.22	.42*	.42*	.43*	.36	-.09	—
Avoidance of reminders	.44*	.46*	.29	.07	.24	-.16	.14	.23	.21	.29	.40

Notes: †Assessed only at first interview. *p < .05; **p < .01; ***p < .001 (using t-test).

This Restoration Orientation is also described on page 9 and developed further in Chapter 6.

Despite what has been said it should be remembered that components of both these modes of reaction are found in most bereaved people; the passive and active styles represent tendencies rather than discrete types of response. It should be noted, further, that defensive reactions such as 'numbness', 'difficulty in accepting the fact of loss', and 'avoidance of reminders' were not significantly intercorrelated, hence there is no support from this study for the notion of a general factor of 'defensiveness'.

APPENDIX 7

Gundel *et al.* (2003) carried out fMRI imaging of the brain while inducing pangs of grief by exposing bereaved women to photographs of the lost person along with words associated with loss. They compared the resulting fMRI images with those produced when the same women were shown photographs of other persons and neutral words. It seems that there is no one location in the brain for the pang of grief, this results from the integrated activity of several parts some of which developed at a very early stage of evolution. Pangs of grief are associated with activation of three regions, the cerebellum, the posterior cingulate cortex, and the medial superior frontal gyrus. The deep nuclei of the cerebellum are linked to the more recently evolved medial superior frontal gyrus in the cerebral cortex. This is responsible for visual recognition, and is an essential part of searching in higher primates (Nagahama *et al.*, 1999; Platek *et al.*, 2004). The cingulate cortex, as we saw on page 37, is a part of Papez's circuit and is involved in the experience and expression of emotion. These parts together subserve the processing of familiar faces, visual imaging, memory retrieval, the processing of emotion and regulation of the autonomic nervous system all of which play a part in searching and grieving.

Another study that used the same techniques was used to compare eleven bereaved women who met criteria for PGD with twelve others who did not. Both groups showed the brain activity typical of grief described above. The PGD group differed from the Non-PGD in showing activity in the nucleus accumbens. Activity in this brain stem nucleus was also correlated significantly with scores of yearning for the deceased person (O'Connor *et al.*, 2008).

The nucleus accumbens plays a central role in the mesolimbic pathway, the brain's reward circuit. Its operation is based chiefly on two essential neurotransmitters: dopamine, which promotes appetitive behaviour (goal-directed seeking), and serotonin, whose effects include satiety and inhibition (which switch off goal-directed seeking). These two effects seem to equate with seeking and finding. Because finding what you seek, and even anticipating successful seeking, is pleasurable it is not surprising that the nucleus accumbens is sometimes referred to as the 'pleasure centre', but O'Connor's research found evidence that in PGD the seeking implicit in yearning for a dead person is correlated with neither positive nor negative affect. This seems to imply that people with PGD somehow maintain a balance between hoping and giving up hope.

It is also of interest that the nucleus accumbens is thought to play a major part in addictions. Here, too, there is repeated activation, by dopamine, of the nucleus accumbens via the mesolimbic pathway. Dopamine was originally thought to mediate the rewarding or hedonic properties of drug and non-drug reinforcers (Wise, 1998), however, evidence obtained subsequently suggests that dopamine affects the motivation to seek a reward, rather than the experience of reward itself (World Health Organization, 2004). It seems that the PGD sufferers and drug addicts have similar levels of craving but that of the PGD sufferer cannot be rewarded.

Drug addiction, it seems, is associated with 'incentive sensitization', the brain becomes more sensitive, or 'sensitized' to the motivational and rewarding effects of psychoactive substances. This is associated with marked changes in the mesolimbic dopamine system. There are both presynaptic changes (increased dopamine release) and postsynaptic changes (changes in receptor sensitivity). Furthermore, many people, from a genetic error, have a reduction of dopamine receptors in the accumbens nucleus, and this is associated with an increased tendency to drug addiction (World Health Organization, 2004). These findings raise the possibility that similar 'incentive sensitization' and genetic factors may play a part in PGD.

APPENDIX 8

Widows in the London Study were asked to rate the frequency of quarrels with their spouse on a 4-point scale ('usually', 'frequently', 'occasionally', 'never'). Half admitted that they did quarrel, and a score of quarrelling derived from this scale was significantly related to three of the mean year scores:

	p	p
Tension as observed at interview	.54	<.02
Ideas of guilt or self-reproach	.51	<.05
Number of physical symptoms from checklist	.60	<.01

and also to:

Few illusions of the dead person during the first month	.48	<.05
Social isolation a year after bereavement	.59	<.01

The assessment of social isolation differed from that of social withdrawal (included in Table 4) in that there was no attempt to discriminate as to the agency – the widow herself or other people – that brought it about. Likewise, no attempt was made to establish who was to blame for quarrels.

APPENDIX 9

The Case-note Study. Parkes' study of the case records of forty-four widows (Parkes, 1964) showed that the consultation rate with the GP rose from a mean of 2.2 consultations per patient per six months during the eighteen months prior to the terminal illness of the husband to a mean of 3.6 during the first six months of bereavement; and for the second and third six-month periods of bereavement the mean consultation rates were 2.6 and 3.0, respectively. The increase is highly significant ($Z = 5.7$; $p < .001$; Wilcoxon matched-pairs signed-ranks test).

In the under sixty-five age group during the first six months there was a 200 per cent increase in consultations for psychological symptoms (i.e. the case notes indicated either a specifically psychological complaint such as depression or insomnia, or the prescription of a sedative, hypnotic, or tranquillizer). This increase was also highly significant ($\chi^2 = 200$; $df = 3$; $p < .001$; Friedman two-way analysis of variance by ranks).

As shown in Figure 3, sedative consumption in the younger age group increased from a mean of 0.7 weeks on sedation per patient per six months prior to bereavement to a mean of 5.0 in the first six months afterwards ($\chi^2 = 10.7$; $df = 3$; $p < .02$; Friedman two-way analysis of variance by ranks).

The small increase (25 per cent) in consultations for psychological symptoms in the sixty-five-and-over age group did not approach statistical significance, and there was no significant change in sedative

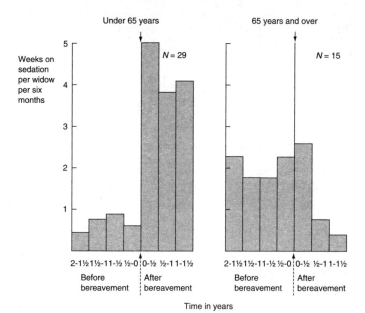

Under 65 years   65 years and over

Weeks on sedation per widow per six months

N = 29

N = 15

2-1½ 1½-1 1-½ ½-0 0-½ ½-1 1-1½   2-1½ 1½-1 1-½ ½-0 0-½ ½-1 1-1½

Before bereavement   After bereavement   Before bereavement   After bereavement

Time in years

Figure 3 Sedative consumption, before and after bereavement, in forty-four widows in two age groups.

consumption in this group. However, there was an overall increase in consultations for non-psychiatric complaints ($Z = 3.96$; $p < .00005$; Wilcoxon test) and this remained significant when the older age group was considered alone ($p < .05$; Wilcoxon test).

When the consultations were broken down by diagnosis the numbers in each diagnostic group were too small for statistical analysis. The exception was consultations for muscle and joint conditions, which in the under-sixty-five age group increased from a mean of 0.11 consultations per six months prior to bereavement to a mean of 0.52 during the eighteen months after bereavement ($p < .05$; Wilcoxon test).

APPENDIX 10

The Harvard Study was confined to a young age group (widows and widowers under forty-five). Respondents were subdivided into those who had only a short time in which to prepare themselves for the death (less than two weeks' warning coupled with a terminal incapacity in the spouse of less than three days) and those who had a longer time (a terminal incapacity of more than three days, whatever the period of warning).

During the first month of bereavement short preparation for death was significantly related to an immediate reaction of disbelief, feelings of anxiety, self-reproach, and depression, as revealed by the fact that 46 per cent of those who had had little time to prepare (compared with 15 per cent of those who had had some time) said that they did not care whether they lived or died, or expressed some positive wish for death.

A year later, the twenty-three who had had the least opportunity to prepare for bereavement continued to be more pessimistic about the future, more inclined to tearfulness, and more anxious and depressed than the forty-five who had had a longer time to prepare themselves. Only three (13 per cent) of the group who had had little opportunity to prepare themselves were rated as having a good overall outcome compared with twenty-six (59 per cent) of the group who had had time to prepare ($p < .001$; Parkes and Brown, 1972).

APPENDIX 11

A score based on the number of major stresses that the London widows reported they had undergone during the two years prior to bereavement was correlated with the mean year scores and outcome scores. Two significant correlations were obtained:

	p	p
Ideas of guilt or self-reproach	0.42	.05
Overall outcome	0.46	.05

This would suggest that those who report a large number of stressors get on less well after bereavement than those who do not. However, since we had no means of checking the reliability of the retrospective information given, a causal connection between stress and poor outcome was not proved in these cases.

APPENDIX 12

There is no space here to give full details of the Love and Loss Study for further details of which the reader is referred to Parkes 2006.

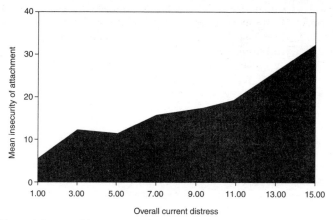

Figure 4 Scores of insecure attachment × overall distress in 181 persons referred for psychiatric help after bereavement.

In the **Love and Loss Study** a retrospective score of insecurity of attachment was obtained by summing together scores of insecure parenting and childhood insecurity. In Figure 4 this score is plotted against a score of distress obtained by summing scores of anxiety/panic, depression/medication, grief/loneliness, and alcohol consumption as reported at the time of referral for help after bereavement. The correlation ($p = 0.4$) is highly significant. Similar findings were obtained in a comparison group of bereaved people who were not seeking psychiatric help. This suggests that the influence of security of attachment on bereavement is not confined to the minority who seek psychiatric help.

Figure 5 shows the intercorrelation between the measure of anxious/ambivalent attachment in childhood, a score of disagreements with the partner and/or the deceased person and the score of grief/loneliness at the time of referral for psychiatric treatment (which was usually more than six months after bereavement). All correlations reached statistical significance. Results are discussed on page 168.

Figure 6 shows the correlations between a score derived from questions about the frequency and duration of separations from either or both parents during childhood and the relationships, coping strategies, and symptom scores of 181 people who sought psychiatric help after bereavement. It seems that high scores of separation are associated with distrust of others in adult life, conflicted

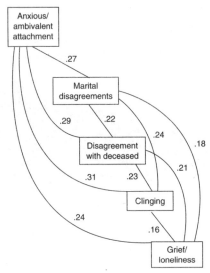

Figure 5 Anxious/ambivalent attachment scores correlated with other variables. Figures are correlations between variables in 181 bereaved
psychiatric patients. Continuous lines indicate significant
correlations.

relationships and a tendency to become very anxious, to cling and/or
to rely on alcohol following bereavement.

Figure 7 shows the correlations between scores of avoidant
attachment in childhood and later coping strategies, relationships
and reaction to bereavement. Avoidant attachments in childhood are
associated with emotional inhibition and distrust in adults. Insofar
as these people relate to others it is often in an assertive, controlling
and/or aggressive manner. It comes as no surprise that their relationships are conflicted. After bereavement they find it difficult to express
grief. In addition the measure of difficulty in expressing grief also
correlated with deep feelings of guilt and self-reproach.

Figure 8 shows the correlations between the measure of disorganized attachment, the response to the end-of-tether questions (see
pages 178–9) and the principle symptoms afflicting people who
sought help after bereavement. It seems that these respondents saw
themselves as helpless in the face of stress. At such times they turned
in on themselves and were more likely than others to admit that they
might 'take an overdose or otherwise harm myself'. This learned

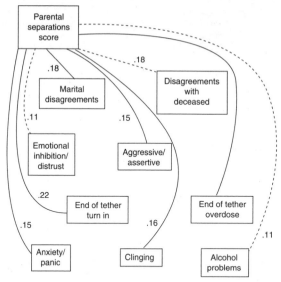

Figure 6 Score of separations from parents during childhood correlated
with other variables. Figures are correlations between variables in
181 bereaved psychiatric patients. Continuous lines indicate significant correlations. Interrupted lines indicate non-significant trends.

helplessness was associated with high scores of anxiety/panic,
depression/medication, and a tendency to use alcohol to excess.

In Figure 9 the mean grief /loneliness score in 181 bereaved psychiatric patients living alone is compared with that in those living
with others at different ages. Although grief/loneliness scores are
consistently higher in those living alone the difference is most pronounced in the over-sixty age group.

APPENDIX 13

Figure 10 shows changes in the expression of overall emotional disturbance (anxiety/depression) during the first three months of
bereavement in twenty-five London widows. (Note that three of
these widows – a, b, and c – were not included in the final analysis
of the study, whose findings have been reported and discussed elsewhere in the book, because they moved away and Parkes was not able
to obtain all the interviews necessary for the full investigation.)

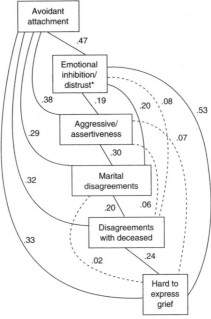

Figure 7 Avoidant attachment scores correlated with other variables. Figures are correlations between variables in 181 bereaved psychiatric patients. Continuous lines indicate significant correlations. Interrupted lines indicate non-significant trends.

Intensity of emotional disturbance was scored on a 5-point scale during interviews at the end of the first and third months of bereavement. Retrospective estimates were then made of the amount of overall upset week by week during the first month and monthly thereafter, based on the widows' own accounts of changes in their feelings.

Emotional upset during the first week of bereavement correlated ($r = .8$) with emotional upset three months later ($p < .01$; Parkes, 1970).

Similar findings come from a study by Levy, Martinowski, and Derby (1994) who found that, although there was a general decline in the mean scores of distress over the first 18 months after bereavement, 22 per cent of their sample of widow(er)s of patients who died from cancer in the Baltimore area experienced initial low levels of distress followed by an *increase* across the 18 months. This applied to

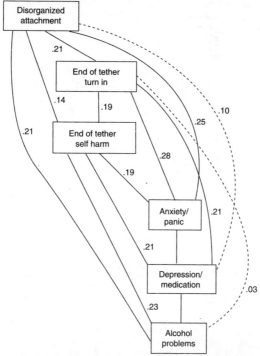

Figure 8 Disorganized attachment scores correlated with other variables. Figures are correlations between variables in 181 bereaved psychiatric patients. Continuous lines indicate significant correlations. Interrupted lines indicate non-significant trends.

both subjective stress (as measured by the Impact of Events Intrusion Scale) and depression (as measured by the Center for Epidemiological Studies Depression scale; CES-D).

APPENDIX 14

Currier, Neimeyer, and Berman (2008) carried out a meta-analysis of 48 peer-reviewed articles and 16 unpublished dissertations reporting 61 controlled studies of bereavement interventions involving 'sustained interaction' with a trained expert. Sixty-three per cent were group, 25 per cent individual and 12 per cent family interventions.

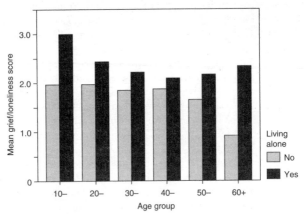

Figure 9 Mean grief/loneliness scores × age group × living alone or with others.

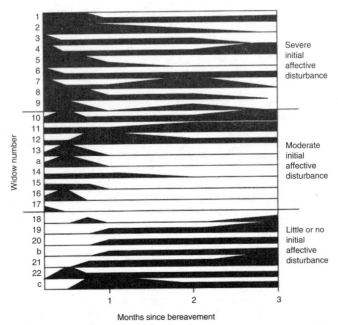

Figure 10 Severity of emotional disturbance in twenty-five widows during the first three months of bereavement.

The interventions included psychotherapy and counselling (63 per cent), professionally organized support groups (17 per cent), crisis intervention (12 per cent), social-activity groups (4 per cent), writing therapies (3 per cent), a visiting service and a staff training programme. Measures of outcome were converted to Cohen's *D*, which is a standardized way of measuring the size and direction of any effects found.

Although there were short-term overall benefits favouring the intervention groups these were no longer present on follow-up. This applied to both random and non-random allocation studies. The samples were broken down into: (1) *Universal* – in which the service was offered to all bereaved persons regardless of need; (2) *Selected* – in which the service was offered only to selected individuals thought to be at special risk (e.g. loss of a child to violent death); and (3) *Indicated* – in which the service was offered either to people with clear symptoms of psychiatric disorder or to others manifesting problems adapting to loss or clinically significant difficulties (e.g. loss-related intrusions, anxiety and guilt feelings).

Table 5 shows that significant post-treatment effects were found in the Selective and Indicated groups but not the Universal. This indicates that both methods of selection of clients are associated with

Table 5 Tests of moderation for targeted population

Variable	No. of studies	Mean effect size	SE	95% CI	Q
Post-treatment effects					
Within group					
Universal	6	0.01	0.11	−0.21–0.22	2.46
Selective	25	0.14*	0.05	0.03–0.24	31.47
Indicated	5	0.53*	0.16	0.22–0.85	8.34
Between group					7.49*
Follow-up effects					
Within group					
Universal	4	−0.06	0.14	−0.33–0.21	4.21
Selective	21	0.03	0.05	−0.08–0.18	17.20
Indicated	2	0.58*	0.21	0.18–0.98	0.72
Between group					7.41*

Nots: A random-effects model was used for these analyses, which accounts for the random variation between studies in addition to variance associated with sampling. *$p < .05$.

significant short-term benefit. Longer term benefit, at follow-up, was confined to the Indicated group.

Studies that strictly intervened with self- and clinician-referred participants generated significantly better post-treatment outcomes (mean $d = 0.40$) than studies using aggressive outreach procedures (mean $d = 0.05$), $p = .03$. There were no significant differences in the benefits that followed individual, group and family interventions, neither were benefits specific to gender, age, violent deaths, type of relationship to deceased person (parent, spouse, etc.), or number of treatment sessions.

APPENDIX 15

Figure 11 is derived from Schut *et al.* (1997b). It shows the mean General Health Questionnaire scores of persons in the Netherlands

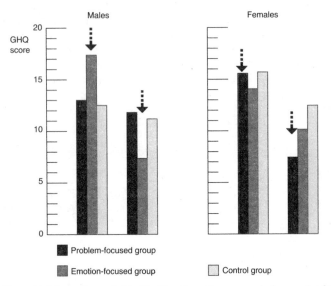

Figure 11 Mean General Health Questionnaire scores before and after intervention in bereaved persons in two therapy groups and a control group.

Source: Redrawn from data in Schut *et al.*, 1997b, Intervention for the bereaved: Gender differences in the efficacy of two counselling programmes. *British Journal of Clinical Psychology*, *36*, 63–72.

with high levels of distress eleven months after bereavement. The three columns on the left of each figure are scores before intervention and those on the right the scores on follow-up. Respondents were assigned at random to three groups, one received 'problem-focused' cognitive therapy, the second 'emotion-focused' therapy as in the Lindemann tradition, and the third were a waiting-list control group. It was only after the data were collected that an unexpected finding emerged, men had benefited from emotion-focused therapy while women benefited from the problem-focused therapy. While these findings need replication and should not be taken to mean that all men need different therapy from all women, they certainly throw doubt on the supposition that each gender knows what is best for it. It is likely that, given a free choice, the men would have chosen the cognitive therapy and the women the emotive.

APPENDIX 16

Shear *et al.* (2005) compared Complicated Grief Therapy with Interpersonal Psychotherapy among patients from a university-based psychiatric research clinic and a satellite clinic focusing on poor and underserved clients. Participants who met criteria for PGD were randomly assigned to receive Interpersonal Psychotherapy ($N = 46$) or CGT ($N = 49$); both were administered in 16 sessions during an average interval of 19 weeks per participant. Treatment response was defined either as an independent evaluator-rated Clinical Global Improvement score of 1 or 2 or as time to a 20-point or better improvement in the self-reported Index of Complicated Grief. Results indicated that both treatments significantly reduced PGD symptoms, but the response rate was much greater for PGD Treatment (51 per cent) than for Interpersonal Psychotherapy (28 per cent; $p = .02$) and the time to response was shorter for PGD Treatment ($p = .02$).

APPENDIX 17

Kissane and Bloch (2002) have developed a Family Risk Index (FRI) to score measures of cohesiveness, conflict and expressiveness within the families of patients in a palliative care service. From these scores they identified five types of family:

1 Cohesive, unconflicted and expressive families.
2 Conflicted but conflicts resolved because cohesive and expressive.
3 Intermediate scores.
4 Low cohesiveness and expressiveness but only low–moderate conflict.
5 Poor scores on all. Conflicts remain unresolved.

Followed up over time, before and after the patient's death, family members from groups 1 and 2 obtain good, declining scores on the Beck Depression Inventory and the Brief Symptoms Inventory, others do less well. Those in groups 4 and 5, which constitute about 15–20 per cent of palliative care families, have high rates of psychosocial morbidity and clinical depression. They can reasonably be regarded as 'dysfunctional'.

In a random-allocation study 81 families were assessed as 'at risk' from FRI scores placing them in groups 3, 4 and 5. A 2:1 randomization resulted in an index group of 53 families who were offered 6–8 sessions of Family Focused Grief Therapy (FFGT). Forty completed all sessions. When compared with 28 unsupported control families significant benefits were found, in groups 3 and 4, six months after the ending of therapy. These benefits were still present at one year in group 4. Groups 1, 2 and 5 did not show benefit (Kissane and Bloch, 2002; Kissane *et al.*, 2006).

It seems reasonable to conclude, with Kissane, that groups 1 and 2 do not need FFGT and that group 5, whom they termed 'hostile', did not benefit. They suggested that this group lacked the ability to make use of group therapies but might benefit from individual approaches.

APPENDIX 18

Goodkin and his colleagues carried out a randomized, controlled, clinical trial of bereavement support provided to homosexuals 97 of whom were themselves HIV positive and 69 HIV negative. Semi-structured groups were provided once a week for ten weeks in 90-minute sessions. All were followed up ten weeks and six months later. Significant differences favouring the group with bereavement support were found on measures of distress at both times and indicators of grief improved more rapidly in the index than the control group (Goodkin *et al.*, 1999). At the six-month follow-up assessment, the intervention groups exhibited significant beneficial effects compared to controls on changes in CD4 cell, total T-lymphocyte, total lymphocyte counts, and plasma cortisol levels. Both CD4 counts and plasma cortisol levels correlated with group attendance. The intervention group made significantly less use of health-care services than the controls, over the six months (Goodkin *et al.*, 1998). Measured only over the ten-week period there was a significant effect of the intervention on the amount of virus in the blood stream as measured by change on the plasma HIV-1 RNA copy number (limited control model, $\beta = -.49$, $p = .02$; extended control model, $\beta = -.37$, $p = .01$; Goodkin *et al.*, 2001).

APPENDIX 19

Widows and widowers of 164 patients who died in St Christopher's Hospice were divided into high- and low-risk groups using a risk assessment measure based on the Harvard Bereavement Study. After excluding a small 'Imperative Need' group of 22 persons in which it was deemed essential to provide immediate support, the remaining high-risk group were divided at random into two samples.

1   A low-risk group ($n = 85$).
2   A high-risk intervention group ($n = 28$).
3   A high-risk control group ($n = 29$).

The intervention group were visited in their homes by volunteer counsellors under the supervision of Parkes. The help given varied from case to case but seldom involved more than three to four visits. These visits, though few in number, were often very lengthy. It was not unusual for them to last for one or two hours.

The control group were not offered help and none of them asked for help from the Hospice.

About twenty months after bereavement all three groups were followed up by a research interviewer who administered a shortened version of the Health Questionnaire that had been used in the Harvard Bereavement Study.

Figure 12 gives the overall outcome in the three groups. It shows first that the predictive questionnaire did, in fact, predict outcome, since the high-risk control group did have a poorer outcome than the low-risk group ($p < .02$); second, that the intervention was successful in that the intervention group had a better outcome than the control group ($p < .03$). In fact it appears that counselling had the effect

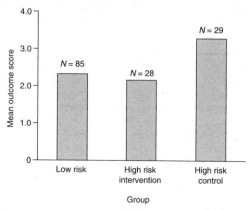

Figure 12 Mean outcome scores in three groups of hospice bereaved.

of improving the adjustment of the high-risk group to about the same level as that of the low-risk group. It is worth noting that no differences between supported and unsupported groups were found during the first few months of the project when our counsellors were still very inexperienced. The above figures refer to results obtained from experienced counsellors. Although the study had not been designed to compare gender differences, and further subdivision caused the differences to drop below significant levels in the women, high-risk males who received support reported significantly less depression than those who were unsupported (Parkes, 1981).

ORGANIZATIONS OFFERING
HELP TO THE BEREAVED

IN THE UNITED KINGDOM

Childhood Bereavement Network (www.childhoodbereavementnetwork. org.uk/), 8 Wakley Street, London EC1V 7QE, UK. Tel. 020 7843 6309.

The Compassionate Friends, mutual help for parents losing a child (www.tcf.org.uk), 53 North Street, Bristol BS3 1EN, UK. Tel. 084 5120 3785.

Cruse Bereavement Care (www.cruse.org.uk), PO Box 800, Richmond, Surrey TW9 1RG, UK. Tel. 020 8939 9530, Helpline 0844 477 9400.

The Foundation for the Study of Infant Deaths (http://www.fsid.org.uk), Artillery House, 11–19 Artillery Row, London SW1P 1RT, UK. Tel. General 020 7222 8001, Helpline 020 7233 2090 (Helpline@fsid.org.uk).

Hospice Information Service, information about services for dying and bereaved people across the world (www.helpthehospices.org.uk/our-services/information-service/). Tel. 020 7520 8222.

Lesbian and Gay Bereavement (LGBT) (www.londonfriend.org.uk). Tel. 020 7403 5969.

The London Bereavement Network, gives contact details in each borough (www.bereavement.org.uk).

The Miscarriages Association (www.miscarriageassociation.org.uk/), c/o Clayton Hospital, Northgate, Wakefield, West Yorkshire WF1 3JS, UK. Tel. Volunteers Manager 01924 339207, Helpline 01924 200799.

RD4U Children and Young People (www.RD4U.org.uk), for address see Cruse Bereavement Care. Tel. Young person's freephone helpline 0808 808 1677.

The Samaritans (www.samaritans.org,uk), The Upper Mill, Kingston Road, Ewell, Surrey KT17 2AF, UK. Tel. 08457 909090.

Support after Murder and Manslaughter (www.samm.org.uk), First floor, Scotia House, 33 Finsbury Square, London EC2A 1PL, UK. Tel. 0207 638 4040.

Survivors of Bereavement by Suicide (SOBS) (www.uk-sobs.org.uk/), The Flamsteed Centre, Albert Street, Ilkeston, Derbyshire DE7 5GU, UK. Tel. Helpline 0844 561 6855.

Winston's Wish, for bereaved children (www.winstonswish.org.uk), Head Office, Westmoreland House, 80–86 Bath Road, Cheltenham, Gloucestershire GL53 7JT, UK. Tel. General enquiries 01242 515157, Helpline 08452 03 04 05.

IN THE UNITED STATES OF AMERICA

Association for Death Education and Counselling, education and accreditation of professionals working with dying and bereaved people (www.adec.org), 111 Deer Lake Road, Suite 100, Deerfield, IL 60015, USA. Tel. 847 509 0403.

Bereaved Parents of the USA (www.bereavedparentsusa.org/), National Contact John Goodrich, PO Box 95; Park Forest, IL 60466–0095, USA. Tel. 708 748 7866 (info@bereavedparentsusa.org).

Compassionate Friends, mutual help for parents losing a child (www.compassionatefriends.org), The Compassionate Friends, PO Box 3696; Oak Brook, IL 60522, USA. Tel. 877 969 0010 (toll-free) ~ 630 990 0010.

The Dougy Center for Grieving Children (www.dougy.org), 3909 SE 52nd Street Avenue, PO Box 86852, Portland, OR 97286, USA. Tel. 1 503 775 683 (ext. 27).

Hospice Education Institute, education on care of dying and bereaved across the world (www.hospiceworld.org/), 3 Unity Square, PO Box 98, Machiasport, ME 04655–0098, USA. Tel. 207 255 8800, Hospicelink 800 331 1620.

The National Center for Post-Traumatic Stress Disorder (www.mentalhealth.va.gov/ptsd/alert.asp). Tel. PTSD Information Line 802 296 6300 (e-mail ncptsd@va.gov).

National Hospice and Palliative Care Organisation (NHPCO) (www.nhpco.org), 1700 Diagonal Road, Suite 625, Alexandria, VA 22314, USA. Tel. 703 837 1500, Member Service Center 800 646 6460.

Parents of Murdered Children, mutual help (www.pomc.com/), 100 East Eighth Street, Suite 202, Cincinnati, OH 45202, USA. Tel. 513 721 5683.

Parents Without Partners (PWP) (http://www.parentswithoutpartners.org/about.htm), 1650 South Dixie Highway, Suite 402, Boca Raton, FL 33432, USA. Tel. Information Line 800 637 7974, International Office 561 391 8833.

RECOMMENDED FURTHER READING

Archer, J. (1999). *The nature of grief: The evolution and psychology of reactions to loss*. London and New York: Routledge.

Bowlby, J. (1969). *Attachment and loss. Vol. 1: Attachment*. London: Hogarth; New York: Basic Books.

Bowlby, J. (1973). *Attachment and loss. Vol. 2: Separation, anxiety and anger*. London: Hogarth; New York: Basic Books.

Bowlby, J. (1980). *Attachment and loss. Vol. 3: Loss, sadness and depression*. London: Hogarth; New York: Basic Books.

Didion, J. (2005). *The year of magical thinking*. New York: Alfred Knopf.

Doka, K. (Ed.). (1989). *Disenfranchised grief*. Lexington, MA: Lexington Books.

Freud, S. (1894/1953). The neuro-psychoses of defence. In *The standard edition of the complete psychological works of Sigmund Freud* (under the general editorship of James Strachey, in collaboration with Anna Freud, assisted by Alix Strachey and Alan Tyson, Vol. 3, pp. 43–61). London: Hogarth Press.

Freud, S. (1917/1953). Mourning and melancholia. In *The standard edition of the complete psychological works of Sigmund Freud* (under the general editorship of James Strachey, in collaboration with Anna Freud, assisted by Alix Strachey and Alan Tyson, Vol. 14, pp. 239–258). London: Hogarth Press.

Freud, S. (1923/1953). The ego and the id. In *The standard edition of the complete psychological works of Sigmund Freud* (under the general editorship of James Strachey, in collaboration with Anna Freud, assisted by Alix Strachey and Alan Tyson, Vol. 19, pp. 3–11). London: Hogarth Press.

Freud, S. (1933/1953). New introductory lectures on psycho-analysis. In *The standard edition of the complete psychological works of Sigmund Freud* (under the general editorship of James Strachey, in collaboration with Anna Freud, assisted by Alix Strachey and Alan Tyson, Vol. 22). London: Hogarth Press.

Gibson, M. (2006). *Order from chaos: Responding to traumatic events*

(3rd ed.). Bristol, UK: British Association of Social Workers, Policy Press. (First published 1991.)

Goodall, J. van L. (1971). *In the shadow of man*. New York: Houghton-Mifflin.

Jacobs, S. (1993). *Pathologic grief: Maladaptation to loss*. Washington, DC, and London: American Psychiatric Press.

Kauffman, J. (Ed.). (2002). *Loss of the assumptive world: A theory of traumatic loss*. New York and London: Brunner-Routledge.

Kissane, D. W., and Bloch, S. (2002). *Family focused grief therapy: A model of family-centred care during palliative care and bereavement*. Buckingham, UK, and Philadelphia, USA: Open University Press.

Klass, D., Silverman, P. R., and Nickman, S. (Eds.). (1996). *Continuing bonds: New understandings of grief*. Washington, DC, and London: Taylor & Francis.

Lewis, C. S. (1961). *A grief observed*. London: Faber. (First published as by N. W. Clerk.)

Marris, P. (1974). *Loss and change*. London: Routledge & Kegan Paul.

Monroe, B., and Kraus, F. (2005). *Brief interventions with bereaved children*. New York and London: Oxford University Press.

Neimeyer, R. A. (Ed.). (2001). *Meaning reconstruction and the experience of loss*. Washington, DC: American Psychological Association Press.

Parkes, C. M. (2006). *Love and loss: The roots of grief and its complications*. London: Routledge.

Parkes, C. M., Laungani, P., and Young, W. (1997). *Death and bereavement across cultures*. London: Routledge.

Parkes, C. M., and Markus, A. (Eds.). (1998). *Coping with loss: Helping patients and their families*. London: BMJ Books.

Parkes, C. M., and Weiss, R. S. (1983). *Recovery from bereavement*. New York: Basic Books.

Stroebe, M. S., Hansson, R. O., Schut, H., and Stroebe, W. (Eds.). (2008). *Handbook of bereavement research and practice: Advances in theory and intervention*. Washington, DC: American Psychological Association.

Stroebe, M. S., Stroebe, W., and Hansson, R.O. (Eds.). (1993). *Handbook of bereavement*. New York and Victoria, Australia: Cambridge University Press.

Walter, T. (1999). *On bereavement: The culture of grief*. Buckingham, UK: Open University Press.

Wertheimer, A. (2001). *A special scar: The experiences of people bereaved by suicide* (2nd ed.). New York and London: Routledge. (First published 1991.)

Whitaker, A. (1984). *All in the end is harvest: An anthology for those who grieve*. London: Cruse Bereavement Care and Darton, Longman & Todd.

Worden, J. W. (2002). *Children and grief: When a parent dies*. London: Guilford Press.

REFERENCES

Abraham, K. (1924). A short study of the development of the libido. In K. Abraham, *Selected papers on psychoanalysis*. London: Hogarth, 1927, new edition, 1949; New York: Basic Books, 1953.

Adamowski, K., Dickinson, G., Wietzman, B., Roessler, C., and Carter-Snell, C. (1993). Sudden unexpected death in the emergency department: Caring for the survivors. *Canadian Medical Association Journal, 149*(10), 1445–1451.

Ainsworth, M. D., and Wittig, B. A. (1969). Attachment and exploratory behaviour of one-year-olds in a strange situation. In B. Foss (Ed.), *Determinants of infant behaviour* (Vol. 4, pp. 129–173). London: Methuen.

Aldrich, C. K., and Mendkoff, E. (1963). Relocation of the aged and disabled: A mortality study. *Journal of the American Geriatrics Society, 11*, 185–194.

American Psychiatric Association. (1987). *Diagnostic and statistical manual of mental disorders* (3rd ed. revised). Washington, DC: American Psychiatric Association.

American Psychiatric Association. (1994). *Diagnostic and statistical manual of mental disorders* (4th ed.). Washington, DC: American Psychiatric Association.

Anderson, C. (1949). Aspects of pathological grief and mourning. *International Journal of Psycho-Analysis, 30*, 48–55.

Archer, J. (1999). *The nature of grief: The evolution and psychology of reactions to loss*. London and New York: Routledge.

Archer, J. (2008). Theories of grief: Past, present and future perspectives. In M. S. Stroebe, R. O. Hansson, H. Schut, and W. Stroebe (Eds.), *Handbook of bereavement research and practice: Advances in theory and intervention* (Ch. 3, pp. 45–66). Washington, DC: American Psychological Association.

Askren, H. A., and Bloom, K. C. (1999). Postadoptive reactions of the relinquishing mother: A review. *Journal of Obstetric, Gynecologic, & Neonatal Nursing, 28*(4), 395–400.

Azhar, M. Z., and Varma, S. L. (1995). Religious psychotherapy as management of bereavement. *Acta Psychiatrica Scandinavica, 91,* 233–235.

Ballard, P. H., and Jones, E. (1975). *The valleys call: A self-examination by people of the South Wales Valleys during the Year of the Valleys, 1974.* Ferndale, UK: Ron Jones.

Bambauer, K. Z., Zhang, B., Maciejewski, P. K., Sahay, N., Pirl, W. F., Block, S. D., *et al.* (2006). Mutuality and specificity of mental disorders in advanced cancer patients and caregivers. *Social Psychiatry & Psychiatric Epidemiology, 41*(10), 819–824.

Barnes, D. (1988). Previous losses: Forgotten but not resolved. In J. Morgan (Ed.), *Bereavement: Helping the survivors* (pp. 27–40). Ontario, Canada: Kings College.

Barrera, M., D'Agostino, N. M., Schneiderman, G., Tallett, S., Spencer, L., and Jovcevska, V. (2007). Patterns of parental bereavement following the loss of a child and related factors. *Omega, 55*(2), 145–167.

Barry, H., Jr., Barry, H., III, and Lindemann, E. (1965). Dependency in adult patients following early maternal bereavement. *Journal of Nervous and Mental Disease, 140*(3), 196–205.

Barry, L. C., Kasl, S. V., and Prigerson, H. G. (2002). Psychiatric disorders among bereaved persons: The role of perceived circumstances of death and preparedness for death. *American Journal of Geriatric Psychiatry, 10,* 447–457.

Bartrop, R., Luckhurst, E., Lazarus, L., Kiloh, L. G., and Perry, R. (1977). Depressed lymphocyte function after bereavement. *Lancet, 1,* 834–836.

Bass, D. M., and Bowman, K. (1990). The transition from caring to bereavement: The relationship of care-related strain and adjustment to death. *Gerontologist, 30*(1), 35–42.

Beck, F. (1966). *The diary of a widow: Rebuilding a family after the funeral.* Boston: Beacon.

Beckwith, B. E., Beckwith, S. K., Gray, T. L., Micsko, M. M., Holm, J. E., Plummer, V. H., *et al.* (1990). Identification of spouses at high risk during bereavement: A preliminary assessment of Parkes and Weiss Risk Index. *Hospice Journal, 6*(3), 35–46.

Benkendorf, J., Corson, V., Allen, J. F., and Ilse, S. (1990). Perinatal bereavement counselling in genetics. *Strategies in Genetic Counselling, March of Dimes Birth Defects Original Articles Series, 26*(3), 138–156.

Bergeron, J. P., and Handley, P. R. (1992). Bibliography on AIDS-related bereavement and grief. *Death Studies, 16*(3), 247–267.

Beutel, M., Deckardt, R., von Rad, M., and Weiner, H. (1995). Grief and depression after miscarriage: Their separation, antecedents, and course. *Psychosomatic Medicine, 57*(6), 517–526.

Birtchnell, J. (1975). The personality characteristics of early-bereaved psychiatric patients. *Social Psychiatry, 10,* 97–103.

Bisson, J. I., Jenkins, P. L., Alexander, J., and Bannister, C. (1997). Randomized controlled trial of psychological debriefing for victims of acute burn trauma. *British Journal of Psychiatry, 171,* 78–81.

Boelen, P. A., and Prigerson, H. G. (2009). The influence of symptoms of prolonged grief disorder, depression, and anxiety on quality of life among bereaved adults: A prospective study. *European Archives of Psychiatry and Clinical Neuroscience, 257*(8), 444–452.

Boelen, P. A., van den Bout, J., and de Keijser, J. (2003). Traumatic grief as a disorder distinct from bereavement-related depression and anxiety: A replication study with bereaved mental health care patients. *American Journal of Psychiatry, 160*, 1229–1241.

Bohannon, J. R. (1991). Religiosity related to grief levels of bereaved mothers and fathers. *Omega, 23*(2), 153–159.

Bojanovsky, J. (1980). Wann droht der Selbstmord bei Verwitweten? *Schweitzer Archive Neurologische Neurochirurgie und Psychiatrie, 127*, 99–103.

Bonanno, G. A. (1994). *The consequences of emotional avoidance and emotional inhibition during bereavement.* Paper read at the 4th International Conference on Grief and Bereavment in Contemporary Society, Stockholm, 12–16th June. Abstract from Swedish Association for Mental Health.

Bonanno, G. A. (2004). Loss, trauma, and human resilience: Have we underestimated the human capacity to thrive after extremely adverse aversive events? *American Psychologist, 59*, 20–28.

Bonanno, G. A., Neria, Y., Mancini, A., Coifman, K. G., Litz, B., and Insel, B. (2007). Is there more to complicated grief than depression and posttraumatic stress disorder? A test of incremental validity. *Journal of Abnormal Psychology, 116*(2), 342–351.

Bonanno, G. A., Wortman, C. B., Lehman, D. R., Tweed, R. G., Haring, M., Sonnega, J., *et al.* (2002). Resilience to loss and chronic grief: A prospective study from pre-loss to 18 months post-loss. *Journal of Personality and Social Psychology, 83*, 1150–1164.

Bonell-Pascual, E., Huline-Dickens, S., Hollins, S., Esterhuyzen, A., Sedgwick, P., Abdelnoor, A., *et al.* (1999). Bereavement and grief in adults with learning disabilities. A follow-up study. *British Journal of Psychiatry, 176*, 297–298.

Bornstein, P. E., Clayton, P. J., Halikas, J. A., Maurice, W. L., and Robins, E. (1973). The depression of widowhood at three months. *British Journal of Psychiatry, 122*, 561–566.

Bowlby, J. (1951). *Maternal care and mental health.* WHO Monograph 2. Geneva, Switzerland: World Health Organization.

Bowlby, J. (1953). *Child care and the growth of love.* London: Pelican.

Bowlby, J. (1961). Processes of mourning. *International Journal of Psycho-Analysis, 44*, 317–340.

Bowlby, J. (1969). *Attachment and loss. Vol. 1: Attachment.* London: Hogarth; New York: Basic Books.

Bowlby, J. (1973). *Attachment and loss. Vol. 2: Separation, anxiety and anger.* London: Hogarth; New York: Basic Books.

Bowlby, J. (1980). *Attachment and loss. Vol. 3: Loss, sadness and depression.* London: Hogarth; New York: Basic Books.

311

Bowlby, J., and Parkes, C. M. (1970). Separation and loss within the family. In E. J. Anthony (Ed.), *The child in his family* (pp. 197–216). New York: Wiley.

Bowling, A. (1988). Who dies after widow(er)hood? A discriminant analysis. *Omega, 19*, 135–153.

Bowman, L. (1959). *The American funeral.* Washington, DC: Public Affairs Press.

Brabant, S., Forsyth, C. J., and Melancon, C. (1992). Grieving men: Thoughts, feelings and behaviour following the death of wives. *Hospital Journal, 8*(4), 33–47.

Brabin, P. (2004). To see or not to see, that is the question. Challenging good practice bereavement care after a baby is stillborn: The case in Australia. *Grief Matters, 7*(2), 28–33.

Bradley, E. H., Prigerson, H. G., Carlson, M. D. A., Cherlin, E., Johnson-Hurzeler, R., Stanislav, V., *et al.* (2004). Depression among surviving caregivers: Does length of hospice enrollment matter? *American Journal of Psychiatry, 161*, 2257–2262.

Breuer, J., and Freud, S. (1893). On the psychical mechanisms of hysterical phenomena: A preliminary communication. In *The Complete Psychological Works of Sigmund Freud* (Standard ed., Vol. 2). London: Hogarth.

Brewin, C. R. (2001). A cognitive neuroscience account of posttraumatic stress disorder and its treatment. *Behaviour Research and Therapy, 39*, 373–393.

Brownstein, M. (1992). Contacting the family after a suicide. *Canadian Journal of Psychiatry, 37*(3), 208–212.

Bunch, J. (1972). Recent bereavement in relation to suicide. *Journal of Psychosomatic Research, 16*, 361–366.

Bunch, J., Barraclough, B., Nelson, B., and Sainsbury, P. (1971). Suicide following the death of parents. *Social Psychiatry, 6*, 193–199.

Burgoine, E. (1988). *A cross-cultural comparison of bereavement among widows in New Providence, Bahamas and London, England.* Paper read at International Conference on Grief and Bereavement in Contemporary Society, London, 12–15th July.

Byrne, G. J., and Raphael, B. (1999). Depressive symptoms and depressive episodes in recently widowed older men. *International Psychogeriatrics, 11*(1), 67–74.

Cain, A. C. (1966). The legacy of suicide: Observations on the pathogenic impact of suicide upon marital partners. *Psychiatry, 29*, 26–28.

Calabrese, J. R., Kling, A., and Gold, P. W. (1987). Alterations in immunocompetence during stress, bereavement and depression: Focus on neuroendocrine regulation. *American Journal of Psychiatry, 144*, 1123–1134.

Cannon, W. B. (1929). *Bodily Changes in pain, hunger, fear and rage* (2nd ed.). London and New York: Appleton.

Caplan, G. (1961). *An Approach to community mental health.* London: Tavistock.

Caplan, G. (1964). *Principles of preventive psychiatry*. New York: Basic Books; London: Tavistock.

Carlson, E. (1998). A prospective longitudinal study of attachment disorganisation/disorientation. *Child Development*, *69*, 1107–1128.

Carlson, V., Cicchetti, D., Barnett, D., and Braunwald, K. (1989). Disorganized/disoriented attachment relationships in maltreated infants. *Developmental Psychology*, *25*, 525–531.

Carr, D., House, J. S., Wortman, C., Nesse, R., Kessler, R. C. (2001). Psychological adjustment to sudden and anticipated spousal loss among older widowed persons. *Journal of Gerontology: B. Psychological Sciences*, *56*(4), S237–S248.

Cerney, M. S. (1985). Imagery and grief work. In E. M. Stern (Ed.), *Psychotherapy and the grieving patient* (pp. 145–149). New York and London: Harrington Park.

Chambers, W. N., and Reiser, M. J. (1953). Emotional stress in the precipitation of congestive cardiac failure. *Psychosomatic Medicine*, *15*, 38–50.

Charlton, R., Sheahan, K., Smith, G., and Campbell, I. (2001). Spousal bereavement–Implications for health. *Family Practice*, *18*(6), 614–618.

Chen, J. H., Bierhals, A. J., Prigerson, H. G., Kasl, S. V., Mazure, C. M., and Jacobs, S. (1999). Gender differences in the effects of bereavement-related psychological distress in health outcomes. *Psychological Medicine*, *29*(2), 367–380.

Cherlin, E. J., Barry, C. L., Prigerson, H. G., Green, D. S., Johnson-Hurzeler, R., Kasl, S. V., *et al.* (2007). Bereavement services for family caregivers: How often used, why, and why not. *Journal of Palliative Medicine*, *10*(1), 148–158.

Christakis, N. A., and Allison, P. D. (2006). Mortality after the hospitalization of a spouse. *The New England Journal of Medicine*, *354*(7), 719–732.

Christakis, N. A., and Iwashyna, T. J. (2003). The health impact of health care on families: A matched cohort study of hospice use by decedents and mortality outcomes in surviving, widowed spouses. *Social Science and Medicine*, *57*, 465–473.

Clark, J., and Franzmann, M. (2006). Authority from grief, presence and place in the making of roadside memorials. *Death Studies*, *30*(6), 579–599.

Clayton, P. J. (1980). Bereavement and its management. In E. S. Paykel (Ed.), *Handbook of affective disorders* (pp. 403–415). Edinburgh, UK: Churchill-Livingstone.

Clayton, P. J., Desmarais, L., and Winokur, G. (1968). A study of normal bereavement. *American Journal of Psychiatry*, *125*, 168–178.

Clayton, P. J., Halikas, J. A., and Maurice, W. L. (1972). The depression of widowhood. *British Journal of Psychiatry*, *120*, 71–78.

Clegg, F. (1988). Grief and loss in elderly people in a psychiatric setting. In E. Chigier (Ed.), *Grief and mourning in contemporary society. Vol. 1: Psychodynamics* (pp. 191–198). London and Tel Aviv, Israel: Freund.

Cleiren, M. P. H. D. (1992). *Bereavement and adaptation: A comparative study of the aftermath of death.* London, Philadelphia and Washington, DC: Hemisphere.

Cochrane, A. L. (1936). A little widow is a dangerous thing. *International Journal of Psycho-Analysis, 17,* 494–509.

Cooley, C. H. (1909). *Social organization.* New York: Scribner.

Cooper, C. L., and Farragher, E. B. (1993). Psychosocial stress and breast cancer: The inter-relationship between stress events, coping strategies and personality. *Psychological Medicine, 23*(3), 653–662.

Cottington, E. M., Matthew, K. A., Talbott, E., and Kuller, L. H. (1980). Environmental events preceding sudden death in women. *Psychosomatic Medicine, 42,* 567–574.

Craske, M. G., and Barlow, D. H. (2007). *Mastery of your anxiety and panic.* Oxford, UK: Oxford University Press.

Currier, J. M., Neimeyer, R. A., and Berman, J. S. (2008). The effectiveness of psychotherapeutic interventions for bereaved individuals: A comprehensive quantitative review. *Psychological Bulletin, 134*(5), 648–661.

Dalgard, O., Bjork, S., and Tambs, K. (1994). Social support, negative life events and mental health. *British Journal of Psychiatry, 166,* 29–34.

Darwin, C. (1872). *The expression of the emotions in man and animals.* London: John Murray.

Dembo, T., Ladieu-Leviton, G., and Wright, B. A. (1952). Acceptance of loss – Amputation. In J. F. Garret (Ed.), *Psychological aspects of physical disabilities* (pp. 80–96). Washington, DC: US Government Printing Office.

Didion, J. (2005). *The year of magical thinking.* New York: Alfred Knopf.

Dillenberger, K. (1992). *Violent bereavment: Widows in Northern Ireland.* Aldershot, UK: Avebury.

Dodd, P., Guerin, S., McEvoy, J., Buckley, S., Tyrrell, J., and Hillery, J. (2008). A study of complicated grief symptoms in people with intellectual disabilities. *Journal of Intellectual Disability Research, 52*(5), 415–425.

Doka, K. (Ed.). (1989). *Disenfranchised grief.* Lexington, MA: Lexington Books.

Doka, K. (2008). Disenfranchised grief in historical and cultural perspective. In M. S. Stroebe, R. O. Hansson, H. Schut, and W. Stroebe (Eds.), *Handbook of bereavement research and practice: Advances in theory and intervention* (Ch. 11, pp. 223–240). Washington, DC: American Psychological Association.

Donne, J. (1609/1839). To the Lady Bedford. In H. Alford (Ed.), *The works of John Donne* (Vol. III, pp. 574–575). London: John W. Parker.

Donne, J. (1624/1933). *Nunc lento sonitu dicunt, morieris* [Now, this bell tolling softly for another, says to me: Thou must die]. Meditation 17. Devotions upon emergent occasions. In H. Grierson (Ed.), *The poems of John Donne* (p. 204). Oxford, New York and Toronto: Oxford University Press.

Dowling, D., Hubert, J., and Hollins, S. (2003). Bereavement interventions in people with learning disabilities. *Bereavement Care, 22*(2), 19–21.

Duke, D. M. (1980). *A study of the effects of bereavement in a sample of those bereaved in the area covered by Horton Parish, South Shields*. Unpublished thesis submitted for MPhil Degree (Council for National Academic Awards).

Duran, A.,Turner, C. W., and Lund, D. A. (1989). Social support, perceived stress and depression following the death of a spouse in later life. In D. A. Lund (Ed.), *Older bereaved spouses: Research with practical applications* (pp. 69–78). New York: Hemisphere.

Engel, G. (1971). Sudden and rapid death during psychological stress. *Annals of Internal Medicine, 74*, 771–782.

Engh, A. L., Beehner, J. C., Bergman, T. J., Whitten, P. L., Hoffmeier, R. R., Seyfarth, R. M., *et al.* (2006). Behavioural and hormonal responses to predation in female chacma baboons (*Papio hamadryas ursinus*). *Proceedings of the Royal Society. B: Biological Sciences, 273*(1587), 707–712.

Erikson, E. H. (1950). *Childhood and society*. New York: Norton; London: Imago, 1951; revised edition, New York: Norton, 1963.

Erlangsen, A., Jeune, B., Bille-Brahe, U., and Vaupel, J. W. (2004). Loss of partner and suicide risks among oldest old: A population-based register study. *Age and Ageing, 33*(4), 378–383.

Esterling, B. A., Kiecolt-Glaser, J. K., and Glaser, R. (1996). Psychosocial modulation of cytokine-induced natural killer cell activity in older adults. *Psychosomatic Medicine, 58*(3), 264–272.

Eysenbach, G. (2005). The law of attrition. *Journal of Medical Internet Research, 7*, e11.

Fagin, L., and Little, M. (1984). *The forsaken families*. Harmondsworth, UK: Penguin Books.

Feeney, J. A., and Noller, P. (1990). Attachment style as a predictor of romantic adult relationships. *Journal of Personality & Social Psychology, 58*, 281–291.

Fenichel, O. (1948). *Psychoanalytic theory of the neuroses*. New York: Norton.

Fisher, S. H. (1960). Psychiatric considerations of hand disability. *Archives of Physical Medicine and Rehabilitation, 41*, 62–70.

Fonagy, P. H., Leigh, T., Steele, M., Steele, H., Kennedy, R., Mattoon, G., *et al.* (1996). The relation of attachment status, psychiatric classification and response to psychotherapy. *Journal of Consulting & Clinical Psychology, 64*, 22–31.

Forte, A. L., Hill, M., Pazder, R., and Feudtner, C. (2004). Bereavement care interventions: A systematic review. *BMC Palliative Care, 3*, 3 (Available at: www.biomedcentral.com/1472-684X/3/3).

Fortner, B. V. (1999). *The effectiveness of grief counseling and therapy: A quantitative review*. Doctoral dissertation, University of Memphis, TN.

Frankl, V. E. (1963). *Man's search for meaning: An introduction to logotherapy* (I. Lasch, Trans.). New York: Washington Square Press. (Originally published in 1946 as *Ein Psycholog erlebt das Konzentrationslager*; Earlier title, 1959, *From death-camp to existentialism*.)

REFERENCES

Freud, S. (1894/1953). The neuro-psychoses of defence. In *The standard edition of the complete psychological works of Sigmund Freud* (under the general editorship of James Strachey, in collaboration with Anna Freud, assisted by Alix Strachey and Alan Tyson, Vol. 3, pp. 43–61). London: Hogarth Press.

Freud, S. (1917/1953). Mourning and melancholia. In *The standard edition of the complete psychological works of Sigmund Freud* (under the general editorship of James Strachey, in collaboration with Anna Freud, assisted by Alix Strachey and Alan Tyson, Vol. 14, pp. 239–258). London: Hogarth Press.

Freud, S. (1923/1953). The ego and the id. In *The standard edition of the complete psychological works of Sigmund Freud* (under the general editorship of James Strachey, in collaboration with Anna Freud, assisted by Alix Strachey and Alan Tyson, Vol. 19, pp. 3–11). London: Hogarth Press.

Freud, S. (1933/1953). New introductory lectures on psycho-analysis. In *The standard edition of the complete psychological works of Sigmund Freud* (under the general editorship of James Strachey, in collaboration with Anna Freud, assisted by Alix Strachey and Alan Tyson, Vol. 22). London: Hogarth Press.

Fried, M. (1962). Grieving for a lost home. In L. J. Duhl (Ed.), *The environment of the metropolis*. New York: Basic Books.

Fry, P. S. (2004). Positive aspects of caregiving and adaptation to bereavement. *The Psychology of Aging, 19*(4), 668–675.

Fulton, R., and Gottesman, D. J. (1980). Anticipatory grief: A psychosocial concept reconsidered. *British Journal of Psychiatry, 137*, 45–54.

Gass, K. A. (1989). Appraisal, coping and resources: Markers associated with the health of aged widows and widowers. In D. A. Lund (Ed.), *Older bereaved spouses: Research with practical applications*. London and New York: Hemisphere.

Gerber, I., Rusalem, R., and Hannon, N. (1975). Anticipatory grief and aged widows and widowers. *Journal of Gerontology, 30*, 225–229.

Gerra, G., Monti, D., Panerai, A. E., Sacerdote, P., Anderlini, R., Avanzini, P., *et al.* (2003). Long-term immune–endocrine effects of bereavement: Relationships with anxiety levels and mood. *Psychiatry Research, 121*(2), 145–158.

Ghosh, A., Marks, I. M., and Carr, A. (1988). Therapist contact and outcome of self-exposure treatment for phobias. *British Journal of Psychiatry, 152*, 234–238.

Gibson, M. (2006). *Order from chaos: Responding to traumatic events*. Bristol, UK: British Association of Social Workers/Policy Press.

Giovinco, G., and Monahan, J. (1994). *Logotherapy and bereavement: A comparison of the grief response of survivors of individuals who died of AIDS and individuals who died of other causes*. Paper read at the 4th International Conference on Grief and Bereavment in Contemporary Society, Stockholm, 12–16th June. Abstract from Swedish Association for Mental Health.

Glare, P., Virik, K., Jones, M., Hudson, M., Eychmuller, S., Simes, J., *et al.* (2003). A systematic review of physicians' survival predictions in terminally ill cancer patients. *British Medical Journal, 327*, 1–6.

Glick, I., Parkes, C. M., and Weiss, R. S. (1974). *The first year of bereavement.* New York and Chichester, UK: Wiley Interscience.

Golan, N. (1975). Wife to widow to woman. *Social Work, 20*, 369–374.

Goldsmith, B., Morrison, R. S., Vanderwerker, L. C., and Prigerson, H. G. (2008). Elevated rates of prolonged grief disorder in African Americans. *Death Studies, 32*(4), 352–365.

Goodall, J. (1971). *In the shadow of man.* New York: Houghton-Mifflin.

Goodkin, K., Baldewicz, T. T., Asthana, D., Khamis, I., Blaney, N. T., Kumar, M., *et al.* (2001). A bereavement support group intervention affects plasma burden of human immunodeficiency virus type 1. Report of a randomized controlled trial. *Journal of Human Virology, 4*(1), 44–54.

Goodkin, K., Blaney, N. T., Feaster, D. J., Baldewicz, T., Burkhalter, J. E., and Leeds, B. A. (1999). Randomized controlled clinical trial of a bereavement support group intervention in human immunodeficiency virus type 1-seropositive and -seronegative homosexual men. *Archives of General Psychiatry, 56*(1), 52–59.

Goodkin, K., Feaster, D. J., Asthana, D., Blaney, N. T., Kumar, M., Baldewicz, T., *et al.* (1998). A bereavement support group intervention is longitudinally associated with salutary effects on the CD4 cell count and number of physician visits. *Clinical and Diagnostic Laboratory Immunology, 5*(3), 382–391.

Goodkin, K., Feaster, D. J., Tuttle, R., Blaney, N. T., Kumar, M., Baum, M. K., *et al.* (1996). Bereavement is associated with time-dependent decrements in cellular immune function in asymptomatic human immunodeficiency virus type 1-seropositive homosexual men. *Clinical and Diagnostic Laboratory Immunology, 3*(1), 109–118.

Gorer, G. (1965). *Death, grief and mourning in contemporary Britain.* London: Cresset.

Gould, M. S., Marrocco, F. A., Kleinman, M., Thomas, J. G., Mostkoff, K., Cote, J., *et al.* (2005). Evaluating iatrogenic risk of suicide screening programs: A randomized controlled trial. *Journal of the American Medical Association, 293*(13), 1635–1643.

Grant, R., Redlener, E., Lynch, L., Paula, S., and Redlener, I. (2003). Mental health services are vital to terrorism preparedness. *Abstracts of Academy of Health Meeting, 20*, Abstract No. 110.

Greer, D. S., and Mor, V. (1986). An overview of national hospice study findings. *Journal of Chronic Diseases, 39*, 5–7.

Grinberg, L. (1964). Two kinds of guilt: Their relationship with normal/ pathological aspects of mourning. *International Journal of Psycho-Analysis, 45*, 366–372.

Gundel, H., O'Connor, M., Littrell, L., Fort, C., and Lane, R. (2003). Functional neuro-anatomy of grief. An fMRI study. *American Journal of Psychiatry, 160*, 1946–1953.

Gundogar, D., Yuksel Bassak, P., Baysal Akkaya, V., and Akarsu, O. (2006). Autoerythrocyte sensitization syndrome associated with grief complications. *Journal of Dermatology*, *33*(3), 211–214.

Hadfield, J. H. (1954). *Dreams and nightmares*. Harmondsworth, UK: Penguin Books.

Hall, M., Baum, A., Buysse, D. J., Prigerson, H. G., Kupfer, D. J., and Reynolds, C. F., 3rd. (1998). Sleep as a mediator of the stress–immune relationship. *Psychosomatic Medicine*, *60*(1), 48–51.

Hall, M., and Irwin, M. (2001). Physiological indices of functioning in bereavement. In M. S. Stroebe, R. O. Hansson, W. Stroebe, and H. Schut (Eds.), *Handbook of bereavement research: Consequences, coping and care* (Ch. 21, pp. 473–492). Washington, DC: American Psychological Association.

Hammack, S. E., Schmid, M. J., LoPresti, M. L., Der-Avakian, A., Pellymounter, M. A., Foster, A. C., *et al.* (2003). Corticotropin releasing hormone type 2 receptors in the dorsal raphe nucleus mediate the behavioral consequences of uncontrollable stress. *The Journal of Neuroscience*, *23*(3), 1019–1025.

Hamner, M. B. (1994). *Endogenous opioid peptides in grief and traumatic stress: Review and hypothesis*. Paper read at the 4th International Conference on Grief and Bereavement in Contemporary Society, Stockholm, 12–16th June. Abstract from Swedish Association for Mental Health.

Harris, T. (2006). Volunteer befriending as an intervention for depression. *Bereavement Care*, *25*(2), 27–30.

Harris, T., Brown, G. W., and Robinson, R. (1999a). Befriending as an intervention for chronic depression among women in an inner city. 1. Randomized control trial. *British Journal of Psychiatry*, *174*, 219–224.

Harris, T., Brown, G. W., and Robinson, R. (1999b). Befriending as an intervention for chronic depression among women in an inner city. 2. Role of fresh-start experiences and baseline psycho-social factors in remission from depression. *British Journal of Psychiatry*, *174*, 225–232.

Harris, T., and Kendrick, T, (1998). Bereavement care in general practice: A survey in South Thames Health Region. *British Journal of General Practice*, *148*(434), 1560–1564.

Heinicke, C., and Westheimer, I. (1966). *Brief separations*. New York: International Universities Press; London: Longman.

Helsing, K. J., Comstock, G. W., and Szklo, M. (1982). Causes of death in a widowed population. *American Journal of Epidemiology*, *116*, 524–532.

Helsing, K. J., Szklo, M., and Comstock, G. W. (1981). Factors associated with mortality after bereavement. *American Journal of Public Health*, *71*, 802–809.

Higginson, I. J., Finley, I. G., Goodwin, D. M., Hood, K., Edwards, A. G., Cook, A., *et al.* (2003). Is there evidence that palliative care teams alter end-of-life experiences of patients and their caregivers? *Journal of Pain Symptom Management*, *25*, 150–168.

Hinton, J. (1967). *Dying*. Harmondsworth, UK: Penguin Books.

Hobson, C. J. (1964, September 24). Widows of Blackton. *New Society*, p. 13.

Holland, J. M., Neimeyer, R. A., Boelen, P. A., and Prigerson, H. G. (2009). The underlying structure of grief: A taxometric investigation of prolonged and normal reactions to loss. *Journal of Psychopathologic Behavior and Assessment* (in press).

Horowitz, M. J. (1976). *Stress response symptoms*. New York: Jason Aronson.

Horowitz, M. J., Bonanno, G. A., and Holen, A. (1993). Pathological grief : diagnosis and explanation. *Psychosomatic Medicine, 55*, 260–273.

Horowitz, M. J., Wilner, N., Marmar, C., and Krupnick, J. (1980). Pathological grief and the activation of latent self images. *American Journal of Psychiatry, 137*, 1157–1162.

Houghton, P., and Houghton, D. (1977). *Unfocused grief: Responses to childlessness*. Birmingham, UK: The Birmingham Settlement, 318 Summer Lane.

Hughes, P., Turton, P., Hopper, E., Slyter, H., and Evans, C. D. H. (2002). Assessment of guidelines for good practice in psycho-social care of mothers after stillbirth. *Lancet, 9327*, 114–118.

Hull, A M. (2002). Neuroimaging findings in post-traumatic stress disorder. Systematic review. *British Journal of Psychiatry, 181*, 102–110.

Hunter, J. (2007–8). Bereavement: An incomplete rite of passage. *Omega, 56*(2), 153–173.

Ide, B. A., Tobias, C., Kay, M., and Guernsey-De-Zapien, J. (1992). Pre-bereavement factors related to adjustment among older Anglo- and Mexican-American widows. Special Issue: Hispanic age and mental health. *Clinical Gerontologist, 11*(3), 75–91.

Illich, I. (1977). *Medical nemesis*. Harmondsworth, UK: Penguin Books.

International Work Group on Death, Dying and Bereavement. (1997–8). Document on violence and grief. (Violence and Grief Work Group, chair R. G. Stevenson). *Omega, 36*(3), 259–272.

International Work Group on Death, Dying and Bereavement. (2005). Breaking cycles of violence. *Death Studies, 29*(7), 585–600.

Ironson, G., Wynings, C., Schneiderman, N., Baum, A., Rodroguez, M., Greenwood, D., *et al.* (1997). Posttraumatic stress symptoms, intrusive thoughts, loss, and immune function after Hurricane Andrew. *Psychosomatic Medicine, 59*(2), 128–141.

Irwin, M. R., and Weiner, H. (1987). Depressive symptoms and immune function during bereavement. In S. Zisook (Ed.), *Biopsychosocial aspects of bereavement* (pp.159–174). Washington, DC: American Psychiatric Press.

Jacobs, B L., Van Praag, H., and Gage, F. H. (2000). Depression and the birth and death of the brain. *American Scientist, 88*, 340–345.

Jacobsen, J. C., Vanderwerker, L. C., Block, S. D., Friedlander, R. J., Maciejewski, P. K., and Prigerson, H. G. (2006). Depression and demoralization as distinct syndromes: Preliminary data from a cohort of advanced cancer patients. *Indian Journal of Palliative Care*, *12*, 8–15.

James, W. (1892). *Psychology*. New York: Holt.

Janis, I. L. (1958). *Psychological stress: Psychoanalytic and behavioural studies of surgical patients*. London: Chapman & Hall.

Johnson, N. J., Backlund, E., Sorlie, P. D., and Loveless, C. A. (2000). Marital status and mortality: The national longitudinal mortality study. *Annals of Epidemiology*, *10*(4), 224–238.

Jones, D. R., and Goldblatt, P. O. (1987). Cause of death in widow(er)s and spouses. *Journal of Biosocial Science*, *19*, 107–121.

Jones, E. (1953). *Sigmund Freud: Life and work* (Vol. 1). London: Hogarth; New York: Basic Books.

Jones, E. (1955). *Sigmund Freud: Life and work* (Vol. 2). London: Hogarth; New York: Basic Books.

Kalish, R. A., and Reynolds, D. K. (1973). Phenomenological reality and post-death contact. *Journal for the Scientific Study of Religion*, *12*, 209–221.

Kaltman, S., and Bonanno, G. A. (2003). Trauma and bereavement: Examining the impact of sudden and violent deaths. *Journal of Anxiety Disorders*, *17*(2), 131–147.

Kaminer, H., and Lavie, P. (1991). Dream repression in adjusted Holocaust survivors. *Journal of Nervous and Mental Disease*, *179*, 664–669.

Kaprio, J., Koshkenvuo, M., and Rita, H. (1987). Mortality after bereavment: A prospective study of 95,647 widowed persons. *American Journal of Public Health*, *77*, 283–287.

Kauffman, J. (Ed.). (2002). *Loss of the assumptive world: A theory of traumatic loss*. New York and London: Brunner-Routledge.

Kaunonen, M., Tarkka, M. Y., Laippala, P., and Punonen-Ilmonen, M. (2000). The impact of supportive telephone call intervention on grief after the death of a family member. *Cancer Nursing*, *23*(6), 483–491.

Kawai, C., and Sasaki, M. (2004). Adjustment to spousal bereavement and successful aging: A 16-year longitudinal study. *Dobutsu Shinrigaku Kenkyu*, *75*(1), 49–58.

Keddie, K. M. G. (1977). Pathological mourning after the death of a domestic pet. *British Journal of Psychiatry*, *131*(2), 1–5.

Keefe-Cooperman, K. A. (2004). Comparison of grief as related to miscarriage and termination for fetal abnormality. *Omega*, *50*(4), 281–300.

Kemmeny, M. E., and Dean, L. (1995). Effects of AIDS-related bereavement on HIV progression among New York City gay men. *AIDS Education and Prevention*, *7*(5 Suppl.), 36–47.

Kemmeny, M. E., Weiner, H., Duran, R., Taylor, S. E., Visscher, B., and Fahey, J. L. (1995). Immune system changes after the death of a partner in HIV-positive gay men. *Psychosomatic Medicine*, *57*(6), 547–554.

Kessler, H. H. (1951). Psychological preparation of the amputee. *Industrial Medicine & Surgery*, *20*, 107–108.

Kirkpatrick, L. A. (1999). Attachment and religious representations and behavior. In J. Cassidy and P. R. Shaver (Eds.), *Handbook of attachment: Theory, research and clinical applications* (Ch. 35, pp. 803–822). London and New York: Guilford Press.

Kirkpatrick, L. A., and Shaver, P. R. (1990). Attachment theory and religion: Childhood attachments, religious beliefs and conversion. *Journal for the Scientific Study of Religions, 29*, 305–334.

Kirsch, I., Deacon, B. J., Huedo Medina, T. B., Scoboria, A., Moore, T. J., Johnson, B. T. (2008). Initial severity and antidepressant benefits: A meta-analysis of data submitted to the Food and Drug Administration. *PLoS Med, 5*(2), e45.

Kissane, D. W., and Bloch, S. (2002). *Family focused grief therapy: A model of family-centred care during palliative care and bereavement.* Buckingham, UK, and Philadelphia: Open University Press.

Kissane, D. W., Lichtenthal, W. G., and Zaider, T. (2007–8). Family care before and after bereavement. *Omega, 56* (1), 21–32.

Kissane, D. W., McKenzie, M., Bloch, S., Moskowitz, S., McKenzie, D. P., and O'Neill, I. (2006). Family focused grief therapy: A randomized, controlled trial in palliative care and bereavement. *The American Journal of Psychiatry, 163*(7), 1208–1219.

Kitson, G. C. (1982, May). Attachment to the spouse in divorce: A scale and its application. *Journal of Marriage and the Family, 44*, 379–393.

Klass, D., Silverman, P. R., and Nickman, S. (Eds.). (1996). *Continuing bonds: New understandings of grief.* Washington, DC, and London: Taylor & Francis.

Klein, M. (1940). Mourning and its relationship to manic-depressive states. *International Journal of Psycho-analysis, 21*, 125–153.

Klerman, G. L., and Izen, J. (1977). The effects of bereavement and grief on physical health and general well-being. *Advances in Psychosomatic Medicine, 9*, 63–104.

Koffman, J., Donaldson, N., Hotopf, M., and Higginson, I. J. (2005). Does ethnicity matter? Bereavement outcomes in two ethnic groups living in the United Kingdom. *Palliative & Supportive Care, 3*(3), 183–190.

Kowalski, K. (1991). No happy ending: Pregnancy loss and bereavement. *Clinical Issues in Perinatal Women's Health Nursing, 2*(3), 368–380.

Kreitman, N. (1964). The patient's spouse. *British Journal of Psychiatry, 110*, 159–173.

Kreitman, N. (1968). Married couples admitted to mental hospitals. *British Journal of Psychiatry, 114*, 699–718.

Krupp, G. R. (1963). Notes on identification as a defence against anxiety in coping with loss. *International Journal of Psycho-Analysis, 46*, 303–314.

Kuhn, R. (1958). The attempted murder of a prostitute. In R. May (Ed.), *Existence* (pp. 365–425). New York: Basic Books.

Kval, V. A. (1951). Psychiatric observations under severe chronic stress. *American Journal of Psychiatry, 108*, 185–192.

Laditka, J. N., and Laditka, S. B. (2003). Increased hospitalization risk for recently widowed older women and protective effects of social contacts. *Journal of Women and Aging*, *15*(2–3), 7–28; discussion 185–187.

Lannen, P., Wolfe, J., Prigerson, H. G., Onelov, E., and Kreicbergs, U. (2008). Unresolved grief in a national sample of bereaved parents: Impaired mental and physical health 4 to 9 years later. *Journal of Clinical Oncology*, *26*(36), 5870–5876.

Larson, D. T., and Hoyt, W. T. (2007). The bright side of grief counseling: Deconstructing the new pessimism. In K. J. Doka (Ed.), *Living with grief before and after the death* (pp. 157–174). Washington, DC: Hospice Foundation of America.

Latham, A. E., and Prigerson, H. G. (2004). Suicidality and bereavement: Complicated grief as psychiatric disorder presenting greatest risk for suicidality. *Suicide and Life Threatening Behavior*, *34*(4), 350–362.

Levav, I., Friedlander, Y., Kark, J., and Peritz, E. (1988). An epidemiological study of mortality among bereaved parents. *New England Journal of Medicine*, *319*, 457–461.

Levy, L. H. (1992). Anticipatory grief: Its measurement and proposed reconceptualization. *The Hospice Journal*, *7*(4), 1–28.

Levy, L. H., Martinowski, K. S., and Derby, J. S. (1994). Differences in patterns of adaptation in conjugal bereavement: Their sources and potential significance. *Omega*, *29*, 71–87.

Lewis, C. S. (1961). *A grief observed*. London: Faber. (First published as by N. W. Clerk.)

Lewis, M., Feiring, C., McGuffog, C., and Jaskir, J. (1984). Predicting psychopathology in six-year-olds from early social relations. *Child Development*, *55*, 123–136.

Li, G. (1995). The interaction effect of bereavement and sex on the risk of suicide in the elderly: An historical cohort study. *Social Science and Medicine*, *40*(6), 825–828.

Li, J., Mortensen, P., and Olsen, J. (2003). Mortality in parents after death of a child in Denmark: A nationwide follow-up study. *The Lancet*, *361*, 363–367.

Lichtenstein, P., Gatz, M., and Berg, S. (1998). A twin study of mortality after spousal bereavement. *Journal of Personality & Social Psychology*, *51*, 797–802.

Lichtenstein, P., Gatz, M., Pederson, N. L., Berg, S., and McClearn, G. E. (1996). A co-twin control study of response to widowhood. *Journal of Gerontology. Series B, Psychological & Social Sciences*, *51*, 279–289.

Lifton, R. J. (1961). *Thought reform and the psychology of totalism: A study of brainwashing in China*. New York: Norton.

Lifton, R. J., Kato, S., and Reich, M. R. (1979). *Six lives, six deaths: Potraits from modern Japan*. London and New Haven, CT: Yale University Press.

Lindemann, E. (1944). The symptomatology and management of acute grief. *American Journal of Psychiatry*, *101*, 155–160.

Lindemann, E. (1945). Psychiatric factors in the treatment of ulcerative colitis. *Archives of Neurology and Psychiatry*, *53*, 322–325.

Lindemann, E. (1960). Psychosocial factors as stress agents. In J. M. Tanner (Ed.), *Stress and psychiatric disorders* (pp. 13–16). Oxford, UK: Blackwell.

Longford, E. (1964). *Victoria RI*. London: Weidenfeld & Nicolson.

Lopata, H. Z. (1979). *Women as widows*. New York: Elsevier.

Lorenz, K. (1937). Uber die Bildung des Instinktbegriffs. *Naturwissenschaften, 25*, 289–331.

Lorenz, K. (1954). *Man meets dog*. London: Methuen.

Lorenz, K. (1963). *On aggression*. London: McEwan.

Lovell, D. M., Hemmings, G., and Hill, A. B. (1993). Bereavement reactions of female Scots and Swazis: A preliminary comparison. *British Journal of Medical Psychology, 66*(3), 259–274.

Lowell, J. R. (1984). After the burial. In A. Whitaker (Ed.), *All in the end is harvest: An anthology for those who grieve* (pp. 53–54). London: Darton, Longman & Todd.

Lund, D. A., Caserta, M. S., and Dimond, M. F. (1989). Impact of spousal bereavement on the subjective well-being of older adults. In D. A. Lund (Ed.), *Older bereaved spouses: Research with practical applications* (pp. 3–16). London and New York: Hemisphere.

Lundin, T. (1984a). Morbidity following sudden and unexpected bereavement. *British Journal of Psychiatry, 144*, 84–88.

Lundin, T. (1984b). Long-term outcome of bereavement. *British Journal of Psychiatry, 145*, 424–428.

Maciejewski, P. K., Zhang, B., Block, S. D., and Prigerson, H. G. (2007). An empirical examination of the stage theory of grief. *Journal of the American Medical Association, 297*(7), 716–723.

Maddison, D. C. (1968). The relevance of conjugal bereavement for preventive psychiatry. *British Journal of Medical Psychology, 41*, 223–233.

Maddison, D. C., and Viola, A. (1968). The health of widows in the year following bereavement. *Journal of Psychosomatic Research, 12*, 297–306.

Maddison, D. C., Viola, A., and Walker, W. (1969). Further studies in conjugal bereavement. *Australian and New Zealand Journal of Psychiatry, 3*, 63–66.

Maher, E. L. (1982). Anomic aspects of recovery from cancer. *Social Science and Medicine, 16*, 907–912.

Main, M. (1991). Metacognitive knowledge, metacognitive monitoring, and singular (coherent) vs. multiple (incoherent) model of attachment: Findings and directions for future research. In C. M. Parkes, J. Stevenson-Hinde, and P. Marris (Eds.), *Attachment across the life cycle*. London and New York: Routledge.

Main, M., and Weston, D. R. (1982). Avoidance of the attachment figure in infancy: Descriptions and interpretations. In C. M. Parkes and J. Stevenson-Hinde (Eds.), *The place of attachment in human behavior* (pp. 31–59). New York: Basic Books.

Malkinson, R., and Bar-Tur, J. K. (2004–5). Long term bereavement processes of older patients: The three phases of grief. *Omega, 50*(2), 103–127.

Manji, H. K., Drevets, W. C., and Charney, D. S. (2001). The cellular neurobiology of depression. *Nature Medicine*, *7*, 541–547.

Mann, J. R. (1987). Psychosocial aspects of leukaemia and other cancers during childhood. In N. K. Aaronson and J. Beckmann (Eds.), *The quality of life of cancer patients* (pp. 135–139). New York: Ravens Press.

Marks, I. M. (2001). *Living with fear* (2nd ed.). Maidenhead, UK: McGraw-Hill.

Marris, P. (1958). *Widows and their families*. London: Routledge & Kegan Paul.

Martikainen, P., and Valkonen, T. (1996). Mortality after the death of a spouse: Rates and causes of death in a large Finnish cohort. *American Journal of Public Health*, *86*(8), 1087–1093.

McCrae, R. R., and Costa., P. T., Jr. (1993). Psychological resilience among widowed men and women: A 10-year follow-up of a national sample. In M. Stroebe, W. Stroebe, and R. O. Hansson (Eds.), *Handbook of bereavement* (Ch. 13, pp. 196–207). Cambridge, UK: Cambridge University Press.

McMahon, B., and Pugh, T. F. (1965). Suicide in the widowed. *American Journal of Epidemiology*, *81*, 23–31.

Mellstrom, D., Nilsson, A., Oden, A., Rundgren, A., and Svanborg, A. (1982). Mortality among the widowed in Sweden. *Scandinavian Journal of Social Medicine*, *10*, 33–41.

Meyer-Holzapfel, M. (1940). Tribbedingte Ruhezustande als Ziel von Appetenzhandlungen. *Naturwissenschaften*, *28*, 273–280.

Miller, D. F. (1961). *Program for widows*. Liguari, MO: Redemptarist Fathers, Liguarian Pamphlets.

Mireault, G., Bearor, K., and Thomas, T. (2002). Adult romantic attachment among women who experienced childhood maternal loss. *Omega*, *44*(1), 97–104.

Mitchell, J. T. (1983). When disaster strikes – The critical incident stress debriefing process. *Journal of Emergency Medical Services*, *8*(1), 36–39.

Mitford, J. (1963). *The American way of death*. London: Hutchinson.

Monk, T. H., Petrie, S. R., Hayes, A. J., and Kupfer, D.J. (1994). Regularity of daily life in relation to personality, age, gender, sleep quality, and circadian rhythms. *Journal of Sleep Research*, *3*, 196–205.

Monroe, B., and Kraus, F. (2005). *Brief interventions with bereaved children*. New York and London: Oxford University Press.

Morley, C., & Fook, J. (2005). The importance of pet loss and some implications for services. *Mortality*, *10*(2), 127–143.

Moss, M. S., and Moss, S. Z. (1995). Death and bereavement. In R. Blieszner and V. H. Bedford (Eds.), *Handbook of aging and the family* (Ch. 20, pp. 422–439). Westport, CT, and London: Greenwood.

Munoz, L. (1980). Exile as bereavement: Socio-psychological manifestations of Chilean exiles in Britain. *British Journal of Medical Psychology*, *53*, 227–232.

Murphy, S. A., Gupta, A. D., Cain, K. C., Johnson, L. C., Lohan, J., Wu, L.,

324

et al. (1999). Changes in parents mental distress after the violent death of an adolescent or young adult. *Death Studies*, *23*, 129–159.

Nagahama, Y., Okada, T., Katsumi, Y., Hayashi, T., Yamauchi, H., Sawamoto, N., *et al.* (1999). Transient neural activity in the medial superior frontal gyrus and precuneus time locked with attention shift between object features. *NeuroImage*, *10*, 193–199.

National Institute for Clinical Excellence (NICE). (2004). *Depression: Management of depression in primary and secondary care*. Clinical Guideline 23. London: National Collaborating Centre for Mental Health.

National Institute for Clinical Excellence (NICE). (2005). *Post-traumatic stress disorder (PTSD): The management of PTSD in adults and children in primary and secondary care*. Clinical Guideline 26. London: Centre for Mental Health National Collaborating.

Neidig, J. R., and Dalgas, P. P. (1991). Parental grieving and perceptions regarding health care professionals' interventions. *Issues of Comprehensive Pediatric Nursing*, *14*(3), 179–191.

Neimeyer, R. A. (2000). Searching for the meaning of meaning: Grief therapy and the process of reconstruction. *Death Studies*, *24*, 541–558.

Neimeyer, R. A. (Ed.). (2001). *Meaning reconstruction and the experience of loss*. Washington, DC: American Psychological Association Press.

Nuss, W. S., and Zubenko, G. S. (1992). Correlates of persistent depressive symptoms in widows. *American Journal of Psychiatry*, *149*(3), 346–351.

O'Connor, M. F., Wellisch, D. K., Stanton, A. L., Eisenberger, N. I., Irwin, M. R., and Lieberman, M. D. (2008). Craving love? Enduring grief activates brain's reward center. *NeuroImage*, *42*, 969–972.

Okabayashi, H., Sugisawa, H., Yatomi, N., Nakatani, Y., Takanashi, K., Fukaya, T., *et al.* (1997). The impact of conjugal bereavement and the buffering effect of social support on the health of elderly people. *Dobutsu Shinrigaku Kenkyu*, *68*(3), 147–154.

Onrust, S. A., and Cuijpers, P. (2006). Mood and anxiety disorders in widowhood: A systematic review. *Aging and Mental Health*, *10*(4), 327–334.

Osterweis, M., Solomon, F., and Green, M. (Eds.). (1984). *Bereavement: Reactions, consequences and care*. Washington, DC: National Academy Press.

Ott, C. H., Lueger, R. J., Kelber, S. T., and Prigerson, H. G. (2007). Spousal bereavement in older adults: Common, resilient, and chronic grief with defining characteristics. *Journal of Nervous and Mental Diseases*, *195*(4), 332–341.

Papez, J. W. (1937). A proposed mechanism of emotion. *Journal of Neuropsychiatry and Clinical Neuroscience*, *7*(1), 103–112.

Parkes, C. M. (1964). The effects of bereavement on physical and mental health: A study of the case records of widows. *British Medical Journal*, *2*, 274–279.

Parkes, C. M. (1965a). Bereavement and mental illness: Part 1. A clinical study of the grief of bereaved psychiatric patients. *British Journal of Medical Psychology*, *38*, 1–12.

Parkes, C. M. (1965b). Bereavement and mental illness: Part 2. A classification of bereavement reactions. *British Journal of Medical Psychology*, *38*, 13–26.

Parkes, C. M. (1970). The first year of bereavement: A longitudinal study of the reaction of London widows to the death of their husbands. *Psychiatry*, *33*, 444–467.

Parkes, C. M. (1971). Psychosocial transitions: A field for study. *Social Science and Medicine*, *5*, 101–115.

Parkes, C. M. (1972a). Accuracy of predictions of survival in later stages of cancer. *British Medical Journal*, *1*, 29–31.

Parkes, C. M. (1972b). Components of the reaction to loss of a limb, spouse or home. *Journal of Psychosomatic Research*, *16*, 343–349.

Parkes, C. M. (1973). Factors determining the persistence of phantom pain in the amputee. *Journal of Psychosomatic Research*, *17*, 97–108.

Parkes, C. M. (1976). The psychological reaction to loss of a limb: The first year after amputation. In J. G. Howells (Ed.), *Modern perspectives in the psychiatic aspects of surgery* (Ch. 24, pp. 516–532). New York: Brunner Mazel.

Parkes, C. M. (1981). Evaluation of a bereavement service. *Journal of Preventive Psychiatry*, *1*, 179–188.

Parkes, C. M. (1991). Planning for the aftermath. *Journal of Royal Society of Medicine*, *84*, 22–25.

Parkes, C. M. (1993a). Psychiatric problems following bereavement by murder or manslaughter. *British Journal of Psychiatry*, *162*, 49–54.

Parkes, C. M. (1993b). Bereavement as a psycho-social transition: Processes of adaptation to change. In M. S. Stroebe, W. Stroebe, and R. O. Hansson (Eds.), *Handbook of bereavement* (Ch. 6, pp. 91–101). New York and Cambridge, UK: Cambridge University Press.

Parkes, C. M. (1995a). Adult orphans: Psychological problems following the loss of a parent in adult life. *Bereavement Care*, *14*(3), 26–28.

Parkes, C. M. (1995b). Guidelines for conducting ethical bereavement research. *Death Studies*, *19*, 171–181.

Parkes, C. M. (1995c). Genocide in Rwanda. *Bereavement Care*, *14*, 3–34.

Parkes, C. M. (1996). Genocide in Rwanda: Personal reflections. *Mortality*, *1*(1), 95–110.

Parkes, C. M. (2006). *Love and loss: The roots of grief and its complications.* London: Routledge.

Parkes, C. M. (2008). Bereavement following disasters. In M. S. Stroebe, R. O. Hansson, H. Schut, and W. Stroebe (Eds.), *Handbook of bereavement research and practice: Advances in theory and intervention* (Ch. 22, pp. 463–484). Washington, DC: American Psychological Association.

Parkes, C. M., Benjamin, B., and Fitzgerald, R. G. (1969). Broken heart: A statistical study of increased mortality among widowers. *British Medical Journal*, *1*, 740–743.

Parkes, C. M., and Brown, R. (1972). Health after bereavement: A controlled study of young Boston widows and widowers. *Psychosomatic Medicine*, *34*, 449–461.

Parkes, C. M., Laungani, P., and Young, W. (1997). *Death and bereavement across cultures*. London: Routledge.

Parkes, C. M., and Markus, A. (Eds.). (1998). *Coping with loss: Helping patients and their families*. London: BMJ Books.

Parkes, C. M., and Sills, C. (1994). Psychotherapy with the dying and the bereaved. In P. Clarkson and M. Pokorny (Eds.), *The handbook of psychotherapy* (Ch. 27, pp. 494–514). London and New York: Routledge.

Parkes, C. M., and Weiss, R. S. (1983). *Recovery from bereavement*. New York: Basic Books.

Parkes, C. M., and Williams, R. M. (1975). Psychosocial effects of disaster: Birth rate in Aberfan. *British Medical Journal*, *2*, 303–304.

Pasternak, R. E., Reynolds, C. F., Schlernizauer, M., Hoch, C. C., Buysse, D. J., Houck, P. R., *et al.* (1991). Nor-triptyline therapy of bereavement-related depression in later life. *Journal of Clinical Psychiatry*, *52*, 307–310.

Peppers, L. G., and Knapp, R. J. (1980). *Motherhood and mourning*. New York: Praeger.

Perkins, W. H., and Harris, L. B. (1990). Familial bereavement and health in adult life course perspective. *Journal of Marriage and the Family*, *52*, 233–241.

Pettingale, K. W., Hussein, M., and Tee, D. E. H. (1994). Changes in immune status following bereavement. *Stress Medicine*, *10*(3), 145–150.

Piaget, J. (1955). *The child's construction of reality*. London: Routledge & Kegan Paul.

Platek, S. M., Keenan, J. P., Gordon, G., Gallup, F., and Mohamed, B. (2004). Where am I? The neurological correlates of self and other. *Cognitive Brain Research*, *19*, 114–122.

Pompili, M., Galeandro, P. M., Lester, D., and Tatarelli, R. (2006). Suicidal behavior in surviving co-twins. *Twin Research and Human Genetics*, *9*(5), 642–645.

Ponzetti, J. J., and Johnson, M. A. (1991). The forgotten grievers: Grandparents' reactions to the death of grandchildren. *Death Studies*, *15*(2), 157–167.

Price, J. (1967). The dominance hierarchy and the evolution of mental illness. *Lancet*, *2*, 243–246.

Prigerson, H. G., Bierhals, A. J., Kasl, S. V., Reynolds, C. F., III, Shear, M. K., Newsom, J. T., *et al.* (1996). Complicated grief as a distinct disorder from bereavement-related depression and anxiety: A replication study. *American Journal of Psychiatry*, *153*, 84–86.

Prigerson, H. G., Bierhals, A. J., Kasl, S. V., Reynolds, C. F., III, Shear, M. K., Day, N., *et al.* (1997). Traumatic grief as a risk factor for mental and physical morbidity. *American Journal of Psychiatry*, *154*, 616–623.

Prigerson, H. G., Frank, E., Kasl, S. V., Reynolds, C. F., Anderson, B., Zubenko, G. S., *et al.* (1995a). Complicated grief and bereavement-related depression as distinct disorders: Preliminary empirical validation in elderly bereaved spouses. *American Journal of Psychiatry*, *152*, 22–30.

Prigerson, H. G., Horowitz, M. J., Jacobs, S. C., Aslan, M., Parkes, C. M., Raphael, B., *et al.* (2009). Field trial of consensus criteria for PGD proposed for DSM-V (Awaiting publication).

Prigerson, H. G., and Jacobs, S. C. (2001). Traumatic grief as a distinct disorder: A rationale, consensus criteria and preliminary empirical test. In M. S. Stroebe, R. O. Hansson, W. Stroebe, and H. Schut (Eds.), *Handbook of bereavement research: Consequences, coping and care* (pp. 613–645). Washington, DC: American Psychological Association.

Prigerson, H. G., and Maciejewski, P. K. (2008). Grief and acceptance as opposite sides of the same coin: Setting a research agenda for studying peaceful acceptance of loss. *British Journal of Psychiatry*, *193*, 435–437.

Prigerson, H. G., Maciejewski, P. K., Reynolds, C. F., Bierhals, A. J., Newsom, J. T., Fasiczka, A., *et al.* (1995b). Inventory of complicated grief: A scale to measure maladaptive symptoms of loss. *Psychiatry Research*, *59*, 65–79.

Prigerson, H. G., Maciejewski, P. K., and Rosenheck, R. A. (2000). Preliminary explorations of the harmful interactive effects of widowhood and marital harmony on health, health service use, and health care costs. *Gerontologist*, *40*(3), 349–357.

Prigerson, H. G., Maciejewski, P. K., and Rosenheck, R. A. (2002). Population attributable fractions of psychiatric disorders and behavioral outcomes associated with combat exposure among US men. *American Journal of Public Health*, *92*(1), 59–63.

Prigerson, H. G., Reynolds, C. F., 3rd, Frank, E., Kupfer, D. J., George, C. J., and Houck, P. R. (1994). Stressful life events, social rhythms, and depressive symptoms among the elderly: An examination of hypothesized causal linkages. *Psychiatry Research*, *51*(1), 33–49.

Prigerson, H. G., Shear, M. K., Jacobs, S. C., Reynolds, C. F., Maciejewski, P. K., Davidson, J. R. T., *et al.* (1999). Consensus criteria for traumatic grief: A preliminary empirical test. *British Journal of Psychiatry*, *174*, 67–73.

Prigerson, H. G., Vanderwerker, L. C., and Maciejewski, P. K. (2008). A case for inclusion of prolonged grief disorder in DSM-V. In M. S. Stroebe, R. O. Hansson, H. Schut, and W. Stroebe (Eds.), *Handbook of bereavement research and practice: Advances in theory and intervention* (Ch. 8, pp. 165–186). Washington, DC: American Psychological Association.

Proudfoot, J., Ryden, C., Everitt, B., Shapiro, D., Goldberg, D., Mann, A., *et al.* (2004). Clinical efficacy of computerized cognitive-behavioural therapy for anxiety and depression in primary care: Randomized controlled trial. *British Journal of Psychiatry*, *185*, 46–54.

Pynoos, R. S., Frederick, C., Nader, K., Arroyo, W., Steinberg,. A., Eth, S., *et al.* (1987b). Life threat and post-traumatic reactions in school-age children. *Archives of General Psychiatry*, *44*, 1057–1063.

Pynoos, R. S., Nader, K., Frederick, C., Gonda, L., and Stuber, M. (1987a).

Grief reactions in school-age children following a sniper attack at school. *Israel Journal of Psychiatry and Related Sciences*, *24*, 53–63.

Range, L. M., Kovac, S. H., and Marion, M. S. (1999). Does writing about the bereavement lessen grief following sudden, unintentional death? *Death Studies*, *24*, 115–134.

Raphael, B. (1977). Preventive intervention with the recently bereaved. *Archives of General Psychiatry*, *34*, 1450–1454.

Raphael, B. (1984). *The anatomy of bereavement: A handbook for the caring professions*. London: Hutchinson.

Raphael, B. (1986). *When disaster strikes*. New York: Basic Books.

Rees, W. D. (1971), The hallucinations of widowhood. *British Medical Journal*, *4*, 37–41.

Rees, W. D., and Lutkins, S. G. (1967). Mortality of bereavement. *British Medical Journal*, *4*, 163–164.

Relf, M. (1994). *The effectiveness of volunteer bereavement support: Reflections from the Sobell House Bereavement Study*. Paper read at the 4th International Conference on Grief and Bereavment in Contemporary Society, Stockholm, 12–16th June. Abstract from Swedish Association for Mental Health.

Reuber, M., Howlett, S., Khan, A., and Grunewald, R. A. (2007). Non-epileptic seizures and other functional neurological symptoms: Predisposing, precipitating, and perpetuating factors. *Psychosomatics*, *48*(3), 230–238.

Reynolds, C. F., 3rd, Miller, M. D., Pasternak, R. E., Frank, E., Perel, J. M., Cornes, C., *et al.* (1999). Treatment of bereavement-related major depressive episodes in later life: A controlled study of acute and continuation treatment with nortriptyline and interpersonal psychotherapy. *American Journal of Psychiatry*, *156*(2), 202–208.

Reynolds, J. J. (2004). Stillbirth: To hold or not to hold. *Omega*, *48*(1), 85–88.

Robertson, J. (1953). Some responses of young children to loss of maternal care. *Nursing Times*, *49*, 382–386.

Robertson, J., and Bowlby, J. (1952). Responses of young children to separation from their mothers. *Courier of the International Childrens Centre, Paris*, *II*, 131–140.

Robinson, L. A., Nuamah, I. F., Lev, E., and McCorkle, R. (1995). A prospective longitudinal investigation of spousal bereavement examining Parkes and Weiss Bereavement Risk Index. *Journal of Palliative Care*, *11*(4), 5–13.

Robinson, M., Baker, L., and Nackerud, L. (1999). The relationship of attachment theory and perinatal loss. *Death Studies*, *23*(3), 257–270.

Rochlin, G. (1965). *Griefs and discontents: The forces of change*. Boston: Little, Brown.

Rogers, C. R. (1961). *On becoming a person*. Boston: Houghton Mifflin.

Rosenblatt, P. C., Spoentgen, P., Karis, T. A., Dahl, C., Kaiser, T., and Elde, C. (1991). Difficulties in supporting the bereaved. *Omega*, *23*(2), 119–128.

Rosenblatt, P. C., Walsh, R. P., and Jackson, D. A. (1976). *Grief and mourning in cross-cultural perspective*. New York: Human Relations Area Files, Inc.

Rosenbloom, C. A. (1993). The effects of bereavement on eating behaviors and nutrient intake in elderly widowed persons. *Journal of Gerontology*, *48*(4), 223–229.

Roskin, M. (1984). A look at bereaved parents. *Bereavement Care*, *3*, 26–28.

Ross, E. K. (1970). *On death and dying*. London and New York: Tavistock.

Rubin, S. S. (1992). Adult child loss and the two-track model of bereavement. *Omega*, *24*, 183–202.

Rush, B. (1835). *Medical inquiries and observations upon the diseases of the mind*. Philadelphia: Grigg & Elliott.

Rynearson, E. K. (1978). Humans and pets and attachment. *British Journal of Psychiatry*, *133*, 550–555.

Santic, Z., Lukic, A., Sesar, D., Milicevic, S., and Ilakovac, V. (2006). Long-term follow-up of blood pressure in family members of soldiers killed during the war in Bosnia and Herzegovina. *Croatian Medical Journal*, *47*(3), 416–423.

Sanua, V. D. (1974). Psychological effects of the Yom Kippur war. *The Source*, *2*(3), 7–8.

Savage, G. (1993). The use of hypnosis in the treatment of complicated bereavement. *Contemporary Hypnosis*, *10*(2), 99–104.

Scheper-Hughes, N. (1992). *Death without weeping: The violence of everyday life in Brazil*. Berkeley, CA: University of California Press.

Schleifer, S. J., Keller, S. E., Kamerino, M., Thornton, J. C., and Stein, M. (1983). Suppression of lymphocyte stimulation following bereavement. *Lancet*, *1*, 834–836.

Schleifer, S. J., Keller, S. E., Meyerson, A. T., Raskin, M. D., Davis, K. L., and Stein, M. (1984). Lymphocyte function in major depressive disorder. *General Psychiatry*, *42*, 129–133.

Schmale, A. H. J., and Iker, H. P. (1966). The affect of hopelessness and the development of cancer: I. Identification of uterine cervical cancer in women with atypical cytology. *Psychosomatic Medicine*, *28*, 714–721.

Schneider, D. S., Sledge, P. A., Shuchter, S. R., and Zisook, S. (1996). Dating and remarriage over the first two years of widowhood. *Annals of Clinical Psychiatry*, *8*(2), 51–57.

Schneider, S. G., Taylor, S. E., Kemmeny, M. E., and Hammen, C. (1991). AIDS-related factors predictive of suicidal ideation of low and high intent among gay and bisexual men. *Suicide and Life-Threatening Behavior*, *21*, 313–328.

Schoevers, R. A., Smit, F., Deeg, D. J., Cuijpers, P., Dekker, J., van Tilburg, W., *et al.* (2006). Prevention of late-life depression in primary care: Do we know where to begin? *American Journal of Psychiatry*, *163*(9), 1611–1621.

Schulz, R., Beach, S. R., Lind, B., Martire, L. M., Zdzniuk, B., Hirsch, C., *et al.* (2001). Involvement in caregiving and adjustment to death of a

REFERENCES

spouse: Findings from the Caregiver Health Effects Study. *Journal of the American Medical Association, 285*, 3123–3129.

Schulz, R., Boerner, K., and Hebert, R. S. (2008). Caregiving and bereavement. In M. S. Stroebe, R. O. Hansson, H. Schut, and W. Stroebe (Eds.), *Handbook of bereavement research and practice: Advances in theory and intervention* (Ch. 13, pp. 265–286). Washington, DC: American Psychological Association.

Schut, H. A. W., de Keijser, J., and van den Bout, J. (1991). *A controlled efficacy study into short-term individual counselling: Client variables.* Paper read at the Third International Conference on Grief and Bereavement in Contemporary Society, Sydney, Australia, 30 June to 4 July.

Schut, H. A. W., de Keijser, J., van den Bout, J., and Stroebe, M. S. (1997a). Cross-modality grief therapy: Description and assessment of a new program. *Journal of Clinical Psychology, 52*(3), 357–365.

Schut, H. A.W., Stroebe, M. S., van den Bout, J., and de Keijser, J. (1997b). Intervention for the bereaved: Gender differences in the efficacy of two counselling programs. *British Journal of Clinical Psychology, 36*, 63–72.

Schut, H. A. W., Stroebe, M. S., van den Bout, J., and Terheggen, M. (2001). The efficacy of bereavement interventions: Determining who benefits. In M. S. Stroebe, R. O. Hansson, W. Stroebe, and H. Schut (Eds.), *Handbook of bereavement research: Consequences, coping and care* (Ch. 30, pp. 705–737). Washington, DC: American Psychological Association.

Segal, N. L., and Bouchard, T. J. (1993). Grief intensity following the loss of a twin and other relatives: Test of genetic kinship hypothesis. *Human Biology, 65*(1), 87–105.

Seligman, M. E. P. (1975). *Helplessness*. San Francisco: Freeman.

Shanfield, S. B. (1979). Social and emotional determinants of the death process. *Arizona Medicine, 36*, 602–603.

Shanfield, S. B., Benjamin, G. A. H., and Swain, B. J. (1984b). Parents' reactions to the death of an adult child from cancer. *American Journal of Psychiatry, 141*(9), 1092–1094.

Shanfield, S. B., and Swain, B. J. (1984a). Death of adult children in traffic accidents. *Journal of Nervous and Mental Disease, 172*(9), 533–538.

Shanfield, S. B., Swain, B. J., and Benjamin, G. A. H. (1985). Parents' responses to the death of adult children from accidents and cancer: A comparison. *Omega, 17*(4), 289–298.

Shear, M. K., Frank, E., Houck, P. R., and Reynolds, C. F. (2005). Treatment of complicated grief: A randomized controlled trial. *Journal of the American Medical Association, 293*, 2601–2608.

Shear, M. K., and Shair, H. (2005). Attachment, loss and complicated grief. *Developmental Psychobiology, 47*, 253–267.

Sikkema, K. J., Hansen, N. B., Ghebremichael, M., Kochman, A., Tarakeshwar, N., Meade, C. S., *et al.* (2006). A randomized controlled trial of a coping group intervention for adults with HIV who are AIDS bereaved: Longitudinal effects on grief. *Health Psychology, 25*(5), 563–570.

Sikkema, K. J., Hansen, N. B., Kochman, A., Tate, D. C., and Difrancisco, W.

(2004). Outcomes from a randomized controlled trial of a group intervention for HIV positive men and women coping with AIDS-related loss
and bereavement. *Death Studies, 28*(3), 187–210.

Silverman, E., Range, L., and Overholser, J. (1994). Bereavement from
suicide as compared to other forms of bereavement. *Omega, 30*(1), 41–52.

Silverman, G. K., Johnson, J. G., and Prigerson, H. G. (2001). Preliminary
explorations of the effects of prior trauma and loss on risk for psychiatric
disorders in recently widowed people. *Israel Journal of Psychiatry and
Related Sciences, 38*, 202–215.

Silverman, P. (1967). Services for the widowed: First steps in a programme
of preventive intervention. *Community Mental Health Journals, 3*, 37–44.

Simon, R. (1982). Bereavement art. *American Journal of Art Therapy, 20*,
135–143.

Smith, E. W. L. (1985). A Gestalt therapist's perspective on grief. In E. M.
Stern (Ed.), *Psychotherapy and the grieving patient* (pp. 65–78). New York
and London: Harrington Park.

Smith, K. R. (1990). *Risk of mortality following widowhood: Sex differences
between sudden and expected bereavement.* Paper presented at the 1990
annual meeting of the Society for Epidemiological Research, Birmingham, AL.

Smith, P. C., Range, L. M., and Ulmer, A. (1992). Belief in an after life as a
buffer in suicide and other bereavements. *Omega, 24*(3), 217–225.

Sobel, S. K., and Cowan, D. B. (2000). Impact of genetic testing for
Huntington disease on the family system. *American Journal of Medical
Genetics, 90*, 49–59.

Solomon, P., and Draine, J. (1996). Examination of grief among family
members of individuals with serious and persistent mental illness.
Psychiatric Quarterly, 67(3), 221–234.

Solomon, R. M., and Shapiro, F. (1997). Eye movement desensitization and
reprocessing: A therapeutic tool for trauma and grief. In C. R. Figley,
B. E. Bride, and N. Mazza (Eds.), *Death and trauma: The traumatology of
grieving* (pp. 231–247). Washington, DC: Taylor & Francis.

Spek, V., Cuijpers, P., Nyklicek, I., Riper, H., Keyzer, J., and Pop, V. (2007).
Internet-based cognitive behaviour therapy for symptoms of depression
and anxiety: A meta-analysis. *Psychological Medicine, 37*, 319–328.

Sroufe, L. A., and Waters, E. (1977). Heart rate as a convergent measure
in clinical and developmental research. *Merrill-Palmer Quarterly, 23*,
3–27.

Steiner, H., Carrion, V., Plattner, B., and Koopman, C. (2003). Dissociative
symptoms in posttraumatic stress disorder: Diagnosis and treatment.
Child and Adolescent Psychiatric Clinics of North America, 12(2),
231–249.

Stengel, E. (1939). Studies on the psychopathology of compulsive wandering. *British Journal of Medical Psychology, 18*, 250–254.

Stengel, E. (1943). Further studies on pathological wandering. *Journal of
Mental Science, 89*, 1050–1054.

REFERENCES

Stirtzinger, R. M., Robinson, G. E., Stewart, D. E., and Ralevski, E. (1999). Parameters of grieving in spontaneous abortion. *The International Journal of Psychiatry in Medicine, 29*(2), 235–249.

Stroebe, M. S., and Schut, H. (1999). The dual process model of coping with bereavement: Rationale and description. *Death Studies, 23*, 197–224.

Stroebe, M. S., Schut, H., and van den Bout, J. (1994). *The dual process model of bereavement.* Paper read at the 4th International Conference on Grief and Bereavment in Contemporary Society, Stockholm, 12–16th June. Abstract from Swedish Association for Mental Health.

Stroebe, M. S., and Stroebe, W. (1993). The mortality of bereavement: A review. In M. S. Stroebe, W. Stroebe, and R. O. Hansson (Eds.), *Handbook of bereavement* (Ch. 12, pp. 175–195). New York and Cambridge, UK: Cambridge University Press.

Stroebe, M. S., Stroebe,W., and Hansson, R. O. (Eds.). (1993). *Handbook of bereavement.* New York and Cambridge, UK: Cambridge University Press.

Stroebe, W., and Schut, H. (2001). Risk factors in bereavement outcome: A methodological and empirical review. In M. S. Stroebe, R. O. Hansson, W. Stroebe, and H. Schut (Eds.), *Handbook of bereavement research: Consequences, coping and care* (Ch. 16, pp. 340–372). Washington, DC: American Psychological Association.

Struhsaker, T. T. (1967). Auditory communication among vervet monkeys. In S. A. Altmann (Ed.), *Social communication among primates* (pp. 281–324). Chicago: University of Chicago Press.

Swigar, M. E., Bowers, M. B., and Fleck, S. (1976). Grieving and unplanned pregnancy. *Psychiatry, 39*, 72–79.

Szanto, K., Shear, M. K., Houck, P. R., Reynolds, C. F., 3rd, Frank, E., Caroff, K., *et al.* (2006). Indirect self-destructive behavior and overt suicidality in patients with complicated grief. *Journal of Clinical Psychiatry, 67*(2), 233–239.

Theut, S. K., Jordan, L., Ross, L. A., and Deutsch, S. I. (1991). Caregivers anticipatory grief in dementia. *International Journal of Ageing and Human Development, 33*(2), 113–118.

Thomas, V., and Striegel, P. (1995). Stress and grief of a perinatal loss: Integrating qualitative and quantitative methods.*Omega, 30*(4), 299–311.

Tinbergen, N. (1951). *The study of instinct.* London: Oxford University Press.

Tomassini, C., Rosina, A., Billari, F. C., Skytthe, A·., and Christensen, K. (1998). A twin study of mortality after spousal bereavement. *Psychological Medicine, 28*(3), 635–643.

Traylor, E. S., Hayslip, B., Kaminski, P. L., and York, C. (2003). Relationships between grief and family system characteristics: A cross lagged longitudinal analysis. *Death Studies, 27*, 575–601.

Tudiver, F., Hilditch, J., and Permaul, J. A. (1991). A comparison of psychosocial characteristics of new widowers and married men. *Family Medicine, 23*(7), 501–505.

Tudiver, F., Hilditch, J., Permaul, J. A., and McKendree, D. J. (1992). Does

333

mutual help facilitate newly bereaved widowers? Report of a randomized control trial. *Evaluation and the Health Professions*, *15*(2), 147–162.

Tyhurst, J. S. (1957). The role of transition states – including disasters – in mental illness. In *Symposium on preventive and social psychiatry* (pp. 1–23). Washington, DC: Walter Reid Army Institute of Research.

Umberson, D. (1987). Family status and health behaviors: Social control as a dimension of social integration. *Journal of Health and Social Behavior*, *28*, 306–319.

Vachon, M. L. S., Sheldon, A. R., Lancee, W. J., Lyall, W. A. L., Rogers, J., and Freeman, S. J. J. (1980). A controlled study of self-help intervention for widows. *American Journal of Psychiatry*, *137*, 1380–1384.

van Baarsen, B. (2002). Theories on coping with loss: The impact of social support and self-esteem on adjustment to emotional and social loneliness following a partner's death in later life. *Journal of Gerontology: B. Psychological Sciences and Social Sciences*, *57*(1), S33–S42.

van den Bout, J. (1994). *Cognitive therapy and rational-emotive therapy of grief-related problems*. Paper read at the 4th International Conference on Grief and Bereavment in Contemporary Society, Stockholm, 12–16th June. Abstract from Swedish Association for Mental Health.

Van der Hart, O. (Ed.). (1988). *Coping with loss: The therapeutic value of leave-taking rituals*. New York: Irvington.

Van Doorn, C., Kasl, S. V., Beery, L. C., Jacobs, S. C., and Prigerson, H. G. (1998). The influence of marital quality and attachment styles on traumatic grief and depressive symptoms. *Journal of Nervous and Mental Disease*, 189, 566–573.

Van Emmerick, A., Kamphuis, J., Hulsbossch, A., and Emmelkamp, P. (2002). Single session debriefing after psychological trauma. *Lancet*, *360*, 736–741.

Vanderwerker, L. C., Jacobs, S. C., Parkes, C. M., and Prigerson, H. G. (2006). An exploration of associations between separation anxiety in childhood and complicated grief in later life. *Journal of Nervous and Mental Disease*, *194*(2), 121–123.

Wagner, B., Knaevelsrud, C., and Maercker, A. (2006). Internet-based cognitive-behavioral therapy for complicated grief: A randomized controlled trial. *Death Studies*, *30*, 429–453.

Waller, W. (1951). *The family: A dynamic interpretation*. New York: Dryde.

Walter, T. (1999). *On bereavement: The culture of grief*. Philadelphia and Buckingham, UK: Open University Press.

Waugh, E. (1948). *The loved one: An American tragedy*. London: Chapman & Hall; New York: Grosset (1949).

Weinberg, N. (1994). Self-blame, other blame and desire for revenge: Factors in recovery from bereavement. *Death Studies*, *18*(6), 583–593.

Weisman, A. D. (1972). *On dying and denying: A psychiatric study of terminality*. New York: Behavioral Publications.

Westermeyer, J. (1973). Grenade amok in Laos: A psychological perspective. *International Journal of Social Psychiatry*, *19*(3), 251–260.

Wiener, A., Gerber, I., Battin, D., and Arkin, A. M. (1975). The process and phenomenology of bereavement. In B. Schoenberg, I. Berger, A. Wiener, A. H. Kutscher, D. Peretz, and A. C. Carr (Eds.), *Bereavement: Its psychosocial aspects*. New York: Columbia University Press.

Wijngaards-de Meij, L., Stroebe, M., Stroebe, W., Schut, H., van den Bout, J., Van der Heijden, P. G. M., *et al.* (2008). The impact of circumstances surrounding the death of a child on parents grief. *Death Studies*, *32*, 237–252.

Williams, K. (2004). The transition to widowhood and the social regulation of health: Consequences for health and health risk behavior. *Journal of Gerontology: B. Psychological Sciences and Social Sciences*, *59*(6), S343–S349.

Wise, R. A. (1998). Drug-activation of brain reward pathways. *Drug and Alcohol Dependence*, *51*, 13–22.

Wittkower, E. (1947). Rehabilitation of the limbless: Joint surgical and psychological study. *Occupational Medicine*, *3*, 20–44.

Worden, J. W. (2002). *Children and grief: When a parent dies*. London: Guilford Press.

Worden, J. W. (2003). *Grief counselling and grief therapy* (3rd ed.). London and New York: Brunner-Routledge.

World Health Organization. (2004). *Neuroscience of psychoactive substance abuse and dependence*. Geneva, Switzerland: WHO.

Wortman, C. B., and Silver, R. C. (1989). The myths of coping with loss. *Journal of Consulting and Clinical Psychology*, *57*(3), 349–357.

Wortmann, J. H., and Park, C. L. (2008). Religion and spirituality in adjustment following bereavement: An integrative review. *Death Studies*, *32*(8), 703–736.

Wretmark, G. (1959). A study in grief reaction. *Acta Psychiatrica et Neurologica Scandinavica*, *136*(Suppl.), 292–299.

Wright, A. A., Zhang, B., Ray, A., Mack, J. W., Trice, E., Balboni, T., *et al.* (2008). Associations between end-of-life discussions, patient mental health, medical care near death, and caregiver bereavement adjustment. *Journal of the American Medical Association*, *300*(14), 1665–1673.

Yamamoto, T., Okonogi, K., Iwasaki, T., and Yoshimura, S. (1969). Mourning in Japan. *American Journal of Psychiatry*, *125*, 1661–1665.

Yerkes, R. M. (1943). *Chimpanzees: A laboratory colony*. New Haven, CT: Yale University Press; London: Oxford University Press.

Young, M., Benjamin, B., and Wallis, C. (1963). Mortality of widowers. *Lancet*, *2*, 454–456.

Zangwill, O. L. (1987). Breuer, Joseph. In R. L. Gregory (Ed.), *The Oxford companion to the mind* (p. 118). New York: Oxford University Press.

Zettel, L. A., and Rook, K. S. (2004). Substitution and compensation in the social networks of older widowed women. *Psychology of Aging*, *19*(3), 433–443.

Zhang, B., Mitchell, S. L., Bambauer, K. Z., Jones, R., and Prigerson, H. G. (2008). Depressive symptom trajectories and associated risks among bereaved Alzheimer disease caregivers. *American Journal of Geriatric Psychiatry*, *16*(2), 145–155.

Zisook, S., Shuchter, S. R., Pedrelli, P., Sable, J., and Deaciuc, S. C. (2001). Bupropion sustained release for bereavement: Results of an open trial. *Journal of Clinical Psychiatry*, *62*(4), 227–230.

Zygmont, M., Prigerson, H. G., Houck, P. R., Miller, M. D., Shear, M. K., Jacobs, S., *et al.* (1998). A post-hoc comparison of paroxetine and nortriptyline for symptoms of traumatic grief. *Journal of Clinical Psychiatry*, *59*, 241–255.

INDEX

absences 1–2
absent grief; after amputation of a
    limb 258; after bereavement 66–7,
    78–9
abnormal grief 216; *see also* grief
    complicated, grief uncomplicated
abortion 159–60; Miscarriages
    Association 305
abuse 174, 178
acceptance 279: of death 263;
    difficulty in 83–4, 127, 263, 286;
    see also reality testing
accidents: mortality 19; in PGD 285;
    see also traumatic bereavement
adoption: and bereavement 158, loss
    of adoptive child 252
adrenaline *see* anxiety physiology of
age: 194, 197 *see also* child, old age
aggression: in non-humans 50, 91;
    dominance/submission 99
Agutainos 10
AIDS: cognitive behaviour therapy
    230; coping style 42; immune
    system in 42; support groups 234,
    302–3; *see also* disenfranchised
    grief, life-threatening illness,
    mutual help
Ainsworth, M. 167, 178; *see also*
    Strange Situation Test
alarm 38–9, 47, 253; after
    amputation of a limb 254–5;
    effects on health 39
alcohol: alcoholism 26, 81, 216; and
    anxious/ambivalent attachments
    294; consumption after
    bereavement 19, 26, 247, 294; and

depression 136; and mortality
    after bereavement 19; risk after
    bereavement 20, 26
Alzheimer's Disease 161 *see also*
    disenfranchised grief
ambivalence 174–180
amok 131
amputations 252, 254–60, 264;
    continuing bonds 256–7;
    depression 259; grief response
    255–8; helping 264; numbness
    259; pathological responses
    257–8; trauma response 254–5;
    see also phantom limb
anaemia after bereavement 22
anaesthesias 1
anger ch.6: after amputation of a
    limb 255; correlation with
    restlessness/tension 40, 91; course
    91, 280; extreme 125, 216;
    management 213; normal part of
    grief 91, 216, 287; quarrelling 94;
    and poor health 40, 91, 282; in
    PGD 284; in PTSD 92; revenge
    196; *see also* blaming, protest,
    traumatic bereavement, murder &
    manslaughter
animals, non-human: bereavement
    26 *see also* chimpanzees,
    companion animals, cows, goose,
    primates
anniversary: reactions 1, 29, 57;
    turning points 218, 265
anorexia *see* appetite
anthropological studies of
    mourning 66–7

anticipation of loss 85, 264–5 *see also* worry work

anticipatory grief 154: validity of concept 88–9; and preparation for bereavement 202

anti-depressants: placebo effect 212, for depression in bereavement 226–7; for sleep 247

anxiety: after bereavement 23, 25, 40, 103, 253; coping 45; and lack of preparation for loss 292; management 221–2, 250, 268; and threat to life 39 *see also* generalised anxiety disorder and separation anxiety

anxious-ambivalent attachment in childhood 88, 136: and alcohol after bereavement 294; and grief/ loneliness 293–4; and relational conflicts 293; *see also* dependence

apathy: and despair 97;

appetites 40: for life 263–4; loss of 24, 59; gain 24; in PGD 285; return of 120 *see also* sexual drive,weight

appetitive behaviour 64, 68

appraisal 87

approach 47

armed conflict 156, 276–7; *see also* Rwanda, genocide in

arthritis 23: rheumatoid after bereavement 22, rheumatism 23

aromatherapy 221

arousal 35–6, 47; physiology of 36, 38

art therapy 250

asthma after bereavement 23

Association for Death Education and Counselling (ADEC) 243, 306

assumptive world: changing assumptions 87–8, 100–104, 264; invalidation 113; nature of 102–3 *see also* psychosocial transitions (PSTs) & shattered assumptions

attachment: before or after birth 206; behaviour 13, 48; bond or tie 64; and complicated grief 128; functions of 11; to a home 261; and loss orientation 9; magnitude of 139; nature of 48–9; new 218; in non-human animals 206; and personality development 12; patterns of 167, 178; security of 139, 167; and vulnerability 165; *see also* abuse, attachment-based psychoanalysis, avoidant attachment, dependence, disorganised attachment, insecure attachments, Love and Loss Study, secure attachments

attachment-based psychoanalysis 230

autoerythrocyte sensitisation syndrome 22

autonomic nervous system 25, 34–8, 40

autonomy 217, 265 *see also* independence

avoidance 171–4, 214: after bereavement 214; after relocation 262; avoidant attachment 172; before bereavement 199; behaviour 47; determinants of 172; delayed grief 127, 171; disbelief 73–4, 280; inhibited grief 127; management 213, 230; physical symptoms 172; in PGD 284; postponement 172; strategy of 178; of traumatic memories 45, 162; of thoughts of loss 78–9, 171; of reminders 79, 125, 127, 287; *see also* attachment-based psychoanalysis, avoidant attachment disorder, disclosure, independence

avoidant attachment in childhood: and aggressive/assertiveness 294–6; disorder 128–9; and emotional inhibition/distrust 294–6; influence on grief 294–6; and guilt 294–6;

Bahamas *see* Caribbean

basic trust xv

Beck, F. 218

belief: in after life 89

bereavement: impact, help 202–3; distress 295–6, 298; losses resulting 8; preparing for 198–202, 291–2; psychological problems after ch. 8; reaction to (recapitulation) 253–4; uncomplicated (normal) 195–6; *see also* grief, grieving, mortality, health risk, determinants of outcome

Bereavement Care (journal) 229, 239, 243

bereavement counsellors 238–9, 241, 243 *see also* Association for Death Education and Counselling (ADEC), Cruse Bereavement Care, volunteers

bereavement services 238–44: in disasters 268; evaluation of 193–8 *see also* Cruse Bereavement Care, groups, mutual help, support groups

Bethlem Study 30, 53–4, 97, 128, 133

bibliotherapy *see* books

bitterness 91–2 *see also* anger

blaming 93–6

books: for treating anxiety and panic 222; for depression 226–7; further reading 307–8

Bowlby, J. 32, 48, 139, 167; protest and calling in non-human species 50, 90–1 *see also* phases of grief

brain: and emotions 37–8; changes during pangs of grief 65–6; in PGD 66 *see also* fMRI scanning

breaking bad news 203–4

Britain 246; *see also* Cruse Bereavement Care, National Health Service (NHS)

burial 207

burn-out 233

calling: 'lost calls' of vervet monkey 50; in human beings 62–3 *see also* crying

cancer 277–8: after loss 19, 22, 281; course 262–3; and disaster 267; and preparation for bereavement 199; in PGD 285; reaction to death by 27–8; recovery from 252; *see also* life-threatening illness

cardiac: *see* heart.

caregivers: ambiguity 214; burden 162; mortality 20

Caribbean 183, 191

Case Note Study 26–7, 132, 165, 290–1

change, resistance to 9, 103–4; changing roles 107–8 *see also* psychosocial transitions

chimpanzees: reaction to bereavement 26, 50

chronic grief *see* prolonged grief disorder

chaplains, hospital: and abortion 160; roles 198; *see also* clergy

child, loss of 58, 142–4: age of child 143; attachment to 144; Bereaved Parents of the USA 306; breaking the news 203–4; Childhood Bereavement Network 305; church attendance 210; cultural influences 143; depression 143; gender of parent 147; health 143; helping 214; mortality 17, 19, 20; and post-traumatic stress disorder 26; preparation for 202; psychiatric problems 142; suicidality 143; *see also* Compassionate Friends, disenfranchised grief, The Foundation for the Study of Infant Deaths, neonatal deaths and stillbirths

childlessness *see* infertility

children: Dougy Center for Grieving Children 306; grief of 52; at home 186–190; risk factors 150–1; as a source of meaning 103; sources of support 214, 306; Winston's Wish 306

Christianity 209–10

cirrhosis of the liver: mortality after bereavement 19; risk after bereavement by 20

Civil Contingencies Act (2004) 269

clergy: roles after bereavement 198, 239, 244–6; visits 25, 245

clinging *see* dependence

clinical depression *see* major depressive disorder

cognitive: behaviour therapy (CBT) 223, 226–7, 230, 250; gender influence on outcome 300–1; restructuring 214

conflict *see* ambivalence

communication: with dying 154; non-verbal 215

companion animals, loss of 158, 252

Compassionate Friends 241, 305–6

complicated grief ch. 5: and attachment problems 128; beneficial interventions 195, 229–31, 301; *see also* delayed grief & prolonged grief disorder

components of grief work 87–8

concentration camps *see* deprivation, extreme

conflict, marital: and anxious/ambivalent attachments 294; bereavement with 289–90

conflict trauma *see* armed conflict

Confucius 181–2

constructive world *see* assumptive world

continuing bonds ch.5 *see also* amputation of a limb, hallucinations, phantom limb

coping: and defence 83; strategies 84 *see also* avoidance, dependence, identification

cot death *see* neonatal death

counselling: for depression 226; *see also* helping bereaved people

counsellors 208; functions of 218

cows 206

creativity and loss 89

cremation 207

crisis 43–4: intervention 299; response teams *see* disasters; theory 43 *see also* trauma

critical incident stress debriefing (CISD) 268, 271

Cruse Bereavement Care 56–7, 229, 241–3, 305: after disasters 269; funding 242; helpline 243; for those with learning difficulties 235; on-line services 243; use of volunteers 243 *see also* Bereavement Care (journal), RD4U

crying: in bereavement 287; for lost home 261; in infancy 48; in greylag goose 50

culture 182, 197, 208–212: cross-cultural comparisons 66, 208–9;

variation in mourning 66, 209; loss of a child 143–4

Currier, J.M. 193–4

Cushing's disease after bereavement 22

Darwin, C. 145; expression of grief in man and other species 51–2

dazed *see* shock

dead persons 182, 205

death: consumer resistance 10; dying 252; prediction of 199; psychological causes of 15–21; registers (GP) 247; registration 203; taboo 248

debriefing *see* critical incident stress debriefing (CISD)

defences 45, 82–4; and coping 83; defensiveness 83–4, 288; functions of 82; pathological 83 *see also* avoidance, denial, depersonalisation, derealisation, dissociation, fugues, grief (absent or delayed), idealisation, postponement, repression

delayed grief 127, 296; and depression 128; and prolonged grief disorder 127;

dementia *see* Alzheimer's Disease

demoralization 263

denial: after amputations 258; of death 73–4; of poor prognosis 74, 262; after relocation 262

dependence: ambiguity 139; interdependence 165; and PGD 166; strategy of 178; on spouse 142; and vulnerability 165–71 *see also* anxious/ambivalent attachment

depersonalisation 77–8

depression: after amputation of a limb 259; after bereavement 23, 27, 99, 135; age 148; and helplessness/hopelessness 87, 178–9, 281; and lack of preparation for loss 292; negative assumptions 227; influence on physical health 22; and passivity 97–8; depressive phase of grief 99, 108, 280; helping in 226–9; physiology of 35; treatment 250;

turning in 179; *see also* anti-depressants, Beck, disorganised attachments, major depressive disorder, Seligman

deprivation 11–12, 191; extreme 162–3

derealisation 77–8, 112, 125, 216

despair 49 *see also* depression

determinants of outcome after bereavement 194: list 140; *see also* risk factors

Didion, J. 49, 114

digestion 40

disabilities and bereavement 233

disasters ch. 17, 267–78: 9/11 269; Aberfan 61, 267, 271, 275; aftermath 272–4; birth rate 275; communal trauma 273–4; crisis response team (CRTs) 268–9, 271–3, 276; illusion of centrality 271; impact 270–2; long-term care 275–6; persons affected by 268; phases of 270; press liaison 274; preparation for 268–70; reactions to 267–8; recoil 272; risk assessment 268; supporting the supporters 271; triage 271; types of 270; Zeebrugge ferry 45–6, 267 *see also* critical incident stress debriefing, psychological first aid, traumatic bereavement, traumatic stress

disbelief: in fact of death 73–4, 76; and lack of preparation for bereavement 292; *see also* denial

disclosure of feelings 213–4

disenfranchised grief 158–61: after AIDS 158; after Alzheimer's Disease 158; helping 232–3

dislocation 265–6

disorganisation 104, 108

disorganised attachments in childhood 178: psychological problems after bereavement 136, 178–9, 294–5 & 297; and suicidality 294–5

disposal *see* burial, cremation

dissociation xiv : in disasters 271; disbelief 73–4, 76; symptoms 1, 133–4; hysteria 2

doctors: blaming 93; and

disenfranchised grief 233; influence 181; roles after bereavement 25, 198, 239; roles before bereavement 201

double knowledge 75

Dougy Center for Grieving Children, The 306

dreams 72–3, 133–4

drugs, excessive consumption of 216 *see also* medications, mutual help

driving: and mortality after bereavement 19

dual process model 59, 84, 163, 169; loss orientation features of 286; and interventions 196; restoration orientation 286–7

emergency room 203

emotion-focussed therapy 230; gender influence on outcome 300–1

emotions 37: intensity 216; physiology of 37–8 *see also* emotion-focussed therapy

endocrine system 25, after bereavement 41, in bereaved baboons 41

ethology 63

evaluation of interventions *see* bereavement services

existential dilemma 113

Eye Movement Desensitisation and Reprocessing (EMDR) 222–3, 268; *see also* PTSD

family 197: changes after bereavement 114–5; conflicts 186, 196; children at home 186–190; dysfunction 196, 232, 301–2; disintegration 116; help at impact 202–3, 221; influence after bereavement 20, 181–2, 185–190, 195, 226; interventions 194; loss of leader 115; and suicidal risk 229; *see also* family focussed therapy

family doctor; *see* general paractitioner (GP)

family liaison officers (FLOs) 269

family focussed grief therapy (FFGT) 198, 232, 302
family risk index 301–2
fathers: influence of 13; loss of 1–3
fears after bereavement 24, 33, 253; management 221–2; see also phobias, panic & shattered assumptions
federal emergency management agency (FEMA) 269
finances: advice 204; change in income 116
finding 68–70 see also searching
flashbacks 45
fMRI scanning xvi–xvii, 37, 65–6, 288–9
forgetting: selective 79–80
The Foundation for the Study of Infant Deaths 305
fragility 112
Frankl, V. 163
free association 2
Freud, S 1–4, 101: and grief work 86–7, 104; mourning and melancholia 96–7
Fried, M 260–2
friends: impact help 203, 221; influence after bereavement 20, 181–2, 198, 215, 226;
frustration 64
fugues: in disasters 271; and the search for a lost parent 54
funeral 76, 92, 203, 207–8; directors 92, 181, 204–5; functions of 182; value of 204–5, 207–8
Funeral Consumer's Association 204

gains 263–4
gender 194, 197: differences after bereavement 143, 146–7; emotion-focussed therapy, reponses 230, 304; and health 147; and mortality 147; and psychiatric problems 142, 147; stillbirths 147; and vulnerability 143, 146
general practitioners (GPs) 29, consultations after bereavement 40, 246, 290–1; roles of 246–9; prescriptions 247; when suicidal risk 229 see also death registers
generalised anxiety disorder 7, 26, 130, 136; and PGD 284; treatment of 193, 226
genetic factors in bereavement 179
gestalt therapy 250
glaucoma after bereavement 22
goal-directed behaviour 63–4; frustration of 64 see also appetites & searching
God: blame 93, 95, 102; cosmic sadist 96; as parent figure 209–210; trust 267; see also beliefs
Goodkin, K. 234
goose, greylag, reaction to loss 50, 97
Gorer, G. 183, 210
government; in disasters 272
grandchild, loss of 146: mortality 17, 144, 146
graves: functions of 182; searching for 162; visiting 60–1
grief: definition xiv, 8; after amputation of a limb 255–6; after life-threatening illness 262; after relocation 260–2; and attachment 9, 293–5; classificatory system 7; complications of ch.8; course of 91, 99, 194; delayed 127; determinants of ch. 9; in Diagnostic Statistical Manual (DSM) 6; disablement 5; dual process model 9; duty to dead 217; expression of 51; medicalization of 196; and mental disorder 4–6, 122–136, 193; mitigation ch.5; loss orientation 9; and mourning 4; nature of 5; neuro-physiology of 65–70, 288–9; normal (see bereavement uncomplicated); outcome 5; pain of 6; as price of love 6; symptoms of 77, 194; restoration orientation 9; roots of 12; stopping 217; work 84, 86, 171; see also absent grief, anticipatory grief, bitterness, delayed grief, disenfranchised grief, grief work, grieving, prolonged grief disorder, TRIG, traumatic bereavement, turning points
grief work 84, 86, 104, 202, 264–5: cognitive restructuring 214; validity of concept 88–9

grieving: absence of 9; dual process of 59; level of 214; patterns of 171; phases (states) of 7, 49, 76, 99, 262–3; problems of 26; process of 7; recovery 7

group interventions: evaluation 194, 299; harmful 196, 218 *see also* mutual help, support groups

guilt: in bereaved psychiatric patients 130; and ambivalence 175, 290; in delayed grief 128; and depression 136, 216; after disasters 267; excessive 216; and hostility 130; and lack of preparation for loss 292; physical symptoms 175; psychoanalytic theory 97; self-reproaches 94–5; and social isolation *see also* restitution

habits 64–5, 101; of mourning 218

hallucinations 70, 216; hypnagogic 216 *see also* continuing bond, illusions, phantom limb

harm *see* interventions harmful

Harris, T. 226, 228

Harvard Bereavement Study 8, 24–5, 30–1, 146, 153–4, 165–6, 175, 205, 291–2, 303

haven of safety 38–9

headaches 1, 24, 40

health: after bereavement 20–8, 282; gender differences 147; influence of marital conflict on 290; in PGD 285; public 265; after relocation 262; *see also* determinants of outcome

health care professionals 232–3, 244 *see also* doctors, nurses

health advice 236

heart: broken 15

heart disease: associated with prolonged grief disorder 126, 285; simulation of 133, risks after bereavement 20, 22; *see also* life-threatening illness, mortality

helpers: selecting 214; self-disclosure 214 *see also* helping bereaved people

helping bereaved people chs. 13, 14 & 15: after the funeral 212–6;

Association for Death Education and Counselling (ADEC) 306; cost-effectiveness 238; individual support 238; when grief is disenfranchised 232–3; evaluation of interventions 193–7, 303–4; in later bereavement 217–8; sources of help 197 *see also* bereavement services, helpers, interventions

helplessness and hopelessness, *see* depression

Henry 45–6

hiding feelings *see* avoidance

HIV *see* AIDS

home: valency 53, 262; change of 115; housing problems 191; loss of 252, 277–8; pining for 260–1; idealization 261; *see also* relocation

homosexuality: Gay Rights 212; The Lesbian and Gay Bereavement Project 305; *see also* AIDS, mutual help, rituals - quilts

hope 114

Horowitz, M. 169, 173

hospices 154, 262: bereavement services 25, 241–2; family support 232; Hospice Education Institute 306; Hospice Information 244, 305; mortality after bereavement 20–1; National Hospice and Palliative Care Organisation (NHPCO) 306

hospital: admissions after bereavement 25; admissions in PGD 285; disaster plans 268; fears of 221; visiting after bereavement 61

hostility *see* aggression

husband, loss of 8

hypertension: after bereavement 22; in PGD 285

hypochondrias 132–5, 221: with delayed grief 128; and identification symptoms 128

hypnosis 2, 250

hysteria *see* dissociation

idealisation: of dead person 81; of lost home 261

identification: with lost person 100,

117–8; with delayed grief 128; during marriage 118; phantom limb 257; symptoms 128, 133–5
identity: changing 84, 100–14
illness: causation 3; classification 6; and dysfunction 5; and grief 5; mental *see* mental illness
illusions: of centrality 271; of the dead 57–8, 69–71, 287; and marital conflict 290
immigrants *see* migration
immortality, modes of 89
immune response system 41–42: in depression 42; in PTSD 42; in AIDS 42, 302–3
Impact of Events scale 297
imprisonment 265–6
incentive sensitization 289
Index of Complicated Grief (ICG) 31, 166, 170, 227, 301; and PGD 126, 283; *see also* Prolonged Grief Index
independence 173–4 *see also* autonomy
infectious diseases: mortality after bereavement 19
infertility 252
inhibited grief *see* delayed grief
insanity *see* psychosis
insecure attachments: distress after bereavement 293
insecurity 11, 180
insomnia *see* sleep
instinct: and learning 13; crying 48
insurance 208
internal model of the world *see* assumptive world
International Work Group on Death, Dying and Bereavement 277
internet services 25, 239–40; for anxiety & panic 222; characteristics 227–8; for depression 227; NICE recommendations 228
interventions: evaluations 299, 303–4; facilitating expression of grief 213; harmful 194–7; individual 194; reactive v. proactive 300; *see also* group

interventions, helping bereaved people, family interventions, mutual help
involvement 139
irritability *see* anger
Islam 246

Judaism: Shiva 210

kinship 141–146 *see also* children, fathers, grandparents, mothers, spouses
Kissane, D.W. 186
Klein, M. 1

learning difficulties 161; volunteer support 234–5; *see also* Cruse Bereavement Care, disenfranchised grief
Lesbian and Gay Bereavement Project 305
levirate marriage 11
Lewis, C.S. 64–5, 80, 96
libido theory 87
life-threatening illness 252: demoralization 263; denial of 199, 263; helping 264; Huntington's disease 252; insight 199; *see also* AIDS, Alzheimer's Disease, cancers, heart, phases of dying
living alone 115; and grief/loneliness 295, 298
Lifton, R. 89, 109 *see also* immortality, modes of
Lindemann, E. 128, 230
logotherapy 163, 250
London Bereavement Network 305
London Study 28–9, 62–3, 81, 85, 91, 94–7, 99, 115, 118, 120, 135, 161, 171, 175, 183, 205–9, 279–80, 282, 285–90, 295–7
loneliness 11, 12, 115, 191; helping 236–7; hospital admissions 236; and panic 130; and sense of presence 70–1
losses: non-death ch.16; divorce 252; and change 277; and gains 263–4; unemployment 252; *see also* amputation, bereavement, companion animal, death, home, infertility, migration

loss orientation *see* dual process
love: bond or tie 64 *see also* ambivalence, attachment
Love and Loss Study 31, 128, 136, 142, 144, 165, 170–3, 186, 191, 210, 228–9, 292–5
lupus after bereavement 22

madness *see* psychosis
major depressive disorder 26; and alcohol abuse 136; after disasters 274; disorganised attachments 136, distinct from prolonged grief disorder 126, 135; family history 136; NICE recommendations 226; proactive intervention 226; and PGD 284; suicidal risk 136, 226; symptoms 135–6; and traumatic bereavements 136; treatment 193, 226–9; unhappy childhood 136
manslaughter *see* murder
Main, M. 178
marital conflict *see* conflicts, marital
maturation 265
media: after disasters 274
medications: from G.P.s 247, for PTSD 223; *see also* anti-depressants, sedatives, tranquillizers
meaning: and assumptive world 114; salience of 113; loss of 89, 102, 114
meaning making 86, 113–4, 214; *see also* cognitive restructuring, immortality, modes of
memorials: quilts 212; roadside 211
memories: and blaming 93; clarity of 79–80, 287; change 80, 216; happy 58; haunting/painful 57–8, 205; images of the dead 57; post-traumatic 44–5, 57, 87; recovery of 81; visual 70, 287 *see also* forgetting, idealisation, reminiscence, situationally activated memories (SAM) and verbally activated memories (VAM)
menstruation: excessive 24
mental illness: after bereavement 25–8; causation 3; classification
6–7; fear of 4; losses caused by 252; nature of 5; *see also* Bethlem Study & Yale Bereavement Study
mental health 265
Mexican Americans 191
migrants 209, 277–8; helping 209 *see also* mutual help
ministers *see* clergy
Mintz, N. 183
miscarriage *see* abortion
missing lost person *see* pining, and preoccupation with thoughts of lost person
misperceptions 58–9, 70 *see also* perception, illusions
Mitchell, J.T. 273
Mitford, J. 204
mode of death ch. 10, 152–63, 194: memories 58 *see also* traumatic losses
monsterisation 82
mortality: after bereavement 15–21, 280–1; awareness of 267; causes of death after bereavement 17–19; 280–1; age 149; factors influencing 19–20; from heart disease 17–19; gender 147; reducing after bereavement 20–1; *see also* child, loss of, twins, widowers, widows
mothers: influence of 12–13, 168; home valency 52–3;
mourning 1, 4, 211: duration 211; *see also* grief
multiple losses *see* disasters
murder (and manslaughter) 156–7; mutual support groups 234; Parents of Murdered Children 306; revenge 156; Support after Murder and Manslaughter 305; volunteer support 234
Muslims *see* Islam
mutilation, feelings of: after amputation of a limb 258; after bereavement 111; after loss of a home 261
mutual help 120; groups 233–4, 240–1; on the internet 239; *see also* Parents Without Partners, stigma, widow-to-widow programmes

Navajo 183

National Association for Loss and Grief (NALAG) 243

National Health Service 223, 250

National Institute for Clinical Excellence (NICE) guidance:for depression 226, 228–9, internet services 228; for PTSD 222

Neimeyer, R. 193–5

neonatal deaths 153–4; The Foundation for the Study of Infant Deaths 305; holding dead baby 206;

nervous breakdown *see* mental illness

neuro-physiology 25; of grief 288; of PGD 288–9

neurosis 3

nightmares 24, 216

nitrazepam 248

non-governmental organisations (NGOs) 272 *see also* ADEC, Cruse Bereavement Care, NALAG, Funeral Consumer's Association, Parents Without Partners

nostalgia 71

numbness 75–7, 286; in amputees 259; phase of grieving 49, 76; pervasive 125, 127; in PGD 285

nurses: blaming 93, community psychiatric 250; in disenfranchised grief 232–3; health visitors 249; roles after bereavement 198, 249; roles before bereavement 201;

obsessions 87

occupation: need for 103

old age 148–150: consultations with GPs 290–1; depression 237; helping 236–7; grief/loneliness 148, 191, 295 & 298; muscle and joint consultations 291; sedative prescriptions 290; mortality 149; social support in 149–50; resilience 66, 148 *see also* disenfranchised grief

oscillation 59, 83–5 *see also* dual process

pain: in chest 24; general aching 24; hypochondriacal 133; of grief 85, 111, 215; in phantom limb 258

palliative care *see* hospice

palpitations 40, 133

pangs of grief 49; duration 49; neuro-physiology of 65–6, 288–9; peak 212; in PGD 284, 288–9

panic 24, 39, 129–30, 205, 216, 250: and delayed grief 128; disorder 26, 130

Papez, J. circuit 37, 288

parent, loss of: in adult life 144–5; suicidality 144–5

Parents Without Partners (PWP) 241, 306

passivity 97–9; and depression 98

perception 55, 113

perinatal deaths *see* neonatal deaths, stillbirths

personality: anxious 173; and attachment 12; and dominance/submission 99; and pathological grief 173; repressers 173

pets, loss of *see* companion animals

phantom limb 256–7

phases (states) of grief 49, 279–80; in infancy 52–3; *see also* protest, numbness, pining, despair, recovery, stages of dying

phobias 24, 130

pining/yearning: after amputation of a limb 255–6; and dependence 166; duration 99; in pangs of grief 49; in PGD 283; and searching 49; phase of 49, 99, 279–80

pity 214 *see also* empathy, sympathy

placebos 212, 227

Pope Pius XII 213

postponement 83

post-traumatic stress disorder (PTSD) 4, 6; after disasters 271, 274; after amputation of a limb 255; after traumatic bereavement 26, 155, 205–6; association with PGD 284; classificatory system 7; CBT 223; distinct from PGD 126, 284; EMDR 222; and memory systems 44–5; National Center for Post-Traumatic Stress Disorder

306; NICE recommendations 222; treatment 222, 250

poverty 191 *see also* deprivation

preoccupation: with thoughts of lost person 57, 78

preparation: for bereavement *see* bereavement preparation for; for disasters 267–8

preventive psychiatry *see* health - public

primary medical care *see* general practitioners (GPs)

primates: vervet monkey 50 *see also* chimpanzees

prisoners 277–8

problem solving therapy 226, 230, 300–1; *see also* cognitive behaviour therapy

professional carers 198 *see also* clergy, doctors, funeral directors, nurses. social workers

project liberty 269

prolonged grief disorder (PGD) 26, 123–9; in amputees 257–8; course 284; and dependence 170–3; diagnostic criteria 126–7, 283–5; different from major depression and PTSD 126; different from normal grief 284; dysfunction 284; incidence after bereavement 27; with life-threatening illness 263; need for recognition 32; neuro-physiology 288–9; after relocation 262; quality of life 284; secure attachments 179; separation anxiety/distress 170, 284; similarity to drug addiction 289; suicidality 126, 284; treatment 194, 231; risk to physical health 126; after deaths by suicide 157; *see also* Index of Complicated Grief (ICG), incentive sensitization, Prolonged Grief Index(PG-13)

Prolonged Grief Index (PG-13) 31; and PGD 126, 301; after suicide 157

protest: and pining 50; in infancy 90; in non human animals 90, phase of grieving 91

pseudocyesis (false pregnancy) 2

psychiatric illness *see* mental illness

psychiatrists: after disasters 274; consults 25; roles after bereavement 249–50; when suicidal risk 229

psychoanalysis 1; the talking cure 2; theory of grief 96–7

psychological first aid 271

psychologists 277: after bereavement 250; after disasters 274; *see also* cognitive therapies

psychopathology 3

psychosis 4: fear of 216; prognosis 4–5; hallucinations not symptom of psychosis 71

psychosocial transitions xiv, 101–04, 265; and restoration orientation 9

psychosomatic disorders: after bereavement 21–25; after relocation 262 *see also* hypochondriasis

psychotherapies (and psychotherapists) 268: after disasters 274; evaluations 299, 301; origin 1; for depression 227; for stigmatised persons 234–5

public health 265

Raphael, B. 267

rash 24

rational emotive therapy 250

RD4U (web site for bereaved young persons) 243, 305

reality testing 84, funerals 207; viewing the dead 205; resistance to 92–3

realization: after amputation of a limb 258–9; after bereavement 84–7, 218; with life-threatening illness 263; *see also* reality testing

recovery: of memories 80; of positive feelings 112

reincarnation 72

relationship with deceased person 141–6, 194 *see also* ambivalence, attachments, dependency, disorganised attachments, kinship, involvement

relationship with parents *see* attachments

relaxation exercises 221

religion 197, 208–212: after disasters 274; church attendance 210; faith 71, 182, 209–210, 245; research into 209 *see also* Christianity, God, Islam, Judaism, rituals
relocating the dead 182–3
relocation 259–62, 264, 277–8; grief 260; psychosomatic problems 262; *see also* home - loss of
remarriage after bereavement 20, 115, 218
reminiscence: function of 85 *see also* obsessions & ruminations
reorganization 112
repression 83
research into bereavement 28; bias 31; ethical aspects 29–30; meta-analyses 193–4, 227, 297, 299; religion 209; retrospective distortion 174; sample size 138; *see also* Case Note Study, Bethlem Study, Harvard Study, Love and Loss Study & Yale Bereavement Study.
resilience 28, 66–7, 136, 148, 164, 170
resistance to reality 92–3
restlessness: in non-human species 50; in bereaved human beings 56, 286 *see also* searching
restitution 95
restoration orientation *see* dual process model
reviewing 85
risk-taking: and mortality after bereavement 19
risk factors after bereavement 88, 194, 303–4: assessment 141; list 140; interventions based on 194, 197, 220, 303–4; *see also* age, childhood experiences, gender, Harvard Study, crises, culture, family, mental illness, mode of death, personality, relationship with deceased, religion, social support, socio-economic status
rites of passage (rites de passage) 208, 211–2, 218, 265
rituals 182, 207–8, 210: after disasters 274; doctor's 212; shiva 210; therapeutic 212, 265; *see also*

funerals, memorials, rites de passage, viewing the dead
Robertson, J. & Bowlby, J. *see* phases of grief
Rogers, C. 110
Roman Catholicism 213
rumination 87
Rwanda, genocide in 277

St Christopher's Hospice 241–2, 303–4
Samaritans, The 305
searching: in bereaved adults 53–7, 70; components of 55–6 ; for a lost home 260; function of 84; in infancy 48; neuro-physiology of 288; and perception 54–7; and separation anxiety 48; urge to search 50; in non-humans 50, 65; *see also* finding
secularisation 183
secure base 13
security of attachment 167: and PGD 179
security 13–14, 96
sedatives 40, 247–8; nitrazepam 248
seizures: non-epileptic, after bereavement 22
self: components of 105–7; empty 125; empirical self 104–5; 'real' self 110; social self 108–9
self-confidence, loss of 103, 180
self-help, guided: for depression 226 *see also* books
self-neglect 236
self-reproach *see* guilt
Seligman, M.E.P. 179
sense of presence: of lost limb 258–9; of lost person 69–71; and age 71; and loneliness 70; within the bereaved person 119; within another person 119–20 *see also* hallucinations, illusions, phantom limb
separation: anxiety 39, 284–5; at birth 206; in infancy 13, 48, 171; and pangs of grief 49
separations from parents: and coping 293–4; and relationships 294; and problems after

bereavement 293–4; and suicidality 295

sexuality 11; frustration of 11, 115; loss of drive 33, 59; increased 59; resurgence 120; social prohibition 115

shadow grief 153–4

Shakespeare 213, 215

shattered assumptions 223–5; treatment by EMDR 225

Shear, M.K. 301

shock 125

shortness of breath 24

showing feelings see disclosure of feelings

shrine see grave

sibling, loss of 145–6 see also twin, loss of

situationally activated memories (SAM) 44–5, 86

sleep after bereavement 23, 33, 40, 71; and PGD 127, 285; and PTSD 46; sedatives 247–8

smoking see tobacco

social class: and sense of presence 71

social influences after bereavement ch.12, 181–92, 214

social isolation 130, 191: and marital conflict 290; support 236–7; see also social withdrawal

social status, loss of 98

social support: after bereavement 20, 190–1, 236–7, 286; for depression 228–9;

social withdrawal: after bereavement 115, 218; in non-human species 50 see also social isolation.

social workers: consults 25; after disasters 269; psychiatric 250; roles 198. 249;

sociologists 277

society desecration of, after disasters 267

spastic colon 125

spiritualism 61

spouse, loss of 8, 28, 39, 141–2, 278: alarm 39; ambivalence 175; dependence 142; mutual help 241; Parents Without Partners (PWP) 241, 306; psychiatric problems 142; PGD 142;

stages: of dying 262; of grief see phases of grieving

starlings, vacuum activities 69–70

sticklebacks, vacuum activities 69–70

stigma 9–10, 233–5; see also mutual help

stillbirths 147

Strange Situation Test 167–8, 172, 178

stress: determinants 47; pre-bereavement 161–2, 292; see also trauma, traumatic bereavements

stunned see shock

sudden infant death syndrome (SIDS) see neonatal deaths

suicidality after bereavement 19–21, 62, 144–5; assessment of risk 229; depression 223, 226; in a hospice 242; ideation 62; management of risk 223, 229; ritual 10; Samaritans 305

suicide, bereavement by 157–8: disclosure of feelings 214; Survivors of Bereavement by Suicide (SOBS) 306; volunteer support 234; see also mutual help

support groups 244: harmful 196; for those bereaved by AIDS 234; see also mutual help, stigma

supporting bereaved people 104, 217 see also social support, support groups

Sushwap 10

suttee 10

Swaziland 183

sweating 24, 33

sympathy 214–5

symptoms: physical 77, 216

telephone calls 217

tension 25, 286

termination of pregnancy see abortion

Texas Revised Inventory of Grief (TRIG) 227

time, sense of 85, and recovery from bereavement 219

thyrotoxicosis after bereavement 22

tobacco: consumption after
  bereavement 247; in PGD 285
tranquillizers 247
transition 265 *see also* psychosocial
  transition
trauma ch. 3, 33-XX, 264; after
  amputation of a limb 354–5; *see
  also* disasters, traumatic
  bereavement, traumatic stress
traumatic bereavement: age at 153;
  anger 156; and attachment to
  parents in childhood 136; after
  violent deaths 155–8; and
  depression 136; and guilt 156;
  interventions for 221–5; reactions
  to 155; mortality after 19; and
  PTSD 155; unexpected deaths
  153–5, 199; *see also* disasters,
  murder & manslaughter, post-
  traumatic stress disorder, suicide,
  viewing the dead
traumatic stress 4: different from
  grief 58; physiology of 34–5 ; *see
  also* armed conflict, disasters,
  post-traumatic stress disorder and
  traumatic bereavement
trust: basic 14, in PGD 284; in self/
  others 14, 125, 180
tuberculosis after bereavement 22
turning points 217–8; *see also*
  meaning making
twins, bereavement 145: mortality
  18; suicide 158

ulcerative colitis after bereavement
  22
unexpected deaths *see* traumatic
  bereavements
unreality, feelings of *see*
  derealisation
untimely deaths 96, 153; *see also*
  traumatic bereavements

vacuum activities 69–70
vagal inhibition 16
verbally activated memories (VAM)
  44–5, 86

veteran support 120 *see also* mutual
  help
Viet Nam 4
viewing the dead 205
violence: cycles of 266, 276–7; death
  by *see* traumatic bereavement
vision: blurring 24
volunteer helpers 198, 220, 241–3,
  250; and depression 226, 228;
  after disasters 273–4; and
  stigmatised persons 234; *see also*
  bereavement services
vomiting 24
voodoo death 16
vulnerability to bereavement,
  personal ch.11, 164–80; and
  attachment 165; grief prone 165;
  and mental illness 164–5;
  implications for helping 225 *see
  also* anxiety disorders, major
  depression, panic

Walter, A. 183
wandering *see* fugues
war *see* armed conflict
Waugh, E. 204
web sites *see* internet, organizations
  offering help to the bereaved
weight: loss of 24, 40, 236; gain
  236
widows: mortality 16–17; image of
  108; widow-to-widow
  programmes 240; *see also* spouse,
  loss of
widowers: mortality 16–18; mutual
  help 240; *see also* spouse, loss of
Winston's Wish 306
withdrawal *see* social withdrawal
Wortman, C.B. 209, 214
worrying: after bereavement 216;
  function of 85; worry work 85,
  202

Yale Bereavement Study xvi,
  31–2, 91, 125–6, 142, 170, 279,
  283–5
yearning *see* pining